Beijing 2008: Preparing for Glory

Beijing 2008: Preparing for Glory – Chinese Challenge in the 'Chinese Century' brings together international scholars with an interest in sport and politics and sinologists with an interest in China – past, present and future – to explore global reaction to the Beijing Olympics – China's anticipated and realised moment of glory on the world stage.

The Beijing Olympics is, first and foremost, a political act and assertion. It is also a statement of national intent, the culmination of ideological effort going back to 1949 and the outcome of political, social, cultural and economic change.

From the moment of the birth of the 'New China' sport has been viewed as a means of internal and external projection illustrating the capacity of the system and people to more than hold their own with those of other nations. In short, sport has been the chosen 'stage' on which the Chinese perform in pursuit of world recognition, respect and esteem.

This assertion is not hard to understand. China's 'century of humiliation' at the hands of first the West and then Japan remains a traumatic experience. Beijing 2008 is to assist the restoration of China's national self-esteem. He Zhenliang, Chairman of the IOC Commission for the Culture of Olympic Education, has remarked pointedly that the most significant outcome of the Beijing Games will be the elevation of the self-confidence and sense of pride of the Chinese people.

Beijing 2008 will be an act of political self-renewal on the world stage.

This Collection demonstrates that sport is inseparable from politics.

This book was previously published as a special issue of the *International Journal of the History of Sport*.

J.A. Mangan is Emeritus Professor, the University of Strathclyde and an internationally recognised academic with a wide range of publications on the political, cultural and social aspects of sport both past and present.

Dong Jinxia is the Director of the Centre for Gender Studies in Sport at Peking University and the author of the acclaimed monograph *Women, Sport and Society in Modern China: Holding Up More than Half the Sky*.

Beijing 2008: Preparing for Glory

Chinese Challenge in the 'Chinese Century'

Edited by J.A. Mangan and Dong Jinxia

Routledge
Taylor & Francis Group

LONDON AND NEW YORK

First published 2009 by Routledge
2 Park Square, Milton Park, Abingdon, Oxon, OX14 4RN

Simultaneously published in the USA and Canada
by Routledge
270 Madison Avenue, New York, NY 10016

Routledge is an imprint of the Taylor & Francis Group, an Informa business

© 2009 Edited by J.A. Mangan and Dong Jinxia

Typeset in Minion by KnowledgeWorks Global Limited, Chennai, India
Printed and bound in Great Britain by MPG Books Ltd., Bodmin, Cornwall

British Library Cataloguing in Publication Data
A catalogue record for this book is available from the British Library

ISBN 10: 0-415-37165-1
ISBN 13: 978-0-415-37165-0

CONTENTS

Series Editors' Foreword   vii

Other Titles in the Series   x

1   Preface: Geopolitical Games – Beijing 2008
J. A. Mangan   1

2   Prologue: Beijing 2008 – The Mixed Messages of Contemporary
Chinese Nationalism
Julia Lovell   8

3   Olympic Aspirations: Chinese Women on Top – Considerations and
Consequences
Dong Jinxia and J. A. Mangan   29

4   Olympian Politics in Beijing: Games but not Just Games
Kevin Caffrey   57

5   Dancing Around the Elephant: The Beijing Olympics – Taiwanese
Reflections and Reactions
Junwei Yu and J. A. Mangan   76

6   Sport as Public Diplomacy and Public Disquiet: Australia's
Ambivalent Embrace of the Beijing Olympics
Peter Horton   101

7   The Dish Might Be Overspiced: Fears, Doubts and Criticisms in
French Perceptions of Chinese Olympic and Other Successes
Thierry Terret   126

8   Creative Tensions: 'Join in London' Meets 'Dancing Beijing' – The
Cultural Power of the Olympics
Vassil Girginov   143

9   Preparing to Take Credit for China's Glory: American Perspectives on
the Beijing Olympic Games
Mark Dyreson   165

10   Epilogue: Sideshow Beijing 2008 – An Absence of Euphoria beyond the
Southern Clouds
Kevin Caffrey   185

Index   203

Series Editors' Foreword

SPORT IN THE GLOBAL SOCIETY was launched in the late nineties. It now has over one hundred volumes. Until recently an odd myopia characterised academia with regard to sport. The global *groves of academe* remained essentially Cartesian in inclination. They favoured a mind/body dichotomy: thus the study of ideas was acceptable; the study of sport was not. All that has now changed. Sport is now incorporated, intelligently, within debate about *inter alia* ideologies, power, stratification, mobility and inequality. The reason is simple. In the modern world sport is everywhere: it is as ubiquitous as war. E.J. Hobsbawm, the Marxist historian, once called it the one of the most significant of the new manifestations of late nineteenth century Europe. Today it is one of the most significant manifestations of the twenty-first century world. Such is its power, politically, culturally, economically, spiritually and aesthetically, that sport beckons the academic more persuasively than ever – to borrow, and refocus, an expression of the radical historian Peter Gay – 'to explore its familiar terrain and to wrest new interpretations from its inexhaustible materials'. As a subject for inquiry, it is replete, as he remarked of history, with profound 'questions unanswered and for that matter questions unasked'.

Sport seduces the teeming 'global village'; it is the new opiate of the masses; it is one of the great modern experiences; its attraction astonishes only the recluse; its appeal spans the globe. Without exaggeration, sport is a mirror in which nations, communities, men and women now see themselves. That reflection is sometimes bright, sometimes dark, sometimes distorted, sometimes magnified. This metaphorical mirror is a source of mass exhilaration and depression, security and insecurity, pride and humiliation, bonding and alienation. Sport, for many, has replaced religion as a source of emotional catharsis and spiritual passion, and for many, since it is among the earliest of memorable childhood experiences, it infiltrates memory, shapes enthusiasms, serves fantasies. To co-opt Gay again: it blends memory and desire.

Sport, in addition, can be a lens through which to scrutinise major themes in the political and social sciences: democracy and despotism and the great associated movements of socialism, fascism, communism and capitalism as well as political cohesion and confrontation, social reform and social stability.

The story of modern sport is the story of the modern world – in microcosm; a modern global tapestry permanently being woven. Furthermore, nationalist and imperialist, philosopher and politician, radical and conservative have all sought in sport a manifestation of national identity, status and superiority.

Finally, for countless millions sport is the personal pursuit of ambition, assertion, well-being and enjoyment.

For all the above reasons, sport demands the attention of the academic. *Sport in the Global Society* is a response.

J.A. Mangan, Boria Majumdar and Mark Dyreson
Series Editors
Sport in the Global Society

Sport in the Global Society

Series Editors: J.A. Mangan, Boria Majumdar and Mark Dyreson

Beijing 2008: Preparing for Glory
Chinese Challenge in the 'Chinese Century'

Sport in the Global Society

Series Editors: J.A. Mangan, Boria Majumdar and Mark Dyreson

As Robert Hands in *The Times* recently observed the growth of sports studies in recent years has been considerable. This unique series with over one hundred volumes in the last decade has played its part. Politically, culturally, emotionally and aesthetically, sport is a major force in the modern world. Its impact will grow as the world embraces ever more tightly the contemporary secular trinity: the English language, technology and sport. *Sport in the Global Society* will continue to record sport's phenomenal progress across the world stage.

Other Titles in the Series

Africa, Football and FIFA
Politics, Colonialism and Resistance
Paul Darby

Amateurism in British Sport
'It Matters Not Who Won or Lost'
*Edited by Dilwyn Porter and
Stephen Wagg*

Amateurism in Sport
An Analysis and Defence
Lincoln Allison

America's Game(s)
A Critical Anthropology of Sport
*Edited by Benjamin Eastman, Sean Brown and
Michael Ralph*

American Sports
An Evolutionary Approach
Edited by Alan Klein

A Social History of Indian Football
Striving to Score
Kausik Bandyopadhya and Boria Majumdar

**A Social History of Swimming in England,
1800–1918**
Splashing in the Serpentine
Christopher Love

A Sport-Loving Society
Victorian and Edwardian Middle-Class
England at Play
Edited by J.A. Mangan

**Athleticism in the Victorian and Edwardian
Public School**
The Emergence and Consolidation of an
Educational Ideology, New Edition
J.A. Mangan

Australian Beach Cultures
The History of Sun, Sand and Surf
Douglas Booth

Australian Sport
Antipodean waves of change
Edited by Kristine Toohey and Tracy Taylor

Barbarians, Gentlemen and Players
A Sociological Study of the Development of
Rugby Football, Second Edition
Eric Dunning and Kenneth Sheard

**Baseball and Moral Authority in
Contemporary Cuba**
Edited by Benjamin Eastman

Beijing 2008: Preparing for Glory
The Chinese Challenge in 'the Chinese
Century'
Edited by J.A. Mangan and Dong Jinxia

'Blooding' the Martial Male
The Imperial Officer, Field Sports and Big
Game Hunting
J.A. Mangan and Callum MacKenzie

Body and Mind
Sport in Europe from the Roman Empire to
the Renaissance
John McClelland

British Football and Social Exclusion
Edited by Stephen Wagg

Capoeira
The History of an Afro-Brazilian Martial
Art
Matthias Röhrig Assunção

Crafting Patriotism for Global Dominance
America at the Olympics
Mark Dyreson

Cricket and England
A Cultural and Social History of Cricket in
England between the Wars
Jack Williams

Cricket in Colonial India, 1780–1947
Boria Majumdar

Cricketing Cultures in Conflict
Cricketing World Cup 2003
*Edited by Boria Majumdar and
J.A. Mangan*

Cricket, Race and the 2007 World Cup
*Edited by Boria Majumdar and
Jon Gemmell*

Critical Events in Baseball History
Class, Race and Politics
*Edited by Benjamin Eastman and
John D. Kelly*

Disciplining Bodies in the Gymnasium
Memory, Monument, Modernity
Sherry McKay and Patricia Vertinsky

Disreputable Pleasures
Less Virtuous Victorians at Play
Edited by Mike Huggins and J.A. Mangan

**Diversity and Division – Race, Ethnicity and
Sport in Australia**
Edited by Christopher J. Hallinan

Doping in Sport
Global Ethical Issues
Edited by Angela Schneider and Fan Hong

Emigrant Players
Sport and the Irish Diaspora
Edited by Paul Darby and David Hassan

Ethnicity, Sport, Identity
Struggles for Status
Edited by J.A. Mangan and Andrew Ritchie

European Heroes
Myth, Identity, Sport
*Edited by Richard Holt, J.A. Mangan and
Pierre Lanfranchi*

Europe, Sport, World
Shaping Global Societies
Edited by J.A. Mangan

**Flat Racing and British Society,
1790–1914**
A Social and Economic History
Mike Huggins

**Football and Community in the Global
Context**
Studies in Theory and Practice
*Edited by Adam Brown, Tim Crabbe
and Gavin Mellor*

Football: From England to the World
*Edited by Dolores P. Martinez and
Projit B. Mukharji*

Football, Europe and the Press
Liz Crolley and David Hand

Football Fans Around the World
From Supporters to Fanatics
Edited by Sean Brown

Football: The First Hundred Years
The Untold Story
Adrian Harvey

Footbinding, Feminism and Freedom
The Liberation of Women's Bodies in
Modern China
Fan Hong

France and the 1998 World Cup
The National Impact of a World
Sporting Event
Edited by Hugh Dauncey and Geoff Hare

Freeing the Female Body
Inspirational Icons
Edited by J.A. Mangan and Fan Hong

Fringe Nations in Soccer
*Edited by Kausik Bandyopadhyay,
Martha Saavedra and Sabyasachi Malick*

From Fair Sex to Feminism
Sport and the Socialization of
Women in the Industrial and
Post-Industrial Eras
Edited by J.A. Mangan and Roberta J. Park

xii   *Other Titles in the Series*

Gender, Sport, Science
Selected Writings of Roberta J. Park
Edited by J.A. Mangan and
Patricia Vertinsky

Global and Local Football
Politics and Europeanization on the Fringes
of the EU
Gary Armstrong and Jon P. Mitchell

Globalised Football
Nations and Migration, the City and the
Dream
Edited by Nina Clara Tiesler and
João Nuno Coelho

Heritage, Sport and Tourism
Sporting Pasts – Tourist Futures
Edited by Sean Gammon and
Gregory Ramshaw

Human Rights in Youth Sport
A Critical Review of Children's Rights in
Competitive Sports
Paulo David

Italian Fascism and the Female Body
Sport, Submissive Women and Strong
Mothers
Gigliola Gori

Japan, Sport and Society
Tradition and Change in a Globalizing
World
Edited by Joseph Maguire and
Masayoshi Nakayama

Law and Sport in Contemporary
Society
Edited by Steven Greenfield and
Guy Osborn

Leisure and Recreation in a Victorian
Mining Community
The Social Economy of Leisure in
North-East England, 1820–1914
Alan Metcalfe

Lost Histories of Indian Cricket
Battles Off the Pitch
Boria Majumdar

Making European Masculinities
Sport, Europe, Gender
Edited by J.A. Mangan

Making Men
Rugby and Masculine Identity
Edited by John Nauright and
Timothy J.L. Chandler

Making the Rugby World
Race, Gender, Commerce
Edited by Timothy J.L. Chandler and
John Nauright

Militarism, Sport, Europe
War Without Weapons
Edited by J.A. Mangan

Modern Sport: The Global Obsession
Essays in Honour of J.A. Mangan
Edited by Boria Majumdar and
Fan Hong

Muscular Christianity and the Colonial and
Post-Colonial World
Edited by John J. MacAloon

Native Americans and Sport in
North America
Other Peoples' Games
Edited by C. Richard King

Playing on the Periphery
Sport, Identity and Memory
Tara Brabazon

Pleasure, Profit, Proselytism
British Culture and Sport at Home and
Abroad 1700–1914
Edited by J.A. Mangan

Rain Stops Play
Cricketing Climates
Andrew Hignell

Reformers, Sport, Modernizers
Middle-Class Revolutionaries
Edited by J.A. Mangan

Representing the Nation
Sport and Spectacle in
Post-Revolutionary Mexico
Edited by Claire and
Keith Brewster

Rugby's Great Split
Class, Culture and the Origins of Rugby
League Football
Tony Collins

Running Cultures
Racing in Time and Space
John Bale

Scoring for Britain
International Football and International
Politics, 1900–1939
Peter J. Beck

Serious Sport
J.A. Mangan's Contribution to the History
of Sport
Edited by Scott Crawford

Shaping the Superman
Fascist Body as Political Icon – Aryan Fascism
Edited by J.A. Mangan

Sites of Sport
Space, Place and Experience
Edited by John Bale and Patricia Vertinksy

Soccer and Disaster
International Perspectives
*Edited by Paul Darby, Martin Jones and
Gavin Mellor*

Soccer in South Asia
Empire, Nation, Diaspora
Edited by Paul Dimeo and James Mills

Soccer's Missing Men
Schoolteachers and the Spread of
Association Football
J.A. Mangan and Colm Hickey

Soccer, Women, Sexual Liberation
Kicking off a New Era
Edited by Fan Hong and J.A. Mangan

Sport: Race, Ethnicity and Indigenity
Building Global Understanding
Edited by Daryl Adair

Sport and American Society
Exceptionalism, Insularity, 'Imperialism'
Edited by Mark Dyreson and J.A. Mangan

**Sport and Foreign Policy in a Globalizing
World**
Edited by Steven J. Jackson and Stephen Haigh

Sport and International Relations
An Emerging Relationship
Edited by Roger Levermore and Adrian Budd

Sport and Memory in North America
Edited by Steven Wieting

Sport, Civil Liberties and Human Rights
*Edited by Richard Giulianotti and
David McArdle*

Sport, Culture and History
Region, Nation and Globe
Edited by Brian Stoddart

Sport in Asian Society
Past and Present
Edited by Fan Hong and J.A. Mangan

Sport in Australasian Society
Past and Present
Edited by J.A. Mangan and John Nauright

Sport in Europe
Politics, Class, Gender
Edited by J.A. Mangan

Sport in Films
*Edited by Emma Poulton and
Martin Roderick*

Sport in Latin American Society
Past and Present
*Edited by Lamartine DaCosta and
J.A. Mangan*

Sport in South Asian Society
Past and Present
*Edited by Boria Majumdar and
J.A. Mangan*

Sport, Media, Culture
Global and Local Dimensions
Edited by Alina Bernstein and Neil Blain

Sport, Nationalism and Orientalism
The Asian Games
Edited by Fan Hong

Sporting Cultures
Hispanic Perspectives on Sport, Text and the
Body
*Edited by David Wood and
P. Louise Johnson*

Sporting Nationalisms
Identity, Ethnicity, Immigration and
Assimilation
Edited by Mike Cronin and David Mayall

xiv *Other Titles in the Series*

Sport Tourism
Edited by Heather J. Gibson

Superman Supreme
Fascist Body as Political Icon – Global
Fascism
Edited by J.A. Mangan

Terrace Heroes
The Life and Times of the 1930s
Professional Footballer
Graham Kelly

The Changing Face of the Football Business
Supporters Direct
*Edited by Sean Hamil, Jonathan Michie,
Christine Oughton and Steven Warby*

The Commercialisation of Sport
Edited by Trevor Slack

The Cultural Bond
Sport, Empire, Society
Edited by J.A. Mangan

The First Black Footballer
Arthur Wharton 1865–1930: An Absence
of Memory
Phil Vasili

**The Flame Relay and the Olympic
Movement**
John J. MacAloon

The Football Manager
A History
Neil Carter

The Future of Football
Challenges for the Twenty-First Century
*Edited by Jon Garland, Dominic Malcolm and
Mike Rowe*

The Games Ethic and Imperialism
Aspects of the Diffusion of an Ideal
J.A. Mangan

The Global Politics of Sport
The Role of Global Institutions in Sport
Edited by Lincoln Allison

The Lady Footballers
Struggling to Play in Victorian Britain
James F. Lee

The Magic of Indian Cricket
Cricket and Society in India,
Revised Edition
Mihir Bose

The Making of New Zealand Cricket
1832–1914
Greg Ryan

**The 1940 Tokyo Games: The Missing
Olympics**
Japan, the Asian Olympics and the Olympic
Movement
Sandra Collins

The Nordic World: Sport in Society
*Edited by Henrik Meinander and
J.A. Mangan*

The Politics of South African Cricket
Jon Gemmell

The Race Game
Sport and Politics in South Africa
Douglas Booth

The Tour De France, 1903–2003
A Century of Sporting Structures,
Meanings and Values
Edited by Hugh Dauncey and Geoff Hare

This Great Symbol
Pierre de Coubertin and the Origins
of the Modern Olympic Games
John J. MacAloon

Tribal Identities
Nationalism, Europe, Sport
Edited by J.A. Mangan

Who Owns Football?
The Governance and Management of
the Club Game Worldwide
Edited by David Hassan and Sean Hamil

**Women, Sport and Society in Modern
China**
Holding up More than Half the Sky
Dong Jinxia

Preface: Geopolitical Games – Beijing 2008

Time present and time past
Are both perhaps present in time future,
And time future contained in time past. [1]

The past is not only with us, but is us, the cause and
context of our every action. What we do is prompted by
what we believed a minute or a year or a century ago. [2]

Arriving at each new city, the traveller finds again a past of his
that he did not know he had : the foreignness of what you no
longer are or no longer possess lies in wait for you in foreign,
unpossessed places. [3]

The *Shorter Oxford Dictionary* defines Geopolitics as political relations between states as influenced by geography but also as a theory which regards the state as an organism with powers independent of and superior to those of its constituent groups or individuals. [4] Both meanings are secreted in the minatory comment by He Zhenliang, Chairman of the IOC Commission for the Culture of Olympic Education that the most significant outcome of the Beijing Games will be 'the elevation of our Chinese people's self-confidence and sense of pride'. [5] This assertion is not hard to understand. China's 'century of humiliation' at the hands of first the West and then Japan remains a traumatic experience and arguably 'has been a driving force... behind China's exertions to press for global status in economics, in science and technology, in global politics and in sport.' [6] Beijing 2008 is to assist the restoration of China's national greatness through the erasing of the memory of a humbled, reduced and subordinate people and its replacement with a confident, risen and superordinate people: physical effort twisted into skeins of political action.

Post 1949 this has been a designated task: 'from the moment of the birth of the "New China"', sport has been... a means of internal and external projection illustrating the capacity of the system and people to more than hold their own with those of other nations. In short, sport has been the 'stage' on which the Chinese perform in pursuit of world recognition, respect and esteem.' [7] New times have given new purpose to this performance as resources in recent decades have allowed stress to be placed on allusive winning 'declamations' in the global theatre of sport. Beijing 2008 will be the loudest.

Vast expenditure, political single mindedness, orchestrated public euphoria and indifference to appeal have meant the IOC has not been much in evidence; less a back seat driver, more a back seat passenger. Beijing 2008 will be remembered not as the gift of the IOC but as the creation of the Chinese. This could be the lasting geopolitical message of the Games. The reason is not hard to find. For historical reasons touched on earlier, Chinese patriotism expressed through sport verges at times on chauvinism: 'In the post-Mao China, the symbolic link between sporting performance and national pride has been constantly [and carefully] maintained.' [8] This is true in spades. Performers, spectators, politicians and the media have produced exceptional 'outbursts of both jubilant and angry nationalism' [9] according to circumstances of victory and defeat. Political 'face' and sporting 'face' have become one: '"When a country is powerful," proclaimed the front page of the *People's Daily* after China's medal success at the Athens' Olympics, "its sport will flourish ... Chinese athletes will make more contributions to realize our nation's *great revival.*"' (emphasis added) [10] Medals are the ambition; world superiority is the intention.

Serious sport, as readers of the visionary George Orwell will be aware, on occasion, 'has nothing to do with fair play. It is bound up with hatred, jealousy, boastfulness, disregard for all the rules...' [11] In his caustic view, it was war minus the shooting! Orwell with abrasive contumacy was dramatically provocative. None the less, he had a point. Only the totally gullible believe that the Olympics are simply about taking part without animosity and winning without acrimony and pursuing national success without geopolitical intent: 'Embedded somewhere within the roseate internationalism of China's... "One World, One Dream" is a confident desire to differentiate a rising China's blueprint for leadership from that of the present Western-dominated status quo, and a willingness to manipulate facts to serve instrumental political purposes innate to all ambitious nationalist elites.' [12]

Sport, of course, is much more. While sport shares with war ubiquity, sport at its finest sweetly seduces the global village: 'it is the new opiate of the masses; it is one of great modern experiences; ... its appeal spans the globe.' [13] With good reason: 'sport is a mirror in which nations, communities, men and women now see themselves. The reflection is sometimes bright, sometimes dark, sometimes distorted, sometimes magnified. The metaphorical mirror is a source of mass exhilaration and depression, security and insecurity, pride and humiliation, bonding and alienation.' [14] Beijing 2008 will prove this up to and beyond the hilt. It will also prove that 'sport for many has replaced religion as a source of emotional catharsis and spiritual passion' with its power to infiltrate memory, shape enthusiasm, serve fantasy. [15] For billions world-wide the Games will mean immediate pleasure not future political purpose. Beijing 2008 is Janus headed; popular and political.

Nevertheless the metonyms of martialism speed along the Chinese internet connections. Here Beijing 2008 can seem like an exercise in revanchism. As Julia Lovell has remarked, 'Visit any of the Olympic chatrooms on major Chinese internet news sites and you will find frank, even aggressive, expressions of popular hunger for Chinese national victory. Military analogues abound, giving the strong impression that Chinese sports fans are far more preoccupied with war than peace. Chinese athletes [and] Olympic prospects are discussed under the heading "preparing for War" (zhanbei); those considering China's medal winning hopes write of "reviewing the troops" (jianyue).' [16] Orwell with his incision seems to have exposed some, if not all, of the components of modern international sport.

What this amounts to is the Chinese intention, conscious and unconscious, of retribution for past indignity-war minus the shooting fought on sports fields and in sports arenas. No extraordinary leap of the imagination is required to recognise this, just a willing ear made available to the Chinese themselves. [17] Equally possible by way of counterpoise is growing international opprobrium at China's rebarbarative state support for repressive policies both at home and abroad which could well result in Beijing 2008 being the source of a global reaction of recrimination; a *succès de scandale*.

The Flame Relay, barely underway at the time of writing, regrettably but understandably has become in its initial stages a symbol not of friendship but of friction, not of harmony but of disharmony, not of peace but of protest. Will it be the last in the present grandiose form? Have the claims for it as a token of amity, unity and concord been cruelly exposed as rhetorical conceits with the sadly anomalous and frankly farcical loading of the Flame on and off vehicles to rush it to empty places to avoid gestures of displeasure, uncomfortable media images and contradiction of purpose? If the Flame Relay in its present form becomes extinct what will have been the geopolitical contribution of Beijing 2008 to its expiry? One action, astounding in the crudity of its diplomatic public relations which will remain in the consciousness of Londoners and others elsewhere in the world, was the sight of the allegedly Chinese Security Service on English soil manhandling its citizens including apparently Sebastian Coe, on the streets of the capital; unfortunate perdurable memories. Indiscriminating intolerance rather than universal tolerance was witnessed world-wide; dysphoric Olympic imagery. [18]

Beijing 2008 contains other paradoxes. On the one hand, 'What are we to conclude from the mixed messages of the 2008 Olympics? Are the Games truly working towards world peace and equality, or do they indicate a cohesive strain of imperialist nationalism that aspires to remake the Western-dominated modern order in the image of a pre-modern. Sino-centric universe? As China resurges, will it seek to humiliate, in turn, the nations it has identified as the authors of its150-year decline?' [19]

On the other hand, 'has contemporary China been seriously overestimated: have the experiences of the past century and a half fully integrated China internationally, tying its identity and self-esteem to external (in reality, Western) recognition? [20] 'Furthermore, 'does the gap . . . between ideal and reality in China's Olympic prepara-tions – in particular, concerns over the severity of environmental problems – suggest that China is not the unstoppable juggernaut feared by Washington's hawks?' [21]

Has Susan Shirk's *China Fragile Superpower* a telling significance? [22] 'Although China looks like a powerhouse from outside, to its leaders it looks fragile, poor and overwhelmed by internal problems.' [23] Is it the case that even if 'China succeeds in hosting an immaculate Olympics, it will be left – after two weeks of escapist spectacle – with severe, longstanding domestic concerns :combating environmental degradation, maintaining economic growth, and limiting the destabilising impact of social inequality'? [24]

It is important also to consider inconsistencies surrounding the Games. Architecture, to offer one example, is frequently a statement about the essence of a nation ideally reflecting in the modern age a blend of national projection and international assimilation. To what extent is this apparent in either the architecture of the Games and indeed its city? 'Beijing's architecture,' it has been stated, 'offers few nods to Chinese identity. The city resembles nothing so much as an instantly created American city – block after block of bland glass offices and hotels connected by broad avenues. A high proportion of the shops are expensive European brands and almost the only indication that you are in China is the scale. Twenty million live here . . .' [25] Is it to be regretted, perhaps, that . . . 'the Chinese [now] have the resources to fulfil Mao Tse Tung's commandment not merely to leave the past behind but to eradicate it.' [26] Is it time for patriotic architectural revisionism? There is little evidence of this in the expensive architecture of Beijing 2008 despite the compelling design of the Bird's Nest Stadium. Historical revisionism awaits the transient Opening Ceremony.

There is, it has been argued, an assured American geopolitical complacency regarding the influence of the United States on the sport of the China of the twentieth and twenty-first centuries. The Christian zeal of the YMCA, at least on the part of some Americans, has been credited with the early transformation of Chinese sport: 'moral transfiguration'. Equally, there is an American conviction that the market forces of American professional sport have been the recent source of change in Chinese sport: 'economic transfiguration'. [27] These 'meta-narratives of American-style sport giving birth to a "new China", though separated by nearly a century, share an important set of common assumptions . . . The Olympic Games will catapult China into the international community, [they] reveal China moving towards a more Western, or more specifically, a more American future. The Olympic Games will render the 'inscrutable Orient' intelligible to the West in general and especially to Americans.' [28] In the case of architecture at least there could be some truth in this! There is another geopolitical dimension of the Games involving America that merits attention. If the Chinese dominate the Games, as they intend, and more especially the medal table, it is a not an unreasonable expectation that America will inject billions of dollars into its athletic systems in time for London 2012. Nationalism cuts more than one way: internationalism sometimes cuts no ice. Sport *realpolitik* is not dead. Ipso facto, the reality of geopolitical sport still exists. In a wider context, will these be geopolitical outcomes of Beijing 2008?

To return to paradoxes: 'A confident ambitious and at times aggressive Chinese nationalism – of which Beijing's Olympic preparations are a grandiloquent emblem – undeniably exists in the contemporary People's Republic. But it is a force compromised by its internal contradictions: by a pride in its imperial history and insecurity about its modern weakness that have generated both a powerful need for external approbation and a compensating rhetoric of strident patriotism. The great conundrum of contemporary China is that most of its messages are, at present, mixed: China is, in short, not fully in control of either its rise or its rhetoric.' [29] Nevertheless, while this may well be true, 'what is clear is that, throughout their long past, China's society, government and culture have historically demonstrated enough flexibility and pragmatism to navigate the political, socio-economic and psychological difficulties that its entry into the modern global system has generated.' [30] However, in the immediate future 'China will doubtless continue to maintain its present, contradictory profile: pushing both patriotism and internationalism; confidently pronouncing on its rise while vying still for foreign approbation and struggling with enormous domestic challenges; combining powerful yearnings for globalisation with tight controls over its media and laws', [31] thus 'making safe predictions over its medium-to long-term future practically impossible.' [32] Is this true? Another commentator comes to a similar conclusion: '...China is caught in a gigantic dilemma. It cannot continue with the current model [massive growth] which is beset by numerous contradictions and which sooner or later will return to earth, provoked either by a banking crisis or simply a crisis of over-investment and excess supply, or some combination of both. The consequent social reaction will provoke a political crisis...It was the fifth generation of communist leaders in the Soviet Union who came to the conclusion that the system was no longer sustainable; it is not inconceivable that after the Beijing Olympics in 2008 some of the incoming fifth generation of Chinese leaders, notwithstanding their apparent conservatism, could come to a similar conclusion.' [33] Is this also true?

And a final paradox: in an emotional comment on the Flame Relay in London, the Chinese ambassador to London, Madame Fu Ying, stated recently that 'a sincere heart is not enough to ensure China's smooth integration with the world. The wall that stands in China's way to the world is thick.' [34] Some would reasonably ask is this the Chinese Internet Firewall or the wall of Chinese incomprehension of sincere international humanitarian concern over human rights in Darfur, Zimbabwe, Tibet and indeed, China? If, as Madame Fu Ying remarks, 'The world has waited for China to join it. Now China has to have the patience to wait for the world to understand China', [35] then the reverse is also true. What part will Beijing 2008 play in promoting necessary symphonious understanding? It is important to be positive and to work for this: West and East. At a recent Oxford conference on Olympic Legacies, none the less, the point was made that one certainty associated with the aftermath of Beijing 2008 was that so much is uncertain. The geopolitical outcomes in the Pacific Rim especially but also beyond, will be watched with interest throughout the world post Beijing 2008.

J. A. Mangan,
Founding and Executive Academic Editor,
The International Journal of the History of Sport

Founding and Senior Editor,
Sport in the Global Society Series

Notes

[1] Eliot, 'Burnt Norton' in *FOUR QUARTETS*, quoted in *The Oxford Dictionary of Quotations*, 270.

[2] Goddard, *Into the Blue*, 291–2.

[3] Calvino, *Invisible Cities*, quoted in *The Oxford Book of Aphorisms*, 57.

[4] *The Shorter Oxford Dictionary*, 1080.

[5] Dong and Mangan, 'Beijing Olympic Legacies', 14.

[6] Ibid., 14–15.

[7] Mangan and Dong, *Beijing 2008: Preparing for Glory*. Publicity flier.

[8] Lovell, 'Prologue: Beijing 2008 – The Mixed Messages of Contemporary Chinese Nationalism', 770.

[9] Ibid.

[10] Ibid.

[11] Crawford, 'Serious Sport': *J.A. Mangan's* Contribution *to the History of Sport*. (See back cover)

[12] Lovell, 'Prologue: Beijing 2008 – The Mixed Messages of Contemporary Chinese Nationalism', 773.

[13] Mangan, 'A Personal Perspective: Twenty-five Years', *IJHS*, 1–2.

[14] Ibid.

[15] Ibid.

[16] Lovell, 'Prologue: Beijing 2008 – The Mixed Messages of Contemporary Chinese Nationalism', 771.

[17] In my own discussions with Chinese at the Beijing Forum in 2008 this was abundantly clear.

[18] See, for example, Knight, 'Torch Guards needed more control, says Jowett', *The Daily Telegraph, April 16, 2008, S24. Tessa Jowell is the British Olympics* Minister. Ken Livingstone, the Mayor of London, was quoted in the same article as saying that it was a mistake to allow the attendants to guard the Torch: 'It should not have happened', he said. 'Had I known, I would have said it was unacceptable'. Sebastion Coe was reliably reported to have called the Chinese attendants 'Thugs'. See *The Daily Telegraph*, April 24, 2008, S19. Equally unfortunate was the attitude displayed by pro-Tibet protestors to jin Jing in Paris, April 13, 2008.

[19] Lovell, 'Prologue: Beijing 2008 – The Mixed Messages of Contemporary Chinese Nationalism', 773.

[20] Ibid.

[21] Ibid.

[22] Shirk, *China: Fragile Superpower*.

[23] Ibid., 255.

[24] Lovell, 'Prologue: Beijing 2008 ...' 773.

[25] Owen, 'Forbidden Cixi: rediscovered', *The Sunday Telegraph*, March 16, 2008, T4.

[26] Ibid.

[27] Dyreson, 'Preparing To Take Credit for China's Glory: American perspectives on the Beijing Olympics', 3.

[28] Ibid.

[29] Lovell, 'Prologue: Beijing 2008 – The Mixed Messages of Contemporary Chinese Nationalism', 773.

[30] Ibid.

[31] Ibid.

[32] Ibid.

[33] Hutton, *The Writing on the Wall: China and the West in the 21st Century*, 339 and 342.

[34] Fu Ying, 'If only the West would listen to China', *The Daily Telegraph*, April 13, 24.

[35] Ibid.

References

Calvino, Italo. Invisible Cities, quoted in *The Oxford Book of Aphorisms, chosen by John Gross.* Oxford: OUP, 1987.

Crawford, Scott A.G.M., ed. *'Serious Sport'; J.A. Mangan's Contribution to the History of Sport.* London: Cass, 2004.

Dong, Jinxia and Mangan, J.A. 'Olympic Aspirations: Chinese Women on Top – Considerations and Consequences'. In *Beijing 2008: Preparing for Glory Chinese Challenge in the 'Chinese Century'*, edited by J.A. Mangan and Jinxia Dong. London: Routledge, 779–806.

——. 'Beijing Olympic Legacies: Certain Intentions and Certain and Uncertain Outcomes'. In *Olympic Legacies: Intended and Unintended – Political, Cultural, Economic, Educational,* edited by J.A. Mangan and Mark Dyerson. London: Routledge, forthcoming.

Dyerson, Mark. 'Preparing to Take Credit for China's Glory: American Perspectives on the Beijing Olympic Games'. In *Beijing 2008: Preparing for Glory Chinese Challenge in the 'Chinese Century'*. London: Routledge, forthcoming.

Eliot, T.S. 'Burnt Norton' in Four Quartets, quoted in *The Oxford Dictionary of Quotations.* Oxford: OUP, 1996, edited by Angela Partington.

Fu Ying. 'If only the West would listen to China'. *The Daily Telegraph*, April 13, 24.

Goddard, Robert. *Into the Blue.* London: Corgi Books, 1995.

Hutton, Will. *The Writing on the Wall: China and the West in the 21st Century.* London: Abacus, 2007.

Knight, Tom. 'Torch Guards needed more control, says Jowett'. *The Daily Telegraph,* April 16, 2008, S24.

Lovell, Julia. 'Prologue: Beijing 2008 – The Mixed Messages of Contemporary Chinese Nationalism'. In *Beijing 2008: Preparing for Glory Chinese Challenge in the 'Chinese Century'.* London: Routledge, 758–78.

Mangan, J.A. 'A Personal Perspective: Twenty-five Years'. *The International Journal of the History of Sport* 23, no. 1 (February 2006): 1–2.

Owen, James. 'Forbidden Cixi: rediscovered'. *The Sunday Telegraph*, March 16, 2008, T4.

Shirk, Susan. *China: Fragile Superpower.* Oxford: OUP, 2007.

Prologue: Beijing 2008 – The Mixed Messages of Contemporary Chinese Nationalism

Julia Lovell

The world has chosen China. ... This is not just about winning the right to host a sporting event; it demonstrates the global status and respect enjoyed by the largest developing country in the world. ... The sons and daughters of the nation are united in their joy ... It is proof of China's exceptional strength. ... China will prove to the world that the International Olympic Committee has made a wise choice indeed. Beijing will give the world the most exceptional Olympics in history.

'One World, One Dream' is a profound manifestation of the core concepts of the Beijing Olympic Games. It reflects the values of harmony connoted in the concept of 'People's Olympics', the core and soul of the three concepts – Green Olympics, High-tech Olympics and People's Olympics ... 'One World, One Dream' ... expresses the firm belief of a great nation, with a long history of 5,000 years and on its way towards modernisation, that is committed to peaceful development, harmonious society and people's happiness. It voices the aspirations of 1.3 billion Chinese people to contribute to the establishment of a peaceful and bright world.

We must be willing to take on more hardship and more intensive training, enduring more pain than average people can ever imagine. Then we can beat all our rivals. [1]

To China, the 2008 Olympic Games represent a great deal more than a fortnight-long sporting spectacular. [2] The 29th Olympiad is the country's international coming-out party: a global recognition of this ancient civilization's euphoric twenty-first-century resurgence. As well as confirming the nation's great-power status, however, the Beijing Olympics is – at least according to official Chinese commentary – as much about world peace as it is about national glory. Its organizers have declared themselves faithful heirs to the modern Olympic ideal of 'promoting a peaceful society concerned with the preservation of human dignity', thereby underlining the benignity of China's own 'peaceful rise'. The 2008 Olympics will, allegedly, be a harmonious fusion of nationalism and internationalism, of Chinese tradition and high-tech modernity: a utopian symbol of China's triumphant – but decidedly non-hegemonic – recovery of a central position in the international political, economic and cultural realm, some 150 years after the country's humiliating nineteenth-century clash with Western imperialism.

While Beijing's publicity machine spins out such idealistic platitudes, however, China's athletes and sports fans seem in little doubt as to China's true mission for 2008: to win as many gold medals as possible – ideally beating their great-power rival the US to the top of the medals table. '[O]ur task in the Beijing Olympics,' the deputy president of the China Olympic Committee has openly stated, 'is to challenge the USA'. [3] The patriotic hunger for Olympic glory is driving some to extraordinary physical extremes. Between June and August 2007, an eight-year-old girl, Zhang Huimin, set herself the personal Olympic challenge of running more than 3,500 kilometres from her home in Hainan, in China's far south, to the Great Wall north of Beijing. 'Olympic spirit, strong body, extreme challenge, honour for the nation' advertised signs pinned to the front and back of her running clothes. [4]

What sense can be made of Beijing's contradictory Olympic enterprise? Will China's global renaissance – exemplified by its 'harmonious' Olympics – truly promote universal goodwill rather than partisan nationalism? How can an event that is, at base, about individual nations' medal placing and (in Coach Liang's words) 'beating all our rivals' spread the gospel of world peace? How are we to reconcile China's emphasis on 'global harmony' with its state-sponsored waves of anti-foreign nationalism, its harsh treatment of domestic political opponents, its heavily polluted environment and its threatening of military action against an independent state (Taiwan) lying off its south-eastern seaboard? If China is so confident about its ancient and contemporary greatness, moreover, why does it require global affirmation through hosting the Olympics? Why do its athletes, coaches and sports fans need to be obsessed with the already-glorious motherland gaining added lustre through sporting triumphs?

These inconsistencies have been generated by the compound of historical experiences and expectations that make up contemporary Chinese nationalism. They spring from the circumstances in which imperial China reinvented itself as a modern nation at the turn of the nineteenth century: circumstances that continue to fuel uncertainties in the international community about the way in which a globally ascendant China will behave over the coming decades. Below, I will set the paradoxes of China's Olympic vision within the broader contexts of Chinese political and cultural history, before exploring the combination of pride and insecurity that has surrounded China's quest, over the past century, to regain global stature.

From Empire to Nation

Until the late nineteenth century, China's rulers largely viewed themselves governing not a nation, but a universal empire (*tianxia*, 'all under heaven'), whose authority – cohering around the moral superiority and sophistication of elaborately literate political and cultural traditions – radiated, in theory, indefinitely outwards to civilize its non-Chinese, barbarian neighbours. Before the incursions by the West, Chinese understanding of the world order was shaped by Sino-centric ideals that went back at least as far as the Han dynasty (206 BC–220 AD). According to the Han five-zone (*wu fu*) theory, since the time of the mythical Xia dynasty (*c.* second millennium BC), China had been divided into five concentric zones: the inner three were ruled directly by the Chinese king, while the outer two were occupied by barbarians. The barbarian zones were tied to the Chinese centre by the system of tributary relations, according to which inhabitants of all five zones owed tribute and ritual obeisance to the Chinese court, thereby affirming their status as dependent vassals. [5] The world, in Sino-centric theory at least, thus revolved around China.

The reality of imperial China's foreign relations was often very different from this ideal: between the Han and Qing dynasties, parts, and sometimes all of China were conquered by tribes from the northern steppe; the last of these conquering tribes founded Qing rule in 1644. Scholarship of the past few decades has carefully demonstrated how the condescending theory of the tributary system – by which inferior 'barbarian' vassals were irresistibly drawn to submit to the civilizing rituals of the Confucian power centre – was frequently not reproduced in practice. The hierarchical façade of tributary homage could serve equally as a pragmatic front for trade; or as a kind of diplomatic protection racket, operating at a financial loss to the empire. The Chinese court would offer subsidies to warlike neighbours (frequently, Mongolian tribes) in exchange for objects of no particular value or use and the promise not to attack Chinese territory. Often enough, the more distant a tributary was from China, the more partial its acceptance of the Chinese ideal of superiority. Far from clinging to a rigidly idealized tributary etiquette, then, imperial China's foreign policy-makers could combine it pragmatically with economic incentives and diplomacy, and even with the laissez-faire 'loose-rein' policy, by which distant barbarians who chose to pay court to the Chinese centre would not be refused, while those who did not would not be forced. [6]

Neither was imperial China chauvinistically convinced of its own self-sufficiency. In her study of Chinese cosmopolitanism from the first millennium BC to the twentieth century, Joanna Waley-Cohen has argued convincingly that China's conventional rhetoric of cultural superiority 'disguised considerable flexibility and open-mindedness. ... Time out of mind, China ... has been energetically and enthusiastically engaged with the outside world, permitting, encouraging, seeking circulation of foreign goods and ideas.' Ranging from the Han dynasty's fascination with Silk Road exotica to nineteenth-century China's readiness to study from the West, Waley-Cohen unearths, from beneath the 'lofty public utterances' of Sino-centric politicians, a significant degree of pragmatic curiosity about foreign offerings on the part of China's rulers and people.

At the same time, however, Waley-Cohen underlines that China's political elites 'have been consistently reluctant to allow free rein to any kind of foreign ideology, for fear of losing political and moral control over that portion of the population for whom the foreign ideology might come to prevail over Chinese values and traditions.' [7] The centrality of Confucian culture, in other words, was the great non-negotiable of the pre-modern Chinese world order. Although Chinese elites were periodically faced with the conundrum of accommodating the humiliation of foreign conquest to the ideal of Chinese cultural superiority, in the end most of these foreign conquerors obligingly bolstered the theory of Sino-centrism by significantly (though far from entirely) sinicizing, by accepting the principles of Confucian culture and government: from the Northern Wei dynasty (386–534), via the Mongol Yuan (1260–1368) to the Manchu Qing (1644–1911).

In asserting the ideal of a universal Chinese empire, pre-modern China's rulers did not rely exclusively on the persuasive attractions of Confucian moral virtue but turned also to more belligerent strategies. Until relatively recently, thanks to the prevailing anti-military bias of Confucian literary elites and to nineteenth- and twentieth-century Western stereotypes of a weak, effete China, the empire's history of militarism has remained one of the significantly obscured narratives of the Chinese past. This is an obscurity that the rulers of contemporary China have been more than happy to encourage, asserting that China has always occupied the moral high ground over other nations and civilizations by striking out only in defence, and not offence; that historically China has been peace-loving, non-confrontational and non-acquisitive in nature – in contrast, implicitly, with the imperialist West. [8]

Western scholarship of the last few years, however, has drawn increasing attention to China's often overlooked traditions of military imperialism. Introducing a 2000 collection of essays on Chinese warfare, Hans van de Ven underlines the vigour of imperial China's military culture across the millennia: its sophisticated use of technology and discipline and 'of offensive strategies ... seeking the annihilation of the enemy'. [9] Focusing on relations between Chinese states and the steppe during the first millennium AD, Nicola DiCosmo has described the 'endemic warfare and ruthless conquest' undertaken during this period, arguing that Chinese sources dwelling on the cultural inferiority of northern peoples were used to justify the subjugation and annexation of these tribes. His work on frontier walls built across north China in the second half of this millennium suggests that the purpose of these barriers – swinging far out into the Mongolian steppe, hundreds of kilometres from farmable land – was more offensive than defensive, designed to enable the Chinese to police peoples whose way of life differed from their own, and to control lucrative trade routes. [10] Those who lay beyond or resisted the Chinese civilising enterprise could be subjected to dehumanizing contempt, described, at benevolent best, as 'birds and beasts' needing to be 'awed' or 'tranquillized' with Chinese 'goodness', or more militantly as 'wolves, to whom no indulgence should be given'. [11]

In an essay on the origins of the tribute system, Wang Gungwu has asserted that it was in fact ancient China's military victories over its foreign neighbours that substantially bolstered, or even generated, China's belief in its cultural centrality and uniqueness. Overturning the Confucian article of faith that, through Chinese history, moral virtue, and not brute force, convinced China's neighbours of China's universal superiority, Wang contests instead that the triumph of force underpinned Sino-centrism from its very inception. [12]

It was under the Manchu Qing dynasty that the projection of China's moral mandate to dominate other cultures was combined with overwhelming military force, to greatest empire-building effect. The Qing absorbed the long-standing universalistic pretensions of Chinese emperorship and gave them real political form by defeating many of the Chinese empire's traditional frontier challengers. Where submission could be attained by culturalist means, the Qing made use of a dense, multi-ethnic – Confucian, Manchu and Tibetan – network of guest ritual and religious codes. Inside the state's civilized velvet glove of ceremonial and diplomacy, however, was an iron fist. Those who violated or defied the norms of the Qing world order risked ruthless elimination – such as the Zunghar Mongols, whom, after almost a century of fighting for their autonomy from Chinese rule, the Qianlong emperor ordered to be ethnically cleansed in the 1750s. [13] Qing military triumphs gave real teeth to the Chinese ideal of 'universal empire', forging by the end of the eighteenth century a state that encompassed, in addition to China proper, Inner and Outer Mongolia, Tibet and Central Asia as far as Lake Balkash, Taiwan and Manchuria.

It was with the high Qing version of the imperial Chinese worldview – a worldview fully capable of openness to the outside world and of pragmatic multiculturalism, but dominated by a confidently grandiose sense of the Chinese empire's universal superiority – that Western imperialist powers violently clashed in the second half of the nineteenth century. [14] Between 1840 and 1895 – years in which China was compelled, by repeated military defeats at the hands of foreign armies unanimously scornful of Chinese civilization, to surrender sovereignty over its borders – the empire's confidence in the validity of universal Sino-centrism steadily collapsed. In 1860, after Anglo-French forces had stormed the imperial

Summer Palace north-west of Beijing, forcing the government to open ten new ports to free trade, to allow free movement of foreigners through China and to permit Western powers to install ambassadors and consuls and assert extra-territorial jurisdiction within designated foreign concessions, the emperor Xianfeng finally pronounced that 'England is an independent sovereign state; let it have equal status with China'. [15] Some 30 years later, China's shocking defeat in the 1894–5 Sino-Japanese War comprehensively demolished the ritual façade of the tribute system, as the Chinese empire found itself vanquished by a country that it had always viewed as a cultural tributary.

Out of this intense, beleaguered perception of crisis and emergency grew modern Chinese nationalism, as reforming elites began to see China no longer as the centre of the civilized world but as one nation among many engaged on a Darwinian struggle for survival in a new modern system invented and dominated by the West. To paradigmatic Chinese thinkers at the start of the twentieth century, the way of nationalism was the key to China's survival and recovery of its ancient greatness. 'Europe has evolved,' concluded the influential intellectual Liang Qichao,

> and the world has progressed since the sixteenth century for no reason other than the enormous power of nationalism ... in today's situation, if we want to counteract the national imperialism of all those world powers so as to save the country from total catastrophe, we must develop a nationalism of our own. [16]

The twentieth-century search by intellectuals and politicians for modern China has been dominated by the quest for a cohesive national polity and culture that will enable China to stand up to the West and become an important global player once more. And having invested so much hope and energy in reinventing China as a modern nation state, China's elites have sought all possible affirmation of their efforts in this direction, namely recognition from the inventor of the modern international system, the West. In the post-Mao era, this desire for recognition has manifested itself in the near-pathological yearning for international prizes and 'face' – for Nobel Prizes, for entry to the WTO, for Olympic gold medals and, of course, for the prestige of hosting the games themselves.

All spheres of cultural and social activity – art, literature, education, fashion, architecture, journalism – have been drawn into China's pursuit of a modern version of itself that will inspire respect, rather than scorn, from the West, but sport has been given particular weight in this effort. Compared, for example, with the intellectual elitism of literature, sport provides a far more straightforwardly populist symbolic framework within which individuals can represent the nation. Athletes strengthen their bodies to strengthen the national body, or compete internationally as members of the national team, to win glory for the motherland, involving, in the process, broad swathes of the Chinese populace as spectators. Consequently, sport has occupied a central place in China's modern nation-building enterprise from its very beginnings. As nationalists at the start of the twentieth century imbibed imperialist views of Chinese racial inferiority, they became fully obsessed with the idea of China as 'the sick man of East Asia', and with the project of curing the weak, diseased national character – spiritually, through literature and art, and physically, through new, Westernized ideas about physical education that attached special importance to sports and military discipline. 'Idealistic reformers throughout modern Chinese history,' summarized a popular Chinese textbook on the Olympics, 'have striven, through developing sport, to transform the national spirit and strengthen the national polity, to rescue China from its state of weakness.' [17]

But the traumatic circumstances in which China transformed itself from a universal empire into a nation have generated a number of serious contradictions at the heart of the modern Chinese national identity. The Chinese project to recover lost imperial glory through winning international – in reality, Western – recognition is one that is doomed to ambivalence, since the global system from which China has sought recognition is dominated by the West, the very source of China's humiliations. A sense of entitlement to Western-based international plaudits reveals both a confident belief in China's superiority *and* an anxious need for that belief to be affirmed by the West. China will never recover its pre-modern, free-standing sense of political and cultural self-confidence in a world order whose centre of gravity has shifted outside it. Insecurity about Chinese national identity and the obsession with a diseased Chinese culture have often produced their inverse: a nationalistic machismo, angrily sensitive to Western slights and affronts, that asserts China's uniqueness and right to global acclaim. Geremie Barmé has summarized this as the tendency towards 'self-approbation and self-loathing' in modern Chinese culture: China is perceived both as a glorious 5,000-year-old civilization deserving of recognition and a humiliated modern culture inferior to the world standard. [18]

The paradoxes of Chinese nationalism – reproduced, in microcosm, in the rhetorical inconsistencies of the Beijing Olympics – have generated many of the doubts about its character and intentions that have troubled Western commentators, particularly in the post-Mao era, following China's assertive re-entry into the international arena. Concerns about China's aspirations have further intensified since the 1990s, when rapid economic development and the growth of (particularly urban) incomes have fuelled a confident, reinforced sense of nationalistic entitlement to global stature. Observers have wondered whether contemporary China is striving only for equality in the global system of nation states, or whether it is permeated with pre-modern imperialist universalism, harbouring ambitions to recover – through whatever means necessary – imperial China's traditional place in the sun. Will its strong international orientation – the importance it attaches to Western-based approbation and its openness to cultural traffic from the West (far in excess, it should be recalled, of the West's openness to Chinese culture) serve as an effective brake on aggressive, competitive confrontation with other countries; or will public memory of nineteenth-century humiliations – kept angrily alive by state-sponsored patriotic education campaigns – tip it in a more aggressive direction?

There is, at present, little consensus on any of these questions, either in academic, governmental or popular debate. [19] One of the most considered perspectives, however, comes from Suisheng Zhao, whose thorough account of Chinese nationalism, while noting its vigour and potential volatility, concludes that it is dominated by a defensively oriented pragmatism: that it is, in David Shambaugh's words, 'assertive in form, but reactive in essence'. Powered by feelings of humiliated pride, Zhao goes on, the 'defensive nature of Chinese nationalism has made China's leaders very assertive in defending China's national interests, particularly on issues concerning national security and territorial integrity. ... The same defensive nature ... [has] prevented China from taking proactive action on issues beyond its immediate concerns and capabilities.' In contemporary China, pragmatic nationalists adapt to 'the predominant international system ... in pursuit of positive compromise'. [20] It is China's aggressive expressions of anti-foreign nationalism that draw international headlines – most prominently, the public outbursts of anger over the NATO bombing of the embassy in Belgrade in 1999, and the death of a Chinese pilot in the spy-plane collision of 2001. And yet, Zhao notes, the government carefully channels and, if necessary, curtails outbursts of anti-foreignism so as not to derail necessary working relationships with Western countries. Although the ultimate aim of pragmatic nationalism remains the pursuit of national strength, it supports the maintenance of a multipolar, anti-hegemonic world system. While pragmatic nationalists want, above all, to see China occupy a prominent position in the world, this is – for the time being – to be achieved through participation in, rather than confrontation with, existing international structures.

Coinciding to some extent with Zhao's analysis, I see contemporary Chinese nationalism – for all its apparent assertiveness and ambition – as currently constrained by the anxieties indigenous to China's experiences over the past century and a half. Drawing on its vast store of historical precedent, China in its official, public dealings with the outside world is capable of both strident self-confidence and abased insecurity, of intransigence and open-minded pragmatism, of universalistic rhetoric and self-interested power-seeking. An unstable consciousness of ancient glory and modern humiliation still haunts contemporary China's self-image, and provides the context against which we must read the mixed messages of the Beijing Olympics – a metonym for the curious phenomenon of modern Chinese nationalism.

Preparing for Glory

1: Self-confidence or self-loathing?

China's earliest public response to the announcement on 13 July 2001 of its successful bid to host the 2008 Olympics was an outpouring of patriotic emotion: in Beijing, an estimated 400,000 people converged on Tiananmen Square, with around one million surging through the streets of Beijing. 'Motherland, I am proud of you!' proclaimed the front page of the *People's Daily* (the broadsheet organ of the Communist Party), describing Tiananmen as a sea of red national flags. A few pages in, another article compiled jubilant soundbites from every corner of the country, including Urumqi in the far north-west ('the greatness of the motherland has brought success to the bid'), Hohhot in Inner Mongolia ('We are victorious!'), Kunming and Shenzhen in the south ('We've won! We've won!') and so on and so forth. Montages of photographs captured images of a nation united in its elation: grinning politicians, delighted national minorities, ecstatic students, all exhibiting a joyful intensity of nationalistic passion that had no analogue in patchy British responses, in 2005, to the announcement that London had won the right to host the 2012 games. [21]

The official Chinese media were quick to gloss the larger symbolism of the decision by the International Olympic Committee. 'Joy reigned supreme, as the entirety of our divine land rose up in celebration,' announced one Party publication:

> China, this ancient eastern civilization, its culture as dazzling as a river of stars, has attracted the attention of the world. ... Beijing winning the right to host the 2008 Olympics is a towering milestone in China, raising its international position: a great event in the grand renaissance of the Chinese race. ... China's struggle to host the Olympics has been the struggle to concentrate national economic, scientific and cultural strength: for international image and national status. The 2008 Beijing Olympics will be the world's fulsome affirmation of contemporary China's economic and social progress. The Chinese people have received the respect of the world. The Olympics have chosen Beijing; the world has chosen China. [22]

Once the veneer of nationalistic triumph has been peeled back from this collection of responses, however, a couple of questions suggest themselves. Would a nation securely confident in the 'dazzling' qualities of its ancient civilization draw such emphatic attention to them? If China is so convinced of its power and glory, why does it look to the IOC for approbation, and respond with such hyperbolic excitement on receiving it? 'Descriptions of China as 'inferior' and 'great',' Peter Hays Gries points out in his 2005 study of contemporary Chinese patriotism,

> cannot be read literally, but must be understood in their historical and political contexts. When tributary missions came to pay obeisance, imperial officials referred to China as 'our inferior nation' (*biguo*) and the tributaries as 'your superior nation' (*guiguo*). They were so confident that China was the undisputed center of civilization ... that they could afford the self-deprecation. By contrast, Chinese diplomats under the People's Republic have routinely referred to China as 'great' (*weida*). These diametrically opposite choices of diction point to an insecurity – central to today's nationalism – about China's international status. [23]

The outburst of exultant self-congratulation that followed the announcement of 13 July was haunted by the vocabulary of modern China's anxious internationalism: by its preoccupation with world 'attention', 'affirmation' and 'respect'. China is, in one breath, a 'divine land', in another 'raising its international position' and embarked upon a 'renaissance'. Recollection of nineteenth-century debacles hung over the celebratory mood, as contemporary China's glorious, vigorous present was contrasted with the sufferings of a century earlier. 'After the Opium Wars, humiliations and defeats cast their pall over the entire nation,' observed the *Journal of the Beijing University of Physical Education.*

> But a nation's sporting achievements are a direct reflection of its economic, scientific and social conditions, and of its national spirit. ... The exceptional performance of Chinese athletes at the Olympic Games has established a gloriously strong and hardworking image for the nation, filling the Chinese people with pride, causing the world to look at us with increased respect, raising our nation's international position and stimulating powerful feelings of patriotism. [24]

To prove that Beijing's successful bid for the 2008 Olympics established China's image as a 'great power', the *Sports Culture Digest* quoted exclusively the responses of foreign newspapers – Japanese, Singaporean, American, British – to the news; China's rise, it seems, still requires external verification from the developed world. [25] 'We thank the international Olympic committee for its faith in us,' the *People's Daily* humbly expressed, below pictures of grinning ranks of Politburo members. 'The Chinese people will not betray expectations but advance with all our might to host successfully the 2008 Olympics.' [26]

Hyperbolic predictions about the exceptional, unprecedented scale of the 2008 Olympics briskly followed the initial eruptions of joy. 'In seven years' time,' pronounced official commentary, 'Beijing will stun the world with the most successful sporting event it has ever seen, striving to compose the most dazzling chapter yet in Olympic history.' [27] As the opening ceremony draws closer, Chinese Olympic fans have filled internet discussion sites with exclamations of patriotic encouragement: 'Keep going, China!'; 'May the Chinese live for ever, and ever, and ever, and ever!'; 'We will bring heaven and earth together to surpass ourselves – to win a glorious victory'; '2008 belongs to China'; and so on. [28]

True enough, every Olympic host recognizes that the games offer an exceptional international PR opportunity for their nation and toils to put on the best show possible, to take advantage of the global media frenzy that will spotlight their efforts. Nonetheless, in its Olympic preparations, China does seem to have striven harder for superlatives than most: to host the 'biggest and most expensive Olympics in the history of the Games'. [29] The torch relay will be longer than all its predecessors, and incorporate an ascent of the highest mountain in the world. Nothing, it seems, can be allowed to stand in the way of this two-week sporting festival: certainly not ordinary civilian residences inconveniently lying on sites earmarked for Olympic development. (While the Chinese government estimates that just over 6,000 people have been relocated to make way for Olympic projects, the Centre on Housing Rights and Evictions in Geneva ups the figure to 1.5 million.) [30] In accordance with the long-established practice of intervening meteorologically to ensure clear skies for events of national importance, the government's weather modification office has openly stated that it will seed the clouds as necessary to guarantee rainless days. [31]

There is, undeniably, a blustering, self-assured swagger to contemporary China's love of massive spectacle and ostentation, reminiscent of the British Empire in its late Victorian heyday. It also, however, betrays a certain undignified desperation to impress that suggests the opposite: a powerful sense that China has something to prove to the world; and an obsession with China's international 'face' and image. The People's Republic of China does have an established record of going that extra (sometimes absurd) mile to overwhelm foreign observers. Decades after they began running lavishly choreographed tours for Western visitors around immaculately faked socialist miracles, contemporary China's rulers a marked fondness for Potemkin display. [32] In preparation for President Clinton's 1998 visit to Beijing, gangs of workers were dispatched to staple plastic leaves onto trees, while swathes of grass were sprayed green before the Olympic Committee's final 2001 inspection, to brighten the sallow capital. Compare a rising China's Olympic frenzy with the relative indifference of post-imperial Britain, in which preparations for the 2012 games have – except for those directly involved in the organization and development – sunk beneath the public radar.

Again in the interests of putting on the most flawless international show possible, the government has been waging mass 'civilization improvement' campaigns across the capital, concentrating on eradicating bad public habits that might disgust squeamish foreigners and tarnish China's image. 'Welcome the Olympics, be civilized' (*ying Aoyun, jiang wenming*) instruct enormous posters pasted throughout the city by the Capital Spiritual Civilization Office, while 'civilization and etiquette practical educational activities' have encouraged groups of civilians to compete against each other in 'civility contests'. [33] In the run-up to the Olympics, the 11th of each month has been named 'queuing day', to indoctrinate citizens in the art of the orderly line, while taxi drivers have been exhorted to brush their teeth, change their clothes and bathe often. [34] The most intense efforts have been poured into eradicating – or at least severely reducing – spitting in public places, to which end the Civilization Office recently revealed that it had spent 1,700 hours monitoring the spitting habits of 230,000 residents in 320 public places. [35]

In its Olympic preparations, China is presented, on the one hand, as an ancient civilization, as 'the most precious pearl in the treasure-house of world culture'; on the other, as a nation of barbarians in urgent need of improvement by the Civilization Police before it is fit for the modern world. [36] This strange juxtaposition of self-esteem and self-disgust goes back to the superiority-inferiority complex that lies at the root of modern Chinese nation-building. 'Our civilization has already advanced two thousand years beyond yours,' the revolutionary nationalist Sun Yat-sen once loftily informed a British consul. 'We are willing to wait for you to progress and catch up with us.' While chastising his compatriots for spitting, burping and farting in public, and failing to brush their teeth, however, Sun complained that 'as soon as foreigners meet us they say that we are barbaric. ... If everyone would devote some systematic effort to cultivating their persons ... then foreigners would certainly respect the Chinese.' [37] For all their bombastic expressions of pride, China's response to and preparations for the 2008 Olympics are notably undercut by an uneasy regard for the foreign – and in particular, Western – gaze. China, it seems, is a rising superpower still far from brashly unilateralist in its self-confidence.

2. One World, Whose Dream?

Almost before the tears of patriotic joy had dried on the face of the nation following the announcement of 13 July 2001, the official media were setting forth how the Beijing Olympics would contribute to international harmony. A rash of slogans ('One World One Dream'; a 'People's Olympics'), articles and handbooks hastened to set out China's benevolent aspirations for the games, and for the world in general. 'While "Harmony of Man with Nature" and "Peace Enjoys Priority",' pronounced the games' website,

> are the philosophies and ideals of the Chinese people since ancient times in their pursuit of the harmony between Man and Nature and the harmony among people, building up a harmonious society and achieving harmonious development are the dream and aspirations of ours. It is our belief that peace and progress, harmonious development, living in amity, cooperation and mutual benefit, and enjoying a happy life are the common ideals of the people throughout the world. 'One World, One Dream' ... is of China, and also of the world. It conveys the lofty ideal of the people in Beijing as well as in China to share the global community and civilization and to create a bright future hand in hand with the people from the rest of the world. [38]

This preoccupation with 'harmony' sets China's Olympic rhetoric squarely within the 'peaceful rise' theory expounded since 2003 by the Chinese Communist Party. Through it, China's rulers have expressly attempted to reassure anxious foreign observers prone to recurring fits of 'Yellow Peril' fear that China's apparently unstoppable re-emergence as a global power will not be accompanied by hegemonic sabre-rattling. China's new strength and influence, they insist, will be a force for international harmony rather than of militant nationalism. 'China persists in its pursuit of harmony and development internally,' runs the 'peaceful rise' manifesto, 'while pursuing peace and development externally; the two aspects, closely linked and organically united, are an integrated whole, and will help to build a harmonious world of sustained peace and common prosperity.'

Theoreticians of China's 'peaceful rise' have pledged their country's enthusiastic support for multilateralism in the international community, resolutely denying that a resurgent China will seek revenge for past humiliations. 'During the 100-odd years following the Opium War in 1840,' the manifesto continues,

> China suffered humiliation and insult from big powers. And thus, ever since the advent of modern times, it has become the assiduously sought goal of the Chinese people to eliminate war, maintain peace, and build a country of independence and prosperity, and a comfortable and happy life for the people. ... The Chinese nation

has always been a peace-loving one. Chinese culture is a pacific culture. The spirit of the Chinese people has always featured their longing for peace and pursuit of harmony. [39]

The Beijing Olympics is, equally, conceptualized as an unprecedented opportunity for China to do good on a global stage: to foster East-West exchange and friendship, to spread the peace-loving principles of ancient Chinese philosophy both in sport and in the world in general. Glossing the slogan 'A People's Olympics', the *Journal of the Beijing University of Physical Education* explained that

> [t]he unique, magical values, culture, philosophy and practice of China's millennia-old sporting traditions will have a deep influence on the Olympic Movement. China's special emphasis on health and longevity will have a corrective influence on the Olympic Movement's obsession with promoting elite sports and muscular strength, and disregard for the harmony of mind, body and nature. The spirit of fairness, honesty, love for fellow man and friendship in Confucian sporting ethics and philosophy will without doubt have a cleansing effect on international sporting competitions plagued by drug use and football hooliganism ... Industrial civilization needs more harmony, and Chinese traditional culture will inevitably benefit the future of mankind. [40]

In insisting on China's universalistic impulses, Chinese commentators have almost unanimously refused to acknowledge the possibility of any conflict between national and international interests – even though realization of the universalistic ideals espoused by the modern Olympic Games has been stymied, since the 'IOC created an institutional structure based on national representation', by nationalistic partisanship. [41] China's official projection of the Olympic Spirit is a mellifluous symphony of nationalism and internationalism, a kind of Westphalian utopia in which China's rise serves only to bolster world peace. 'The Olympics will promote exchange between East and West,' observed a *People's Daily* commentary, 'increasing contacts between the people of China and the people of the world ... [and] powerfully stimulate the patriotic feelings of everyone and every nationality in the country. ... [It] is an opportunity for China, and an opportunity for the world.' [42]

Beijing's harmonious Olympic rhetoric, however, poses almost as many questions as China's 'peaceful rise' theory. First of all, how should we square China's claim to be the true inheritor of the idealistic Olympic spirit with its hunger to top the medal tables, triumphantly dislodging the US – the contemporary world's one undisputed superpower – in the process? Since the People's Republic returned to the Olympics in 1984, after an absence of 32 years, it has been obsessed with increasing its medal count. In post-Mao China, the symbolic link between sporting performance and national pride has been constantly maintained – among professional sportsmen, spectators and in the media – and the country's re-entry into the international sporting realm has spurred some of its most public outbursts of both jubilant and angry nationalism: the passionate rejoicing at the victory of the Chinese women's volleyball team over Japan in the 1981 World Cup; the riot that followed the defeat of the Chinese football team by Hong Kong on 19 May 1988; and, of course, the strenuous efforts made by the Chinese government to win the right to host both the 2000 and 2008 Olympics. As the Chinese men's team made its early exit from the 2002 Football World Cup finals, web commentators raged that the players had 'lost face' for China as a whole. 'When a country is powerful,' proclaimed the front page of the *People's Daily* after China's medal success at the Athens Olympics, 'its sport will flourish ... Chinese athletes will make more contributions to realize our nation's great revival.' [43]

Although, throughout the run-up to the Beijing Olympics, its organizers have stressed their encouragement of mass physical education, resources have been overwhelmingly concentrated on developing elite sports. China's sporting philosophy, Fan Hong, Ping Wu and Huan Xiong summarize, is not '"fair play", but winning no matter at what cost.' [44] Visit any of the Olympics chatrooms on major Chinese Internet news sites and you will find frank, even aggressive, expressions of popular hunger for Chinese national victory. Military analogies abound, giving the impression that Chinese sports fans are more preoccupied with war than peace. Chinese athletes' Olympic prospects are discussed under the heading 'Preparing for war' (*zhanbei*); those considering China's medal-winning hopes write of 'reviewing the troops' (*jianyue*). [45] 'Thanks to the Olympics, we can show how great our country is,' a plain-speaking taxi-driver explains. 'We will finish top of the medal table. There is no doubt about it. And when we win, I will be so excited my blood will boil.' [46] China, it seems, has a furious appetite for Olympic glory that does not sit comfortably with its universalistic verbiage.

A historically-minded critique of both China's 'peaceful rise' and 'One World, One Dream' manifestos, moreover, would rather undermine their monochrome take on China's eternal, harmony-loving traditions. China's past has been probably about as full of violence and ethnocentric imperialism as that of any successful empire in human history. Neither does a cursory appraisal of contemporary China give much sense of a society in which anyone has particularly internalized ancient principles of harmony and health. 'The Chinese tradition of "Treating humans as important above all else" (*yi ren wei ben*) will be realized in Beijing's Olympic practice,' waxed one exponent of the 'People's Olympics' slogan. 'Everything will be considered so as to be of greatest benefit to the athletes, referees, officials, journalists, supporters, tourists and locals.' [47] Yet within the lyrical expositions of how Chinese humanist traditions are about to make the world a better place, mention of human rights – the key issue on which China is most frequently criticized in the international community – is for the most part conspicuously absent. Some argue that the Western media, meanwhile, repays the compliment by often omitting to emphasise the dramatic progress the PRC has in fact made in human rights over the past thirty years: in lifting hundreds and millions out of poverty, in the widespread growth of personal freedoms for the majority, and so on. [48] As the year-long countdown to the Olympics began, foreign journalists were detained for attending a press freedom protest, while Amnesty and Human Rights Watch issued critical reports on China's human rights record. 'We find no consolation or comfort in the rise of grandiose sports facilities,' prominent Chinese citizens and public intellectuals protested in an open letter to the government,

> or a temporarily beautified Beijing city, or the prospect of Chinese athletes winning medals. We know too well how these glories are built on the ruins of the lives of ordinary people, on the forced removal of urban migrants, and on the sufferings of victims of brutal land grabbing, forced eviction, exploitation of labor, and arbitrary detention. [49]

With a year to go to the opening ceremony, air pollution in Beijing was so bad that the iconic Bird's Nest Stadium in which the Olympic opening ceremony will be staged was barely visible and the head of Australia's Olympic Committee advised athletes against long stays in China, due to the risks of respiratory and gastric illness. [50]

But even if we accept at face value the professed desire for world harmony in the 'peaceful rise' and 'One World, One Dream' doctrines, closer examination brings out a rather less universalistic edge to them. Both seem to be based on saccharine versions of Chinese history out of which China's unharmonious past and present have been efficiently edited, in the interests of asserting the moral superiority of Chinese tradition and its inexorable resurgence. In his exploration of the experiences and consequences of the first few years of China's 'peaceful rise', Joshua Kurlantzick finds mixed results: despite the notable successes of Beijing's 'charm offensive', Kurlantzick expresses concerns that, in its need to secure energy sources, China is shoring up a number of repressive, natural resource-rich dictatorships around the globe (especially in Africa); exporting beyond its borders its poor performance on environmental, human rights and corruption issues; and starting to look politically and militarily overbearing in the Asia region. Critics of Chinese foreign policy have labelled recent African ventures as little more than economic imperialism. While the Beijing government upholds that recent trade, investment and aid initiatives directed at African nations are a 'win-win proposition' for both sides, sceptics assert that China's hunger to extract Africa's raw materials and to flood its markets with cheap manufactured goods 'is not progress. It is colonialism.' [51]

A similar ambiguity can be detected in Beijing's stated quest for Olympic harmony. On one level, the Beijing Olympics are presented as an idyllic, multicultural encounter between Eastern and Western traditions; on another, however, commentators and interpreters of the 'People's Olympics' manifesto often hint at a kind of Sino-centric self-importance in which China will rise up as the leader of 'The East' to challenge successfully Western supremacy. Peng Yeren and Chen Huinuo begin a 2007 article in the journal *Sports Culture Guide* entitled 'Globalisation, Post-modernism and the Renaissance of Eastern Sports Culture' with the proposition that world sports culture should be divided into two traditions, the Western (America and Europe) and the Eastern (encompassing India, Japan and Islamic countries, but represented by China). After bemoaning the stranglehold in which Western sports now hold the world and blaming serious problems in the Olympic movement (commercialization, politicization, alienation of athletes) and in the world at large (the global spiritual and environmental crisis) on Western philosophy, the authors pronounce that Western culture 'has shown itself to be unable to adapt to the human-centred problems of the post-modern era. With its emphasis on harmony, Chinese culture, by contrast, is fully able to adjust. ... The future of world culture ... [foreigners observe] is the resurgence of Chinese culture.' [52]

Reading their conclusions, one is struck first by the obvious rebuttal that Peng and Chen's portrait of an exclusively harmonious Chinese tradition is one that is economical with historical truth and for which there is little evidence in the Chinese present. Secondly, their analysis demonstrates a powerful regard for global hierarchy – their unhesitating election of China as the leader, or representative of 'the East', their preoccupation with Eastern rise over Western crisis and decline – that sits uneasily with the supposed universalism of Confucian harmony and postmodernism. If a culture is committed to world peace, one cannot help wonder why questions of 'resurgence' are so important. 'A large river without many tributaries will dry up,' analogizes another academic, Wu Xiaoyang, in the same journal. 'The culture of the Chinese nation is a vast tributary second in size only to the river of world culture itself. And so we must promote and advance our national culture, for which the Beijing Olympics is a great opportunity.' [53]

Embedded somewhere within the roseate internationalism of China's 'peaceful rise' and 'One World One Dream' is a confident desire to differentiate a rising China's blueprint for leadership from that of the present, Western-dominated status quo; and a willingness to manipulate facts to serve instrumental political purposes innate to all ambitious nationalist elites.

Conclusion

What are we to infer from the mixed messages of the 2008 Olympics? Are the games truly working towards world peace and equality, or do they indicate a cohesive strain of imperialist nationalism that aspires to remake the Western-dominated modern world order in the image of a pre-modern, Sino-centric universe? As China resurges, will it seek to humiliate, in turn, the nations that it has identified as the authors of its 150-year decline? Or has contemporary China been seriously overestimated: have the experiences of the past century and a half fully integrated China internationally, tying its identity and self-esteem to external (in reality, Western) recognition? Does the gap, moreover, between ideal and reality in China's Olympic preparations – in particular, concerns over the scale of environmental problems – suggest that China is not the unstoppable juggernaut feared by Washington's hawks? Even if China succeeds in hosting an immaculate Olympics, it will be left – after two weeks of escapist spectacle – with severe, long-standing domestic concerns: combating environmental degradation, maintaining economic growth and limiting the destabilizing impact of social inequality.

There is, confusingly, some truth in all these observations. A confident, ambitious and at times aggressive Chinese nationalism – of which Beijing's Olympic preparations are a grandiloquent emblem – undeniably exists in the contemporary People's Republic. But it is a force compromised by its internal contradictions: by a pride in its imperial history and insecurity about its modern weakness that have generated both a striking commitment to openness and powerful need for external approbation, and a compensating rhetoric of strident patriotism. The great conundrum of contemporary China is that most of its messages are, at present, mixed: China is, in short, a rising power not fully in control of either its rise or its rhetoric.

What is clear is that, throughout their long past, China's society, government and culture have historically demonstrated enough flexibility and pragmatism to navigate the political, socio-economic and psychological difficulties that its entry into the modern global system has generated. In the short-term, China will doubtless continue to maintain its present, contradictory profile: pushing both patriotism and internationalism; confidently pronouncing on its rise while vying still for foreign approbation and struggling with enormous domestic challenges; combining powerful yearnings for globalization with tight controls over its media and laws; and making safe predictions over its medium-to-long-term future practically impossible.

Notes

[1] The initial three quotations are drawn, respectively, from Sun, 'Shijie xuanze Zhongguo'; 'One World One Dream,' available online at http://en.beijing2008.cn/spirit/beijing2008/graphic/n214068253.shtml, accessed 3 Aug. 2007; and Lindsay Hilsum, 'Girl, 8, Slave to the Olympic Spirit', *The Observer*, 5 Aug. 2007, available online at http://www.guardian.co.uk/china/story/0,,2142037,00.html, accessed 5 Aug. 2007.

[2] Where this essay uses the large term 'China', I have tried, as far as possible, to deploy it advisedly, to reflect the non-specific, generalising way in which it is used in Chinese sources. At other points, I have tried to specify the subjects of my analysis: China's government, intellectuals, internet users and so on. In some instances, I have made use of 'China' for reasons of concision when referring to broadly apparent patterns of thought, and where several unclearly overlapping political, social and economic groups are involved. I do not mean to efface the very significant political, social and intellectual diversity present in contemporary China. I have, however, periodically made judgements about what I consider to be fairly dominant and widespread modes of political and intellectual consciousness.

[3] Hong *et al.*, 'Beijing Ambitions', 525.

[4] Hilsum, 'Girl, 8'.

[5] Although tributary practices can be traced as far back as the Shang period (second half of the second millennium BC), they were first fully institutionalized under the Han, reaching a peak of maturity and complexity during the Qing dynasty. For more details see, for example, Fairbank, *The Chinese World Order*; Yü, 'Han Foreign Relations', 377–83.

[6] Yang, 'Historical Notes', 32.

[7] Waley-Cohen, *The Sextants of Beijing*, 4–5.

[8] See discussion of China's 'peaceful rise' below, and also comments in Lorge, *War, Politics and Society*, 1–14.

[9] Van de Ven, 'Introduction', 2–3. See also, for example, Lorge, *War, Politics and Society*; and Graff, *Medieval Chinese Warfare*.

[10] Di Cosmo, *Ancient China*.

[11] Yang, 'Historical Notes', 25.

[12] Wang, 'Early Ming Relations', 36–7.

[13] See Perdue, 'Culture, History', for an excellent summary of Qing strategic culture.

[14] The intensity of this conflict was exacerbated by an unfortunate historical coincidence. By the middle of the nineteenth century, the essential flexibility with which China's elites had, over history, demonstrated themselves able to put the Sino-centric ideal into practice happened to have largely absented itself from imperial policy-making. The move to stage an outright confrontation with British demands for diplomatic equality and free trade was not the decision of a court united in an intractable Chinese superiority complex, but was driven rather by the chance resurgence of an ambitious clique hoping to commandeer imperial favour through anti-foreign propaganda. This rigidity was only further entrenched in the years that intervened between the two Opium Wars, as British aggression elicited an equal and opposite reaction on the Chinese side, in the form of a hostile xenophobic intransigence to foreign demands. See Waley-Cohen, *The Sextants of Beijing*, 142–3.

[15] Zhao, *A Nation-State*, 48.

[16] Ibid., 49.

[17] Ren, *Aolinpike yundong duben*, 429. See also Brownell, *Training the Body for China*.

[18] Barmé, *In the Red*, 265–72.

[19] See summaries of various conflicting viewpoints in Gries, *China's New Nationalism* and Scott, *China Stands Up*.

[20] See Zhao, *A Nation-State*, 289, 259 and 248–90 *passim*.

[21] *Renmin ribao*, 15 July 2001, 1, 5 and 4 respectively.

[22] 'Aoyun shenghuo: ni zhongyu lai le!'

[23] Gries, *China's New Nationalism*, 9.

[24] Wang and Chai, 'Dui Beijing chenggong shenban', 591. See also Huang and Gu, 'Zonglun Beijing', 117.

[25] Cheng, '2008 nian Aoyunhui', 14.

[26] *Renmin ribao*, 14 July 2001, 1.

[27] 'Aoyun shenghuo'.

[28] See, for example, the popular sports news and discussion site at http://bbs.sports.sina.com.cn/?h=http%3A//bbs.sports.sina.com.cn/g_forum/00/20/00/&g=4, accessed 15 Aug. 2007.

[29] Jonathan Watts, 'Welcome to Beijing', *The Guardian*, 11 Aug. 2007, available online at http://www.guardian.co.uk/china/story/0,,2144249,00.html, (accessed 12 Aug. 2007.

[30] Clifford Coonan, 'The Human Cost of the Games: Standing Up to the Beijing Bulldozers', *The Independent*, 13 Aug. 2007, available online at http://news.independent.co.uk/world/asia/article2859069.ece, accessed 14 Aug. 2007.

[31] 'Beijing to Shoot Down Olympic Rain', CNN, 9 June 2006. http://edition.cnn.com/2006/WORLD/asiapcf/06/05/china.rain/index.html, accessed 21 Aug. 2007.

[32] See, for example, Hollander, *Political Pilgrims*.

[33] Capital Spiritual Civilisation Committee, *Aolinpike zhishi*, 114.

[34] 'Organizers strive for a 'civilized' sheen', CNN 8 Aug. 2007, available online at http://edition.cnn.com/2007/WORLD/asiapcf/08/03/olympics.manners/index.html, accessed 21 Aug. 2007.

[35] Jonathan Watts, '"We Must Start by Eradicating Bad Habits"', *The Guardian*, 9 Aug. 2007, available online at http://www.guardian.co.uk/china/story/0,,2144422,00.html, accessed 14 Aug. 2007.

[36] *Aolinpike zhishi*, compare pages 122 and 114.

[37] Fitzgerald, *Awakening China*, 46 and 11 respectively.

[38] 'One World One Dream', available online at http://en.beijing2008.cn/spirit/beijing2008/graphic/n214068253.shtml, accessed 3 Aug. 2007.

[39] 'China's Peaceful Development Road', *People's Daily Online*, 22 Dec. 2005, http://english.peopledaily.com.cn/200512/22/eng20051222_230059.html, accessed 5 Aug. 2007.

[40] Sun, 'Beijing 2008 nian aoyunhui', 437.

[41] Guttmann, *The Olympics*, 2.

[42] 'Puxie Aoyun shi shang zui zhuangli de pianzhang' ['Compose the most glorious chapter in Olympic history'], *Renmin ribao*, 14 July 2001, 1.

[43] 'Wuxing hongqi wo wei ni jiao'ao: relie zhuhe woguo tiyu jianer zai Aoyunhui shang qude youyi chengji' ['I am proud of the five-starred red flag: warm congratulations on the victory of our national sporting heroes at the Olympics'], *Renmin ribao*, 30 Aug. 2004, 1.

[44] Hong *et al.*, 'Beijing Ambitions', 519.

[45] See, for example, http://2008.sohu.com/, accessed 15 Aug. 2007.

[46] Watts, 'Hello Beijing!' *The Guardian*, 9 Aug. 2007, available online at http://www.guardian.co.uk/china/story/0,,2144258,00.html, accessed 10 Aug. 2007.

[47] Sun, 'Beijing 2008 nian Aoyunhui', 437.

[48] For example Daniel A. Bell, 'Badmouthing Beijing', 2 April 2008, available online at http://commentisfree.guardian.co.uk/daniel_a_bell/2008/04/badmouthing_beijing.html, accessed 10 April 2008.

[49] 'One World, One Dream, Universal Human Rights', http://crd-net.org/Article/Class9/Class15/200708/20070807140359_5310.html, accessed 7 Aug. 2007.

[50] Richard Spencer, 'Beijing Smog Endangers Olympic Countdown', *Daily Telegraph*, 8 Aug. 2007, available online at http://www.telegraph.co.uk/news/main.jhtml?xml=/news/2007/08/08/wchina108.xml, accessed 15 Aug. 2007.

[51] Kurlantzick, *Charm Offensive*. For an example of international (American, Japanese, Indian, Taiwanese) concerns over China's military spending, see Daniel Griffiths, 'Fears Over China Military Build-up', BBC News, 15 Feb. 2007, available online at http://news.bbc.co.uk/2/hi/asia-pacific/6365167.stm, accessed 29 Aug. 2007. For more details on China's controversial interventions in Africa, see Lydia Polgreen and Howard W. French, 'China's Trade in Africa Carries a Price Tag', *New York Times*, 21 Aug. 2007, available online at http://www.nytimes.com/2007/08/21/world/africa/21zambia.html, accessed 24 Aug. 2007.

[52] Peng and Chen, 'Quanqiuhua, houxiandai'.

[53] Wu, 'Aolinpike yundong', 29. Many Mainland commentators have strenuously underlined the unique Chinese qualities of the 2008 Olympics, asserting that Beijing is 'surpassing' previous games (see Zheng Xiaojiu, 'Lun Beijing Aoyunhui dui Aolinpike lunli jingshen de chaoyue') and 'Sinicizing' the Olympics (for example, Qiu Ruilang, 'Aolinpike zhuyi de Zhongguohua quanshi'); or dwelling on the games' deep connections with Chinese tradition (see Zhu Ling, 'Aolinpike yundong yu Zhongguo chuantong wenhua'). It is hard to imagine a parallel effort being made, for example, to 'Anglicize' the 2012 London Olympics.

References

'Aoyun shenghuo: ni zhongyu lai le!' ['The sacred Olympic torch has come at last!']. *Dangyuan zhi you* 8 (2001): 1.

Barmé, Geremie. . *In the Red: On Contemporary Chinese Culture*. New York: Columbia University Press, 1999.

Brownell, Susan. *Training the Body for China: Sports in the Moral Order of the People's Republic*. Chicago: University of Chicago Press, 1995.

——. *Beijing's Games: What the Olympics Mean to China*. Lanham, MD: Rowman and Littlefield, 2008.

Capital Spiritual Civilisation Committee, ed. *Aolinpike zhishi shimin duben* [A citizens' Olympic reader]. Beijing: Beijing chubanshe, 2005.

Cheng Chuanyin. '2008 nian Aoyunhui dui Zhongguo zhengzhi de yingxiang' ['The political effect of the 2008 Olympics on China']. *Tiyu wenhua daokan* 2 (2002): 14–15.

Di Cosmo, Nicola. *Ancient China and Its Enemies: The Rise of Nomadic Powers in East Asian History*. Cambridge: Cambridge University Press, 2002.

Fairbank, John K., ed. *The Chinese World Order*. Cambridge, MA: Harvard University Press, 1968.

Fitzgerald, John. *Awakening China: Politics, Culture, and Class in the Nationalist Revolution*. Stanford, CA: Stanford University Press, 1996.

Graff, David A. *Medieval Chinese Warfare 300–900*. London: Routledge, 2002.

Guttmann, Allen. *The Olympics: A History of the Modern Games*, 2nd edn. Urbana, IL and Chicago: University of Illinois Press, 2002.

Gries, Peter Hays. *China's New Nationalism: Pride, Politics and Diplomacy*. Berkeley, CA: University of California Press, 2004.

Hollander, Paul. *Political Pilgrims: Travels of Western Intellectuals to the Soviet Union, China and Cuba 1928–1978*. New York and Oxford: Oxford University Press, 1981.

Hong, Fan, Ping Wu and Huan Xiong. 'Beijing Ambitions: An Analysis of the Chinese Elite Sports System and its Olympic Strategy for the 2008 Olympic Games'. *The International Journal of the History of Sport* 22, no. 4, (July 2005): 520–9.

Huang Xiaohua and Gu Yafen. 'Zonglun Beijing shen Ao chenggong de juda yingxiang he jiazhi' ['A summary of the enormous influence and value of Beijing's successful Olympic bid']. *Guangzhou tiyu xueyuan xuebao* 21, no. 3, (Sept. 2001): 117–22.

Kurlantzick, Joshua. *Charm Offensive: How China's Soft Power Is Transforming the World*. New Haven, CT: Yale University Press, 2007.

Lorge, Peter. *War, Politics and Society in Early Modern China, 900–1795*. London: Routledge, 2005.

Peng Yeren and Chen Huinuo. 'Quanqiuhua, houxiandai yu dongfang tiyu wenhua de fuxing'. *Tiyu wenhua daokan* 1 (2007): 11–12.

Perdue, Peter. 'Culture, History and Imperial Chinese Strategy'. In *Warfare in Chinese History*, edited by Hans Van de Ven. Leiden: E.J. Brill, 2000.

Qiu Ruilang. 'Aolinpikezhuyi de Zhongguo quanshi' ['An explanation of the sinicization of Olympism']. *Tiyu yu kexue* 28, no. 2, (March 2007): 35–8.

Ren Hai, ed. *Aolinpike yundong duben* [A reader on the Olympic Movement]. Beijing: Renmin tiyu chubanshe, 2005.

Scott, David. *China Stands Up: The PRC and the International System*. Oxford: Routledge, 2007.

Sun Baoli. 'Beijing 2008 nian aoyunhui 'renwen Aoyun' linian chutan' ['A preliminary exploration of the Beijing Olympics' concept of a "People's Olympics"']. *Beijing tiyu daxue xuebao* 5 (2002): 436–7, 457.

Sun Tianzuo. 'Shijie xuanze Zhongguo' ['The world chooses China']. *Pingpang shijie*, Aug. 2001: 3

Van de Ven, Hans. 'Introduction'. In *Warfare in Chinese History*, edited by Hans Van de Ven. Leiden: E.J. Brill, 2000.

Waley-Cohen, Joanna. *The Sextants of Beijing: Global Currents in Chinese History*. New York: Norton, 1999.

Wang Gungwu. 'Early Ming Relations with Southeast Asia: A Background Essay'. In *The Chinese World Order*, edited by John K. Fairbank. Cambridge, MA: Harvard University Press, 1968.

Wang Xiangdong and Chai Youzhi. 'Dui Beijing chenggong shenban 2008 nian Aoyunhui de yinsu fenxi' ['An analysis of the reasons for Beijing's successful Olympic bid']. *Beijing tiyu daxue xuebao* 25, no. 5, (Sept. 2002): 590–1, 604.

Wang Xiaohua. 'Aolinpike wenhua yu rujia wenhua de gongming' ['The resonance of Olympic culture with Confucian culture']. *Tiyu shijie – xueshu* 2 (2007): 78–9.

Wu Xiaoyang. 'Aolinpike yundong de renwen neihan – jiantan 2008 nian Beijing Aoyunhui de 'renwen Aoyun' linian' ['The humanistic implications of the Olympic Movement: and a discussion of the 2008 Beijing "People's Olympics"']. *Tiyu wenhua daokan* 6 (2002): 28–9.

Yang, Lien-sheng. 'Historical Notes on the Chinese World Order'. In *The Chinese World Order*, edited by John K. Fairbank. Cambridge, MA: Harvard University Press, 1968.

Yü Ying-Shih. 'Han Foreign Relations'. In *The Cambridge History of China*, vol. 1: *The Ch'in and Han Empires, 221 BC–AD 220*, edited by Dennis Twitchett and Michael Loewe. Cambridge: Cambridge University Press.

Zhao, Suisheng. *A Nation-State by Construction: Dynamics of Modern Chinese Nationalism*. Stanford, CA: Stanford University Press, 2004.

Zheng Xiaojiu. 'Lun Beijing Aoyunhui dui Aolinpike lunli jingshen de chaoyue' ['On the Beijing Olympics' surpassing of the Olympic spirit']. *Guangzhou tiyu xueyuan xuebao* 27, no. 2, (March 2007): 17–19.

Zhu Ling. 'Aolinpike yundong yu Zhongguo chuantong wenhua' ['The Olympic Movement and traditional Chinese culture']. *Hubei tiyu keji* 26, no. 2, (March 2007): 128–9.

Olympic Aspirations: Chinese Women on Top – Considerations and Consequences

Dong Jinxia and J. A. Mangan

Preamble: Political Context

To begin with anticipatory comments on a new global era: an article entitled 'Chinese Century' in the American *Times Weekly* in January 2007 contained the following remark: 'Now China is turning ... commercial might into real political muscle, striding onto the global stage and acting like a nation that very much intends to become the world's next great power.' [1] Three years earlier, a prescient article in the British *Daily Telegraph* in August 2004, included the following statement:

> As the Athens Games drew to a close, Jacques Rogge, the president of the International Olympic Committee, made repeated reference to China's perfor-mance in Athens, and, while he coupled this with praise for Japan and other Asian countries – calling it ' the awakening of Asia' – it was the Chinese performance that took the eye; third in the medal table with 63 medals overall and their 32 gold only three behind the United States ... it is appropriate that Beijing should follow

Athens, the country that invented the Games, handing the torch to the country that wants to proclaim itself as the greatest in the world. [2]

These two disparate observations, at first sight, seemingly separate in both time and topic, are not unrelated: Chinese political ambitions and Chinese sporting ambitions for the twenty-first century are two sides of the same coin. Within China itself there is now candid acknowledgement that 'the country is a rising power. Chinese openly admit that China is now turning from a regional to a world power.' [3]

As one Chinese academic has predicted merely on the economic front, 'Chinese GDP will reach 17.5 per cent of the world's total by 2015, surpassing America'. [4] This is only one of several straws in the wind blowing to China's advantage in 'the Chinese Century' – a wind it intends to ride to a favourable outcome.

These Chinese ambitions exist in an atmosphere of occasionally febrile nationalistic feeling growing ever more intense, a culmination of a massive state patriotic programme.

> In September 1994 the Central Committee of the Chinese Communist Party, advised by the Central Propaganda Department, issued an 'Outline for Conducting Patriotic Education'. The 'Outline' established patriotic education from the nursery school to the university as a key party aim ... grounded on a proclivity ever present in the population at large: defiance aimed at the allegedly predatory foreigner. The message was blunt: 'China had to be on permanent guard against its enemies.' [5]

At present the Foreigner in Chinese immediate sights is the United States of America.

At least one distinguished American observer has noted that the CCP propaganda department in recent years has remained in Cold War mode, relentlessly railing against American 'hegemonism', a term that for the Chinese encapsulates America's desire 'as the most powerful nation in the world, to remain dominant by keeping down emerging powers like China'. [6]

There are self-evident reasons for Chinese suspicion, antagonism and resentment: the nineteenth-century American humiliations of China both military and diplomatic; an awareness that the view America in past decades had of its black population was not dissimilar to its view of the Chinese people; and a corresponding realization that falsehoods about the supposed inferiority of both, had taken 'deep root in the minds of white Americans'. [7]

A more recent cause of anger was the American attempt to ensure that China did not get the 2000 Olympics which, it has been argued, has left 'a lasting legacy of resentment towards the United States for trying to rob China of its Olympic glory'. [8] Consequently, despite official government policy to go gentle on America to allow concentration on pressing problems of internal social stability, just under the surface the Chinese continue to suspect US intentions and the gap between emotional public resentment and conciliatory foreign policy is considerable. [9]

American past and present imperialism is, therefore, a challenge to nascent Chinese 'imperialism'. Although most, if not all, Americans are in self-denial about the nation's imperial posturing, in fact

American 'imperialism' has taken many forms. Domination of other nations and cultures through selected sports is merely one of them. This has been nowhere better exemplified than in the Olympic Games. [Consequently] China's blatant ambition is to 'bury America' at Beijing 2008. Past political humiliation at the hands of the West is the spur. In the case of China, therefore, too much should not be made of a too narrowly focused Saidian cultural imperialism. A fuller conceptual analysis than the merely cultural and a longer time scale than Beijing is the sine qua non of an adequate understanding of the Chinese psyche. In time, and sooner rather than later, China's impact on the East and beyond will dwarf that of Japan's in the late twentieth century – materially, culturally and politically. Beijing 2008 is simply a down-payment on a long term investment. [10]

As those with even the smallest knowledge of Chinese history appreciate:

The truth of the matter is that the Chinese have their own logic far older than anything imported from the West. It is that China was once at the centre of the world, and now seeks relentlessly to be so again. China fully agrees with the Queen in *Through the Looking Glass and What Alice Found There*: 'It's a poor sort of memory that only works backwards'! [11] Thus, if as has been suggested, critical events are crucial tests of strength and tests of strength include the politics of culture, then Beijing 2008 could be interestingly crucial. It raises interesting questions: will the Games be the harbinger of other tests ahead for America beyond the sports arena? Will they be a symbolic crucial event in sport but with an import beyond sport? [12]

If it is a truth universally acknowledged 'that the United States is the pre-eminent great power [and] China is now its potential challenger' [13] then there is a further truth associated with Beijing 2008 closer to the Chinese mainland. The reality is that regionally China is ideologically isolated, adjacent to powerful political and commercial rivals and surrounded by various smaller fearful nations. Little wonder, therefore, that as China begins 'to flex its muscles as an Asian power, Americans and Europeans ... have little idea how edgy and raw relationships are between China and the surrounding states. ... The region frequently sounds and feels more like pre-1914 Europe than part of the twenty-first century globalisation.' [14] At this level, the political genealogy of the Beijing 2008 in the history of the Chinese nation state leaps into prominence. China's utilization of the Olympics as a political statement of hegemonic intent concerns the regional countries, not least Taiwan. It is against this background also that Beijing 2008 should be viewed. Without question in the Chinese case, the genealogy of the nation state looks different if it includes the Olympics. [15]

Women and Sport in Modern China: A Brief Evolutionary Perspective

Due to the astounding global appeal of the Olympic Games, Beijing 2008 will have clear implications for China's fast-rising impact on world affairs. The games will provide, literally, a golden opportunity for the Chinese to fulfil their persistent dream of becoming the leading Olympic power; an athletic sublimation of a wider intent – the intention to become the leading superpower. Many Chinese believe that Beijing

2008 will be an engine that will accelerate the thrust towards 'the Chinese century' and it is reality not fantasy that women will be the most important 'cogs' in the engine. They will propel the Chinese sports machine into pole position. For centuries, physically crippled by a grotesque former Chinese cultural obsession, the tradition of 'footbinding', in this new century after their release from the abhorrent practice in the last century, they will be in the vanguard in the race to snatch metaphorically the Olympic laurel wreath, and more than the wreath, from the head of the United States.

In view of their remarkable performances in many aspects of modern sport, for the most part achieved in the space of less than 50 years, some questions beg to be asked: how has it come about that Chinese women are expected to cast such a dominant shadow over Beijing 2008, how realistic is this anticipation and if it is realized, what will be the impact of this expected success on Chinese sportswomen, the sports system and gender relations, and on Chinese women beyond sport? And what might be the significance for the wider emancipation of Asian women?

The athletic transformation had a modest beginning. In the wake of gradual, if oscillatory, social change in the first part of the twentieth century the position of, and possibilities for, Chinese women slowly improved. [16] One outcome was that in the 1920s women participated more and more in national and international competitions. [17] Then in 1936 Li Shen earned a place in the pantheon of Chinese sportswomen. She was the only woman in the Chinese delegation of 22 athletes to participate in the Berlin Olympics.

However, due to civil war and foreign invasion for virtually all of the 1930s and 1940s, mass organized sport for women did not and could not exist. After the Communist Party took power in China in 1949, fundamental changes took place in every aspect of society. Sport was immediately chosen to serve the purposes of improving national physique and establishing a positive image of the New China. One after another sports institutions were established after 1952 and sport gradually became extensive, specialized and bureaucratized. [18] Meanwhile, in keeping with the Communist principle of equality between men and women, women were encouraged to break down traditional gender barriers and to enter male-dominated fields including sport. Attitudes to women and sport gradually became more and more positive. Women now took up elite sport as a career. Communism then brought about literally revolutionary changes which embraced sport. Between 1954 and 1957 women athletes created new national records on average in 25 events each year. [19] Confidently able women were now integral to Chinese sport – 'new' spring-heeled women of the 1950s in stark contrast to the 'old' literally crushed 'feet-bound' women of the 1850s. By 1957 there were 43 regional women's basketball teams with full-time coaches. [20] In the same year women actually outnumbered their male counterparts in the athletic events in which both competed (see Table 1). The most famous of these new women athletes was the high jumper Zheng Fengrong, who broke the world record in 1957. This produced a general surge of optimism and the ambition to match and, if possible, outperform Western women in the future.

Table 1 Number of female and male athletes in major athletic events

	sprint	400m	800m	hurdle	high jump	long jump	shot put	disc	javelin	other	total
F	120	46	40	52	63	51	29	41	45	128	615
M	105	36	48	52	38	34	22	40	52	87	514

Source: Beijing tiyu xueyuan, *61 nian tiyu gongzuo huiyi cankao wenxian*, 1–160.

Interestingly, this ambition moved closer to fulfilment in the disastrous short-lived Great Leap Forward (1958–60). Ambitious targets were set for various aspects of Chinese society including sport; [21] in sport some were realized. There was a rise in the number of sportswomen. In 1962 those in elite sport numbered some 3,552, more than a third of the total. [22]

These women steadily infiltrated global consciousness. Internationally they were increasingly a force to be reckoned with. Their earlier ambition to equal, and if possible to better, the performances of the rest of the world was making progress. It was a beginning.

And behind them was a resolute government determination that the New China would win international respect and force from the rest of the world recognition of an ideological and national transformation brought about by a revolution only some ten years in place. Without this political support, women would not have thrust themselves to the centre of the world's sport stage at anything like the speed achieved.

Things steadily got better and better for many talented Chinese sportswomen and by extension for ideological and national priorities. By 1965, some five years after Mao's piquant and distinctive plea for their equality to the people of China from the podium on the wall of the Forbidden City – 'women hold up half the sky' – they had more than justified his faith in them. In time they would, in both national and international sport, eventually come to hold up *more* than half the sky – an aspiration that is certainly demanded of them in Beijing 2008. Preparing for a triumphant 2008, in reality, took a remarkably short time. The seed bore ripe fruit in the 1960s. Progress, however, was not without problems. As the Great Leap Forward painfully 'advanced' and China improved internally slowly in some ways if not others, international relations deteriorated. The hitherto ostensibly warm 'fraternal' relationship between China and the USSR cooled due to different approaches to social development but more essentially to different political aspirations. Simultaneously, tension with the United States grew over the issue of Taiwan. [23] Then, due to the recognition of 'two' Chinas by the IOC and eight other international sports organizations in 1956, [24] in protest, China withdrew from them all in 1958. This was a notable action. It reduced international possibilities for Chinese athletes, both men and women, and resulted in their international anonymity for more than two decades.

Nevertheless, progress on elite sport did not come to an end. It developed steadily at the national level. Women were very much involved. The National Games were inaugurated in 1959. A third of the 10,658 competitors who participated in the final phase of the games were women (3,670). They took part in 24 and men in 36 events. Three women parachute jumpers broke the world record for group precision landing from an altitude of 1,000 metres, and a woman shooter broke the 50m and 100m world records. [25] Then in 1959 eight women including Pan Duo [26] climbed the 7546-metre-high Muztag Mountain (a range in the Xinjiang autonomous region) – the highest height reached by women at the time. Two years later, she and another female climber, Xi Yao, once more established a new record by reaching 7,595 metres on the Kongur Jiubie Shan, the second highest summit of the Kunlun mountains, also in Xinjiang. These were not simply statistics of relative excellence; they were also statements of relative empowerment.

In this way sportswomen forced themselves upon public attention. The momentum was unstoppable. In 1961 China was badly affected by famine caused by disasters, both natural and man-made, in the latter case a result of Mao's inordinate and unrealistic ambition adopted during the Great Leap Forward (1958–60), [27] but the elite sports bandwagon rolled on, and the first-ever Chinese world sports event – the World Table-tennis Championships – took place in Tianjin in Hebei province. To ensure Chinese success, 108 of the best players from the whole country were brought together to practise for a year! They were given priority and wanted for nothing. As a result, the Chinese achieved outstanding success. One of the three gold medals won by Chinese players was won by a woman, Qiu Zhonghui. [28] The championship gave notice to the world that China was intent on making its mark in world sport. Mind-numbing national disaster was peripheral to this aim; player preparations and privileges were central. The writing for Beijing 2008 has long been on the wall! In the short space of ten years, Chinese women had arrived at a position of parity, in some sports at least, with women of the leading sports nations. By 1965, Chinese women ranked second in speed-skating, third in volleyball, fifth in basketball and seventh in gymnastics in the world championships, and broke several world records in shooting. [29] These achievements delighted the Chinese people. They wanted more. They were accustomed to pain; they wanted unaccustomed pleasure. To bring this about, the nation swallowed its immediate pride with a view to greater long-term pride. Daimachu Hirofumi, the leading Japanese coach from the paramount 'enemy' nation, was invited to coach the Chinese volleyball players in April, 1965. Thus the early signs that Chinese women would eventually shoulder responsibility for the nation's ascent to world supremacy in sport were already visible in the sixties. The government was not slow to realize this and provided enthusiastic support. [30]

With full government backing and with support systems and structures in place, women's elite sport expanded steadily in spite of severe upheaval – the result of the chaotic and cruel 'Cultural Revolution' (1966–76). [31] The absolute number of performers actually increased from 3,552 (33.3 per cent) in 1962 to 6,348 (38.3 per cent) in 1978. [32] Then China rejoined the IOC after an absence of 20 years. Chinese athletes were now determined to conquer the world. Women were in the vanguard of the charge. The 15-year-old girl gymnast Ma Yanhong won a world title in the World Gymnastic Championships in December 1979. In the following decade, China produced women champions in fencing, judo, shooting, diving, table tennis and badminton. [33]

The ponderous slogan, first voiced by the Chinese diving team in 1980, summed a general aspiration: 'Go beyond Asia and join the advanced world ranks'. A year later the Chinese women's volleyball team (CWVT) turned a cumbersome mantra into a stunning reality, defeating Japan in the final of the World Cup and then winning five world titles in succession between 1982 and 1986. [34] The impact on the nation was remarkable. These women became icons of a newly confident China, symbols of resuscitated national self-esteem and, not least, representatives of a new generation of increasingly assured Chinese women.

At the time China had just opened its doors to the outside world and the gap between China and the advanced nations was so wide that many Chinese were depressed. The indomitable spirit of the women's volleyball team raised their spirits. In a march celebrating the volleyball victories in 1981, students from the prestigious Peking University for the first time chanted this patriotic clarion call: 'Unite together, revive the Chinese nation' [*tuanjie jilai, zhenxing zhonghua*]. [35] It caught perfectly the mood of a previously backward and now determinedly renascent people.

The players assumed almost beatific status. They provided sustenance for a nation hungry for international respect. The press portrayed them as exemplars of the essential Chinese character. Through their exceptional success, they exemplified for the Chinese a 'certification of uniqueness', a collective cultural uniqueness and a sense of distinctive community identity. To put it colloquially, they allowed the Chinese people 'to walk tall' on the world stage, setting a standard for future Chinese women in sport that had loud resonances for Beijing 2008. They were part of the preparation for glory. It has been written with verisimilitude 'that sport is a mirror in which nations, communities, men and women now see themselves. The reflection is sometimes bright, sometimes dark, sometimes distracted, sometimes magnified. This metaphorical mirror is a source of mass exhilaration and depression, security and insecurity, pride and humiliation, bonding and aberration'. [36] These Chinese women, without doubt, were a source of national exhilaration, pride and bonding. And they were the descendants of generations of culturally denied, restricted and abused 'foot-bound' predecessors. In a very real sense, they were 'a new breed' of women.

In the 1980s, while it is not the whole truth it contains some truth, as a by-product of earlier emancipation gender boundaries steadily dissolved. Whatever brought esteem to China was now a legitimate activity for women, endorsed by government and sanctioned by society. In sport a sea-change in sexual attitudes had occurred. Women seriously and successfully took up hitherto 'men-only' sports, including weightlifting and association football. It was on the football pitch that they most showed up men, demonstrated their national value and underlined their contribution to the positive image of New China across the globe. The Chinese women's team won the Asian Championships in 1988, reached the semi-finals of the first Women's World Soccer Championships in 1991, then won the Olympic silver medal in 1996 followed by the World Cup silver medal in 1998. The men's national team won nothing and came nowhere near winning anything. The contrast could not have been greater.

Inexorably, women were achieving international successes that revealed their potential for the future, ensured increasingly powerful support from the authorities and created a set of expectations that will come to an apogee with Beijing 2008.

And as a consequence of a golden age of women's sport in the last decade of the twentieth century, these expectations, like Topsy, have grown and grown. The prospect of Olympic glory appears to be more and more both an anticipated outcome of ability and a preordained reality – for one good reason. In the golden age, of the 923 world championships won by Chinese between 1990 and 2000, some 575 (62.3 per cent) were won by women. [37] This resulted in a widely discussed controversial phenomenon: *yinsheng yangshuai* (the blossoming of the female and the withering of the male). [38] The evidence seemed incontrovertible. Consequent to the 'Best Ten Athletes of the Year' contest launched in 1978, selected women made up 62.3 per cent in the 25 years between 1978 and 2003, and in 1998, only *one* of the best ten athletes was a man! [39] Women's success in international sport, together with the associated financial and social benefits, had helped elevate sportswomen in the public's esteem, promoted their status both in the sports community and society at large and created high expectations of them for the twenty-first century. In the twenty-first century, while some men have had glittering success in some sports – for example, the 110m hurdler Liu Xiang won in the Athens Olympic Games in 2004 and broke the world record in 2006, and triumphed in the world championships in 2007 – women continue to play the major part in ensuring Chinese success in international sport. Women won 64.3 per cent (270) of the 420 world titles won by Chinese athletes between 2003 and 2006. [40]

National Assertion, Olympic Ambitions, Symbolic Sportswomen

China has a long history as a powerful nation, first unified under the Qin (221–206 BC) and the Han (202 BC–2002 AD) and more strongly united under the Tang (618–906 AD) It has had a distinct identity for over 2,000 years. This impressive heritage, coupled with traumatic humiliations inflicted by the West in the nineteenth century and the hideous atrocities of Japan in the twentieth century, gave a powerful impetus to Communist ambitions after 1949 to create a strong, respected and powerful China. International success in sport was seen as one means of achieving this. It was early official policy. The 'Report on the Improvement of People's Sport and Physical Education', issued by the Central Sports Committee in 1953, pointed out that Chinese sports performances were well below international level and not proportional to the national status of China. Sports training was strengthened. This policy was endorsed at the highest level. Premier Zhou Enlai predicted in 1954 that 'if our sports policy works well, in six years, namely by 1960, some good athletes will emerge'. [41]

Winning Olympic medals was the most obvious way to project a forceful new image. The 1952 Helsinki Olympic Games provided the newly-founded Communist regime with an immediate chance. China sent a 41-strong delegation: 24 men and two women athletes. In fact, only one man actually took part due to the late arrival of the Chinese. [42] Subsequently, as noted earlier, on account of the ambivalent position of the IOC on the issue of 'two Chinas', in 1958 Communist China withdrew from the IOC and eight other international sports federations. Its image reconstruction via international sporting success was put on hold. Its seat on the IOC was not regained for 21 years. These years were not wasted.

In the period between retiring from and returning to the IOC, China made enormous internal strides in sport – in every way, from the structural to the competitive. The outcome was 15 gold medals in the 1984 Olympics (five won by women). The global image of Chinese sport was transformed. Within China new ambitions surfaced. Olympic success stimulated intense nationalism and an equally intense hunger for even greater Olympic success.

To achieve even better results in future Olympics was now official policy. The 'Notice on Further Developing Sports and Physical Education' issued by the Central Government in 1984 aimed: 'to turn China into a sports power in the [twentieth] century'. [43] A year later an 'Olympic Strategy' was drafted by the National Sports Committee. Wu Shaozu, the Minister of Sport (1988–2000), was unequivocal: 'The highest aim of Chinese sport is success in the Olympic Games. We must concentrate our resources on it. To raise the flag at the Olympics is our major responsibility.' [44] The succeeding Minister of Sport, Yuan Weiming (2000–4), made clear his continued support for the policy when he declared that given the now general economic condition of China and the specific progress made in sport, 'the Olympics-centred elite sports strategy is a reasonable choice for Chinese'. [45]

The emphasis now in sport shifted dramatically to Olympic performance. Resources were concentrated on potential Olympic winners. Planning, however, does not invariably lead to the realization of objectives. There was forward and backward movement in the struggle for Olympic supremacy. In 1988 China 'captured' only five gold medals, well below the number anticipated. This made the Chinese even more determined to become an Olympic power to be reckoned with whatever the cost, although there was a fierce debate over the goals of China's sport and the relationship between elite and mass sport. [46] International image won out. 'The lost advantages must be recaptured and the laggard sports should catch up through making various measures', declared state official Li Jieying. The result was that in 1989, 18 Olympic sports were supported. In 1980 it was 13, and in 1984 16.

This determination was certainly assisted by economic advances that boosted the prosperity of China and ensured in turn increased financial backing for its Olympic aspirations. In the 1990s market-oriented reform was introduced in China and the consequence was a boost in both living standards and the confidence of the Chinese. The intended consequence was not a secret. As Samuel P. Huntington pointed out in 1996, the Chinese increasingly declared their intention to resume the historic role of 'the pre-eminent power in East Asia' and 'to bring to an end the overlong century of humiliation and subordination to the West and Japan'. [47] Sport and the Olympics were to play their part.

With Olympic victory considered talismanic for China's rising world status, in the 1990s the national Olympic-oriented policy led to re-organization of provincial and municipal sports teams. Non-Olympic sports teams were substantially reduced. In the events programme of the 1987 National Games half were non-Olympic sports. In the 1997 National Games there were only Olympic sports events and traditional Chinese martial arts. As a result, by 1995, non-Olympic athletes comprised *only* 7.34 per cent of the total. [48] In addition, team sports that required more investment than individual sports and that had no medal potential were abandoned in most provinces and municipalities. The number of sports teams dropped significantly. Women's volleyball teams in the national league, for example, were reduced from 35 in the 1980s to 20 in the mid-1990s. [49] Basketball players in various sports schools fell from 50,529 in 1980 to 30,640 in 1995, and the coaches fell by 28 per cent from 2,794 in 1980 to 1,995 in 1998. [50] Nevertheless, and significantly, in spite of the decline in terms of the total number of elite athletes of both sexes from 16,982 in 1990 to 13,374 in 1994, the percentage of women actually increased (by 44 per cent in 1994). [51] This was the clearest evidence of their importance to national ambitions.

The advantages of increased affluence born of economic reform were quickly apparent. To secure victory at the Olympic Games, the 'Olympic Honour-winning Plan' was drafted in 1994 and introduced in 1995. It continued the policy of Olympic sports in the elite sports programme. In the same year, a special fund for Olympic-related sports facilities, nutrition and sports research was established. This budget, in its first year, was 65 million yuan (US$8.13 million) and over 200 researchers were involved in 56 Olympic-related projects. [52] Its budget then increased annually.

All this paid off. In the last decade of the twentieth century China consolidated its fourth position in the Olympic medal rankings (16 gold medals at the Barcelona and the Atlanta Games respectively in 1992 and 1996). In the new millennium, China advanced to third position in the medal count both in the Sydney and Athens Games. These achievements were largely due to *Chinese women* (see Figure 1); they raised their profile to ever higher levels; and they laid down a marker for 2008.

Nothing illustrates the confidence of coaches, administrators, politicians and public in their women athletes, demonstrated starkly in their 'overrepresentation' in Olympic delegations between 1992 and 2004 (see Figure 2) more than the self-effacing practice on the part of men strongly favoured by government endorsement of 'training with male counterparts' [nan pei nv liang], adopted widely and regarded as a major reason for the outstanding performances by Chinese women. This 'women first' policy in the cause of national image is dramatic evidence of the example of a

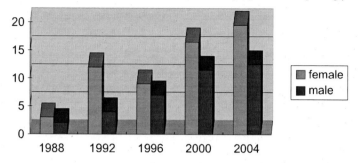

Figure 1 Comparison of Chinese men and women in terms of Olympics gold medal count

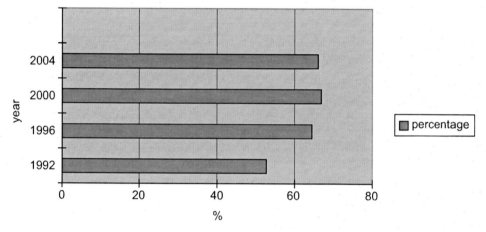

Figure 2 Percentage of women in Chinese Olympics teams

contemporary 'breed' of physically normal and vigorous women and the consignment to history of physically abnormal and feeble women – in part, in the interests of Chinese glory in sport by means of Olympic pre-eminence.

It is worth repeating that these measures were possible due to a centralized sports administration system that had been gradually put in place, steadily refined and firmly insisted upon from the 1950s onwards. Women's advance onto the world sports stage and the Olympic stage was the product of both long-term planning and long-held political ambitions. Irrespective of the various decentralized reforms introduced in sport since the 1980s, such as the club system, athlete registration and national league competition, the centralized system has *not* undergone fundamental change as it still best serves the long-asserted purpose of securing Olympic success through concentrating all resources, finance and attention on the key athletes and teams with medal potential. Olympic victory is the ultimate prize and the national glory it brings is valued above all else in Chinese sport. Centralization continues to support this ambition. This will become clear later.

A recent illustration of the value of this centralized system and the benefits of it for women, incidentally, is to be found in the steady rise of Chinese women tennis players to world dominance in the last decade. In 2001, the State Tennis Management Centre selected women's tennis for 'breakthrough' status, and located, trained and then sent promising players to competitions abroad to gain experience and improve their skills with the eventual aim of Olympic medals. [53] This strategy, utilizing the resources, financial and material, of a state centralized system, was successful in a remarkably short time. The double players Li Ting and Sun Tiantian advanced from 171st in the world in 2002 to Olympics championship winners in 2004. The priorities given to women, incidentally, led to complaints by men that their opportunities to go abroad to compete were of no importance to the authorities and were ignored. [54] Here was further evidence of the realistic attitude to success in Olympic sport that has reconstructed gender relations and favoured elite women performers in the interest of national image.

And paradoxically there has been another advantage for women in the wake of moves to a market economy, which up to a point has challenged a centralized sports system. Successful sports women can now win substantial rewards. The tennis double players Zheng Jie and Yan Zi, who won the Australian Open in 2006, for example, were given 200,000 yuan (US$25,000) each by their home province Sichuan on top of the Open AUS$440,000 prize money. In addition, the Tennis Management Centre gave them 500,000 yuan (US$65,789) each as a reward for their world top ten ranking. The Olympic tennis double champions Li Ting and Sun Tiantian have obtained about 2 million yuan (US$250,000) from state, province and city bonuses as well as commercial fees. [55] Rewards have come in other forms. Some successful athletes have been promoted to high-level coaching and administrative positions. Sun Jingfan, the former volleyball player, is now the director of the National Tennis Association; Tang Jiuhong, the seven-times world badminton champion in the 1990s, was promoted to deputy director of the Hunan Provincial Sports Administration in 2004. The table-tennis star Deng Yaping, a graduate from the University of Tsinhua, is now a Ph.D. student at Cambridge University, a member of the IOC Athletes' Commission and a member of the National Olympic Committee of China. Furthermore, in recent decades outstanding sportswomen have become media celebrities and have been feted as media heroines.

And there has been a knock-on effect in society. Women's success in international sport in conjunction with the consequent professional, financial and social benefits, has raised sportswomen in the public's esteem and to an extent influenced beneficially the status of women in the community.

It is wise to introduce here a note of caution. The path to full equality has significant pitfalls. The tradition of male predominance is deeply entrenched in Chinese society; women will face increasingly the double pressure of home and career commitments as those in the West have found; the setting-aside of the one-child policy which has to come to ensure China has the young to service its economy in the decades ahead and the 'time-bomb' of an ageing population, with its demands on daughters, will all have an influence on women's freedom. The success of Chinese sports, however impressive, can only do so much for the egalitarian cause.

In essence, then, successful sportswomen have become a distinctive stratum of society: elevators of the national image abroad and confidence-creators for their sex at home. They have contributed to the raised morale of the public in general and women in particular. If they ensure glory for China in 2008 they will be seen as avatars of a political system, a rising nation and a gender revolution.

Economic Reform, Diversity and Sportswomen

Mention has been made briefly above of the consequences for exceptional sportswomen of the post-1990s market reforms. They merit fuller investigation. They have resulted in profound changes in social values that have not yet run their course. The pursuit of profit is now a common aim. This has had consequences for women's sport. Values, relationships and systems have become increasingly diversified. The last decade of the twentieth century and the first decade of the twenty-first century have witnessed complex, and at times, confrontational change.

Reforms in the wider community post-1992 were speedily imitated in the sports community. First, in 1993 a decentralization of sports institutions took place and resulted in the establishment of management centres for specific sports. These centres obtained freedom from the National Sports Administration. It no longer exclusively managed sport from planning to implementation. In addition, a club system, a professional league competition and registration of athletes were introduced, initially for men's football and later for basketball, tennis and other sports. [56] Furthermore, since the mid-1990s the Western 'professional model' of management has been adopted in women's tennis, for example, within the framework of a State Tennis Management Centre. Those with potential for excellence are now given full support, secure funding to play in international professional tournaments and, if successful, receive bonuses. Moreover, the State Tennis Management Centre itself has the freedom to host more and more competitions sponsored by international tennis organizations in order to provide Chinese players with greater opportunities for high-level competition within China. As a result, the number of international competitions in China rose from ten in 2001 to 19 in 2004, while the total winning bonus increased from 10,000 yuan (US$1,315) in 2001 to 500,000 yuan (US$65,789) in 2004. [57]

In short, Western-type changes in management structure and access to greater resources on the back of increasing national prosperity have led to greater autonomy, affluence and freedom to act independent of central control, direction and interference. The successes of Chinese women in the 2004 Olympics, and in the Australian Open and Wimbledon tournaments in 2006, would seem to bear testimony to the practical value of these changes.

One change that requires close consideration because of its impact on performance, motivation and success is the encouragement of corporate sponsorship. As part and parcel of the sports reforms, the system of sports funding has undergone radical change since the mid-1990s. In the past sport was exclusively financed by the State Sports Administration. Now that market-oriented reform has been introduced in sport, corporate sponsorship has become an increasingly important supplement to government funding. [58] It thus augments government funding and allows the government the flexibility to juggle resources more than in the past. Situations in which corporate sponsorship is generous offer the government the opportunity to divert funds. For example, while the government funding for sport increased from 1,318.4 million yuan (US$164.8 million) in 1991 to 2,256.7 million yuan (US$282.9 million) in 1995, its funding for the football association decreased from 3 million yuan (US$375,000) to 2 million yuan (US$ 250,000). [59] This means more government money went to other sports.

The introduction of sponsorship, however, is not without its drawbacks. Less popular sports such as women's football, despite its record of international success, find it hard to get sponsorship and have to exist on the limited and fixed government budget. Strangely this is not generous. The salaries and bonuses of players and coaches as well as living and training conditions are not as attractive as is the case of those sports with sponsorship. This inequality has had a deleterious impact on the women's game. The Chinese women's football team that won silver medals in the 1996 Olympics and the 1998 World Cup has suffered due to insufficient sponsorship. The salaries of the players are between 2,000 and 3,000 yuan (US$250–375) a month, and some players earn as little as 1,000 yuan (US$125) – in 2005, the average monthly income was 1,167 yuan (US$146) per head nationally. This situation discourages young girls from playing football. Partly because of the lack of promising young players, the national team's performance has declined in the recent years. This state of affairs appears to fly in the face of keen support for successful performers projecting the national image. The brutal reality is that the co-existence of government funding and corporate sponsorship has created unexpected difficulties for some sports. Women footballers are a case in point and have felt the have felt the chill wind of the profit-motive.

By the mid-1990s, individual sponsorship had become pervasive. Celebrated athletes, such as the Olympic diver Guo Jingjing [60] and the speed skating champion Yang Yang, [61] endorsed a number of products following their successes in the Olympics and other major competitions. However, only the successful, confident *and beautiful* sportswomen are likely to attract commercial companies. Liu Xuan, the Olympic champion in gymnastics in 2000, nicknamed 'Xuan beauty', is now a film and media star and an endorser of a number of products. The less successful and less pretty girls are not so fortunate. Zhou Chunlan, the national weightlifting champion in 1988, ended up as a masseuse in a bath house, with a daily income of 4.5 yuan. When this was reported in the media, it aroused heated debate on post-athletic jobs and acute concern about athletes' lives after sport.

Zhou Chunlan was merely the tip of a metaphorical iceberg. Post-sport job assignment had been a thorny issue for years. A number of famous sportswomen, including some of the 'Ma Family Army', are unemployed at the time of writing. [62]

The reasons are not hard to find. Due to years of commitment to sport, most athletes have very low academic qualifications. Athletes in China begin professional training at an early age. This adversely affects academic study. Low educational achievement makes it difficult to obtain attractive post-sport jobs. In an attempt to remedy the situation, at least for the most famous, early in the mid-1980s, the National Sports Commission issued the following regulation: 'Athletes who have won world top three places can enrol at universities without passing an entrance examination and complete degree courses in between five and nine years.' [63] This policy was later extended to cover the top eight places in the Olympics, Asian champions and national champions, but on condition that their educational achievement reached high-school standard. Obviously, this policy favours only the most successful athletes. Ordinary athletes have to take entrance exams. However, sports colleges sympathetically have devised specially designed exams for athletes. Local provinces have also established policies to ensure that former athletes receive special consideration on application to higher education. These policies have created a channel between elite sport and higher education for some , but the fundamental cause of poor post-sports careers for many others has not yet been addressed, namely low scholastic ability caused by concentration over many years on sports training at the expense of academic studies. One temporary solution has been that the state decided in 1995 not to assign jobs to retired athletes but to provide them with financial subsidies. It has been estimated that the annual budget for this is now about 100 million yuan (about US$13.16 million); a small price to pay, some might argue for national glory. As there are now about 3,000 retired athletes each year, each one receives about 30,000 yuan (about US$3,947). [64]

This is not all. The situation may be satisfactory for women performers at the top of the medal ladder but some are well down the ladder. While there have been post-sports career problems for sportswomen, their sports careers have not been without difficulties largely as the result of traditional attitudes. In the past, there was emphatic inequality: superior coach and inferior athlete – a state of affairs determined by a master/pupil and man/woman legacy. Despite continuous and often dramatic political, cultural and economic change in recent decades, the Confucian legacy is still a living reality in Chinese society. While women's equality is stressed, female obedience, self-sacrifice, discipline and humility are stressed in the sports community, school and family. It comes as no surprise, therefore, that sportswomen are expected to be more obedient and thus easier to manage than men. However, times are changing. In 2006, the long distance runner Sun Yingjie [65] with three others [66] demanded that their coach Wang Dexian return their bonuses and salaries kept by him for years. They sued him. [67] This event attracted maximum media attention and led to skeletons tumbling out of the sports community closet. [68] There was precedent. In the 1990s the 'Ma Family' athletes and the skater Chen Lu challenged their coaches over monetary issues. [69] While financial concerns were the compelling immediate cause for these confrontations, also involved was the growing confidence of women and their desire to control their own lives – athletically, financially and socially. Increasingly, sportswomen have vehemently voiced their opposition to the manipulative control and overbearing domination of their coaches. At the same time, some have been understandably ambivalent in attitude. The international marathon champion Ai Dongmei stated that 'if he [her coach Wang Dexian] had not pushed me into this situation [no money to raise her child; her salaries and bonuses during the years of training had been taken by Wang] I would not have sued him. After all, without him I could not have achieved so much. To tell you the truth, I admire him a lot.' [70]

These women have mounted a challenge to past, and still extant, ideas of subservience, loyalty and sacrifice of individual interest – the foundations of the past performance expectations. This challenge demonstrates some progress towards women's emancipation. Sport is serving as a vehicle for the re-interpretation of the relationship between men and women. And the potency of the re-interpretation stems in part from the success of sportswomen, their value to the nation and their increasing self-assurance.

This self-assurance has been accelerated by foreign gender relations. The employment of foreign coaches has, to a extent, accelerated a change in the relationship between coaches and athletes. After the State Sports Administration issued a regulation encouraging the employment of foreign coaches in 2003, [71] more and more national teams including softball, handball, archery, fencing and rhythmic gymnastics have recruited overseas coaches. Their presence has helped improve Chinese performances and improved coaching standards. It also brought about changes in the relationship between coach and athlete. As one woman softball player has pointed out: 'Before the Canadian coach Michael came, we kept our coaches at a respectful distance, rarely embraced them. We never expressed our thoughts to them frankly.' [72] Shen then added: 'Michael has become a good friend. We would tell him directly if we are not happy and he listens to us carefully without disapproval. Then he gives us his opinion and advice'. [73] Without doubt, the open-door policy on foreign coaches has had an impact on the relationship between coach and performer. A more relaxed, more equal and less formal interaction is developing which women prefer and consider beneficial.

Beijing 2008: Opportunities and Challenges

Since Beijing obtained the 2008 games in 2001, unprecedented national attention has been given to sport. To ensure Chinese success in 2008, the 'Plan to Win Glory in the 2008 Olympics' was drafted by the State Sports Administration in 2002. According to the plan, the Chinese plan to win 180 medals and over 80 per cent are calculated to be won by women. [74] Clearly, in the Beijing games women will again play a major part in ensuring Chinese success. With regard to gold medals, it is estimated that Chinese have the potential to win in 40 events; it is expected that 25 of these medals could be won by women. [75]

This assessment is based on past success and present performance. Chinese women won 19.5 gold medals in 12 events in the 2004 Athens games, excelling in diving, judo, table-tennis, shooting, badminton, weightlifting and Taekwando. These plus gymnastics are listed as the 'superior sports' in the Olympic Glory Plan 2008. Logically, t is believed that women's dominance will be in these events in the 2008 games. [76]

It is a truism that the economic strength of a nation is basic to development of its sport. Chinese economic growth has soared in the past decade. According to the State Statistics Bureau, the GDP per capita increased from less than US$1,000 in 2001 to US$1,700 in 2005. [77] China moved from sixth largest world economy in 2001 to third in 2007. Growth continues. China is expected to be the world's leading economic power by 2050. An expanding economy has financed elite sport. In 2002 the SSA had a special budget of 14 million yuan (US$1.75 million) for 49 Olympic-related research projects comprising 144 studies. In 2005 the government invested 480 million yuan (US$60 million) in elite sport and 270 million yuan (US$33.75 million) in mass sport. [78] Furthermore, there has been ever-increasing investment from private sources in recent years. [79] All this has provided, and will continue to provide, a solid fiscal basis for improved performances on the part of the nation's athletes.

No stone is being left untouched to bring about success. Merely one illustration, with domination of the 2008 games in mind and with women with a key role in this: China sent a lot of fresh female faces to the 2004 Athens Olympics. Of the 407 athletes there, 323 were participating for the first time and 269 of these were women, including the youngest, the 14-year-old girl swimmer Zhang Tianyi. [80] This Athens experience will be invaluable for Beijing 2008.

Everything outlined above illustrates Chinese determination to achieve global sports supremacy. Nevertheless, intentions are never without difficulties. Chinese women face a number of challenges in preparation to the coming Beijing games.

First, despite obvious bilateral advantages, confusion regarding the centralized system and the market-oriented system caused by sports reforms could affect women's performances if not handled well. Western professional management models have been advocated now for over ten years, but the system of centrally planned and financed administration established in the 1950s, as stated earlier, is far from moribund, and when Western professional practices were introduced into centralized Chinese sport, criticism of the past and conflict over control inevitably resulted. Prior to the establishment of the Tennis Management Centre, Li Na, the top-ranked woman tennis player in China at the time, criticized the national tennis team for both its inability to provide adequate coaching and its outdated coaching methods. In addition, inadequate funding for high-level competitions hindered players' improvement. Peng Shuai, a young promising tennis player, wanted to quit the national team in 2005. [81] Women in other sports have expressed dissatisfaction and challenged unfair or unsatisfactory aspects of the national system. The rhythmic gymnast Ding Ning, for example, attacked the bias of the judging at the National Games. After winning merely a bronze medal for 500m speeding skating in the Asian

Winter Games in January 2007, Wang Meng criticized the coaching methods of the head coach of the national team. [82] The two incidents dominated the media headlines for days. They reflect the complications generated by recent sports reform. In addition, they also indicate that sportswomen in the twenty-first century have become more independent, more individualistic and more self-assertive. Confrontation is essentially the product of a new self-assurance on the part of women athletes who now are ever more conscious of their rights, their power and their opportunities. The main bones of contention are twofold: the authoritarianism of national officials who fail to move with the times and the unacceptable distribution of winning bonuses and prizes. Women themselves, as discussed briefly earlier, have exerted massive pressure on doctrinaire and dogmatic coaches, and the SSA is considering giving most of any winning bonuses and rewards to the performers. Athletes have initiated change and now are part of change.

This has come about because they have displayed the universal human proclivity for dignity, justice and equality. What these women have insisted upon and have brought about is an impressive pragmatic pluralism. They have successfully demanded fairness, consistency and dignity of treatment and consideration for their concerns. Extrapolation here is legitimate: arguably they are in the vanguard of a wider movement in sport and beyond sport: 'As for China, the next phrase of the growth will probably be accomplished by more and certainly not less pluralism.' [83]

It is a truism, of course, that the pluralism is not easy to achieve in authoritarian conditions, and certainly not easy to sustain, but these women have made more than a mere gesture. Nonetheless, the fact remains 'that pluralism does not just happen; it is a precious quality that has to be protected and nurtured. China has a long way to travel.' [84] The evidence for this is set out below.

All in Chinese sport as it impacts on women is far from idyllic. The plain fact remains that the actions of some sportswomen have tested the limits of administrators' tolerance and rocked the foundations of the centralized sports system. This has produced a bureaucratic backlash.

Performer's discontent and dissent may be indicative of a new female franchise. However, to confront the current system is difficult, if not impossible. After leaving the national tennis team for a short while, Peng Shuai had to eat humble pie and returned to the national team. The reasons for her humiliation are simple and compelling: without affiliation to the national team, she would have no chance to represent China in the Olympic Games and other major competitions; without national support she cannot afford all the cost of training and competition. Her predicament illustrates that while change is in the air, traditional forces are resilient and cultural change is neither straightforward nor smooth. [85] Change *and* continuity are a recurrent theme of Chinese sport in the twenty-first century. This brings advantages and disadvantages.

Progress, whatever the desire and the intention, is seldom linear. While women in some aspects of sport go from strength to strength supported by centralization, whatever its shortcomings, and are further assisted by recent managerial reforms which have resulted in Western-type institutions such as the Tennis Management Centre, some aspects of women's sport are not party to this steady advance. Two striking examples are volleyball and soccer As noted earlier, in the mid-1990s the provincial and municipal sports teams were re-organized in accordance with the Olympic strategy and as a consequence the team sports that demanded more investment than individual sports were reduced significantly in number. Women's volleyball teams in the national league declined from 35 in the 1980s to 16 in 2005. [86] The national sports system hived off women's football to commercialism. This has been a disaster. Though there are about 7,000 women football players in the country, the game has virtually no commercial appeal. Enterprises will not sponsor women's teams and events, and there are few spectators. [87] This has had serious consequences. The women's game, which brought international esteem through its performances in the late twentieth century in terms of these international performances, has gone from very good to very bad. In the 2004 Athens games the Chinese team was beaten badly by Germany in the first round. This was really a slap in the face for the Chinese.

In spite of unsatisfactory treatment and performances, the Chinese still have high expectation for the national women's football team that once won the silver medals in the Olympics and the World Cup. The team is expected to win a medal in 2008. The Chinese Football Association has learnt from past mistakes. It is making belated efforts to atone for past errors. International success still counts for something. The Chinese Football Association has recently made concerted attempts to ensure Olympic success and more coaches and advisors, including one from Germany, are now working with the team.

Despite the consequences of the Olympic Strategy, unsurprisingly the women's volleyball team is more hopeful than the football team of winning medals in 2008. The resurgent volleyball team won the world championships in 2003 and the Olympic Games in 2004. However, this team is also facing a shortage of young talent – the direct result of the reduction in players since the 1980s. Chinese women also once achieved good results in softball, basketball, handball and hockey as well as football and volleyball, but there is little hope of Olympic gold medals in these activities. They too have been adversely affected by the Olympic Strategy. The hockey and softball teams, both coached by Koreans, have made progress in recent years and were both ranked fourth in the 2004 games. They might win medals for China in 2008 but they have systematically been denied adequate and sustained financial support. The truth of the matter is that funding successful athletes is expensive and funds are not unlimited.

And there are other problems. Talent is the prerequisite of success. The clamour has been for years for sufficient young and capable Chinese athletes. This clamour becomes louder when experienced world-standard athletes retire from competition. Unfortunately, a number of world-famous women athletes, including Sun Wen (football) [88] and Luo Xuanjuan (swimming) retired recently. They cannot be easily replaced. Their absence will weaken China's chances of gold medals in 2008. Then there is the fact that sportswomen in the rest of world have improved. To add to

China's woes, more and more countries have increasingly talented women in Olympic competition. Chinese women will face severe challenges from Australia, Europe and America in swimming, athletics, football, volleyball and gymnastics.

Furthermore, in the wake of ever increasing and rapid prosperity, the extension and diversification of career opportunities could affect commitment to sport. In this new century, Chinese women are faced with unprecedented career choices. Women now are to be found in many occupations and play an important part in virtually every aspect of society. Indeed, 'numerous women are changing and renewing themselves so rapidly that men who have long dominated the society feel perplexed and even the Western women who have struggled for over a hundred years, are surprised'. [89] According to a recent survey, some 69.1 percent of Chinese women are optimistic about their future. [90] Opportunities for advancement now go well beyond sports fields and areas. Talented sportswomen in the future may choose other routes to success – less arduous and more lasting.

In summary, sport is entwined intimately with national politics, economics *and* social change. The changing status of sportswomen in the future will have an impact on training, performances and results. With the increase of assertive and increasingly mature and married athletes, managing different ages and experiences will be a challenge to coaches used to the traditional 'semi-military' way of management. If this management is handled badly, the morale of teams and individuals will be affected. Add to this the fact that athletes are now not only more assertive but also more demanding. With the transformation to the market economy, they have become much more aware of their marketing potential. This, of course, is two-edged sword. Sponsorship has drawbacks, as noted, including increasing disparity in income between different sports and between the successful and the unsuccessful and increasing jealousy over financial returns. Alert to the possibility that commercial activities can distract athletes, can adversely affect performance and can impair team spirit, in 2006 the SSA stated that until after the Beijing games athletes in national teams must refuse invitations for commercial work unless they are approved by the SSA. Balancing the interests of the nation, team and individual will be crucial to the motivation, performance and standing of athletes, coaches and administrators in 2008. Nevertheless, morale is high and expectations are high. With the renascence of China, 'there is a rallying cry for Chinese everywhere ... China's time has come ... it will rise in the world to the place it deserves'. [91] The elite sportswomen of China in 2008 will endeavour to bring this about sooner rather than later.

Concluding Comments and Reflections

For advocates of the study of significant events in history as prefigured, the Beijing Olympics offers clear attractions. Present Chinese attitudinal logic is lodged in the past, Beijing 2008, in a real sense, is ' a preprogrammed novelty' [92] that locates sport in larger political and gender 'histories'. Major events in history seldom if ever stand alone. They are meshed into political, cultural and social structures. Such events gain exceptional significance as expressions of crisis – appreciated and unappreciated. And they not only express new crises but reveal new resolutions. They are tests of strength for new realities.

There are critical events that shape the life of nations, new modes of action and intention, that redefine traditional ways of seeing the obvious. New political actors emerge to give form, expression and fulfilment to new visions. The state, of course, still attempts to control collective memories and assert political priorities and does this through appointed political agents. They become the sanctioned image of the state. And in the process they experience self-extension and self-realization. Their events become transformative events in the history of the state, nation, people and themselves.

In this regard the Beijing games will be a moment of truth for the Chinese. Success could point to a confident future beyond sport; failure will raise all the issues of past insecurity discussed in the Prologue. There is a great deal riding on the games for the Chinese and their future. Arguably, it is a political gesture of national assertion similar in intent but exceeding them in effort and expectation to the pronounced nationalistic 1936 Berlin Games – the projection of a nation into the future through sport. However, in terms of capital cost, infrastructure reconstruction and psychological preparation it is, and may well remain in the future, unique.

And in this extraordinary and exceptional staged event in the history of Chinese sport, and Chinese history, it is women who are in the spotlight. Tradition is turned in on its head; modernity has a female face. In the delivery of glory, after years of the most intense preparation and centuries of the most complete subordination, Chinese women are expected to play the major part. Their national and international visibility has never been greater in the long history of China. In 2008 they are expected to hold up the larger portion of the 'sky'. It is a responsibility of momentous significance. Not only China but the world expects much of them; in a phrase, to be on top of the world in August 2008, both literally and figuratively. That is the measure of the task they face.

None of this means that the realist loses sight of the realities of a nation that has travelled far, will travel further but still has a long way to travel. Women, in association with large swathes of the population, both men and women, are some distance from the finishing post of true equality; the gap between urban rich and rural poor widens; the population ages without a basic national pension scheme for all; there is as yet no effective national health service; free education is not widely available, and so on. All this was candidly admitted, explicitly or implicitly, by President Hu Jintao at the 17th Party Congress in Beijing in 2007.

Nevertheless, to strike a justifiable and resonating note of optimism, 'in every epoch Chinese have made use of resources they have inherited – material, intellectual and institutional – to set goals to respond to new challenges, protect themselves and advance their interests'. [93] In the specific context of Beijing 2008, can be added with respect to women, the acquisition of 'new' feats and a new life for them to advance themselves and the fame of China in the twenty-first century.

The crucial question to be asked is: will the emblematic 'new' women, who have already in their earlier performances struck a solid rather than a glancing blow for nationalism, pluralism and emancipation, strike further blows and in a phrase pregnant with possibilities, 'unsettle our sense of contemporary institutions' [94] and enlarge our understanding of the changing contours of hitherto 'political givens' at home and abroad?

How heavy the blows and how lasting their impact are questions to be determined in the coming decades, but blows have been struck and have had an undeniable impact.

And a further question – if Chinese women succeed in Beijing 2008, what might be the consequences *inter alia* for gender relations not only in China but in South-east Asia? Might it be that in this region the twenty-first century could be in increasing measure 'a women's century' on the back of 'the Chinese Century' propelled forward by Beijing 2008 – a spur to increased regional female empowerment, equality and opportunity? Or in the final analysis is Beijing 2008 simply a gargantuan sports festival – with geopolitical overtones and undertones – as simple as that? And a final question specifically for China and its women: will Beijing 2008 prove to be a watershed in international gender history or, to shift the metaphor on to a higher geographical level, if Chinese women come out on top in Beijing 2008 will Asian women climb closer to the top of the equalitarian peak? One thing is clear: Chinese sportswomen in recent decades have been leading climbers. Are other women in Asia roped to them? Only time will tell.

Notes

[1] Michael Elliott, 'The Chinese Century', *Times* Weekly, 11 Jan. 2007.
[2] Mihir Bose, *Daily Telegraph*, 31 Aug. 2004, S.6.
[3] Shirk, *China: Fragile Superpower*, 107.
[4] Live broadcast keynote speech by Hu Angang from the Chinese Academy of Science, 22 March 2003, available online at http://business.sohu.com/52/19/article207441952.shtml, accessed 6 April 2004.
[5] Hutton, *The Writing on the Wall*, 249.
[6] Shirk, *China: Fragile Superpower*, 222.
[7] The source of the quotation – made, incidentally, by the iconic black baseball player, Jackie Robinson – is the stimulating article by John D. Kelly, 'Baseball and Decolourization: The Caribbean, 1945–1975', 821.
[8] Shirk, *China: Fragile Superpower*, 226–7
[9] Ibid., 220
[10] Mangan, 'Epilogue: "Empire in Denial"', 1195–6.
[11] Carroll, *Through the Looking Glass*.
[12] Mangan, 'Epilogue', 1196.
[13] Hutton, *The Writing on the Wall*, 1.
[14] Ibid., 24
[15] Kelly, 'Baseball and Decolourization', 823.
[16] Women ceased to be constrained by the cruel practice of footbinding. Women got access to formal education, including university education, in spite of very limited numbers.

[17] Women played volleyball at the Eighth Guangdong Provincial Games in the Old China of 1921, and debuted at the National Games in 1922.

[18] For detail, see Dong Jinxia, *Women, Sport and Society in New China*, ch. 1.

[19] Women appeared in most sports, except football and weightlifting, in which Chinese men participated.

[20] Rong Gaotang, *Dandai zhongguo tiyu*, 218, 269.

[21] Lu Tingyu, *Zhonghua renming gongheguo lishi ji shi*,75.

[22] Guojia tiyu wenshi xinxi bianji weiyuan hui, *Tiyu shiliao*, 88–9.

[23] Yongjin Zhang, *China in International Society*, 23.

[24] Kanin, 'Ideology and Diplomacy', 268.

[25] Pinglun yuan [editorial], 'Feiyue qianjin de woguo tiyu shiye' [Chinese Sport greatly leaping forward], *Renmin ribao* [People's Daily], 25 Oct. 1959.

[26] The seven others were Qi Mi, Xi Rao, Cha Mujin, Wang Yiqin, Wang Guihua, Zhou Yuying and Cong Zhen.

[27] In agriculture, a production target for 12 years under normal circumstances was now shortened to one or two years. In industry, steel production increased tenfold within half a year (Lu Tingyu, *Zhonghua renming gongheguo lishi ji shi*, 75).

[28] Qiu is the first Chinese woman to win the world table-tennis championships. After stopping training, she continued to work in the field, first as a coach and then as a researcher. In the 1990s she ran a sports goods shop named after her.

[29] Rong Gaotang, *Dangdai zhongguo tiyu*.

[30] Ibid., 221.

[31] For details, see Dong Jinxia, *Women, Sport and Society in New China*, ch. 3.

[32] Zhonghua renmin gongheguo guojia tiyu yundong wei yuan hui, *Quanguo tiyu shiye tongji zhilaio huibian*, 101.

[33] Luan Jujie ranked second at the Youth World Fencing Championships in 1978 and the World Fencing Championships in 1981. She became an Olympic champion in 1984. Chen Xiaoxia won the women's platform diving title in 1979. Gao Fenglian won the World Judo Championships successively between 1986 and 1989. Wu Lanying broke shooting world records many times between 1981 and 1989.

[34] They include the 1981 and 1985 World Cup, the 1984 Olympics and the 1982 and 1986 World Championships.

[35] Liu Man, 'Bashi niandai: cong danyi zouxiang duoyuan' [The 1980s from singularity to plurality], *Nanfang doushi bao* [Nanfang Daily], 4 Aug. 2004.

[36] Mangan, 'A Personal Perspective', 1.

[37] '21–28 World Championships Won by Chinese Athletes', available online at www.stats. gov.cn/english/statisticaldata/yearlydata/YB2002e/htm/u2128e.htm, accessed 4 Jan. 2006.

[38] This phenomenon arose when women made more remarkable achievements in international competitions than men in the early 1980s. It was also reflected, incidentally, in show business. More actresses than actors won international recognition.

[39] Yuan Honghen, 'Benjie 'shijia' pingxuan, huojianzhe nannu bili wei 1:9: zhongguo tiyu yinsheng yangshuai toushi' [The ratio of 'the best ten' athletes selected this year was 1:9: The exploration of the female blossoming and the male withering in China's sport], *Beijing wanbao* [Beijing Evening Daily], 9 April 1999.

[40] One gold medal in a mixed event is equal to 0.5. Data come from the Elite Sports Department of State Sports Administration, availableonline at, http://www.sport.gov.cn/jjty/jjty-gzzg.htm, accessed 19 Jan. 2007.

[41] Wu Shaozu, 'Zhou Enlai yu xin zhongguo tiyu shiye de fazhan' [Zhou Enlai and the development of the sports cause of new China], Zhou Enlai Memorial Hall.

[42] Regarding the reasons for late arrival, see Kolatch, *Sport, Politics, and Ideology in China*, 171–4.

[43] Zhen Yan, 'Quanguo tiyu fazhan zhanlve taolun hui zongshu' [Review of the National Seminar on the Strategy of Sports Development], *Tiyu kexue* [China Sports Science] 1 (1986).

[44] Wu Shaozu, 'Shixing aoyun zhanlve yao zuodao suoduan zhanxian, tuchu zhongdian' [To implement the Olympic Strategy necessitates shortening the battleline and emphasizing the focal points], *Zhongguo tiyu bao* [China Sports Daily], 14 March 1989.

[45] Liu Xiaoli, Chao Huo, Cui Linna, '2004 nian quanguo tiyu juzhang huiyi bimu' [The conference of Sports Directors at Provincial and National levels across the Country concluded], available online at http://www.sport.gov.cn, accessed 27 Feb. 2004.

[46] 'Zhongguo jianshe tiyu qiangguo yao zhuanghao "liangge zhangye" – benbao zhaokai de lilun taolun hui fayang zhaiyao' [China must insist on the 'Two Strategies' to become a sports power – Extracts of speeches remarked in the theoretic seminar held by the Sports Daily], *Tiyu bao* [Sports Daily], 2 May 1988, 2.

[47] Huntington, *The Clash of Civilizations*, 229.

[48] Guojia tiwei jihua caiwu shi, *Tiyu shiye tongji nianjian* (1994), 20–3.

[49] Shu Shuicher, 'Zhongguo tiyu jie mianlin shichang jinji de tiaozhang' [Chinese sport community faces the challenge of the market economy], *Cankao xiaoxi* [Reference News], 12 Aug. 1994, 4.

[50] Wang Jiali, 'Nunan shangxin dao heshi', 8–11.

[51] Zhang Yao, '1995 nian wuoguo shengqushi suoshu youxiu yundongdui qingkung fenxi'.

[52] Zhang Tianbai, 'Di 26 Jie aoyunhui ji zhongguo tiyu daibiaotua cansai qingkuang'.

[53] Hua Xinyi, 'Ba nian kangzhan nvpai duoguan, sun jingfang: nannv pingdeng yaoqiu butong' [Eight years fighting, women's volleyball won world title; Sun Jingfang: equality between men and women, but different requirements], *Xinmin wanbao* [Xinmin Evening News], 11 March 2005.

[54] Liu Xiaoxing, 'Zhongguo wangqiu pang "nannv pingedng"' [Chinese tennis waits for 'equality between men and women']' *Dongnan zaobao* [Dongnan Morning Post], 27 Sept. 2006.

[55] 'Nvxing "zhifu", liuzhong wuqi: fu mingxia ru haomeng, guo jingjing linglei tianhou' [Female stars "become rich" with six weapons: Fu Minxia married a rich and powerful family, Guo Jingjing is another kind of queen of heaven], available online at http://www.sportsmkt.com, accessed 18 Oct., 2006.

[56] For example, table tennis, volleyball and athletics.

[57] Wang Jing, 'Zhongguo wangqiu he tianjing de meihao jiyi: "zou chuqu" dailai de chengxiao [Good memories of China's tennis and athletics: effect from the 'walking out'], *Zhongguo tiyu bao* [Sports Daily of China], 15 July 2004.

[58] Ma Bangjie, 'Wang Zijiang 'na shenme zhengjiu ni, zhongguo nvzu' [What can save you, Chinese women's football], *Beijing wanbao*, 5 Oct. 2003.

[59] Guojia tiyu zongju, *Tiyu tongji nianjian* (1994,1995–1997,1998).

[60] Born in 1981, Guo Jingjing dominated the headlines after she won two Olympic gold medals in 2004, and especially after her rumoured 'love affair' stories with the equally famous male diving champion Tian Liang and then the son of influential Hong Kong businessman He Yindong were exposed by the media. Though her charge for an endorsement has increased from 600,000 yuan to 1 million yuan, more than 20 manufacturers wait for her to endorse their products in a queue. At moment, she is endorsing nine products with an income of 9.5 million yuan.

[61] Yang Yang, winner of the 500m and 1000m speed skating events at the 2002 Winter Olympics. She was selected as one of the top ten athletes in the country in 2002 and received the China's Top Ten 'Ronlence' Champion's Award in 2004. She was admitted into the prestigious Tsuinghua University to study in 2002 and became a member of the IOC Women and Sport Committee in 2006. She is going to co-host a TV programme called *Olympic China*. Besides,

she has been involved in many charity events and working with international sports organizations. She was the endorser of the Shengyan Ince and Snow Festival event.

[62] For example, the former Ma Family athletes Wang Yuan, Wang Xiaoxia and Liu Li were unemployed after stopping training. Chen Yubei became a miner. (Source from Zhang Ye, 'Ma Jiajun mingjiang jin an zai?' [Where are the famous athletes of the Ma Family Army/the world champion Chinese women runners in the early 1990s], *Gansu Ribao* [Gansu Daily], 26 June 2003).

[63] Li Zhenhui and Dai Jinshong, 'Tiyu mingxin "jinjun" daxue ketan' [Sports stars "march" to university classroom], *Beijing wanbao*, 12 Sept. 1998.

[64] 'Yige qunti de shiluo: zhou Chunlan shijian hou de guanjun tuiyi zhi huo' [Loss of a group: puzzle of the retired champions reflected by the case of Zhou Chunlan], available online at http://sports.china.com, accessed 31 March 2006.

[65] Sun Yingjie. the 5000m and 10,000m champion at the 2002 Asian Games, was caught drug-positive at the National Games in 2005. Though she was banned for two years, she is still training and hoping to participate in the 2008 games.

[66] They are Ai Dongmei, Guo Ping and Li Juan.

[67] Zhang Ying, Wang Wei, 'Xiri malasong guanjun, yishuang canjia du yusheng' [The past Marathon champions, a pair of damaged feet to lead their remaining lIves], *Fazhi wanbao* [Legal Evening Daily], 10 Sept. 2006.

[68] It was claimed that coach Wang once beat Sun badly. The toes of the athletes who sued the coach to the court became obviously disfigured and, even worse, they are now unemployed and lead very difficult lives.

[69] For details see Dong Jinxia, *Women, Sport and Society in New China*, ch. 5.

[70] 'Zhang ying, 'wang wei, xiri malasong guanjun, yishuang canjiao du yusheng' [The former marathon champion spends her life with a pair of deformed feet], *Fazhi wanbao*, 20 Sept. 2006, BO1.

[71] It is illustrated in the Regulation on the Management of Employing Foreign Coaches by the National Teams ('guojia pinqing waiji jiaolian guanli guiding'). This regulation was initiated for the 2004 Olympic Games.

[72] 'Liu ziyuan, 'zhongguo nvlei yao yongbao buyao xiuse' [Chinese softball players want embrace not shyness], *Fazhi wanbao*, 22 Sept. 2006.

[73] Ibid.

[74] Guojia tiyu zongju jingji tiyu si, 'Ge sheng zizhiqu zhixia shi beizhan 2004 nian 2008 nian aoyunhui diaoyan qingkuang baogao'.

[75] Wu Xilin, 'Aoyunhui jubanguo cansai xiangmu dejin youshi de yanjiu'.

[76] 'Juzhang dahui dianmin nvpai xu nuli, nvwang ticao tupo cheng kaimo' [The Women's Volleyball Team, named by the Director of the SSA Liu Peng at a meeting, needs to make great effort, Women's tennis and gymnastics become role models for making breakthrough in performance], available online at http://sports.sina.com.cn, accessed 18 Jan. 2007.

[77] Zhang Yi and Wang Yu, 'Rushi wunian zhongguo jingji shehui fazhan chengjiu jushi zhumu' [Chinese achievement in social and economic development is remarkable after entering the WTO five years ago], available online at http://www.jrj.com, accessed 10 Dec. 2006.

[78] 'Yige qunti de shiluo, Zhou Chunlan shijian hou de guanjun tuiyi zhi huo' [The loss of a group – perplexity about retired champions behind the case of Zhou Chunlan](3)', available online at http://sports.china.com,http://sports.china.com, accessed 31 March 2006.

[79] Take the Volleyball Association as an example. Between 1998 and 2000, the association received 12 million yuan from the government, but it obtained 108 million yuan through marketing activities over the years 1996–2000 (Source: Gao Shenyang, 'Zhongguo paiqiu xiehui 1996 nian zhi 2000 nian caiwu qingkuang baogao', 56–7).

[80] 'Shuzi hua zhongguo aoyun juntuan' [Digital Chinese Olympic delegation], *Dongnan kuaibao* [Southeast Express], 10 Aug. 2004.

[81] The direct reason is again the issue of money. In 2005 Peng Shuai obtained US$260,000 from the WTA series, but she had to hand in 65 per cent of this income according to a regulation laid down by the SSA. Feeling that relying on current domestic coaching made it hard for her to make a breakthrough in her ranking, that the Tennis Management Centre was unable to provide her with sufficient funding for her to employ an experienced foreign coach and cover her costs for travelling abroad for competitions and that her own proportion of any bonus was not enough to employ a foreign coach either, she decided to leave the national team and become a professional player in the real sense.

[82] She later had to apologize for her action at the team meeting and was disqualified for the World Short-track Championships and World Team Championships.

[83] Huntington, *The Clash of Civilizations*, 185.

[84] Hutton, *The Writing on the Wall*, 193.

[85] Dong Jinxia *Women, Sport and Society in New China*, 108.

[86] Qu Beilin and Xu Zheng, 'Xu Li: zhongguo nvpai zialin huaji' [Xu Li: Chinese Women's Volleyball meets the blossom season again], available online at www.xinhua.net, accessed 25 Dec. 2004.

[87] 'Zhongguo nvzu zhuangkuang – renshu shjie pai diyi, shichang kaifa wei ling' [The situation of Chinese women's football – first in terms of the number of athletes, but virtually no marketing], available online at http://sports.tianjindaily.com.cn/content/2006-11/17/content_55311.htm, accessed 19 Jan. 2007.

[88] The 33-year-old player intended to continue playing until the Beijing games, but her conditions, to be an assistant coach of the team, were rejected. Faced with marriage pressure and other concerns, she had to make the decision to leave.

[89] Hu Fayun, *Di si dai nvxing*, 350–4.

[90] Zhao Mingyu, 'Shekeyuan nvxing shenghuo lanpi shu: Beijing nvxing xingfu gan quanguo disan' [The blue book of women's lives by the Social Science Academy: Beijing women rank third nationally in terms of the feeling of happiness], *Beijing yule xinbao* [Beijing Entertainment Newspaper], 1 Sept. 2006.

[91] James R. Lilley, 'Nationalism Bites Back', *New York Times*, 24 Oct. 1996.

[92] Kelly, 'Baseball and Decolourization', 823.

[93] Ebrey, *The Cambridge Illustrated History of China*, 336.

[94] Kelly, 'Baseball and Decolourization', 823.

References

Beijing tiyu xueyuan [BIPE] (ed.), *61 nian tiyu gongzuo huiyi cankao wenxian* [Reference Document of the 1961 Sports Conference]. Beijing: Tiyu xueyuan, 1964.

Carroll, Lewis. *Through the Looking Glass and What Alice Found There*. New York: The Macmillan Company, 1899.

Dong Jinxia. *Women, Sport and Society in New China*. London: Cass, 2003.

Dyreson Mark and J.A. Mangan, eds. *Sport and American Society: Insularity, Exceptionalism and Imperialism* (Special issue of *The International Journal of the History of Sport* 22, no. 6, (2005)).

Ebrey, Patricia Buckley, ed.*The Cambridge Illustrated History of China*. Cambridge: Cambridge University Press, 2003.

Gao Shenyang. 'Zhongguo paiqiu xiehui 1996 nian zhi 2000 nian caiwu qingkuang baogao' [Report on the financial situation of Chinese Volleyball Association between 1996 and 2000]. In Zhongguo paiqiu xiehui [Chinese Volleyball Association], *Zhongguo paiqiu xiehui di liu ci huiyuan daibiao dahui wenjian huibian* [Collection of Documents of the Sixth Congress of the Chinese Volleyball Association], Sept. 2001.

Guojia tiwei jihua caiwu shi [Planning and Finance Department of the NSC]. *Tiyu shiye tongji nianjian (neibu ziliao)* [Statistics Yearbook of Sports Cause] (internal materials), 1994.

Guojia tiyu wenshi xinxi bianji weiyuan hui [Editorial Commission of State Sports Literature and History Information], ed. *Tiyu shiliao* [Sports History Information], 11. Beijing: Renmin tiyu chuban she, 1984.

Guojia tiyu zongju [State Sports Administration]. *Tiyu tongji nianjian* [sports statistics] (1994, 1995–7, 1998). Beijing: People's Sports Press, 1995, 1998.

Guojia tiyu zongju jingji tiyu si [Department of Competitive Sport in the National Sports Administration]. 'Ge sheng zizhiqu zhixia shi beizhan 2004 nian 2008 nian aoyunhui diaoyan qingkuang baogao' [Survey report on the preparation of provinces, autonomous regions and municipalities for the 2004 and 2008 Olympic Games]. In *Quangguo jingji tiyu gongzuo huiyi canyuan cailiao zhiyi* [Reference Materials for the National Work Conference of Competitive Sport], 2003.

Hu Fayun. *Di si dai nvxing* [The fourth generation of women]. Beijing: Changjiang wenyi chuban she [Changjiang Arts Press], 2000.

Hutton, Will. *The Writing on the Wall: China and the West in the 21st Century*. Free Press: Simon & Schuster, 2006.

Huntington, Samuel P. *The Clash of Civilizations and the Remaking of the World Order*. New York: Simon & Schuster, 1996.

Kanin, David B. 'Ideology and Diplomacy: The Dimension of Chinese Political Sport'. In *Sports and International Relations*, edited by Benjamin Lowe. Champaign, IL: Stipes Publishing Company, 1978.

Kelly, John D. 'Baseball and Decolourization: The Caribbean, 1945–1975'. In *Muscular Christianity in Colonial and Post-Colonial Worlds*, edited by John J. MacAloon (Special issue of *The International Journal of the History of Sport* 23, no. 5, (2006)).

Kolatch, Jonathan. *Sport, Politics, and Ideology in China*. New York: Jonathon David, 1972.

Lu Tingyu. *Zhonghua renming gongheguo lishi ji shi: quzhe fazhang* [Historical record of the PRC: Zig-zag developments] *(1958–1965)*. Beijing: Hongqi chuban she, 1994.

MacAloon John J., ed. *Muscular Christianity in Colonial and Post-Colonial Worlds* (Special Issue of *The International Journal of the History of Sport* 23, no. 5, (2006).

Mangan, J.A. 'Epilogue: "Empire in Denial": An Exceptional Kind of Imperialism'. In *Sport and American Society: Insularity, Exceptionalism and Imperialism*, edited by Mark Dyreson and J.A. Mangan (Special issue of *The International Journal of the History of Sport* 22, no. 6, (2005).

Mangan, J.A 'A Personal Perspective: Twenty-Five Years, IJHS'. *The International Journal of the History of Sport*. 23, no. 1, (Feb. 2006).

Rong Gaotang. *Dangdai zhongguo tiyu* [Modern China's Sport]. Beijing: Zhongguo shehui kexue chubanshe, 1984.

Shirk, Susan L. *China: Fragile Superpower: How China's Internal Politics Could Derail Its Peaceful Rise*. London: Oxford University Press, 2007.

Wang Jiali. 'Nunan shangxin dao heshi' [When Will the Women's Basketball Stop Grieving]. *Xin tiyu* [New Sport] 7 (1998).

Wu Xilin. 'Aoyunhui jubanguo cansai xiangmu dejin youshi de yanjiu' [A study of the advantages of Olympic host countries in terms of winning gold medals], unpublished paper, 2006.

Yongjin Zhang. *China in International Society since 1949: Alienation and Beyond*. London: Macmillan Press Ltd, 1998.

Zhang Tianbai, 'Di 26 Jie aoyunhui ji zhongguo tiyu daibiaotua cansai qingkuang' [The Situation of the Chinese Delegation at the 26th Olympic Games]. *Tiyu gongzuo qingkuang* [The Situation of Sports Affairs], 624–5 (16–17) (1996): 14.

Zhang Yao. '1995 nian wuoguo shengqushi suoshu youxiu yundongdui qingkung fenxi' [Analysis of the Situation of the Elite Sports Teams Attached to Provincial, Autonomous Regions and Municipal Commissions in 1995]. *Tiyu gongzuo qingkuang* [The Situation of Sports Affairs], 610, no. 2, (1996): 6–8.

Zhonghua renmin gongheguo guojia tiyu yundong wei yuan hui [The National Sports Committee of the PRC]. *Quanguo tiyu shiye tongji zhilaio huibian* [Collection of Statistical Information on Sport in China] (1949–1978)]. Beijing: Renmin tiyu chuban she, 1979.

Olympian Politics in Beijing: Games but not Just Games

Kevin Caffrey

Introduction

The old adage is that 'politics is who gets what', and it is a sentiment that rings true to our modern logics of limited-resource competitive capitalist societies. However, such questions are never quite so simple as Adam Smith would have us believe. Politics is also who 'who' is, who is positioned where and how smoothly all this is accomplished. It is something multi-faceted, and the Olympic Games have come to be one of these facets for a growing world society. The 2008 games in Beijing seem set to be exemplary in this respect, with most commentators observing that the games are political except the official acolytes of the party state itself. [1] Suggesting that the games are a form of politics by other means has become something of a commonplace, so without becoming too inequitably critical we will take up the example of how the 2008 Beijing games are the latest result of an old project that has seen muscular Christian motivations in China morph into notions of 'face' that articulate with China's 'higher weight-class' geopolitical position in the world today. The Beijing games are analysed here as a two-front communicative ritual operation aimed both inwardly at the Chinese populace, and outwardly at an international audience of global neighbour-states – though both fronts are properly geopolitical. What follows are observations about the many aspects of this greater geopolitical reckoning of the 29th Olympiad.

Sport as Politics

The International Olympic Committee (IOC) enjoys holding forth on its apolitical character, but few interested observers actually believe them. [2] Its charter defines the 'Olympic spirit' from the eyes of an individual, steering clear of reference to statehood and intending to promote peace and human dignity while prohibiting discrimination based on 'race, religion, politics, gender' or anything otherwise incompatible with belonging to the 'Olympic Movement'. [3] Despite this hopefulness, the charter nonetheless frames the mechanism of running the games through existing geopolitical nation states. In order to compete, one has to be selected by one of the 202 national Olympic committees (NOC) and be a national of that NOC country. While NOCs are supposed to preserve their autonomy from government, [4] public office-holders often govern the NOCs. They are also not provided independent sources of funding, depending financially on the national governments from which they 'maintain separation'. When the practical issues of the games are so financially and otherwise dependent on national governments, the Olympics cannot live up to its ideal as a politics-free venue for sport competition. Rather, political tension and propaganda have at times substantially darkened the modern history of the games. Hitler tried to showcase the athletic superiority of the Aryan race during the 1936 games in order to justify his Nazi plan to the world. Terrorists killed 11 athletes in the 1972 Munich games as part of Israeli-Palestinian terror politics. The US and USSR also boycotted the 1980 Moscow and 1984 Los Angeles games as part of Cold War geopolitics. In short, there is a wealth of evidence to suggest that they are a venue for international geopolitics. On the academic front there is even work to suggest that the games are expressly political, and MacAloon has formulated the games as a Turnerian ritual process, suggesting that the very structure of the Olympic rituals resonate with the logic of inter-group interaction rituals. [5] As the political logic of the modern nation state developed, an ancient Greek idea about sport as ritualized war without weapons and bloodshed was to undergo a renaissance, as seen reflected in the opinion of a German sporting newspaper from 1913: 'The Olympic idea in the modern age symbolizes a world war that is not expressed through open military action, but that gives anyone who knows how to read sports results a fair idea of the hierarchy of nations.' [6]

The charitable interpretation of these trends suggests that sport can also be a lesson in peace. [7] According to the sociological work of Elias and Dunning, international-level sporting events such as the Olympics or the World Cup are regular occasions for states to congregate publicly. [8] Games allow each state's proxies to compete without killing each other. The IOC seems to use such ideas to exaggerate the

Olympic movement's high moral purpose, but in the end it *is* undeniable that the games allow a trans-national view of the world and its peoples which can militate against prevailing national insularities. In a working paper during the Barcelona Olympics, MacAloon suggested that the venue is unique and almost ideal for both explicit and back channel politics. [9]

The analogy of war by other means is a felicitous one, and the pragmatic hopefulness in the idea is reasonable. Yet the machinations of the official, the wealthy and the well-placed are not the only considerations here, and these international sporting events have little to structurally direct them away from the at least as likely result of their feeding chauvinism and xenophobia in national populations. The sentiments of the not wealthy and the poorly-placed masses are unpredictable, and if Chinese history is any indication, they are potentially transformational. In the light of this, it becomes difficult to maintain a simple position that the games resolve international disputes and rivalries between countries when we must also recognize this potentially xenophobic result.

The Olympics as war by other means is analogically the same as to invoke Clausewitz's famous argument that war is politics, and this 'games=politics' logic plays to the hierarchical element of the Olympics. While every country is an equal competitor in the games, there are clear leaders and followers – no more than one team or person stands at the top of the pyramid winner's platform. There is something about China that has an affinity with the idea of politics relating to the management of hierarchy, since relative hierarchy has been something worth going to war for in China – as we know from its cosmological politics and the first line of Sun-Tzu's *Art of War*, that 'war is a vital matter of state' (*bing zhe guo zhi da shi ye*). Though not a 1:1 relationship, it is fair to say that China's approach to the games has a clear geopolitical hue to it. Dong suggests that '[Sport] does not occur in a vacuum …it reflects, and is reflected by, the dominant social structures and values of the society in which it exists'. [10] This is a pregnant notion worth unpacking on many levels, but suffice it to say that in the consideration of the games for China, it reflects a new awareness on the part of the state that it is operating with an audience of equally sovereign neighbour states in a tightly interconnected world. Witness the recent attempt by the Chinese state to change its mascot. Knowing that other states see the dragon as an aggressive icon, Chinese image engineers suggested the panda be used instead. This set off a firestorm of commentary, claiming everything from exaggerated political correctness and poor understanding to weakness and outright stupidity. It is now unclear what will be done, but the attempt to ditch the dragon was a sign of awareness that what others think is a key aspect of this Olympics as a venue for political manoeuvring.

Sport, put in anthropological terms as an abstract practice, seems to be something like competition within particular ritualized parameters. The act of competition itself can be seen as merely the potential to succeed, since one does not *compete* when there is no chance of winning or losing – a situation that would be all ritual rather than competitive sport. It is a small leap from this to Beijing's 2008 spandex geopolitics, and the approach is readily documented by attention to the small events leading to Beijing. Competition and triumph were, for example, the tropes that energized China's being awarded the 2008 games. Almost every Chinese newspaper covering the awarding of the games to Beijing splashed something like the phrase 'We won!' (*women yinle!*) over their front pages. [11] The structure of the modern sports in the Olympics is fixed by international rules, but in its Chinese avatar these political games have a significant charge of Chinese historical characteristics. Susan Brownell contends that

> [S]ports were emptied of their muscular Christian moral content and replaced with contents that suited the needs of the politics and tenor of the times in China. The muscular Christian morality [*sic*] of fair play, citizenship, and democracy was replaced over time with Chinese discourses about national prestige and international competition. [12]

Athletic bodies can here be seen as a relatively new idea for the intended expansion of new Chinese state influence, which is still imperial in a non-territorial manner – interestingly, this ancient mode is very much in keeping with more recent modes of empire like that of the US. Hardt and Negri's argument about the nature of the new world order [13] is perhaps useful here in that it shows how a dominance over the ways in which political, social, and economic interactions are made meaningful at a global level is a new kind of more subtle 'empire'. If the Olympic Games have taken on newer importance in the Beijing event, it is likely because of the challenges of this new 'empire' aspect of global interaction – a spectacle of emerging world culture with its explicit or implicit impositions of a meaningful governing mechanics of national interaction that might not be as new as we thought. The games might now also be a site where the playing out of a new global political order can be seen, half engaged with the older system of nation states and half engaged beyond it with a new global order of interaction.

In order to properly situate how the Beijing Olympics are meaningful as particularly Chinese politics, we turn to some historical background of contextualizing importance. An image increasingly associated with Beijing 2008 is that of Zheng He, the great Ming Dynasty admiral who sailed seven voyages to and through the India Ocean, reaching as far as the Middle East and the east African coast. Little is actually known about him, but imagined likenesses are appearing regularly in Olympics propaganda as the man who went out into the rest of the world to spread the light of Chinese civilization. [14] As the once and now again poster-boy for China's (re)engagement with the world, he presents something of a revelatory coincidence for our understanding of Chinese Olympic geopolitics, [15] and there may be more similarity to his activities as a tool for Chinese engagement in the world than is immediately apparent. His mission seems interesting in that there is increasing argument over whether it was exploratory or a maritime colonial operation. [16] Since it wasn't 'our' kind of colonialism, which is to say directly economic and extractive, and was instead tasked more overtly with collecting relationships of tributary quality all the way to Africa, we might split the difference and call it some kind of imperialism with Chinese characteristics. Surely the Chinese, who were imperial far earlier than the modern Western countries, can have some claim to their own brand of imperialism. Note too the recent commentary storm about China's forays into African and South American 'resource diplomacy'. Western, especially American, pundits have over-exerted themselves in their efforts to argue this new behaviour into convenient imperial categories, when the very Chinese desire for and careful engineering of productive relationships describes it better. Re-engagement in the world and the opportunity to show off Chinese skills, logistical abilities and modern advancement have a happy affinity, then, as the stated goals of hosting the games and the unstated political goals of the Beijing government coincide. They are nonetheless political.

Not a coincidence in this politics is the use of the image of Zheng He's great treasure boats to signal China's re-engagement with the world. A replica of what one of the boats is thought to have looked like is being constructed in Nanjing, and in 2008 it will sail on a new voyage of image-building, the politics of which resonate with what we now like to call 'public relations'. [17] It will cost about US$10 million to build, and will be the largest wooden ship in the world. It is slated to travel to countries along the ancient maritime 'Silk Road' to promote 'bilateral relationships', and if we care to look closely we can see that this 'modern legendary ship' is a kind of physical metaphor for the way Chinese want to see their intended rise to world position unfold. The ship looks the part of a traditional vessel, with an oak plank shell and a configuration thought to be that of the Zheng He vessels. Yet outward appearances hide key differences, since it is also to have three modern engines, computers and air-conditioning, with a speed capability almost twice that of other large 'sailing' vessels. This is the way China's new geopolitical image will engage the world: a physical statement that the dragon fleet is ready to set sail as the biggest, fastest operator, with both its traditional forms and its modern sciences intact and deployed to good effect. [18] Consider the comparison to the world's next biggest wooden vessel, Sweden's *Gothenborg*. It was constructed as an austere, relatively compact vessel closely approximating a recognized past and with its own technological limitations. China's new Zheng He vessel, immediately described as a 'treasure ship', emphasizes exquisite structure and decoration in a spectacle of Chinese skill – very much in keeping with traditional Chinese cosmological practice, as it turns out. 'Practical' vs. 'spectacle', only this time the spectacle has some serious practical in it. It is of course also revelatory how the sense of 'tradition' is working in this example, and since nobody really knows what the great treasure ships of Zheng He's fleet looked like, [19] this 'traditional' form is something of a best-guess rendition that lives up to newfound 'nostalgia'.

Just as this fifteenth-century Chinese Muslim admiral was sent on seven expanding voyages to engage with the wider world than that well known by the Chinese court at the time, his twenty-first-century image signals a re-engagement with the larger world. Six hundred years ago the great treasure fleet carried with it spectacular gifts made to represent the civilizing light of the Chinese son of heaven, and today Zheng He is a masthead for the programming that will present a spectacular China re-engaging with a receptive world through the spectacle of the Olympic Games. The games will showcase Chinese development – the sine qua non for inexpensive goods that fuel the Western world's consumerist cultures – and its recent infrastructural wonders. Counting on its newfound economic wealth to gain it mainstream legitimacy in the community of nations, Beijing is hoping that the games as a political instrument of broadcasting will accentuate the positives of it meteoric rise while suppressing the negatives. Whether the world will parse the data in the way China hopes remains to be seen, but the voyage will not be exactly smooth sailing.

Credit Where Credit Is Due

China can legitimately use the opportunity of the Beijing games to exhibit the successes of the state, its logistical abilities and its potential for the future. Most of the country has improved access to almost everything; it is an economic development superstar; its success at infrastructural development is a logistical masterstroke that India publicly envies; and a greater general national wealth is evident. Beginning with infrastructure-building projects, China has achieved the spectacular. The new Beijing-Lhasa rail line, said to have been declared unfeasibly difficult by the Swiss who were consulted beforehand, was completed last year. Total railway mileage has increased dramatically, with a China-Europe line said to be on schedule for completion in 2008–9. Total Chinese highway infrastructure is to exceed that of the US interstate highway system soon, and an 'Asia Highway' linking China, Vietnam, Laos, Thailand and Burma to Europe is due in 2010. Airports have been built, with the new Beijing airport to be the biggest in the world when it is completed in 2008, and air travel is booming. Symbolically and actually, China is no longer the 'sick man of Asia'.

'Yellow Peril' Chinaphobes in the West often like to pontificate about how China's fast economic growth will be offset and even reversed by a lack of political reform, causing collapse because the state is unable to deal with the forces it is unleashing. In this particular brand of wish-dream, China must follow 'our' development parameters, whether it wants to or not. Modernization liberals, on the other hand, are content with remaining hopeful about China's rise. The cargo-cult like payoff of being able to sell every Chinese person a pair of socks that is always just beyond the horizon involves a myth of the China market 'Great Pumpkin' that continues to motivate the neoliberal classes, whose exercise in fancy reinforces their own bias that evolution towards an Anglo-American style capitalist democracy is an unavoidable course that all states must follow. The notion that China is a lumbering giant, poorly equipped to respond effectively to its problems or strike its own path towards development, has been shown to be more than a little clumsy by a fairly responsive 'brush-fire' method of addressing social problems that seems to have worked so far.

Ten years ago government revenues were 10 per cent of GDP, and prospects for addressing serious internal issues seemed bleak. And yet today's 20 per cent of GDP and tightly run fiscal policies make it more likely that it will be able to address its social problems. Some commentators suggest that Chinese corruption is of the 'lubricating' kind resembling America's nineteenth-century gilded age – monumentally corrupt, rapid economic growth – but not the 'kleptocratic' zero-sum type that has destroyed Africa. [20] Tight control of its development process has paid off, with the decision to maintain state corporations having had benefits in being able to avoid some of the excesses seen in the former Soviet developmental sequence. The monumentally corrupt Shanghai land bubble, for example, ended in the Shanghai party boss being jailed last year for his offences. To combat income inequality the government has chosen to stress equality of opportunity as a state responsibility, thereby investing huge amounts in education, quadrupling the number of university graduates in the past five years and making public education in the poorer inland provinces free up to grade nine. After SARS, China has taken its head out of the sand in terms of the danger it faces from possible epidemics, recently demonstrating that it can address these types of issues. Its AIDS control attempts are far superior to India's, with progress on tuberculosis detection and treatment having also soared. Even the environment has finally appeared on the Chinese radar as a potential threat, with much rhetoric and even some attention to the matter being attempted. These indicators of progress will be the raw material of China's Olympic presentation to the world, with medals won a nice icing on the cake.

A more subtle and quiet advance is also happening behind the scenes. Governance has seen a transformation from engineering approaches to legal, economic, management and historical methods – evidenced by the kinds of degrees held by most of the next generation of officials. Nearly 200,000 officials have been shifted around lately, and preference has been given to younger officials who have experience dealing with poverty and rural development issues. This is a beneficial change since the last generation of officials was almost all technocrat engineers, and the 2008 Beijing games will present this transformation as a milestone in the progress of Chinese development. [21] The power of this positive narrative for the Olympics 2008 coverage will be significant, but every milestone has its millstone.

Felt But Unseen Difficulties

It is important to recognize the new and improved conditions in China today, but it is equally significant to recognize that the ways in which China has secured them are nonetheless 'brush-fire' methods of addressing social problems unleashed by its development. This is not necessarily bad, but the doubtfulness of whether addressing the symptoms are enough to change their causes takes some of the hopefulness out of the observations. The brush-fire method of social problem-solving, successful though it has been so far, does seem to suggest that the government has lost some or all of the initiative in the development process, and is now in many ways only reacting to it rather than driving it. Operating on the observation that the Olympic Games are also high politics, like other political operations it necessitates an accounting of the negatives that accompany its positives. Though spectacles like the Olympic ritual have a place in the system of modern nation states, such grand performances can also obfuscate the unequal mechanics that are often its conditions of possibility. It does not well serve a thinking audience to politely endure this obscurity, nor does it do justice to the human price being paid to underwrite the spectacle or its associated development track. Just as any empire's expansion needs an accounting of what it is costing to expand, there must be a reckoning for the cost of an empire-turned-nation-state's full reengagement with the international system of states. To this end, let us look again at the positive elements of China's performance.

Improved access to almost everything, economic development, infrastructural advances and national wealth are evident, and China has managed to ride the whirlwind of development effectively. Both Chinaphobes and modernization liberals are having to recognize that China has demonstrated flexible and attentive governance, and is capable of choosing its own path rather than having it dictated by the forces of an unleashed capitalism. Today's 20 per cent of GDP government revenues and tightly run fiscal policies allow better ability to address its social problems, but are they successfully managing to do so? First, accurate data on Chinese finance or any other kind of economic indicator are difficult to come by and should be considered approximate. Second, corruption is still a monumental problem, and while the suggestion that it is of the 'lubricating' rather than kleptocratic variety seems hopeful on its face, the analogy with America's gilded age is misleading. The idea that Chinese corruption is 'lubricating' has a pedigree in the notion that there is a particularly Chinese form of capitalism, and that idea has merit. However, the suggestion that Chinese corruption is not kleptocratic 'of the type that has destroyed Africa' [22] seems more problematic. I find it difficult, for example, to allow for the idea that the jailed Shanghai party boss, whose accepted bribes were in the millions and who acted more as a gate-keeper than a facilitator, would have been practising lubricating rather than kleptocratic corruption.

In early March 2007 the topic of the Beijing Olympics even came up in the National People's Congress meeting, and the news was not all good. Corruption and cost overruns were the topic of discussion, with the arrest of Deputy Mayor Liu Zhihua (the official in charge of Olympic projects) for corruption and other embarrassing habits being an issue of note. [23] This is in fact a brute example of how corruption is out of control, and it provides for exactly the kind of parasitic businessmen-elite (of the type found in Latin and South America) that some commentators suggest is not a fixture of Chinese development. [24] In 2006 the official number of deaths reported in China's mining industry was 5,000, with candid assessments putting that number far higher. [25] In Shanxi the party and government heads often drive Hummers, but the mines are considered some of the most deadly. In a country like China, famously assumed to be authoritarian, we might think repeated reform directives from Beijing on the authority of top national leaders would produce results. Not so. In fact, central government efforts to rein in local authorities have been not only ignored but actually blocked. In October 2006 Beijing announced that it was delaying until 2010 a plan that would have forced the closure of the thousands of illegal mines that account for the majority of deadly accidents. According to the official Xinhua News Agency, the plan foundered because of opposition from local governments, which see mines as their 'major capital sources'. That, said Xinhua, led 'many local authorities to protect unsafe mines for financial gain'. [26] It is difficult to see how these actions are 'lubricating' when they seem at least as kleptocratic. [27] While money is made and lives develop, not all lives. The image of poor people being sacrificed for the privileged, when it appears in Olympic coverage broadcast to the world, can have a strong blowback potential.

Stressing equality of opportunity to combat income inequality has a nice American 'rugged individualist' tone to it that plays well in today's neoliberal justification for the way the world 'is', but it is characteristically dissembling about the way the world should or could be. Money invested in education can only be a good thing, but quadrupling the number of university graduates and free public education in the poorer inland provinces is not without its own resulting problems when tens of thousands of these graduates fail to find jobs every year. [28] Wealth inequality and unequal access to opportunity will almost surely be a high-profile topic of discussion when thousands of foreign journalists are given free access to China, as was required by the IOC in order to award the games to Beijing. The post-SARS wake-up *has* demonstrated that China can address healthcare concerns, and its AIDS control attempts may be superior to India's even despite the embarrassing habit of arresting the best of the AIDS doctors and activists. Still, in much of the country there is little or no access to healthcare *at all*, marking a division between first- and second-class citizens demarcated by whether or not one can endure a major illness without dying due to, or sending one's family into, dire poverty. An unhappy example then is the nexus between a particularly kleptocratic corruption and the healthcare system, seen recently in a hospital scandal in response to much reader-generated complaining about predatory health profession practices. It was reported by the courageous *Southern Weekly* that out of ten samples of 'urine' sent in to coastal hospitals for diagnostic analysis, six of them returned a diagnosis that the patient had a urinary tract infection requiring over $US100 worth of medicine (a vast sum for most Chinese) – all despite the fact that the 'urine' sent in was actually just tea. Aside from not being at all a 'lubricating' form of corruption, what this indicates is that healthcare access at the actual human level is still very much a serious and pervasive problem. Any suggestion that vast strides have been made since the time of China's 'barefoot doctors', who at one time had provided a minimal level of free healthcare even to the far edges of the Communist empire, needs to be moderated by practical reflection. Health and reasonable healthcare are particularly sentimental issues that promise to take a significant place in the human interest segments of Olympic coverage, and these predatory conditions will likely be covered even by the charitable foreign media. And when it comes to China, few foreign media tend to be charitable.

When it comes to governance, the transformation from engineering approaches to legal, economic, management and historical perspectives can again be a positive. If engineers are the ones who know *how to do things right*, and governors, economists, managers, historians and other social scientists are the ones who know *what the right things to do are*, then a balancing progress *is* being made. But realizing that not everything that counts can be counted and not everything broken can be fixed mechanically is only a beginning step. Beijing 2008 marks this transition from engineering to managing an actual human population, and the subsequent age/term limits for official positions help to insure receptive and flexible governance into the future. However, it remains to be seen if the state will effectively develop past its current brush-fire method of addressing the social problems generated by the challenges of development. Addressing the symptoms may not be enough to transform their causes, thereby taking some of the hopefulness out of observations about China's future. If this loss of initiative in development is the case, then the future may hold only a waiting game of brush-fire events until the fires get too big to stamp out.

Spectators have been led to believe that all Chinese citizens stood up and cheered when the 2008 games were awarded to Beijing. Dong wrote that 'Virtually all of China, from the government to its citizens, pledged all-out support for Beijing's bid to host the 2008 Olympic Games', even citing a poll showing 98.7 per cent support. [29] The strong internal support for the Beijing games seems to come largely from the coastal regions that have the largest middle-class urban populations, but some of the rest of the country seems to have been underrepresented in this support. I have no doubt that Beijing exploded in rapture at the news, but that this 'all-out support' was not forthcoming from many people elsewhere seems to have been lost in the festivities of self-congratulation. There is much resistance, aggravation and ambivalence hidden behind this narrative; it is not 'all-out support' and it is worth outlining to serve our cause of accounting for a downside to China's new globalization and re-engagement games. In the rural areas labouring under increasing relative poverty, routinized labour migration and other forms of deprivation characterizing the underclass of neoliberal Chinese development, priorities often lie elsewhere. One illegal shaft coal miner I met in Sichuan in 2002, between jokes about how well he would do the day hauling coal out of a tiny, black tunnel became an Olympic sport, voiced this sentiment in his comments on Beijing being awarded the games. '*That* China has reason to be happy, *this* China has more practical things to worry about than games,' he said with a matter-of-fact grin.

I was living on China's south-western Yunnan frontier at the time the news that Beijing had been awarded the games was published in the newspapers, and the number of people who were visibly excited about it was a bit surprising – surprising because there were so few. Most who were very animated about it were tourists from eastern China, a few students and anyone connected to the operations of the party-state. The rest seemed to shrug it off as yet another of Beijing's plans that will likely not benefit Yunnan or its people. One way to parse this was that people who were far removed from the needs of the common citizen were more likely to engage in self-congratulatory rapture than were the actual common people. Perhaps it is the faraway quality of the frontier – the popular sentiment there being 'the mountains are high and the emperor is far away' – that makes this blasé approach to this latest imagination of national pride possible, but it pays to remember that a great deal of China is frontier. And even more of it is marginal, where even in more urban places the disenfranchised can reflect this view on the orgy of Olympic support in China. One Mr Song, a Beijing restaurant owner whose restaurant was flattened to make way for new construction that was supposed to make Beijing look better for the Olympics, pointed out how he was neither compensated for the loss of livelihood nor reimbursed for the rent he had already paid in advance. He said: 'Holding the Olympics will directly benefit real estate contractors with special connections. How can I support Beijing's Olympic bid when I'm not sure how I'm going to feed my children now?' [30]

The artificial patriotic high of Olympics mania will end after two weeks of ritual games in 2008, and the country will then be left with the often very stark conditions of developing China. When the country can win gold medals in badminton and Shanghai can produce Ferrari-driving *Forbes* 500 list members, but the inner regions of China continue to be dominated by poverty, poor health care access, a manufactured lack of voice, massive inequality and a hyper-visible wealth disparity, Yunnanese can feel (not without good reason) like there are problems with Beijing's priority list. It isn't that the people of the frontiers think the Olympics are at fault, but rather that there are other pressing issues yet to be taken care of before China spends money on international spectacles. As a result, they find it difficult to get carried away in the Olympic spirit. This lack of enthusiasm in the face of priority disagreements highlights the domestic price that China is paying for its emphasis on the Olympics. The increase in patriotism for the relative 'haves' may be an effective strategy for Beijing's development course, but as an internal control tactic its success is predicated on the condition that people do not consider themselves as relative have-nots who have lost out on the benefits of the games and see patriotism as a poor substitute for food with which to feed their children.

There are other examples of potential disagreement along these lines, with other relative 'have nots'. Against all manner of advice, China intends to run the Olympic torch to the top of Mount Everest. Aside from climbing professionals who consider it lunacy of the first order, the fact that Everest is in Tibet has made the issue a lightning-rod for political comment. On one hand this plan is understandable as the nation state 'encompassing' its geobody by the semiotic light of that particular nation-reinforcing torch. On the other hand, Tibet as a colonial territory of the world's oldest empire casts this spectacle of torchlight in roughly the same terms as the new Beijing-Lhasa railway – i.e. as a neo-imperial vehicle of expansion. Consider this new 'world's highest' railway. The shiny new Canadian-made Bombardier train-cars and the sheer engineering marvel of the line would seem to be a laudable success for China, and that is just the way Chinese media will present it for Olympic coverage. And yet only about ten per cent of the jobs constructing the railway were held by Tibetans; between 3,000 and 5,000 *additional* soldiers will be stationed along the route for 'security'; and the new access to Tibet further facilitates an inflow of Chinese migrants to Tibet that is already the most hated aspect there of China's control. The Dalai Lama has already observed that the new railway is politically motivated to bring about cultural change, even invoking a notion of 'cultural genocide'. These 'domestic' concerns, by warrant of the relative greater legitimacy the Dalai Lama enjoys internationally regarding Tibet, become international issues of geopolitical significance for Beijing that will factor prominently in the lead-up to and aftermath of the 2008 games. And once the media have enjoyed the unprecedented freedom mandated to them for the Olympics coverage, it will be difficult to put the genie back in the bottle, and the price for attempting to do so will be high.

China is perhaps the world's most impressive neoliberal development success, and a final indicator for this success is the recent legislation ensuring private property. [31] This success has been effective at controlling China's internal concerns, but unrest shows that it may be encountering diminishing returns on its brush-fire methods. In trying to meaningfully account for the increasing rate of unrest in China, we catch a glimpse of this discord's pace. A 2004 protest in Sichuan against corruption surrounding a dam project was 100,000 strong, and it was only one of 74,000 'mass incidents' that year. That number increased to 83,000 the next year, and these are just the statistics to which the state has admitted. One of the ways China has tended to deal with internal discord is to displace it by manipulating internal sentiment to an external location – America not being the only government adept at manipulating its population's xenophobic sentiments in order to fertilize the fields of its geopolitical interests. With a sense of the obstacles to China's presentation as an international success story, it is these geopolitical interests to which we now turn.

Geopolitical Significance

As we can see, several of the relatively hidden aspects of China's development performance have important international geopolitical implications. The Beijing Olympics are the culmination of an effort going back to 1949, an internal political act directed at its populace, and a geopolitical assertion of international scope about the intended direction China plans to take for its ascendance to the status of fully peer state. Since 1949 the government had an oscillating engagement with the Olympics movement, before settling into an 'elite sports system' as a winning strategy. The games and their political complex are therefore the outcome of dramatic diplomatic, political, social and economic change born of ideological commitment. This commitment has an analogue in Beijing's plans for international stature, including the politics of relationship in Asia and the rest of the world. In addition to this nearby concern, China is expanding its influence into regions such as Africa, the Middle East and South America in its quest for resources to power its economic development – often coming into new tensions with already existing political relationships in these regions.

As we saw hinted in its willingness to change mascot from the 'threatening' dragon to the cuddly panda, China is wisely concerned with its international image because it remains quite negative despite recent improvement (a trend helped, no doubt, by recent political idiocies by the United States, which seem designed to universally antagonize). While some reports have suggested that recent polls show how Asians have begun to see China less as a threat to them, ethnographic data gathered in South-East Asia, Taiwan, Japan and India seems to suggest rather that people in these areas maintain a less rosy view of China's rise. [32] Compared to the recent behaviour of the United States, China looks downright benign; but not everyone is interested in comparing these two imperial giants. Many countries are more interested in the ramifications of China's rise. The games being in Beijing is an opportunity for China to get its message out in order to rebuild its image, a venue where the host benefits from the charge of positive sentiment usually extended to it because of its need to adhere to internationalist standards of cordial interaction agreed upon by the world sporting community. The Olympic ritual event is a sign of the nation for the Chinese that the international stature of modern China is something worthy of pride, but it is also a sign to the international audience of an agreed-upon interaction ritual. Of course, as with games in general, something is at stake; and these stakes are what China's neighbours are watching more intently.

The government's position is that all nation states can coexist in harmony, but in the realpolitik-dominated age of nation states this can only really be taken as a place-holder for when the state is politically capable of disregarding this harmony in its interests, and everyone knows it. [33] It is one thing to say that China wants only peaceful, harmonious growth or that its re-engagement with the world should be accepted this way. It is quite another thing to actually have reason to believe that is all there is to it. Just as Zheng He's voyages were both relationship-building engagement *and* maritime imperialism, so China's expansion now is resource relationship-making *and* good old fashioned influence expansion. Hosting the games is something to be proud of, but China's new diplomatic weight-class means that the competition is also aware of a new presence in the ring – and new contenders can get knocked out. China well understands the symbolic importance of face, and abstracting the concept to the level of the nation diminishes this understanding only a little, since its own international relations theory is often spoken of in this way. Indeed, this grandiose calculation of public image in a kind of Goffmanian mechanics writ large has a long history. [34] The order of traditional Chinese polity was organized as a symbolic hierarchy-making process that enticed or required other polities to accede to Chinese orderings of the world assembled concentrically and hierarchically by relations of tribute. China has for 2,000 years had its own logic of empire, and it seems reasonable to suspect that all these mysteries of recent manifestation and conception that are seen to coalesce around the 2008 Olympics also reflect this historical imperial logic. The major transformation in China's geopolitical approach now as apart from its historical one is that the traditionally default centre-of-the-world self-positioning has been replaced with one of nominally equal competitors with the opportunity to succeed.

There are several ongoing concerns involving China's policies in Asia that will surely be part of the message it wants to broadcast to its neighbour states, and therefore will certainly colour the image-engineering attempt presented in the games. Even a short list of these Asia policies, when viewed for their interconnected relationships, constitutes something of an 'alliance haze'. Of more immediate scope is China's recent interaction with India, which, though usually civil, has still been quite competitive. The new Beijing-Lhasa rail line is too stark a colonial instrument to put Tibetan minds at ease, and the further shrinking of China's buffer with India has given *that* country cause to heighten its attention to China's moves in the region. The opening of the Nathu La Pass, a Himalayan pass on the old Silk Road, occurred last year, and bilateral trade between the two Asian population giants reached US$21 billion in 2005, up 38 per cent from 2004 and expected to reach US$50 billion by 2010. There are those in India, such as Gujarat's infamous Chief Minister Modi, who look to the Chinese development model as the only suitable model for Indian development. However, a larger and less morally bankrupt consortium of Indian military experts has warned that the new openings will allow 'Chinese spies and agents on subversive missions' to enter India. [35] Of course, most of this is predicated on the situation of India vis-à-vis Pakistan, and of greater concern to India is the close relationship China has with Pakistan and Burma. Pakistan's relationship is signalled by the Chinese-assisted Gwadar Deep Water Port project, which gives economic benefits to China, because it is only a few hundred miles from the energy-rich Persian Gulf, and strategic benefits to Pakistan and its naval forces. Burma's (Myanmar's) relationship to China is shown by cross-border trade and the fact that China is one of the very few countries that routinely defend its pariah-state behaviour – the product of successful resource and access diplomacy – in the UN, and by the fact that it serves to contain Indian's own potential to expand its influence. The close relationships these countries have with China have in turn played a large part in India's new closeness with the US, unfolding as a traditional balancing act for the region. And where there is traditional balancing along the realist model of international relations, there is the matter of military strength.

According to Jiang Enzhu, a spokesman for the National People's Congress, Beijing has also accelerated its military spending. China's military budget is to be increased 17.8 per cent this year to about 350 billion yuan (almost $45 billion). [36] Taiwan already has something of an arms race going with China, regularly purchasing US weapons and technology, and ensuring US involvement in that relationship. Presenting this military build-up as benign during the Olympics will likely follow the tried and true path of suggesting that it is for internal protection rather than external projection, and there is more than a little truth to this. But this is something of a two-edged sword that demands attention to why it needs the *internal* protection of a national army rather than a police force.

Japan presents China with a complex range of issues designed to complicate Beijing's plans for Asia, allied as it is with both Taiwan and the US along both political and economic lines. US bases in Japan mark it as a cooperator with the containment policies of the Cold War; a 'missile shield' being considered to protect Japan and Taiwan in case of a Chinese attack is also in the works; the remilitarization of the country has been given the green light; and the aggravating refusal of Japan to apologize for its atrocities in China during the Second World War energize certain conditions of possibility for further contention between the two Asian powerhouses. Colonial memories of Japanese invasion die hard in China, and it is to this day extremely difficult to find a person in or from Nanjing that has anything good to say about Japan. Japan does indeed have much to answer for, and Beijing's hospitality during the Olympics will likely highlight this by its exacting charm and diplomacy in the face of morally questionable Japanese decisions of late. With all attention focused on the camaraderie of the games in Asia, the powers of the Pacific Rim will be on high image alert while furiously positioning themselves under Olympic cover. As MacAloon suggests, there will likely be much back-channel politicking obscured by the reasonable comment that 'we are just here for the games'. [37]

There are loose ends in this diplomatic haze and development narrative, of course. China's total highway infrastructure is to exceed that of the US, but occupying any significant portion of it with automobile density to the degree that the US has carelessly allowed would be economically infeasible and an environmental suicide involving its neighbours. With global warming rightly becoming the unavoidable cause celeb for the twenty-first century, and China having a nearly hopeless record in this regard, environmental concern will be a theme for which it will have to answer many tough questions. Internally, flooding due to over-cutting of timber in the headwaters of the Yangtze is still a cause of great concern. Geopolitically, environmental dangers are an already sensitive point with Russia because a recent chemical spill poisoned a river running into Russian communities north of China. The 'Asia Highway' also develops ties to and through Central Asia that require Russia to interface with Chinese plans as well, so these relationships are not inconsequential. These development projects are natural moves for a growing, globalizing state, but the potential for projection of Chinese influence, particularly in Central Asia and the Middle East, concerns its global neighbour-states for a variety of economic, environmental and political reasons. Virtually nothing can be done beyond its own borders without activating an entire system of interpenetrating alliances already formed in the international community, and the Beijing games will be the window into China's thinking and behaviour on these issues.

China should not be unrealistic about the games' impact on its image. The event will not change the political economics of unrest in the country, and it may even contribute to it. If Beijing is unwilling or unable to parlay the higher profile it achieves through the Olympics into a new image in the international community that emerges from its troubled past – all despite the fact that conditions seem set for at least half of the world media coverage having a decidedly critical tone to it – then the new mandarins will have only a stark and troubled social landscape to return to, not much will have changed and they will be paying off a large debt that many disgruntled Chinese saw coming. The games will also not change the suspicion that China represents in Japan and India. We have discussed how the Olympics serve as a meaningfully political act at least as much as they are a sporting event, and media attention so far seems to agree – at least until the games actually start. China's ambitions to dominate the 2008 Olympic Games have been shown here to be something of a political analogy for the logic of its greater ambitions in Asia and the world, and the fact that its major geopolitical competitors are the US, Japan, India and Russia indicates something of the scope of its ambitions.

Late in the writing of this article it became necessary to include reference to two revelatory examples of Chinese geopolitical wrangling that draw this discussion into clearer relief. Exacerbation of the Sudan situation by Chinese road-blocking in the UN has left Beijing's protestations of harmony-building somewhat embarrassingly bloodied, with everyone from Hollywood directors and multinational corporations (!) decrying the injustice and making the obvious link between China's hopes for a great Olympics and its providing cover for crimes against humanity. Beijing's very late attempts to influence their African partner's behaviour is too clearly the result of massive international outrage at China rather then a visibly laudable willingness to help for greater international harmony. Its late decision to send a company of peacekeeping military engineers to Sudan will not untarnish their reputation in time for a shiny Olympics – no matter how good they are at kung fu. [38] Similarly, the very recent forestalling of UN Security Council motions to condemn Burma's lethal crackdown on peaceful protest seems to have struck the Western media audiences as something like moral cowardice of sacrificing lives on the altar of politics. One does not have to think hard to reach that conclusion, since that is largely what it is; but the outcome of the situation promises to be a repeat of the backward-thinking reaction, 'too little too late' response and unsubtle result of the Sudan situation so far. Perhaps these actions have been overdetermined by the importance of resource access for a precariously balanced Chinese development machine, but too obviously these manoeuvrings are the actions of crass realpolitik for anyone to mistake them for anything like the harmonious rhetoric spun from Beijing. Having to take it on the chin from other global heavyweights the year before the 2008 games will doubtless have an effect on China's presentation, and running interference (in any recognized form) for two of the most bloodstained regimes in the world promises to be a hot topic of discussion in 2008.

Several of the articles in this volume document various vantages on China's ambitions in the world, and in the process they take on a realpolitik visage. Many of the articles flesh out specific instances and aims of China's political games by exploring the background to this Olympic commitment as seen from the vantage of China's global neighbours, and in one case from inside China where the vantage is from the position of women athletes. The multiple perspectives on the means by which China was able to impress the world and win the games provide an informed comment on the background to the spectacle, meaningfulness and politics of the 2008 games. Like the long list of similar states who have in the past more visibly conducted politics under guise of games, China is in the business of calculating its interests. This recent instrumentalization of the Olympics (perhaps Olympization of instrumentality is more accurate?) has taken on Chinese form in its stated stress on harmonious relationship-building. [39] China has much to be proud of in the reform contemporary period because it has come a long way, and its accomplishments have been, well, Olympian. But it would be unwise of world punditry – indeed, it has been unwise of them – to look too rosily on China's many positive accomplishments without giving a matter-of-fact accounting of their negative conditions and consequences. China's Olympians will be standing on the shoulders of their less fortunate countrymen, and their plight should not be ignored during the grandiosity of the games – even if the Beijing government does not have a strong record of recent concern for them. We have discussed how some of China's more recent accomplishments are inextricably tied to enduring social problems and risks worth *not* ignoring, and how these concerns become geopolitical concerns.

Notes

[1]   A good example of this would be Beijing former vice mayor Liu Jingmin, who, not being quite clear on the concept, maintained that 'We want to separate politics from the Olympics'.
[2]   Boniface, 'Weaponless War', 3.
[3]   IOC Charter Fundamental Principles, Clauses 2 and 5, available online at http://multimedia. olympic.org/pdf/en_report_122.pdf.
[4]   IOC Charter, Rule 28.6.
[5]   MacAloon, *This Great Symbol*.
[6]   Boniface, 'Weaponless War', 3.
[7]   Federic Paxson at the turn of last century imagined that athletic fields could serve as a proxy for expansionist foreign policy in a world of shrinking available frontiers – imperialism by other means. Dyerson, 'Prologue: The Paradoxes', 940.
[8]   Elias and Dunning, *Quest for Excitement*.
[9]   MacAloon, 'Politics and the Olympics', 14.
[10] Dong Jinxia, 'Women, Nationalism', 538.
[11] A few of the Beijing tourists I interviewed on the south-west frontier could not understand how blasé the locals were about it, saying to me that the locals just 'did not have a sufficient understanding of how hard China had struggled to get the games'. The local Yunnanese had little use for this idea, and one retired official who overheard this statement later explained to me that local people understood very well what the Olympics was, but unlike the 'inner Chinese' (meaning Beijingers in this case) they knew how much the games would cost – how much normal Chinese people would have to struggle *because* the games were awarded to Beijing. See below.
[12] Brownell, *Training the Body for China*.
[13] Hardt and Negri, *Empire*.
[14] 'China To Revive Zheng He's Legend', *China Daily*, 4 Sept. 2006.
[15] Unlike in the Ming, when being a Muslim was just another way of being 'Chinese' – a category that had everything to do with sociopolitical practice and almost nothing to do with anything

we would now call 'ethnic' – now Islam is racialized by a relatively recent ethnic paradigm. Now the fact that he was Muslim and descended from the Prophet will not likely be one of the qualities most commonly cited in support of his symbolic power.

[16] Wade, 'The Voyages of Zheng He: A Reassessment'.

[17] When complete, this replica will be about 71 metres long, 14 metres wide and five metres tall.

[18] The best of the traditional and modern is not a new goal for China. Once before the ideal of using 'Western science' synthesized with 'Chinese culture' had been the marching orders of some Republican revolutionaries before the 1911 Revolution.

[19] Jealously at court and an extreme policy shift at Zheng He's death (1433) saw the great ships left to rot, their plans destroyed and all records of the voyages burnt. These extreme shifts in the ancient world are interestingly resonant with Chinese politics of the last half-century even after 600 years.

[20] A. Kroeber, 'The Underestimated Party-state', *Financial Times*, 26 Feb. 2007.

[21] Also, newer age and term limits for official positions ensure than those older than 65 (locally) or 70 (nationally) do not continue to hold power. As a check and balance, it seems fairly anaemic. But for a country that has tended towards gerontocracy, this is a veritable leap in protecting against an irrational durability of bad policy ideas.

[22] Kroeber, 'The Underestimated Party-state'.

[23] Mr. Liu was removed from his position because he had taken so many bribes he was found to have his own resort pleasure palaces stocked with young women. Also discussed in regard to the games was the arrest of the party secretary of Qingdao, though less is known about that case. Such sexy topics are far too attention-grabbing to pass up for any mainstream media operation.

[24] Kroeber, 'The Underestimated Party-state'.

[25] One Hong Kong NGO estimated that as many as 20,000 die each year.

[26] S. Flegant, 'Where the Coal Is Stained with Blood', *Time*, 2 March 2007, available online at www.time.com/time/magazine/article/0,9171,1595235,00.html, accessed 20 April 2008.

[27] Given the structure of Chinese governance and the intimate relationship the party and the government have with development capital, the future seems rather more likely to be something like Japan's corporate government... with Chinese characteristics, of course, though an uncharitable observer may start thinking 'kleptocracy' along these lines.

[28] Approximately 30,000 each year. One would also expect that, as in America where the mantra of opportunity is also a dominant and poorly veiled manipulation of public sentiment, eventually what the range of opportunity is may be shrinking and tightly controlled by circumstance.

[29] Dong Jinxia, 'Women, Nationalism', 538.

[30] R. MacKinnon, 'Beijing-Going for Gold', CNN Online, 19 Feb. 2001, available online at http://archives.cnn.com/2001/WORLD/asiapcf/east/02/19/china.olympics/index.html, accessed 20 April 2008.

[31] 'China Passes New Law on Property', BBC News, 16 March 2007, available online at http://news.bbc.co.uk/z/hi/asia-pacific/6456959.stm, accessed 20 April 2008.

[32] This even as they (correctly, I think) see America's recent behaviour as *even more* of a threat.

[33] This is especially true of the US, which has deployed the subtleties of just this technique even if the recent administration has embodied the dangerously thick and uninterested lack of subtlety that animates its commander in chief.

[34] E. Goffman, *Interaction Ritual: Essays on Face-to-Face Behavior*.

[35] Stakelbeck, 'For Commerce or Conquest'.

[36] J. Yardley and D. Lague, 'Beijing Accelerates Its Military Spending', *New York Times*, 5 March 2007.

[37] MacAloon, 'Politics and the Olympics', 4.

[38] Richard Spencer, 'China's Kung Fu Peace-keepers Head for Darfur', *DailyTelegraph*, 17 Sept. 2007, available online at http://www.telegraph.co.uk/news/main.jhtml?xml=/news/2007/09/17/wdarfur117.xml, accessed 20 April 2008.

[39] 'Philosophy of Harmony', *China Daily*, 27 Sept. 2006.

References

Boniface, P. 'Weaponless War at the Olympics'. *Le Monde Diplomatique*, Aug. 2004: 3.

Brownell, S. *Training the Body for China: Sports in the Moral Order of the People's Republic*. Chicago: University of Chicago Press, 1995.

Dong Jinxia. 'Woman, Nationalism and the Beijing Olympics: Preparing for Glory'. *The International Journal of the History of Sport* 22, no. 4, (July 2005): 530–44.

Dyerson, M. 'Prologue: The Paradoxes of American Insularity, Exceptionalism and Imperialism'. *The International Journal of the History of Sport* 22, no. 6, (Nov. 2005): 938–45.

Elias, N. and E. Dunning. *Quest for Excitement: Sport and Leisure in the Civilizing Process*. Oxford: Blackwell. 1986.

Fan Hong, Ping Wu and Huan Xiong. 'Beijing Ambitions: An Analysis of the Chinese Elite Sports System and its Olympic Strategy for the 2008 Olympic Games'. *The International Journal of the History of Sport* 22, no. 4, (July 2005): 510–29.

Goffman, E. *Interaction Ritual: Essays on Face-to-Face Behavior*. New York: Pantheon, 1982.

Hardt, M. and A. Negri. *Empire*. Cambridge, MA: Harvard University Press, 2000.

MacAloon, J. *This Great Symbol: Pierre de Coubertin and the Origins of the Modern Olympic Games*. Chicago: University of Chicago Press, 1981.

——. 'Politics and the Olympics: Some New Dimensions', available online at http://www.recercat.net/bitstream/2072/1338/1/ICPS128.pdf, accessed 20 April 2008.

Stakelbeck, F. 'For Commerce of Conquest?' MonstersandCritics.com, 19 Oct 2006, 19:00, available online at http://www.freerepublic.com/focus/f-news/1725288/posts, accessed 20 April 2008.

Sun-Tzu [Sunzi]. *Sun-Tzu The Art of Warfare*, trans. Roger Ames. New York: Ballantine Books.

Wade, G. 'The Zheng He Voyages: A Reassessment'. Asia Research Institute, Working Paper Series, no. 31. Singapore: National University of Singapore, October 2004, available online at http://www.ari.nus.edu.sg/docs/wps/wps04_031.pdf, accessed 20 April 2008.

Dancing Around the Elephant: The Beijing Olympics – Taiwanese Reflections and Reactions

Junwei Yu and J. A. Mangan

Introduction [1]

> One of my ... achievements during my 20 years of the IOC presidency is, without a doubt, presence of People's Republic of China and its athletes at the Games of XXIII Olympiad in Los Angles in 1984, after an absence of 32 years, and after having found a historical agreement with Chinese Taipei. [2]

This statement above made by Juan Antonio Samaranch on the triangular relationship between Taiwan, China and the International Olympic Committee (IOC) highlights an occasional reality: sport can be a bridge bringing antagonistic nations closer. Personal as well as political actions can also serve the same purpose. IOC members from Taiwan or China, for example, worked as one to rescue the Taiwanese reporter Huang Debei, arrested by the People's Republic of China (PRC) on the grounds of spying in Tiananmen Square in 1989. [3] Conversely, of course, sport can reinforce antagonism between nations, when they are at odds with each other over foreign policy, national interests or universal values. The initial claim during 1950s and 1960s by the Republic of China (ROC) located in Taiwan to represent the whole of China, and the subsequent response by the People's Republic of China (PRC) to label Taiwan a rebel province, resulted in the turning of allegedly apolitical sport into political sport and to 'sports wars' fought predominately on IOC terrain.

In the past 20 years, adversarial political relations between the ROC and the PRC have undergone significant changes that will impact on the 2008 Beijing Olympics, towards which the Taiwanese government, media and people have very mixed feelings. These will be explored here under following four headings: Modern Sport and Politics; Taiwan and China and Beijing 2008 – Historical Antecedents; Taiwan and China and Beijing 2008 – Immediate Antecedents; and finally, Taiwan and China and Beijing 2008 – 'Postcedents'.

Preamble: Modern Sport and Politics

It is now a tired truism to state that politicians cannot afford to ignore sport and run hard to jump on its bandwagons, especially national bandwagons carrying as freight international victories by successful national teams, triumphant representative individuals and major hosting bids. Presidents, kings, queens, prime ministers, cabinet ministers and parliamentarians (where they exist) crowd onto the available spaces on the bandwagon. The fundamental reason is transparent:

> The merging of memory, capitalism, consumerism and sport has produced its own 'long cultural revolution' increasingly, inexorably and unrelentingly impacting on more and more millions as modern decades slip by. The human memory, stimulated in specific cultural circumstances, feeds the appetite for sensation and much else. For this reason, capitalism through consumerism has been able to utilize sport successfully in the pursuit of profit. 'The vulgarity of intruding masses' has been welcomed; the media mass spectacle has triumphed; moments made into memories are marvellously marketable and mostly because memory holds open the door to active and passive pleasures. [4]

Furthermore, 'Sport seduces the teeming "global village"; it is the new opiate of the masses; it is one of the great modern experiences; its attraction astonishes only the recluse; its appeal spans the globe.' [5] It may also be said without fear of contradiction that 'sport is a mirror in which nations now see themselves. The reflection is sometimes bright, sometimes dark, sometimes distorted, sometimes magnified. This metaphorical mirror is source of mass exhilaration and depression, security and insecurity, pride and humiliation, bonding and alienation.' [6]

The consequence is that no politicians can afford to ignore the significance of national success in sport for political popularity. This fact has been well learnt by politicians worldwide. Illustrations are numerous. The most recent one at the time of writing involved the 2007 Rugby World Cup. It occasioned the following observation regarding, for its past policies, the once globally diplomatic pariah now widely, for its present policies, a diplomatic 'pet'. Following the cup-winning success of the South African national rugby team, under a newspaper headline banner 'World Cup Success Unites Rainbow Nation' was the following: 'The team had been left in no doubt that the whole country was supporting them—a message delivered in person by state president Thabo Mbeki, who visited the team hotel ... to thank them for *uniting* [emphasis added] the nation.' [7]

For the PRC, Beijing 2008, the greatest sports event in China's history, has several important roles. A great deal is at stake internationally and nationally – not least domestically, the enhanced cohesion of a huge population of different ethnicities, groups, classes and religions – a continual concern of the Communist leadership:

> The worst nightmare of China's leaders is a national protest movement of discontented groups – unemployed workers, hard-pressed farmers, and students – united against the regime by the shared fervour of nationalism. Chinese history gives them good reason to worry. The two previous dynasties fell to nationalist revolutionary movements. Mass movements that accused leaders of failing to defend the nation against foreign aggression brought down the Qing Dynasty in 1911 and the Republic of China in 1949. No wonder China's current leaders are obsessed with the fear that the People's Republic of China could meet the same fate, and strive to stay ahead of the wave of popular nationalism sweeping the country.
>
> In 1989, the regime was shaken to its roots by nationwide student protest and divisions within the leadership over how to handle them. If the military had refused to obey Deng Xiaoping's command to forcibly impose order or if it had split, the Chinese Communist Party might have followed its Soviet counterpart into the dustbin of history. [8]

It has been argued on good evidence that after the closest of calls in 1989:

> China's leaders became fixated on what they call 'social stability'. They use that euphemism to convince the Chinese public that Communist Party rule is essential for maintaining order and prosperity, and that without it, a country as large as China would descend into civil war and chaos. In their speeches, the leaders make no secret of their anxieties about social unrest. [9]

Increasingly, it is recognized that nationalism, not Communism, is the 'cement' of the nation – as a new cement to bond the people to it. Truistically, social stability is assisted and promoted by great national events and achievements. Beijing 2008 is intended to be a great event leading to great achievements. The PRC wishes to present itself to the world through the games as a twenty-first-century Communist nation equipped with the appurtenances and potentialities to be a presence in world affairs. Beijing 2008 is a Chinese visiting card in reverse – for visitors not hosts, outlining the hosts' putative credentials for future superpower status.

However, Beijing 2008, as viewed by the Taiwanese, is simply a costly, meticulous, purposeful and gargantuan exercise in political propaganda. This fact explains Taiwan's determined effort to take strenuous action in 2008 to declare, assert and promote itself as a nation state. It throws light on Taiwan's response to Chinese plans for the torch relay and on Taiwanese counteractive international sports programmes – both deliberate negations of what it sees as the aggressively political Beijing Olympics. These conjoint rebuffs serve notice to the world that the Taiwanese see themselves as less and less Chinese and more and more Taiwanese. Thus Beijing 2008 for both Chinese and Taiwanese offers a global opportunity for declamatory political averment. What follows is an outline of past events that have provoked Taiwanese negativity.

Taiwan and China and Beijing 2008: Historical Antecedents

In 1945, the Chinese Civil War erupted. Four years later, the Chinese Communist Party (CCP) emerged victorious. The defeated Chinese Nationalist Party (KMT) retreated to Taiwan, which became its last refuge. The next two decades saw the KMT clinging tenaciously to its optimistic claim to represent the whole of China. 'Reconquering the Mainland and vanquishing the Communists' was its foremost slogan – and policy. This, and the further slogan 'Han Chinese and bandits cannot stand together' ensured mutual hostility between the ROC and the PRC through the 1950s and 1960s, and indeed later.

This hostility on political and military fronts spilt over into sport. The burning issue was who legitimately represented China at international events. Lacking unanimous IOC support, the ROC delegation withdrew from the 1952 Helsinki Olympics. [10] Then followed a period of prolonged and bitter sporting confrontation between the ROC and the PRC lasting some three decades. The main struggle was for the support of the IOC. It lasted over a decade and steadily increased acrimony between the two nations, with each attempting to prevent the other from taking part in international competitions. Enmity progressively reached ever higher levels of intensity. It manifested itself in various actions and reactions.

In 1954, the 'Chinese problem' was raised at the annual IOC meeting. The problem was the suitability of the term 'China Olympic Committee' with reference to the KMT after the KMT's relocation from Mainland China to Taiwan. The PRC wanted to join the IOC and oust the ROC's China Olympic Committee. The IOC created a precedent by recognizing *both* Chinese members, now named respectively as the 'Chinese Olympic Committee – National Amateur Athletic Federation' and the 'Comité Olympique de la République Chinoise'. [11] Having failed to block the participation of the ROC in the 1956 Olympic Games, the PRC withdrew its delegation in Melbourne and subsequently withdrew from the IOC and eight other international sports organizations. Nevertheless, the IOC still asked Taiwan's Olympic Committee to change its name, because it did not represent the whole of China. On 8 June 1959, less than two weeks after the request was made, the ROC attempted to adopt the title 'the Republic of China Olympic Committee'. This was rejected by the IOC. It considered a title containing the word 'China' was inappropriate. Taiwan's Olympic Committee tried again to register as the Republic of China Olympic Committee at the 1960

Olympic Games in Rome. Taiwanese athletes also wished to take part in the Rome Olympics under the abbreviated name of ROC, but the IOC did not accept either proposal, and instead suggested 'Taiwan' or 'Formosa' in place of 'China'. Furious at not allowing ROC characters to be shown on athletes' uniforms, Lin Hongtan, head of the delegation, marched in the opening ceremony holding a banner on which were written the words 'Under Protest'. In the 1964 Tokyo Olympic Games, the ROC logo was allowed on the uniforms of Taiwanese athletes, but the IOC used Taiwan in place of China when referring to the Taiwan Olympic Committee. Four years later, in 1968, the IOC finally agreed formally to use the term ROC Olympic Committee, though it was more popularly called China ROC.

Taiwan endeavoured to have the field entirely to itself in international competitions. On any occasion when Taiwan discovered it had to compete with China, it would ask its delegation to withdraw. For example, the ROC had a golden opportunity to enter the 1958 Football World Cup, but learning that the Fédération Internationale de Football Association (FIFA) planned to allocate the ROC to the same group as the PRC in the World Cup qualifiers, it withdrew. [12] Personal boycotts as well as national abstention were part of this political vendetta. Athletes from China and Taiwan were banned from contacting each other. In addition, every opportunity was taken for individual denigration. Accusations of cheating were bandied about. Yang Chuanguang, the ROC decathlon silver medallist in 1960 Rome Olympics, claimed that he would have won the gold medal in the 1964 Tokyo Olympics if he had not been drugged by his teammate, Ma Qingshan, allegedly a 'closet communist'! Ma Qingshan immediately defected to the PRC. [13]

In the early 1970s, the tide of Western support started to turn against Taiwan. The American table tennis team's China tour of 1971 set the stage for President Nixon's epoch-making visit to Beijing the following year. *Time* magazine spoke of a 'ping heard round the world' in response to plays executed by the political players in this now famous 'ping-pong diplomacy'. 'Never before in history has a sport been used so effectively as a tool of international diplomacy', said the then Chinese Premier Zhou Enlai. [14] Juan Antonio Samaranch, then President of the IOC, commented piously: 'The ping-pong diplomacy that pushed forward Sino-US relationships in the early 1970s has vividly demonstrated the positive role that sport can play in promoting world peace. It can serve to strengthen the friendship and mutual understanding of peoples from all countries.' [15]

As is widely known, the coming together of American and Chinese table tennis players paved the way for Kissinger's visit to the PRC and the subsequent announcement of President Nixon's visit. As a result, Taiwan suffered heavily on the diplomatic front. In October 1971, the PRC was admitted to the United Nations (UN), and the ROC lost its seat. This eventually led to American de-recognition of the ROC in 1979. After the mid-1970s, Taiwan became a pariah in the international community, most of whose members chose to recognize the PRC as the legitimate government of China. As General St John Barclay suggested, 'Israel, Chile and Taiwan and … South Africa [formed] part of the Fifth World. All had common characteristics. They were ruled by immigrants or their descendants; they surpassed their neighbours in economic and political development and were envied for this; and they had all become targets of communist onslaught.' [16]

The diplomatic humiliation of expulsion from the UN produced a domino effect. Taiwanese sport suffered. Firstly, a group led by Iran and Japan orchestrated the admission of the PRC into the Olympic Council of Asia (OCA) in 1973 and simultaneously expelled Taiwan. The following year, Taiwan was excluded from the international governing bodies of fencing, wrestling, volleyball and weightlifting, and had its basketball membership suspended. In the 1976 Pan-Pacific Championship, the Japanese volleyball team refused to play against Taiwan, whose membership was revoked. [17] China then made further inroads into the IOC by winning more and more open support from PRC sympathizers. This eventually bore full fruit in 1979. These developments, as noted earlier, turned Taiwan into an international outcast banned from the UN and barred from many sports organizations.

As a direct result of this hostile international environment, the ROC began to intervene politically and financially in domestic baseball. The purpose of this was to raise the game's domestic profile and improve its domestic performance to distract attention from global isolation, to get closer to America through its highly popular game and to attract the favourable attention of the overseas Chinese. The international community might recognize the PRC as the legitimate government of China, but the ROC encouraged summer camp-type little league baseball (LLB) triumphs held in Williamsport in America, where Taiwanese children acted as surrogate warriors for the nation, to win friends and influence people in the West and to raise the morale of the Taiwanese. As political optimism in Taiwan deteriorated with the withdrawal of US recognition in 1979, baseball was seen as the most effective form of unconventional diplomacy with which to forge links with 'significant others'. [18] In addition to the LLB, Taiwan also held unofficial international tournaments such as the William Jones Basketball Cup, which enabled domestic teams to play foreign teams. Sport played its part in keeping Taiwan before the eyes of at least some influential parts of the world.

The Co-existence of Three-Nos Policy and the 'Olympic Formula'

In 1982 Deng Xiaoping proposed the 'One Country, Two Systems' formula, which allowed Taiwan to enjoy a high level of autonomy, to have independent troops, a different socio-economic system and links with other countries, but no diplomatic recognition. Ironically, Deng's innovation created a chance to allow both the PRC and the ROC to compete together on the world's sports stage. He agreed to let Taiwan compete internationally on condition that 'the name has to match the status of being a local sporting body, and its flag, emblem and anthem need to be changed correspondingly'. [19] Under no circumstances was the national squad to use the term 'Republic of China' or 'Taiwan': the PRC wanted to totally erase Taiwan's use of the term 'Republic of China' or 'Taiwan'. Nevertheless, the PRC was eager to maintain good relations with Taiwan in order to create favourable conditions for reunification. Thus the PRC permitted Taiwan to participate in non-governmental organizations so long as the official term ROC, the national flag and the national anthem were not used.

Then at an executive council meeting at Montevideo in 1979 the IOC recommended that the PRC rejoin the IOC as the 'Chinese Olympic Committee, Peking'. and now referred to its Taiwan counterpart as the 'Chinese Olympic Committee, Taipei'. But the PRC strongly objected to the proposal. Subsequently, the IOC passed a resolution in Nagoya that the IOC official names be changed to Chinese Olympic Committee and the Chinese Taipei Olympic Committee respectively. The Taiwanese government, in turn, contested this revision, appealing to the Swiss court in Lausanne that it was a violation of the IOC charter. As a result, the IOC made an amendment to the requirements for participation in the Olympiad: participants were to represent their Olympic committee not their country. At the same time, however, the Chinese Taipei Olympic Committee (CTOC) had to observe the regulation that no ROC national flag was to be displayed in Olympic-held competitions.

These arrangements, known as the 'Olympic Formula', were formalized when Shen Jiaming, the president of CTOC, signed a protocol with Juan Antonio Samaranch in Lausanne on 24 March 1981. Since then, Taiwan has been able to participate in the Olympic Games. Taiwan's IOC vice-president, Ding Shanli, argued later that 'it is a compromise, not a concession' and further stated that 'survival means hope, life will be meaningless without survival'. [20] Thus the CTOC compromised. To ensure participation in the Olympic Games, it agreed to lower its national flag at this and related events. Needless to say, for the CTOC and the ROC, it was not an ideal but a pragmatic decision.

With China once again a member of the IOC, in 1980 the Communist Party formulated its 'Olympic Strategy' to promote 'competitive sports diplomacy'. Training regimes and organizational structure were reformed to achieve good results in the 1984 and 1988 Olympics. This 'strategy' laid a solid foundation for future bids to host the games. [21] China, the soon-to-be sporting colossus, was quickly a force to be reckoned with. The PRC's debut at 1984 Olympic Games was impressive. It won 15 gold medals and was ranked fourth behind USA, Romania and West Germany. Two years later, China won 94 gold medals in the Seoul Asian Games. To add to this success must be added another. China's surging economic strength from the late 1970s onwards made it one of the most attractive countries in the world for foreign investment. This had unfortunate consequences for Taiwan. Nations with official ties with Taiwan could not resist China's commercial allure, to the detriment of Taiwan. In 1984, South Korea, a staunch anti-Communist partner of Taiwan, even persuaded Taiwan not to display its national flag during basketball games between the two nations. This was not simply international diplomacy but an instance of blatant personal interest. Seo Cheong-hwa, president of the South Korean Basketball Association, wanted to expand his business links with China! [22] Japan was also now anxious not to offend China. Yomiuri Giants, the most popular team in the Japanese professional baseball league and the club of the home-run king and Chinese-descendent Sadaharu Oh, did not want Oh to visit Taiwan in case it damaged Sino-Japanese relations. [23]

Taiwan fought back as best it could. Irritatingly for Mainland China, it continued to stress its nationhood. Although the ROC and the PRC were able to compete in international tournaments at neutral venues, the ROC president Chiang Ching-kuo was far from happy and proposed the 'Three Nos policy' (no negotiation, no contact, no compromise) to counter the PRC's 'One Country, Two Systems' policy. From 1979 this Taiwanese policy applied to all Communist countries. The 'Three Nos' posed a major problem. Taiwan could not hold genuine international tournaments since performers from Communist countries could not compete in Taiwan. In 1984, Yan Xiaozhang, president of the Chinese Taipei Baseball Association, persuaded the government and media to host an international baseball invitation tournament, but had to exclude the baseball giant Cuba due to national policy. This rather defeated the purpose of the exercise. However, the government did show sensible flexibility in the 1982 Women's Softball World Championship, which was the biggest international sporting event ever to be held in Taiwan. Although there was controversy concerning the participation of the PRC, the public generally approved the hosting of the tournament. Consequently, demonstrating purposeful realism rather than pointed obduracy, Chiang Ching-kuo endorsed the entry of the PRC national team. [24] At least, the endorsement showed some intelligent flexibility in government policy. In the end, however, the PRC decided not to attend the competition. Incidentally, there was a loophole of a sort in the Chiang arrangement. Taiwan could hold 'friendly' international tournaments, but his concession over Mainland China exposed its limitations. Nevertheless, Taiwan was not prepared to be a political pushover and mutual political exasperation on the part on the part of Mainland China and Taiwan remained the order of the day.

'Brothers Across the Straits are from the Same Family'

Thanks to the 'Olympic Formula', the long-awaited 'rematch' between the ROC and PRC was made possible at the 1984 Los Angeles Olympics. However, the Taiwanese had to face both a Chinese sporting powerhouse and waning international support. China's sports successes had captured the hearts of overseas Chinese, many who were previously sympathizers of the ROC government but now more intent on ridding China of that insulting and demeaning hundred-year tag of 'Sick Man of East Asia'. To add insult to injury, the PRC's sports propaganda machine caught the ROC off guard. Television stations covering the 1984 Los Angeles Olympics could not avoid publicizing the strong performances of Chinese athletes wearing the red star. Although attempts were made to reduce the highly visible nature of China's success, they failed. One anonymous ROC official admitted that the Chinese athletes' outstanding achievements had a profound psychological impact on the Taiwanese when compared to the lacklustre performance of their own participants. [25] Furthermore, one of Taiwan's best-selling newspapers, *The China Times* (US edition), carried the headline 'Chinese Pride' to describe the PRC's excellent results. This infuriated the ROC leaders, who accused the publisher of propaganda on behalf of Communism and ordered the suspension of money remitted to the paper, thus bringing about in its eventual closure. [26]

There now occurred a momentary halt to Taiwanese/ Chinese political bickering. In 1987, both domestic and external pressures forced the ROC to jettison its 38-year-long martial law and this was followed by the freedom to visit relatives in Mainland China. All of a sudden, it became fashionable to travel to the mainland, regarded by many Taiwanese as the 'Motherland'. A more peaceful and optimistic atmosphere now characterized cross-straits relations. 'We are descendents of Yan and Yellow Emperors [legendary forefathers of the Chinese nation]' was the view expressed by both sides. A *Lianhebao* (United Daily) survey showed that most Taiwanese wanted reunification. [27] In addition to internal 'China-mania', external pressure was brought to bear to solve the China/Taiwan Olympic issue peacefully. In particular, Juan Antonio Samaranch, the then president of the IOC, wanted to settle the intricate triangular relationship – Taiwan, China and the IOC – during his tenure. The Taiwanese themselves now made their own self-interested gesture of goodwill. After witnessing powerful Chinese contingents winning countless medals, Taiwan's sports associations now invited distinguished Chinese athletes to Taiwan both in order to both improve Taiwanese performances and strengthen mutual understanding and trust. Initially, however, only non-Communist party members were welcome. In 1989, the table-tennis player Teng Yi was the first to arrive. [28] Shortly afterwards, however, the regulations were relaxed to allow in Communist athletes.

The Tiananmen Square incident resulted in the ROC government reasserting its no-go policy, but public opinion rejected the government's decision. When Ding Maoshi, Minister of Foreign Affairs, intended to ban sports delegations from competing in China, the decision produced dissatisfaction both in the sports world and among legislative members. It drew concern also from Juan Antonio Samaranch. Surveys by three major Taiwanese newspapers showed that over half of interviewees supported sending delegations to the Beijing Asian Games. [29] Faced with intense pressure from the general public, the government changed the law to enable teams to take part in China-held tournaments.

Despite gestures of this sort, there was no fundamental shift in Taiwanese political implacability. The ROC still considered the PRC a rebel regime that unlawfully governed China. Indeed, it was not until the abolition of 'Temporary Provisions Effective during the Period of Communist Rebellion' in 1991 that the civil war with the China legally ended. Prior to 1991 the Taiwanese still regarded the ROC as the legitimate government of China. Symbolically, Beijing was still called Beiping throughout the 1990 Asian Games because Beiping was the name the KMT had used when it ruled China.

When Beijing won the bid for the Asian Games, theoretically the stage was set to implement the 'One State, Two Systems' policy under which both sides could compete according to the 'Olympic Formula'. Samaranch anticipated that sports exchanges would now bring dialogue and eventual peace. Indeed, 'Brothers across the Straits are from the Same Family' was the optimistic slogan used during the games. Such was the spurt of optimism in some quarters that the possibility of organizing a joint Chinese team for the Asian Games was aired prior to the event by Zhang Baifa, vice-president of the Asian Games Organizing Committee, who pragmatically welcomed an arrangement that might increase the chances of a 'united Chinese nation' winning medals. [30] However, the PRC stressed that such an arrangement was only possible in accordance with to the 'One China' principle. The ROC was far from enthusiastic and the sanguine conception produced a stillborn offspring. A residual warmth, however, among some Taiwanese remained despite the ROC's frosty reception of China's insistence on the implementation of the 'One China' principle.

This was evident when time moved on and China bid to host the Olympics. There were differences of opinion in Taiwan. Pro-unionists welcomed the idea of Beijing's bid for the Olympics to show to the world that the new millennium was potentially a Chinese era. The pro-independents were less welcoming, viewing the bid as both a direct and an indirect act of Chinese political hegemony replete with unacceptable overt and covert messages of ultimate reunification. The mainland-born Taiwanese Wu Jingguo, an IOC member, supported the Beijing bid and in response to immediate criticism was forced to make it clear that he voted for Beijing as the 2000 Olympics venue only because of filial loyalty: 'you have to remember you are Chinese', his parents apparently instructed him. [31] He ran counter to official policy. The ROC position was to oppose to Beijing's bid for the 2000 Olympic Games. President Li Denghui's government did not support Beijing hosting the Olympic Games, and delivered a veiled criticism of Wu, stating that 'from our government's stance, [Beijing's] requirements for hosting Olympics are immature, but we will respect his [Wu's] rights and decision'. [32] This cautious official line was due, of course, to the IOC's top-down structure, in which IOC members were assigned by the IOC to each national Olympic committee (NOC) instead of being appointed directly by the nation they represented; thus IOC members had the liberty to contradict government policy. And Wu was able, therefore, to vote as he did.

The Beijing bid continued to have consequences for China/ Taiwan relations. After the pro-independence DPP (Democratic Progressive Party) took power in Taiwan in 2000, the PRC refused to return to the negotiating table. Nevertheless, some Taiwanese politicians and some members of the public thought the Beijing 2008 mega-event could offset this setback and lead to peace and stability in the region. Some, including Taiwan's vice-president and independence hardliner Lü Xiulian, even argued that political brinkmanship could well be averted in the run-up to Beijing 2008 as it could serve as a safety valve for seven years; [33] the Chinese would not dare invade the island and thus incur condemnation from the international community and jeopardize their ambition of wooing the world to Beijing. Some sports-inclined unificationists made their views clear. Over 3,000 Taiwanese joggers joined a ten-city run, from Taipei to Beijing, in support of China's bid for the games.

A congratulatory slogan was thought up for the event: 'Olympics in Beijing, Pride of Chinese Nation'.

Then the Chinese put in their political pennyworth. Xu Shiquan, a Chinese expert on Taiwan issues, made a placatory goodwill gesture when he proposed that some Olympic venues could be moved to Taiwan. [34] The Taiwanese President Chen Shuibian also showed interest in the plan. Other Taiwanese were seduced by the idea. 'The co-hosting of international sports competitions by two or more Olympics Committees will definitely contribute to world peace and friendship, which reflects the Olympic spirit', suggested Huang Dazhou, the head of CTOC. [35]

In the event even this friendship of brief duration proved unstable. .Just before the IOC bid vote, the director of the Taiwanese Sports Affairs Council (SAC), Xu Yixiong, made it clear that co-hosting the Olympics had to be conducted with 'equality, reciprocity and dignity'. [36] Not surprisingly, the idea quickly faded into oblivion as the PRC insisted that this could only be achieved by subscription to the 'One China' principle, by which the Taiwanese government had to recognize Taiwan as part of China. Needless to say, it refused. The pursuit of joint global esteem and applauded compliance with Olympic ideals did not mean that the Taiwanese government was willing to come under China's political control. The price was simply too high.

The firm response to the beguiling possibility of a shared Olympics was not only a reaction to a blunt Chinese declaration, it was also, in part, the outcome of persistent Chinese endeavours to make the point that no matter what Taiwan announced to the contrary, it was part of China. Currently the 'Olympic Formula', as noted earlier, enables Taiwan to participate in international sporting events. However, the PRC attempts continually to exploit the formula to create an image of Taiwan as a constituent of China. Moreover, China in its direct dealings with Taiwan treats Taiwan as a province of China and demands that other IOC members do the same. In short, it leaves no stone unturned in its efforts to avoid giving the impression that Taiwan is on an equal footing with other nations.

There are various other sources of contention. One major problem the ROC has had to deal with down the years has been the Mandarin translation of 'Chinese Taipei'. China has wanted to downgrade Taiwan to the status of a province bearing the title Taipei, just like China Hong Kong or China Macao. The main conundrum for Taiwan has been the Chinese translation of 'Chinese', insignificant to foreigners but a matter of life and death to the ROC. The English world 'Chinese' can be translated into Chinese in two ways. One is *Zhonghua*; the other is *Zhongguo*. Basically, *Zhonghua* means Chinese in the broadest cultural and ethnic sense, while *Zhongguo* has a political connotation. Therefore the English words 'Chinese Taipei' could be translated as *Zhonghua Taibei* or *Zhongguo Taibei*. Taiwan prefers to use *Zhonghua Taibei*, implying that the Taiwanese are ethnic Chinese but not part of the PRC – now, of course, synonymous with China as a political entity and recognized as such by the international community. But the PRC prefers to use *Zhongguo Taibei*, thus making Taiwan a part of China. Juan Antonio Samaranch, after listening to explanations from both representatives on the issue, naively professed himself baffled, saying 'What is the difference between *Zhonghua* and *Zhongguo*? I cannot understand you Chinese people, who make such a big fuss just because of one word.' [37] Nevertheless, despite Olympian bewilderment, understandably it did cause a big fuss. The Taiwanese government threatened to pull out of all the competitions held in China in 1989, if Taiwan continued to be referred to as *Zhongguo Taibei*. After lengthy negotiations, the PRC's IOC member, He Zhenliang, finally conceded that Taiwan could participate under the name of *Zhonghua Taibei* and on 6 April 1989 signed an agreement dealing specifically with the Chinese translation of Chinese Taipei.

Although the issue was 'solved' after China made this critical concession, the PRC media had a trick up their sleeves and continued to use *Zhongguo Taibei* to refer to Taiwanese teams. According to China's *Opinions on how to Correctly Use Propaganda Phrases Involving Taiwan*, published in 2002, 'In international sporting competitions held by us [China], Taiwanese delegations can use the Chinese words of *Zhonghua Taibei*, but our media reports should still call them *Zhongguo Taibei*. The document also pointed out that the Taiwanese delegations who take part in non-governmental organizations cannot be called from 'Taiwan' or 'Taipei' but from 'China Taipei' or 'China Taiwan'. [38] Thus China, whatever concessions it ostensibly has made to Taiwanese sensibilities before the gaze of the world, remains clearly determined in the eyes of speakers of Chinese to linguistically treat Taiwan as a province, deliberately creating the impression that it is under China's jurisdiction whatever was signed to appease Olympians in 1989.

Provocation goes well beyond the refusal to abide by that agreement. Various tricks and gimmicks have continually been used to interfere with Taiwan's participation in international sporting events. China does not always abide by IOC protocol, which allows the Chinese Taipei team to enter the arena at the opening ceremony in Group T and China in Group C, so that Taiwan is not seen as part of China. At the 2001 World University Games (*Universiade*) held in Beijing, for instance, China tried to tamper with the established marching order by putting 'Chinese Taipei' in Group C. [39] Furthermore, Taiwan's education minister, Zeng Zhilang, was forced to forego attending the *Universiade* after the Chinese government demanded he apply for a special visitor's permit commonly known as a Taiwan Compatriots Visa rather than being granted a VIP card, which would have explicitly recognized Zeng as a government official. [40]

The case of the Sina basketball team provides the clearest evidence of a Chinese determination to downgrade Taiwan to provincial status despite the generally non-political nature of sport migration. Following the collapse of the Taiwanese domestic professional league in 2000 due to the limited market and the consequent withdrawal of television contracts, Sina planned to recreate itself by joining China's professional league. [41] This decision impacted on both sides of the straits. The PRC wanted to take advantage of this opportunity to implement its pan-China project; in response, the ROC government predictably endeavoured to assert its independence. Although Sina was mostly composed of Taiwanese players, its new venue was located in Suzhou, in the eastern part of China. The China Basketball Association (CBA) deliberately asked Sina to use the name 'Taiwan' or 'Taipei', rather than Suzhou, as part of its team name. This sparked controversy. The Taiwanese government refused the team's permit to travel to the Mainland. As Cai Yingwen, chairman of the Mainland Affairs Council, said: 'I am worried that the team's designation would undermine national integrity'. [42] The saga eventually ended peacefully, with the team using a bizarre and elongated name: Suzhou (Taiwanese Investors) Sina Lions Club. Thus China did not wholly accomplish its name-changing objective, but was successful in getting Sina to insert 'Taiwanese Investors'; more importantly, from a Chinese point of view, it now had a Taiwanese team in a Chinese domestic league. The naming issue also raised its head in the case of a Chinese women's football team, who wished to be called 'Motherland Female Football Team', when visiting Taiwan. [43] Taiwan again took umbrage. The team came and the Taiwanese media showed that they, like the Chinese media, had a way with words. The team was referred to as 'the Mainland Women's Football Team'. There was no reaction from China.

Perhaps the most striking recent act of Chinese provocation was not to do with titles but torches. It involved the unilateral announcement by the Chinese of the Olympic torch relay route via Hong Kong, Macao and Taiwan. The ROC swiftly rejected the plan, thus becoming the first IOC member to decline to be included in the route. It accused China of undermining Taiwan's sovereignty by deliberately creating the impression that Taiwan was part of China. It demanded that the route came to Taiwan from a third country and left it via another third country. However, Jiang Xiaoyu, the executive vice-president of the Beijing Organizing Committee, made available several documents signed by Cai Chenwei, the CTOC president, pledging Taiwan's participation, clearly implying that the CTOC had agreed to the route. Cai later stated that 'I can only say there is different opinion [in Taiwan] between sport officials and government officials'. [44] In fact, Hao Longbin, the mayor of Taipei and a member of the KMT, welcomed the route passing through the capital and urged the government to accept it. 'Please do not interfere with the relay and damage Taiwan's international reputation by mixing sports and politics,' he urged politely. He was making precisely the same point as Cai – but from a different perspective. ROC officials stuck to their guns. The route was not accepted. Cai had proved his point.

The issue of titles, incidentally, has not gone away. The Taiwanese government recently has announced that the Taiwanese delegation will withdraw from the Olympics if Beijing refers Taiwan as *Zhongguo Taibei* (China Taipei) during the tournament. This was a risky decision, as Tang Mingxin, a senior sports adviser, has argued that China has nothing to lose by the absence of the 'rebel province'. China could accept, in fact, an independent group comprising pro-China Taiwanese as 'independent Olympic participants' (IOP), which would reinforce the image of Taiwan as part of China. [45]

Determined audacity, however, on the part of the ROC has paid off. Again compromise has been reached, Beijing has acknowledged the IOC protocol agreed in 1989 and has promised it will use the term *Zhonghua Taibei* in 'areas under the China

Olympics Committee jurisdiction', outside which the press and media are free to use either term. [46] The ROC has stated that this is satisfactory. One very good reason for the ROC's acceptance of the compromise is the fact it has already invested substantial time and money in Beijing 2008.

Creating a Separate Identity

As time goes by, fewer communalities may be found between the Taiwanese and the Chinese, given the latter's persistent oppressive attempts to block Taiwan's international visibility as a nation. The PRC does not give an inch on flag and anthem. Understandably from its perspective, it remains highly sensitive to the existence of both these global manifestations of national sovereignty which blatantly implies 'Two Chinas' or 'One China, One Taiwan'. In the 1988 Calgary Winter Olympics, Taiwan nearly had its NOC membership suspended because its bobsleigh athletes displayed a national flag emblem. The IOC issued this grave warning:

> In order to demonstrate that we regard this matter as extremely important, the IOC hereby give your NOC formal notice that any future violation of the agreement between the IOC, Chinese Olympic Committee and the Chinese Taipei Olympic Committee will result not just in disqualification of the athletes and officials involved, but in suspension of the Chinese Taipei Olympic Committee for such period as the IOC considers appropriate in the circumstances. [47]

No equivocation or room for misunderstanding there!

In the 1996 Atlanta Olympics, one excited Taiwanese student waved the ROC flag in a table tennis final featuring the Taiwanese Chen Jing. He was immediately handcuffed and fined by the American police. [48] During a taekwondo contest in the 2000 Sydney Olympics, one Taiwanese spectator was told to remove his ROC flag-embossed cap. [49]

Not surprisingly, in the face of China's intransigence, fewer and fewer Taiwanese regard themselves as Chinese. A National Chengchi University survey conducted in 2006 revealed that 60 per cent of interviewees regarded themselves as Taiwanese, 5 per cent as Chinese, while 33 per cent saw themselves as both. [50] This shows how much things have changed since the lifting of martial law in 1987 and the subsequent introduction of democratic principles and practices. 'Taiwan's democratization', it has been recently claimed, 'is strengthening the island's sense of a separate identity and driving its politics towards formal independence despite growing economic ties with China'. [51] In the survey only 14 per cent of Taiwanese welcomed the success of the Chinese Beijing Olympic bid. The majority were indifferent. A political straw in the wind. While most Taiwanese still think themselves as Chinese, this is in the sense of being ethnically Chinese as opposed to being 'Chinese citizens'. Two factors in particular, over and above democratization, have contributed to an increasingly Sinophobic feeling: firstly, China's continual harassment of Taiwan in international affairs has led to great resentment and secondly, the fact that successive Presidents Li

Denghui and Chen Shuibian have been strongly pro-independent and their policies have systematically sought to sever bonds with China.

Added to these phenomena are sports successes. As is commonplace elsewhere in the world, they have increasingly bonded the Taiwanese people and this has progressively weakened China's claim of a single nation separated in space only by narrow straits. These successes have strengthened Taiwan's image of itself as an 'imagined community' and reinforced the feeling of 'deliberate nationalism'. [52] Arguably gold medals do this better than virtually anything else. Zhu Muyan's gold medal in taekwondo in the 2004 Athens Olympics sent millions in Taiwan into ecstasy. It was a symbol of nationhood made more emphatic by Zhu's opening words at his winner's press conference: 'I am from Taiwan' he announced to the world in the world's international language, English. He wanted no mistranslation by the Chinese translator! He translated the message himself. The *Taipei Times* reporter Lin Chienyu spoke for millions when said that 'this [gold medal] encourages the morale of the country and creates more nationalism for independence'. [53] Olympic 'one-world-in-unity' idealism may be supranational, but when it is confronted by national reality it frequently takes second place. So it has proved in the case of Taiwan. Nothing exposed the latent hostility to Mainland China on the part of the Taiwanese than the furore provoked following the taekwondo gold medal success at the Athens Olympics and the subsequent action of the medallist. When the Taiwanese taekwondo gold medal winner Chen Shixin, revealed that she had accepted a coaching assignment from the Shanghai Qingpu Martial Arts School in China after her gold-winning triumph, it produced a national outcry. The thought that she might improve the performances of 'the enemy' offended many. Chen had to make a formal announcement denying acceptance. The SAC had demanded that she rejected the offer because the act was in severe breach of national interests allegedly jeopardized by China's potential to win taekwondo gold medals in the 2008 Olympics. [54] Ultimately, the Taipei College of Physical Education and Sport, in an unprecedented move, awarded her an associate professorship with merely a master's degree. [55] She stayed in Taiwan.

These instances make one thing very clear. Taiwan may have threatened to withdraw from the Beijing Olympics but the likelihood was always slim. The cold reality is that sport is a useful 'glue' to bind the nation together; a bonding agent that fuses political, ethnic and social differences, and the Olympic Games is the most efficient 'glue' producing a tight grip. There is irony in the fact that a Chinese Olympics may help unite Taiwan. Unity through sport can sometimes be more effective than any agent other than war. For this reason, the Taiwanese Sports Affairs Council in the late 1990s proposed a 'Challenging 2008 Golden Plan' with the objective of winning seven gold medals in taekwondo, archery, shooting, weightlifting, table tennis, badminton and judo. A four-year budget of $34 million has been made available to cover training at home and abroad and the recruitment of top class foreign coaches. [56]

Taiwan is thus determined to use various sports as 'building blocks' to raise the edifice of a nation. It is not only events like the Olympics that provide raw material from which to make 'blocks' to achieve this. The ROC assiduously promotes sports stars for their propaganda value in the West as well as the East. They too are national 'building blocks'. This is apparent from the 'star-status' carefully and purposefully allocated to the American major league baseball icon, the Taiwanese Wang Jianmin, a starting pitcher with the New York Yankees and now a national hero. The ROC sees considerable diplomatic value in projecting Wang nationally and internationally, not only because he matches the Chinese basketball 'mega-star' Yao Ming in regional prominence, but also because his talent focuses the attention of the American public, if only fleetingly, on Taiwan. In an enterprising marketing move, the Taiwan Tourism Bureau used images of Wang from sponsoring ESPN's *Baseball Tonight* to promote Taiwanese scenery, cuisine and other attractions throughout America to put Taiwan on America's map of the modern democratic world.

Interestingly, China has taken note. It now has its potential stars in Liu Kai and Zhang Zhenwang, who have professional contracts with the New York Yankees. The Seattle Mariners have signed other two Chinese players. Self-interest is served all round! The clubs want the world's best players, the players want the most lucrative contracts, the nations want the world publicity. This Chinese invasion of American baseball is not a pleasing development for the Taiwanese. If China has more American baseball stars than Taiwan, then Taiwanese morale will suffer. For China to outperform Taiwan in a sport considered peripheral in China and central in Taiwan will be a bad blow to Taiwanese confidence. The 'feel-good' factor in sport is a phenomenon no nation can ignore especially when locked in a global diplomatic public-relations war.

In other ways Taiwan is determined to use sport for self-advertisement. Aware that there will be little room for self-display in China-held competitions, especially the extravagant Beijing Olympics, for some time Taiwan has been launching a sports diplomatic offensive by every possible means to increase its international visibility, and this has caused concern in Chinese circles. In 1997, when China sent a national squad to the Asian Baseball Championships, held in Taipei, the squad found a large Taiwanese flag-waving crowd in the stadium at the opening game, coincidentally against Taiwan. Chinese sensitivity on this issue has been discussed above. So furious was the Chinese deputy leader Cai Jizhou that he threatened to pull out of the competition unless Taiwan abided by the 'Olympic Formula'. The organizers had to call for restraint from the Taiwanese people. [57] Because of this embarrassing experience, the PRC issued a 'Relevant Notification of Further Strengthening Sports Exchanges with Taiwan'. It had four main points: The PRC was opposed to Taiwan sending leading political figures to international sporting events; it was against Taiwan bidding for international sporting events; it would no longer send athletes to international sports events held in Taiwan; it would prevent Taiwan from using attendance at international sports events to sabotage the 'Olympic Formula'. [58] Self-evidently it has not gone down well in Taiwan. With regard to China refusing to attend competitions in Taiwan, however, China has been self-interestedly selective. If a sport is not its strong point, it does not appear. If it is strong at a sport, then it appears. China pulled every level of national team out of baseball competitions held in Taiwan during 2001 despite later being penalized by the Baseball Federation of Asia. However, it chose to take part in the Women's Football Championship held in Taipei and faced the possibility of ROC flags because the chance to win medals was high. Sensitivity is clearly calibrated.

The tentacles of Chinese sensitivity to Taiwan's projection of itself through sport are octopus-like. Not only is China opposed to any effort by Taiwan to assert itself through diplomatic recognition, it is afraid of Taiwan using sport as a cover for diplomacy. In 1993, the OCA president Sheikh Ahmad Al-Fahad Al-Sabah issued an invitation to the Taiwanese President Li Denghui to attend the 1994 Hiroshima Asian Games. This created a massive political storm in the IOC. China reacted most fiercely, threatening to boycott the Asian Games if President Li was allowed to go to Japan. In the end, a Taiwan spokesman had to announce on behalf of President Li that the president had decided 'not to attend the Hiroshima Asian Games for the sake of solidarity and harmony in Asian sport'. [59] Chinese pressure of this nature does not win friends in Taiwan. Taiwan, on this occasion, seemingly had a friend in Japan. The Taiwanese Vice-Premier Xu Lide, however, was allowed to attend the opening ceremony. China was not mollified. It viewed this also as an act of separatism due to Xu's official status. In retaliation for Japanese lack of cooperation on the issue, China suspended a senior official's visit to Japan and aborted a non-governmental organization's cultural exchange. [60]

The truth of the matter is that Taiwan and China have been playing a cat-and-mouse game in international sports arenas and on sports fields and other venues for decades, with Taiwan refusing to act the intimidated 'mouse'. The game shows no sign of ending. In 2004, the Taiwanese President Chen Shuibian's wife, Wu Shuzhen, led Taiwan's Paralympics delegation to Athens and this evoked protest from China, which demanded that the International Paralympics Committee (IPC) ask Wu to avoid all public appearances and cancel her National Paralympics Committee card, a top-class VIP card given to delegation leaders. Once again, Taiwan stood up for itself. Huang Zhifang, a technical staff member, threatened to hold a conference and release all the official documents exchanged with the IPC which clearly revealed IPC's bias against Taiwan. The tactic worked. Wu maintained her accreditation and attended the opening ceremony. [61] However, this was a rare victory.

The 'game' is played on other sites and in other circumstances. As a member of the IOC, Taiwan shares the same rights and obligations as other members. Accordingly, it is entitled to file a bid for international tournaments. Since 1987, Taiwan has bid to host a number of major sports events. At least five attempts have been made, including the 1998 and 2002 Asian Games, the 2001 and 2007 World University Games and the 2009 East Asian Games. These all have failed because of PRC intervention and pressure. The most notable example was 1995 when Taiwan's Gaoxiong bid for the 2002 Asian Games. The PRC backed the rival bidder, South Korea's Busan, which subsequently won the majority of votes based on a show of hands instead of a secret ballot. Taiwan vehemently questioned a system that deterred pro-Taiwan members from casting 'yes' votes because of Chinese pressure and fear of Chinese reprisals. Crushing defeat led to strong criticism by Zhang Fengxu, the CTOC president, of Juan Antonio Samaranch, who allegedly leaned towards Beijing on the ground of cohesion within the organization. It was estimated that the failed bid cost Gaoxiong $1 billion in lost construction and sponsorship. [62]

Taiwan finally broke through the Chinese ' blockade' by winning the 2009 World Games, a quadrennial competition of sports not included in the Olympics. Due to past strained relations between China and Taiwan resulting in Chinese obstruction, the Taiwanese government and media sensibly agreed not to leak any information on the bid to head off Chinese interference. The strategy worked. The bidding, in almost absolute secrecy, resulted in enough votes for Gaoxiong to host the first IOC-endorsed competition. [63]

The Beijing Olympics will ensure that the sports spotlights of the world are focused on China. Taiwan is acutely conscious of this fact. To avoid being marginalized by the games, Taiwan decided to host its own mega-event Taiwan Expo in 2008 aimed at diverting at least some the global glare from China. [64] The four-month-long exposition, estimated to cost $608 million, was to showcase Taiwan's vitality and creativity in culture, tourism, science and technology and was intended to deflect at least some attention away from Beijing. It was estimated that it would attract 5.5 million tourists, generate $156 million in revenue and provide 13,000 job opportunities. [65] However, humiliatingly the project was aborted because the opposition-party-dominated legislators would not support the bill. In an attempt to save face, Wu Jingguo, the Taiwanese IOC member, fallaciously reassured the nation that irrespective of its location, Taiwan would benefit hugely from the games. They would increase cross-straits sporting links and provide Taiwanese investors with access to booming construction and other opportunities in Beijing. [66] However, the reality is that most Taiwanese investors have not been able to jump on the Olympics bandwagon owing to the financial and political restrictions imposed mainly by Taiwan.

Taiwan has been imaginatively enterprising in its attempts to project itself through sports sponsorship. Ironically, in this regard it has found itself in direct competition with China in a most unlikely sport. Cricket, a sport virtually unknown to both Taiwan and China, recently and extraordinarily became a main publicity battlefield between the two nations. Diplomatic sports skirmishing between the two cross-Strait rivals extended to politically insignificant Caribbean countries where the Cricket World Cup was held in 2007. The construction of world-class cricket stadiums had fallen far behind schedule. But generous financial assistance from both Taiwan and China ensured that the venues were completed on time. According to ABC News, China spent a remarkable $132 million on cricket facilities in the West Indies over the past few years compared to the International Cricket Council's ten-year budget of $70 million to promote cricket globally! Taiwan was not to be left out. It responded with gifts of $21 million to St Kitts and Nevis and $12 million to St Vincent and the Grenadines respectively: [67] 'It's been quite fun in a meeting to express how well the

Taiwanese are doing on a stadium ... you see the Chinese contractors looking at each other and making up the time very, very quickly,' Chris Dehring, chief executive officer of the Cricket World Cup, remarked with amusement. He added somewhat unnecessarily: 'They certainly wanted to demonstrate that they were equally capable.' [68]

Taiwan and China: Beijing 2008 – 'Postcedents'

In the case of the Beijing Olympics, undoubtedly, the combination of publicity, tourism and advanced communications infrastructure is a powerful mix. It will ensure global attention and emphasize China's dramatic rise. Taiwanese leaders, media and people have mixed feelings about this. The Taiwanese President Chen Shuibian's address to the National Day Rally in 2004 catches this ambivalence perfectly:

> Taiwan is pleased to witness the steady progress, reforms and peaceful emergence of China. We also extend our best wishes to the other side of the Strait as it prepares for the 2008 Beijing Olympics; and we hope that it will be a successful event conducted in accordance with the Olympic spirits of peace and equality. Nevertheless, the international community should be wary of and yet hope for the emergence of China to be accompanied by a 'peaceful awakening' rather than a hegemony of belligerence and aggression. [69]

This 'hegemony of belligerence and aggression' down the decades has systematically destroyed trust in and affection for Mainland China. China has relentlessly used 'hard' power and 'soft power' interchangeably to achieve its ultimate objective of reunification. Traditional 'hard power' exerted through military and economic means to coerce Taiwan has been a continuous feature of PRC policy. Consequently Taiwan's government has shown little interest in engaging the Chinese Communists in cross-strait talks. These have stalled since the mid-1990s because of Taiwan's responsive shift towards independence. This has resulted in increased attempts by the PRC at military intimidation. In 2005 China ratified the Anti-Secession Law that established the legal basis for the use of force should Taiwan declare independence. Such 'hard power' action proves to be highly unpopular in Taiwan.

'Soft power', too, has not been neglected. Joseph S. Nye coined the term 'soft power' to denote 'the ability to get what you want through attraction rather than coercion' to describe the ways governments and businesses influence others' actions through the appeal of their ideals and values. [70] China will seize the opportunity of the games to improve the country's global status by presenting a polished image to the world. It is soft power calculated also to appeal to some Taiwanese. Some Taiwanese regard the games as a source of pride for the whole Chinese people, and pro-unionists especially hope the Olympic torch relay will pass through Taiwan. And many Taiwanese investors are interested in business opportunities the games may still offer.

China's successful bid for the games has long-term implications for China's neighbours. They have long been hoping for the Beijing Olympics in order to provide some protection against the growing dragon. However, they fear possible over-reaction by a chauvinistic Chinese people. They are well aware of the power of public pleasure but even more aware of the power of public displeasure:

> Whenever the public pays close attention to an issue, leaders feel they have to act tough to show how strong they are. Like Chinese Clark Kents, they abandon their usual mild-mannered international demeanor, and reveal themselves as nationalist superheroes. Throwing caution to the wind, they take risks to defend China's national honor. This more emotionally volatile side of China's split personality – we might call it China's 'id'. [71]

After Beijing won the bid to host the of 2008 Olympics, the *Economist* wrote: 'No one wanted to deal with a sullen China, bent on finding scapegoats for its defeat.' [72] In turn, the success of the games is crucial not only to China but also to its neighbours and even the world, who all fear a disappointed nation and a frustrated nationalism that might turn its frustration on Taiwan among others. Some have suggested that not only organizational success but medal victory in 2008 will be the only way to preserve stability in Asia and for this reason are rooting for a triumphant games this summer. [73] Many Taiwanese consider that success in presenting and performing the games has become vital to China's global self-esteem. Any loss of esteem could have unfortunate consequences.

The Chinese government's official 2008 Olympic theme, as is now well known, is 'One World, One Dream' and the Beijing Olympic Committee's stated objective is to host an 'open, green, and humane Olympics'. At a videoconference with foreign journalists in 2005, the Taiwanese President Chen Shuibian declared pointedly in response that

> We still hope that the Olympic theme 'One World, One Dream' can become 'One World of Peace, One Dream of Freedom'. We also hope that China will conform to the Olympic theme and not consider the Olympics to be one thing and its military expansion and intimidation to be another. [74]

Whether or not the games will be successful, Taiwanese leaders and society fear that they will add momentum to China's attempt to marginalize the island.

The Japanese expert Kenichi Ohmae, among others, has predicted that future Chinese expansive economic trends will be unstoppable, and it will be difficult for Taiwan not to join a Greater China federation if it wants its economy to grow. He has suggested that if Taiwan does not join a Chinese federation before the games, it will be economically marginalized. [75] The former Taiwanese President Li Denghui has taken another tack and argued that 2008 will be the most flamboyant year in the history of China, and '[Chinese] nationalism will be grotesquely powerful. If Taiwan does not take countermeasures, it would be at someone's [China's] mercy.' [76] And the impact of the games will be cultural and psychological as well as economic and political. Lin Zhongbin, executive director of the Taiwanese Foundation on

International and Cross-Strait Studies, suggested that China may invite the Tibetan spiritual leader, the Dalai Lama, to attend the opening ceremony of Beijing Olympics to further the image of a magnanimous nation, when hundreds of countries and leaders from across the globe will come to the new 'Middle Kingdom'. [77]

With so many future uncertainties and with such significant potential outcomes, the Taiwanese government and people are split on how to handle the games. The Ma Yingjiu-led opposition KMT party wants conciliatory engagement to replace the present administration's hostile isolationism. In contrast, the pro-independence *Ziyou shibao* has warned of the danger of jumping enthusiastically onto the Beijing Olympics bandwagon. China's games it argues, are essentially a political action to unite the vast nation and a diplomatic irredentist exercise to assist the process of regaining Taiwan. [78] For this reason, although Taiwanese political responses to the games hinge upon which party wins the presidential election in March 2008, there is general consensus among the public and politicians that Taiwan's sovereignty should not be negotiable whoever wins the presidency in March 2008.

Conclusion

Beijing's successful bid for the Olympic Games is a political milestone in the history of the Chinese nation as well as a global festival. The event increases the international status and visibility of the PRC. Mainland politicians claim that passionate involvement allegedly on the part of Hong Kong, Macao and Taiwan demonstrates Chinese national cohesiveness and conveys the message of a 'unified' China to the world. This tactic to attract pro-China Taiwanese to its side has had some success, but there remains a threat of coercion which alienates many Taiwanese. China still views Taiwan as a province, and it wishes to suppress any action connected to separatism, such as Taiwan's flying of its national flag and the playing of its national anthem. A final example: in 2000 the famous singer Amei was blacklisted by China merely for singing the ROC anthem at President Chen Shuibian's inaugural ceremony.

While of the same ancestry as the Mainland Chinese, the Taiwanese have been increasingly frustrated by the PRC's Janus-headed tactics. Every Chinese move is thoroughly scrutinized for fear that it is an attempt to implement the 'One China' policy. Consequently, Taiwan has completely ignored China's reunification messages transmitted, either overtly or covertly, via the Beijing Olympics. Years of direct or indirect coercion have taken their toll. The majority of Taiwanese are no longer proud of being Chinese, and this has resulted in a growing demand for independence. Furthermore, despite occasional efforts made to thaw the frozen relations between the two sides via sport, Taiwan feels that China persists in using sport to achieve its political goals. And Taiwan reciprocates. To counterbalance attempted Chinese hegemony, symbolized in sport most grandiosely by the Beijing Olympics, Taiwan is implementing its own modest plans through sport to construct a cohesive identity, to seek recognition from the international community and to avoid being engulfed by its mainland neighbour. It is not surprising that Taiwan uses sport as a means to further its national identity. Other nations, including China, do it. As Eric Hobsbawn shrewdly observes, 'the imagined community of millions seems more real as a team of eleven named people'. [79] Since both nations adamantly stick to their national ambitions, intentions and aspirations, confrontation on sports fields and in sports arenas in all probability will continue for years to come.

Notes

[1] This article employs the Pinyin romanization system, which is used in Mainland China and also is internationally recognized, since the systems used in Taiwan are quite confusing. Except for Taipei, and references that are originally written in original fashion, all are in Pinyin style.
[2] He, *Aolin pike yu beijing*.
[3] *Mingbao* [Ming Pao Daily], 11 July 1989.
[4] Mangan, 'Series Editor's Foreword', xi.
[5] Mangan, 'A Personal Perspective', 1–2.
[6] Ibid.
[7] A. Colquhoun, 'World Cup Success Unites Rainbow Nation', *Daily Telegraph*, 22 Oct. 2007, S9.
[8] Shirk, *China: Fragile Superpower*, 7.
[9] Ibid.
[10] Tang, *Woguo canjia aoyun cangsang shi xiapian*, 8–20.
[11] Chen, 'Wo aohui mingcheng zhi yanbian', 22–9; Xu, *Woguo aohui huiji fanzhanshi zhi yanjiu yu fenxi*, 52.
[12] He, 'Jinjun shijiebei zhuqiu saishi', 162–4.
[13] *Ziyou shibao* [Liberty Times], 29 Jan. 2007.
[14] *Time*, 26 April 1971, available online at http://www.time.com/time/magazine/article/0,9171,902878-1,00.html, accessed 30 June 2007.
[15] *Zhongguo wang* [China.com], available online at http://www.china.org.cn/english/2002/Sep/42150.htm, accessed 1 June 2007.
[16] Vale, 'South Africa and Taiwan', 101.
[17] *Lianhebao* [United Daily], 25 Aug. 1976.
[18] Yu, *Playing in Isolation*, 37–90.
[19] Lin and Zheng, 'Haixia liangan tiyu jiaoliu de huigu yu zhanwang', 17–19.
[20] *Lianhebao*, 24 March 1981.
[21] Guojia tiwei, 'Guojia tiwei guanyu jiasu tigao tiyu yundong shuiping'.
[22] *Lianhebao*, 8 April 1984.
[23] Suzuki, *Wang Zhenzhi*, 26–9.
[24] Taylor, *The Generalissimo's Son*, 370.
[25] *Lianhebao*, 17 Aug. 1984.
[26] Zhang, *Tibi wei shidai*, 59–65; *Zhongguo shibao* [China Times], 10 April 2002.
[27] *Lianhebao*, 11 June 1989.
[28] *Lianhebao*, 16 Aug. 1989.
[29] Li, 'Haixia liangan tiyu jiaoliu xingtai bianqian zhi yingxiang yinsu fenxi', 27–41.
[30] *Lianhebao*, 15 July 1989.
[31] Wu and Zeng, *Aoyun changwai de jingji*, 126.
[32] Ibid., 122.
[33] *Lianhebao*, 5 Dec. 2000.
[34] *Washington Times*, 28 Sept. 2002.

[35] *Lianhebao*, 21 June 2000.
[36] *Lianhebao*, 6 June 2001.
[37] Wu and Zeng, *Aoyun changwai de jingji*, 97–106.
[38] Liu and Wang, *Tongyi zhanxian wenjian huibian*, 231–5.
[39] *Ziyou shibao*, 19 June 2001.
[40] *Ziyou shibao*, 21 Aug. 2001.
[41] The CBA granted Sina several prerogatives to ensure its accession. For example, Sina was allowed to circumvent division two and promoted to division one. Furthermore, Taiwanese players in Sina were regarded as domestic players, while Chinese players, in contrast, became 'domestic foreign players'.
[42] *Taipei Times*, 29 Sept. 2001.
[43] *Lianhebao*, 18 Jan. 2000.
[44] *Lianhebao*, 26 April 2007.
[45] Mingxin Tang, 'Aoyun dianran zhengzhi huati qing huigui tiyu bing zunzhong zhuanyan', 30 April 2007, available online at http://www.npf.org.tw/particle-2091-3.html, accessed 1 June 2007.
[46] *Lianhebao*, 28 June 2007.
[47] Chinese Taipei Olympic Committee website, available online at http://www.tpenoc.net/File/folder/D830041014381.doc, accessed 3 June 2007.
[48] *Lianhebao*, 3 Aug. 1996.
[49] *Ziyou shibao*, 13 Nov. 2005.
[50] *Lianhebao*, 28 Nov. 2006.
[51] Shirk, *China: Fragile Superpower*, 260.
[52] Anderson, *Imagined Communities*; Billig, *Banal Nationalism*.
[53] Associated Press, 28 Aug. 2004, available online at http://www.taiwantp.net/cgi/TWforum.pl?board_id=3&type=show_post&post=279, accessed 11 June 2006.
[54] *Lianhe wanbao* [United Evening News], 29 Dec. 2004.
[55] *Minshengbao* [Mingsheng Daily], 7 Sept. 2005.
[56] Sports Affairs Council, available online at http://www.meworks.net/allsports/files/gold_plan_2008.doc, accessed 1 June 2007.
[57] *Lianhe wanbao*, 1 June 1997.
[58] Guojia tiyu zongju, 'Zhongguo dalu guojia tiwei', 63–5.
[59] Wu and Zeng, *Aoyun changwai de jingji*, 63.
[60] *Lianhebao*, 30 Sept. 1994.
[61] *Taipei Times*, 29 Sept. 2004.
[62] *Jingji ribao* [Economic Daily News], 24 May 1995.
[63] *Minshengbao*, 15 June 2004.
[64] *Ziyou shibao*, 12 Aug. 2003.
[65] *Taipei Times*, 7 Jan. 2005.
[66] *Lianhebao*, 5 May 2001.
[67] Pal Pramit Chaudhuri, ABC News International Opinion, 26 March 2007. available online at http://abcnews.go.com/International/story?id=2980988&page=1, accessed 15 June 2007.
[68] *Taipei Times*, 11 March, 2007, available online at http://www.taipeitimes.com/News/editorials/archives/2007/03/11/2003351858, accessed 25 May 2007.
[69] Available online at http://constitution.president.gov.tw/article/article.php?Type=2&rowid=354, accessed 25 June 2007.
[70] Nye, *Soft Power*, x.
[71] Shirk, *China: Fragile Superpower*, 11.
[72] 'Beijing Gets the Gold', *The Economist*, 16 July 2001.
[73] Ibid.

[74] Office of the President of the Republic of China, available online at http://www.roc-taiwan.org/RU/ct.asp?xItem=5566&ctNode=1596&mp=212, accessed 30 July 2007.
[75] *Taipei Times*, 15 April 2003.
[76] *Lianhebao*, 25 July 2002.
[77] *Lianhebao*, 27 July 2006.
[78] *Ziyou shibao*, 11 July 2001.
[79] Hobsbawm, *Nations and Nationalism*, 143.

References

Anderson, B. *Imagined Communities: Reflections on the Origins and Spread of Nationalism*. London: Verso, 1991.

Billig, M. *Banal Nationalism*. London: Sage Publications, 1995.

Chen, J. 'Wo aohui mingcheng zhi yanbian' [Development and change in our Olympic membership]. *Aolin pike jikan* [Journal of Olympics] 23 (1993): 22–9.

Guojia tiwei [National Sports Committee of China]. 'Guojia tiwei guanyu jiasu tigao tiyu yundong shuiping de jige wenti de qingshi baogao' [The report of several questions on enhancing sports standards by the National Sports Committee of China], unpublished official report, 28 March 1980.

Guojia tiyu zongju [State Sport General Administration of China]. 'Zhongguo dalu guojia tiwei bangongting banbu guanyu zuohao taiwai lai dalu tiyu jiaoliu renshi jiedai gongzuo de tongzhi' [The notice related to sports exchange with Taiwan]. In *Zhongguo tiyu nianjian – 1998* [China Sports Yearbook – 1998]. Beijing: Guojia tiyu zongju, 1999.

He, C. 'Jinjun shijiebei zhuqiu saishi' [History of qualifying for Football World Cup] in *Zhonghua zhuqiu nianjian* [Chinese Football Yearbook], edited by Zhonghua taibei zhuqiu xiehui. Taipei: Zhonghua taibei zhuqiu xiehui, 1998: 162–4.

He, Z., ed. *Aolin pike yu beijing* [Olympics and Beijing]. Beijing: Wenming zazhishe, 2006.

Hobsbawm, E. *Nations and Nationalism since 1780*. Cambridge: Cambridge University Press, 1990.

Li, J. 'Haixia liangan tiyu jiaoliu xingtai bianqian zhi yingxiang yinsu fenxi' ['The analysis of impact factors in sport exchange patterns across the Taiwan Straits']. *Dazhuan tiyu xuekan* [Journal of Physical Education in Higher Education] 7, no. 3, (2005): 27–41.

Lin, J. and X. Zheng. 'Haixia liangan tiyu jiaoliu de huigu yu zhanwang' [The retrospect and prospect of sports exchange across the straits]. *Tiyu xuekan* 8, no. 4, (2001): 17–19.

Liu, X. and D. Wang. *Tongyi zhanxian wenjian huibian* [Document collections on United Front]. Beijing: Zhongyang bianyi chubanshe, 2007.

Lowe, B., D.B. Kanin, and A. Strenk, eds. *Sport and International Relations*. Champaign, IL: Stipes Publishing Company, 1978.

Mangan, J.A. 'Series Editor's Foreword'. In *Sport and Memory in North America*, edited by S.G. Wieting. London: Frank Cass, 2001.

Mangan, J.A. 'A Personal Perspective: Twenty-five Years'. *The International Journal of the History of Sport* 23, no. 1, (Feb. 2006): 1–2.

Nye, J. *Soft Power: The Means to Success in World Politics*. New York: Public Affairs, 2004.

Shirk, S.L. *China: Fragile Superpower*. Oxford: Oxford University Press, 2007.

Suzuki, H. *Wang Zhenzhi: Bainian de guixiang* [Wang Zhenzhi: Coming home for one hundred years], trans. S. Li. Taipei: Xianjue chubanshe, 2005.

Tang, M., ed. *Woguo canjia aoyun cangsang shi xiapian* [The authentic history of our participation in the Olympics, vol. 2]. Taipei: Zhonghua taibei aolin pike weiyuanhui, 2000.

Taylor, J. *The Generalissimo's Son: Chiang Ching-kuo and the Revolutions in China and Taiwan*. Cambridge: Harvard University Press, 2000.

Vale, P. 'South Africa and Taiwan: Pariahs, International Redemption, and Global Change'. In *Taiwan's Expanding Role in the International Arena*, edited by M. H. Yang. New York: M.E. Sharpe 1997.

Wu, J. and Y. Zeng, *Aoyun changwai de jingji – Wu jingguo de wuhuan shiyue* [Competition outside the Olympics: Wu Jingguo's vow under five rings]. Taipei: Tianxia yuanjian, 2001.

Xu, W. *Woguo aohui huiji fanzhanshi zhi yanjiu yu fenxi* [Research and analysis of membership development of our Olympic Committee]. Taipei: Gaoli chubanshe, 1992.

Yu, J. *Playing in Isolation: A History of Baseball in Taiwan*. Lincoln, NE: University of Nebraska Press, 2007.

Zhang, H. *Tibi wei shidai: yu jizhong* [Pick up the pen for our time: Yu Jizhong]. Taipei: Shibao chubanshe, 2002.

Sport as Public Diplomacy and Public Disquiet: Australia's Ambivalent Embrace of the Beijing Olympics

Peter Horton

Introduction

China has been acclaimed as the 'next superpower'. [1] If the markers of military, economic, political and cultural power are enlisted in the analysis of this statement, then the notion that China is fast emerging as a force that will possibly end the global dominance of the USA [2] does not seem an unreasonable proposition. Upon reflection China's hard power potential, represented by its military expenditure, [3] continued firm dialogue with the Taiwanese government and annexation of Tibet and its economic growth [4] presents an almost irresistible argument for this claim. However, many observers [5] feel that China's real advance is being made through the enlistment of soft power, [6] which embraces: diplomacy; trade incentives; aid and cultural and educational exchanges in an effort to shape other nations' diplomatic preferences and, as a corollary, their perception of China. [7] Consistent with Joseph Nye's description of soft power, this process involves the use of neither 'sticks nor carrots'. [8] China inexhaustibly and very competently utilizes its soft-power resources and is currently taking advantage of the USA's preoccupation with its very costly military engagements in Iraq and Afghanistan to usurp the United States' position as the global master of soft power. [9] It would appear that China has adopted a heightened level of soft power as a major weapon in its 'foreign policy arsenal' [10] and in doing so deflects attention from the storm produced by the harder elements of its growing power – its economic rise and the continual growth of its military force. Despite the evident rise in China's soft power, it still faces international resistance in terms of 'desired foreign-policy outcomes', [11] as concern still exists arising in the main from its human rights record and policies regarding Tibet, Xinjiang and Taiwan. [12]

The reversal in China's international credibility that followed the Tiananmen Square 'crackdown' on the student-led pro-democracy demonstration on 4 June 1989, during which several hundred students were killed, [13] and the collapse of the Soviet Union in the same year, left China with no geopolitical option other than to normalize diplomatic relations with the US. [14] At the same time, domestically, China had to build the people's confidence in their government by generating national pride, and by forcefully driving economic growth. By the end of the twentieth century China's move into the global market economy had precipitated a growth in its trade figures that was some eight times bigger than that of world trade in general. [15] Following its poor attempt to regionally assert itself militarily in the mid-1990s [16] and the fact that globally China had little chance of confronting America using hard power, [17] the nation's leaders shifted their diplomatic tack to one with which they could attempt to undermine the US using soft power. [18] The US's soft power cupboard had been left quite bare by the end of the 1990s and China filled the vacuum, pouring billions of dollars of aid into Third World countries such as Venezuela, Sudan, East Timor, Papua New Guinea and Iran, and by setting up its own Peace Corps and expanding educational and cultural links, particularly in South East Asia. [19]

Sport was explicitly embraced by the Chinese government in the 1970s when athletes were enlisted to promote China's diplomacy in the Third World through cultural diplomatic exchanges and the emphasis of these policies was 'friendship first, contests second' (*youyi diyi, bisai dier*). [20] Sport was explicitly being embraced as an instrument of politics by 'other means' [21] and its use during this period was most significant, as this deliberate policy led to the famous era of 'ping-pong diplomacy', which began with China's ground-breaking decision to accept an invitation from the Japanese Table Tennis Association in 1971 to compete in the 31st World Table Tennis Championships. [22] Supported by Mao Zedong, these initiatives precipitated the thawing of the ice of the impasse that existed between China and the US and essentially the whole of the Western world. Henry Kissinger met Premier Zhou Enlai in July 1971 to pen the Shanghai communiqué, which President Richard Nixon and

Mao Zedong jointly issued on 21 February 1972. This ushered China's re-emergence as a member of the international community. [23] As Xin Xu succinctly suggested, the small-ball diplomacy (*ping pong*) soon led to diplomatic engagements that figuratively moved the 'big ball' (the globe). [24]

China's self-imposed exclusion, particularly from the Olympic Games from 1959 to 1979, [25] precipitated by the International Olympic Committee's (IOC's) sanctioning of the independent participation of Nationalist China (Taiwan) in the Olympic Games, [26] had frustrated China's international integration. However, the normalization of diplomatic relations between the USA and China in 1979, and China's subsequent readmission into the Olympic movement, foreshadowed its emergence as a future world power. The successful hosting of the 1990 Asian Games proved to be critical in re-establishing China's international diplomatic credibility following the Tiananmen Square 'event' in 1989. The emphatic crushing of the students' demonstration precipitated China's diplomatic isolation from the majority of democratic Western nations; it had also negatively impacted upon foreign trade and investment. [27] The Olympic Games, as an avenue of China's soft-power diplomacy, thus assumed more political significance following the collateral damage that had emanated from the harrowing events of 4 June 1989. [28] Leading Chinese politicians had noted the impact of hosting such sport festivals as the Olympic Games, and they were well aware of their diplomatic potency. Chinese leaders, including, most importantly, Deng Xiaoping, soon urged the nation's sport officials to make a bid to host the Olympic Games. [29]

In 1991, buoyed by the success of hosting the 1990 Asian Games, and at the insistence of the nation's leaders, the Chinese Olympic Committee submitted an application to enter the bidding process to host the 2000 Olympic Games. [30] It was at this point that the Olympic histories of China and Australia converged. Sydney was selected to host the 2000 games ahead of Beijing, winning the final vote by just two votes. Some felt that the loss represented a new schism in 'West-Rest' relationships; [31] however, it is suggested that the IOC (and probably the leaders of the major Western powers) felt that China had not sufficiently lost the taint of the events in Tiananmen Square and needed more time on the periphery to further develop its claim to be a member of the core of Olympic nations. Sydney's successful bid and the subsequent unrivalled success of the Sydney 2000 Olympic Games, dubbed at the closing ceremony by the then president of the IOC, Juan Antonio Samaranch, as the 'best-ever' Olympic Games, [32] has already had a direct impact upon the upcoming Beijing Olympic Games.

This article will examine the development and the complexity of the relationship between China and Australia as the Beijing Olympics approach. There are many levels of the Sino-Australian relationship and sport, particularly the Olympic Games, has been enlisted as a feature of the diplomatic interface between the two Asian Pacific nations. Critical to Australia's view of China is the nation's growing trade with China. In 2007 China became Australia's biggest trading partner, overtaking Japan and the US. [33] China, as an emerging regional if not global superpower, has continually used sporting ties and exchanges since the 1970s, [34] while Australia, being a 'mid-ranking power in the Asia Pacific' [35] must, pragmatically, engage in a wide-ranging public diplomacy strategy to promote 'overseas understanding of our [Australian] society, people and values', [36] and sport features large in the public diplomacy policies of the Australian government. [37] Sport and other cultural exchanges are central dimensions of the Australian government's diplomatic strategy regarding its relationships with China, as this statement from a recent Senate Report entitled 'Opportunities and Challenges: Australia's Relationship with China' indicates: 'Communication through culture and sport is a highly effective means of promoting understanding and awareness and bringing people together. It can have flow-on benefits for the economic and political community in Australia.' [38]

Since the 1970s, Australia's diplomats have worked assiduously to establish a Sino-Australian relationship with qualities that approach the level and form of the enigmatic Chinese cultural-form of *guanxi*, [39] which literally means 'relationships' though, with its cultural roots in Confucian communitarian tradition, it is centred more upon the nature of the interconnections between the parties involved than upon the characteristics of the individuals involved. [40] *Guanxi*, once believed to be 'inaccessible to non-Chinese outsiders', [41] now forms the basis of much foreign business negotiation and diplomatic activity with China. [42] Australia has worked long at initiating, building and using its *guanxi* with China and the mutual trust, commitment and loyalty, which are vital in the actualization of such relationships, [43] are certainly apparent in Australia's current diplomatic activity with China. The consequent mutual embrace of China by Australia's politicians and diplomats and its resources, industrial and commercial sectors, is matched by the nation's 'Olympic industry' fraternity, who are eagerly looking forward to the hoped-for profits that they believe will be generated by their involvement in the Beijing Olympic Games. This profitable embrace could, ethically, be viewed as being less than faultless, as concerns continue to be raised expressing a sense of public disquiet emanating from the Australian people's perception of China. [44]

Major issues still resonate as to China's hegemonic neo-imperialist aspirations in the Asia Pacific region, which potentially could impact upon Australia's regional status and security, while its hard line on Taiwan and occupation of Tibet represent stumbling blocks to China's attempts to be viewed as being a benign and benevolent global power. Domestic human rights issues still attract condemnation internationally from, not unexpectedly Amnesty International [45] and also from groups calling for a boycott of the Beijing games, including the largely French organization, the Collective for the Boycott of the Beijing Olympic Games, [46] which has among its contributors the long-time critic of the Olympic movement, Jean-Marie Brohm. [47] Yet in the Australian media it is the issue of the air quality in Beijing and at the rowing venue that appeared to be holding sway with a year to go before the opening ceremony. It has even been suggested by the IOC that because of the quality of the air in Beijing certain events may have to be rescheduled. [48] The following analysis will elucidate how Australia has negotiated the paradoxes that have emerged and that will continue to do so because of its active association with China's Olympic efforts and from the implicit support for the policies and actions of the Chinese government as both nations navigate a course through the oceans of public diplomacy and soft power en route to Beijing 2008.

Sport, Public Diplomacy, Soft Power

The very different Olympic histories of China and Australia have merged as they approach Beijing 2008. The sporting routes they have travelled are as different as the nations are – historically; culturally; politically; demographically and geographically. However, there have been similarities, as discussed below. Furthermore, as China further entrenches itself in the global market economy and Australia is drawn closer, culturally, as an outcome of globalization processes, [49] such differences are becoming more tolerable. Australia, a foundation member of the modern Olympic club, has competed in all previous summer Olympic Games; it has hosted them twice and the Olympic team, particularly the swimmers, are national icons. [50] China, as a nation, has tremendous 'Olympic' ambitions as demonstrated by its overwhelming industry, motivation and the political embrace of the potential success that the forthcoming Beijing games offers the nation. They are, in fact, 'obsessed by Olympic gold medals'. [51] Similarly, during the Sydney Olympic Games in 2000, Australia as a nation was preoccupied with the medal tally, which was relentlessly driven by the media. During the games success for the average Australian meant only one thing: the number of gold medals the nation would win. The final tally of 16 gold (58 medals overall) placed Australia fourth In the unofficial table, three places better than it had achieved in the two previous Olympics – Barcelona in 1992 and Atlanta in 1996. [52] Consequently, considerable nationalistic pride was generated, which typically was very well used by politicians. However, for China the quest for Olympic gold medals and indeed sport per se has always had very specific political overtones and, as Fan Hong *et al.* suggest, from the Maoist era 'sport has never escaped the shadow of politics'. [53] It must be noted that Australia's sport history and particularly its Olympic history is similarly replete with overt political incursion and manipulation. The establishment in 1981 of the Australian Institute of Sport (AIS), the hub of the nation's elite sport system, was a consequence of direct federal government intervention following the Olympic team's poor performance at the Montreal games in 1976 when Australia won just one silver and four bronze medals. An initial proposal to create an institute of sport had previously emerged in 1973 in a report from a study group chaired by University of Queensland academic Allan Coles, but little formal development occurred. The unacceptable results at Montreal and the urgent call for a revision of the whole elite sport programme from Olympic team manager Julius (Judy) Patching in his official report, [54] however, precipitated immediate government action. The nation had suffered too much grief and lost too much face internationally: [55] sport was, and still is, a central feature of Australia's sense of itself, its morale and how Australians (particularly politicians) believe the rest of the world sees them, so in sport they must succeed. [56] The AIS, locally referred to as 'the gold medal factory', [57] still receives criticism for its elitist and mechanistic rationale, and its embrace of 'good old Eastern Bloc tradition'. [58]

As divergent as the two nations' Olympic journeys have been, in the eyes of their people, it is the medal count that really matters. Fan Hong *et al.* suggest that 'the Olympic gold medal fever among ordinary Chinese people is derived from a mixture of extreme pride and extreme inferiority', [59] and this could also be the case for Australians, with the inferiority stemming from its colonial heritage – as a nation Australia aggressively asserts its national identity through its sporting victories, particularly those over the motherland (England) in the traditional sports of cricket and rugby. China has previously adopted sport, particularly Olympic sport, as a means to validate its political ideology, now it is actively embracing international sport in its efforts to promote its ascent to first nation status. [60] Elite sporting achievement is now viewed, as Fan Hong *et al.* observed, as a clear indicator of the nation's economic and cultural 'revival'. [61] To the Chinese government, the Beijing Olympic Games represent the pinnacle of this particular climb to international acceptance, and this is a definitive example of China's soft-power diplomacy at work. Hosting an Olympic Games offers the host city and the host nation an ideal opportunity to seduce not only visiting countries and spectators and global television audiences but also its own people. China's enlistment of the tools of culture as features of its global strategy has been a feature of its diplomacy since the end of the Cold War. [62] The era of ping-pong diplomacy, as significant as it was historically, almost pales into insignificance against the current scope and range of the public diplomacy and soft-power initiatives that China now adopts. This soft power is so pervasive and accomplished that China is viewed by observers such as Joshua Kulantzick to be actually using it to transform the world. [63] Increasing cultural exchanges of all kinds has been a central part of China's 'new public diplomacy' [64] which has, since the end of the Cold War, moved well away from the form of 'pure propaganda'. [65] The promotion of their Olympic ambitions has been and continues to be a major dimension of their diplomatic efforts, as depicted by the front-page editorial of the People's Daily (*Renmin Ribao*) on 30 August 2004, which celebrated the close of the Athens Olympic Games and the 'heroic' efforts of China's athletes who had just competed at the Athens Olympic Games:

> When a country's powerful, its sport will flourish. Chinese athletes' excellent performance at the Olympic stage is inevitably proof of our great achievements in economic reform and modernization....The achievements at the games have showed China's ability to stand proudly and independently among the other nations in the world....Chinese athletes will make more contributions to realize our nation's great revival. [66]

The comment foreshadows the impact the Beijing games would have on China's international standing, coupling this, as He Zhenliang, China's IOC delegate, suggested, with the 'far-reaching impact of China's access to the World Trade

Organization' [67] – and if the predicted foreign investment targets in China from the 'Invest in Beijing' campaign, launched in April 2004, are reached, the 'impact' will be immense. It has been suggested that foreign investment attracted by this campaign will reach $US365 billion. [68] This hoped-for direct investment far outdoes the actual cost to Beijing of hosting the Olympics, which is currently estimated to be $US36 billion. Amazingly, this is 'double the initial estimate and 32 times the cost of the Los Angeles Olympics'! [69]

The Australian Olympic fraternity that so successfully delivered the Sydney 2000 Olympics has been closely involved in Beijing's preparation for the 2008 Olympics since its bid was launched. So defined is this role, involving Australian businesses, individuals, NGOs and governments at all levels (territory, state and federal) that it is not unreasonable to suggest that the greatest and most profitable feature of the legacy of the Sydney Olympic Games will in fact be the Beijing games. Immediately China decided to bid for the 2008 games (not that any decision *had* to be made, for hosting the Olympics and becoming a sport superpower was central to the Communist Party's and the central government's policy well before 2000), [70] Australia's help was sought and Australia's Olympic organization enthusiastically offered its total support. There was no need for the Australians to prevaricate on the grounds of sympathy after their very 'fortunate' and, some say, suspiciously close win in the bidding war for the 2000 Olympics; [71] the forces of public diplomacy and economic pragmatism, as well as common sense, underpinned these moves. So entrenched and interconnected did the Australian Olympic army become that they were actively engaged at every stage of the strategic planning, design and construction of the new Olympic infrastructure, and the development of the policies and planning of security systems, the environmental master plan for the games, the volunteers' programme and the transport and telecommunications systems. [72] For the Australians this offered not only a very profitable opportunity to promote Australian companies and products; it also provided a highly productive diplomatic conduit to further closer relations with the emerging superpower.

China's global 'charm offensive' [73] is unparalleled, even outdoing that of the US, which it is suggested 'has alienated many of its oldest friends' [74] while China has been wooing the world with its soft power. [75] However, Australia, mindful of its intertwined trade relations and the new strategic interface with China's burgeoning presence in the Pacific region, has been earnestly realigning its geopolitical position vis-à-vis China, as can be gleaned by reviewing the extent and intensity of the bilateral political relationships between China and Australia since 21 December 1972, when diplomatic relations were formally established. [76] Pertinent to the current discussion was a series of visits by government ministers with sport portfolios from both nations in the late 1990s, which featured a visit to Australia by Wu Shaozu, president of the Chinese Olympic Committee and Minister of State for the Administration for Sports of China who signed a 'Memorandum of Understanding (MOU) on Cooperation in the Field of Sports between the State Administration for Sports of China and the Australian Sports Commission (ASC)'. [77] Thus it can be seen that the overt alliance between the two countries' Olympic bodies was well supported at a governmental level, indeed upon meeting President Jiang Zemin in Shanghai on 20 October 2001, ahead of the APEC meetings that year, Australia's Prime Minister, John Howard, not only warmly congratulated the president on the 'fine arrangements' [78] but also commented that

> he was satisfied at the sound development of bilateral ties and is pleased with China's imminent entry into the World Trade Organization (WTO). He also congratulated China on Beijing's successful bid to host the 2008 Olympic Games, adding that Australia, having just hosted the Sydney Olympic Games, is willing to offer any assistance Beijing might need. [79]

The intertwining of the two topics, China's entry to the WTO and its success at winning the bid to host the 2008 Olympics, is evidence of how both nations view international sport and of their leaders' attitudes to the political and social centrality of such sporting festivals. (As shown above, He Zhenliang certainly echoed this view in 2004.) The direct and unconditional offer from the leader of the Australian government to help China prepare for the Beijing Olympics at such a significant political moment is a very clear indication of the level of importance bestowed upon the Olympic Games by both countries.

Beijing 2008: With a Little Help from Your Friends

The Australian Senate's report that considered the opportunities and challenges that emanate from Australia's relationship with China, published in 2005, [80] could be considered as the definitive report that reflects upon Australia's complete relationship (*guanxi*) that exists with China. A section of this very expansive Senate inquiry report deals specifically with 'Public diplomacy, culture and sport, and the Chinese-Australian community'; though sport does not receive particularly expansive treatment, specific reference is made to the 2008 Beijing Olympic Games, [81] which are immediately characterized as providing an opportunity to create new levels of cooperation between the two nations. [82] The report also points to the 2005 MOU between the ASC and China's State General Administration of Sport outlining the key points of the agreement. This section of the report concludes rather positively calling for government activity to do more to further the recognition of the efforts of the Chinese-Australian community:

> Public diplomacy, cultural and sporting interaction, promotes awareness of China and, at a broader societal level, mutual understanding. It fosters a greater awareness of the Chinese-Australian community's contribution to Australia and encourages greater tolerance and understanding. It builds bridges between the two countries. The committee believes that the Australian government should continue to demonstrate its support for public diplomacy including ensuring that there is adequate funding for the cultural and sporting organisations actively engaged in establishing and maintaining their links with China. [83]

This is evidence of a general acceptance that sport is a domain that can be productively enlisted in the promotion of cultural relations between the two nations, though the almost naive level of recognition of the extent of the engagement, particularly with regard to the synergy between the two Olympic fraternities, is an issue. Similarly, the closing comment from Richard Tan, president of the Chung Wah Association, in the chapter of the report dealing with human rights, demonstrated he was also apparently unaware of the collaborative industry that was afoot as the Beijing Olympics neared:

> With respect to culture and other ties, in talking about the Chinese market we should take note that recent exchanges between Australia and China have been predominantly trade and business related. Few are to do with culture and sports and other things.... Real and genuine friendship can be developed through promoting mutual understanding and appreciation of each other's culture and traditions. Thus, while emphasising economic gains, we should not lose sight of the long-term benefits of exchanges in other areas. I would also like to appeal to the Commonwealth to allocate appropriate funding to promote closer links in the other areas of the arts, sport, and tourism. [84]

The report does not recognize the extent of the very constructive and extremely profitable industry the Australian Olympic 'army' had begun undertaking several years before the report was published. Following the success of the Sydney Olympic Games, which was most efficiently and effectively conducted by the Sydney Olympic Games Organising Committee (SOCOG), the Beijing Organizing Committee for the Olympic Games (BOCOG) began to court the expertise of the Australians. Beijing's bid was very specifically well supported by members of the SOCOG executive, including the chief executive officer, Sandy Hollway. Hollway, plus three other senior SOCOG staff were recruited by Endeavour Consulting, [85] which was very closely involved in the preparation of Beijing's bid to the extent that Hollway actually accompanied the official Beijing party to the final IOC meeting in Moscow in July 2001 at which the announcement was made. [86]

In 2002 direct intervention and action was also taken by the New South Wales (NSW) government (host state of the 2000 Sydney Olympics) after it had, somewhat belatedly, recognized the immense commercial potential the Beijing Olympics offered the Olympic-savvy companies of NSW. The NSW government initiated an inventive scheme, proposed by its Department of State and Regional Development (DSRD), that established, in association with the Premier's Department and the Sydney Olympic Park Authority, the Sydney-Beijing Olympic Secretariat, which sought to join the Australia China Business Council and Austrade [87] in managing a coordinated programme of commercial, consultancy and industrial activities related to the preparation and conduct of the Beijing Olympics. The Olympic expertise gained at Sydney 2000, much of which, obviously, was held in Sydney-based companies, was eagerly sought by BOCOG, and this relationship continues to heighten as the games approach. [88] The extent of Australian corporate involvement in the Beijing 2008 Olympic Games is very extensive and represents an extremely committed level of activity and investment by the companies involved. [89] The investment naturally affords potential profits; however, most significantly, what it does indicate is the extent of the business trust and confidence Australia has in China. The magnitude of the two countries' economic interconnectedness is indicated by fact that China, as noted earlier, is now Australia's biggest trading partner: they had a two-way trade of $52.7 billion in the financial year up to March 2007. [90] Not surprisingly, since 2005 the two have been negotiating the establishment of a free trade agreement (FTA). In June 2007 the ninth round of negotiations produced some a reasonable level of progress but little real advance on issues regarding market access. [91] Perhaps the next few scheduled rounds may be more productive with the Beijing Olympics on the horizon and becoming more diplomatically critical. However, the 'push and pull' factors that underpin the symbiotic 'Olympic' relationship between the two nations and how they balance out, or are rationalized, are grounded in the very same philosophical issues that pervade discussion of the future FTA. The Olympic activity is but a single element of the wider economic and diplomatic relationship between the two nations, the significance of which has yet to be fully tested, yet it may eventually play a decisive role in the facilitation of the efforts to establish this bilateral free trade agreement. The FTA for Australia may, in the future, be the 'best managerial device – the answer to our prayers' [92] with which to handle its future inevitable close engagement with China.

The Olympic relationship between Australia and China is framed by the geopolitical context, just as all economic activities are. In 2005 English *et al.* suggested that three main issues remained as 'points of possible contention' [93] that could negatively impact upon Sino-Australian relations: 'the China-Taiwan issue, Australia's regional relationships, and the question of human rights in China'. [94] Yet as the 2008 Olympics draw near, these no longer seem to be arousing political heat and are not the most prevalent issues being discussed in the Australian media. Much discussed, however, are, as previously mentioned, the poor quality of the air Australian athletes will have to compete in (called in one article a 'toxic soup'), [95] and the concern over the poor quality of toys being imported into the country from China. [96] It would appear that these 'fortunate' and not particularly 'difficult' diplomatic matters may have obfuscated the more harrowingly complex issues mentioned by English *et al.* However, in Australia, where sport is perhaps the pre-eminent cultural icon and means of distraction, [97] it is difficult to see issues of global, regional or internal politics, human rights or the environment causing the average Australian, let alone politicians such as ex-Prime Minister, John Howard, to ponder upon the moral implications of their support of the 'Aussie' Olympic team in Beijing.

What then are Australia's wider political motivations for its almost absolute support of the Beijing games and thus, implicitly, of China's current geopolitical position? The growing prominence of the dimensions of trade, cultural engagement and sport in the bilateral relations between China and Australia are in themselves significant. [98] Yet the overarching factor is China's emerging global superpower status, not just in terms of its economic power, but in regard to the Asia-Pacific region and its growing military strength, which in some quarters is seen to be moving China 'onto the offensive'. [99] The regular yearly increase in military spending by the Chinese of nearly 18 per cent [100] does leave some doubt as to the veracity of its more overt soft-power policies. In the light of this, the discussion of Australia's own public diplomacy policies and actions, and the possibility that there exists some political ambivalence in the regard to China is worthy of serious cogitation, particularly, as Australian ex-Prime Minister Paul Keating remarked, China 'would not cross the road to doff its hat to Australia' were it not for Australia's mineral wealth. [101] However, Australia does have the minerals China wants, and does stand as a major political and diplomatic, if not military, presence in the Asia Pacific region. China, as one of the world's major manufacturers of a range of goods from toys to electrical appliances, requires the support of the world's biggest markets, the US and the EU; and, though avidly courting the developing nations, it still relies upon the mineral resources of Australia to produce these goods. The interconnectedness that exists between China and Australia and their mutual reliance may well allow Australia to exert a level of sanction upon the emerging superpower. The tension produced in this symbiotic relationship and its potential significance in global terms and its playing out in such arenas as the Olympic Games gives credence to the apparent diplomatic ambivalence of Australia's embrace of Beijing Olympic Games in 2008.

Australia's Ambitions for Beijing 2008

Just as the Beijing Olympic Games provide an opportunity for China to showcase its emergence as a 'major player in the mainstream of international affairs', [102] it has also given Australia a multi-layered opportunity to further its already strong relationship with China. The primacy and the enthusiasm with which all levels of government and industry in Australia promoted and supported 'the cooperative 'Olympic' links with China' [103] are indicative of its particular significance. Success in these games will have far more than the 'usual' nationalistic sporting connotation for Australia; the success of the games as a mega-sporting festival for China will be viewed as a victory for all the Australian organizations, companies and individuals that were involved in bringing the 2008 Olympic Games to fruition. If they are a success, Australia's involvement will be viewed by the public service in Canberra, if it is not already so, as a major diplomatic achievement. Since 2001, when China won the bid to host the 2008 games, the interaction and collaboration between the two nations has generated an immense level of goodwill in China towards Australia. [104] The actual successful presentation of the 2008 games with such a high level of support from Australia will, as John Bowan, former Australian diplomat and senior adviser on international relations to the Bob Hawke government from 1983 to 1990, suggests, further 'the already strong and important relationship between Australia and China'. [105] The kudos to be gained from the recognition of its technical and organizational competencies and the ostentatious showcasing of its economic power will promote

China internationally as a potential global superpower; it will also, domestically, be a very potent means of solidifying popular support and nationalistic sentiment. Politically, for Australia the alliance built on these soft-power interactions will also create an impact domestically by improving the image of China, which is, after all, its greatest trading partner and the most powerful strategic force in Asia. The implicit promotion of Sino-Australia relations that can emerge from the close interaction during the preparation and conduct of the games will far outdo the meagre budget of the Australia-China Council, which has annually under $1 million to fund its wide range of activities. [106] Gill Bates and Yanzhong Huang expressed doubt that China's soft-power resources had little, if any, flow-on to the policies made by other nations. [107] Although the diplomatic embrace of sport, particularly if characterized by the Olympic Games, with its highly political and commercial character, may be viewed as hardly 'soft' diplomacy, the extent of direct policy initiatives that have emerged at both federal and state government levels in Australia from the Beijing games alone tends to refute their contention. It is suggested that the effectiveness of both China's and Australia's public diplomacy activity, of which culture and sport are central, is critical to their future geopolitical interrelatedness.

However, the value and importance of Australia's future relationship with China cannot be simply centred upon the issue of finance; it must but have wider and deeper social and cultural dimensions – both countries must gain a more expansive understanding and appreciation of the people and culture of each other. Sport, and particularly the great sports festivals and competitions such as the Olympic Games, are excellent vehicles for such interface, and the Beijing Olympic Games, as far as Australian diplomats are concerned, offer an excellent springboard to future interactions on a far wider stage. [108] Cultural exchanges, including sport, at all levels can be very productive in developing cultural awareness. Just as the hard-power dimensions of political, formal diplomatic and economic interactions need to be undertaken at all levels to conduct international affairs, so can cultural, educational, scientific and sporting exchanges be utilized to demonstrate not only goodwill but also a country's attractiveness to others or, as Kurlantzick calls it, the country's 'brand'. [109] The Australian diplomatic corps is, by definition, heavily engaged in the promotion of 'brand Australia'; however, its current diplomatic policy is also pragmatically directed at promoting 'brand China':

> Cultural exchange provides a means whereby Australians can tell other nations about Australia and its people. It enables Australians to demonstrate how we conceive of ourselves, where we have come from, and where we are going as a nation. Similarly, exposure to the cultural products of other nations, such as China, enables us to learn about them. [110]

The public diplomacy efforts of the Australian foreign affairs department in changing the domestic perception of China has very evidently worked, as indicated in the first part of a study, *Australians Speak 2005*, conducted by Ivan Cook for the Lowy Institute, entitled 'Our Place In the World'. This looked at 'Australians' views of our national character, about how we fit in the world, and about how we relate to the global leadership'. [111] Cook's study, which involved surveying 1,000 subjects, demonstrated that the respondents placed China ahead of the US in most categories in which they were directly compared. Significantly, when asked 'about the countries and regions of the world with which we are closest geographically, culturally and as trading partners', [112] they gave China 69 per cent, which put it five places higher than the US, which received only 58 per cent. Not surprisingly New Zealand was the most favoured nation with 94 per cent, followed by the UK (86 per cent), Europe (85 per cent), Japan (84 per cent) and Singapore (83 per cent). China's growing power did not pose a major threat to Australians, with only 16 per cent registering that they were 'seriously worried' about them, with only a further 19 per cent indicating that they were 'fairly worried' about China. [113] The resonance of Australia's growing trade relationship with China was apparent, with 51 per cent of the sample having a positive perception of Australia's proposed FTA with China, while a meagre 34 per cent positively viewed the existing FTA with the US. Some 32 per cent viewed the FTA with the US negatively, while only 20 per cent thought the proposed agreement with China would have a 'bad' effect. [114] To what extent these perceptions are the direct or indirect outcome of the public diplomacy efforts of the Australian government or the efforts of the nation's major commercial and industrial companies is difficult, if not impossible, to assess. However, the fact is that, despite all the efforts of a not insignificant number of lobby and protest groups internationally and in Australia such as Amnesty International, the Collective for the Boycott of the Beijing Olympic Games, [115] the Australia Tibet Council (with their 'Race for Tibet' protest) [116] and the Falun Dafa (Australia), [117] there appears to be no weakening of brand China's high market standing in Australia. The diplomatic efforts in Australia have, it appears, stemmed the tide of human rights protest thus far and, predictably, as previously mentioned, only the environmental aspects of the Olympic venues garner any continual negative press.

Stumbling Blocks

The outcome of the diplomatic efforts the Australian government and other agencies are enlisting to change the perception of China in the minds of its people relies on a good deal of prudent management of several well-publicized 'stumbling blocks'. These hazards need to be negotiated by all Australian agencies promoting stronger and closer ties with China, and with a matter of months to go to the opening ceremony of the Beijing Olympic Games on 28 August 2008 many issues still provoke concern and even indignation in some quarters of society. Public disquiet, though hushed, still exists; the push and pull factors of Australia's favoured-nation status and its close engagement with China, which in regard to the Beijing Olympics has a very public face, are yet to be reconciled. The importance of the Beijing Games to Australia goes well beyond sport; it goes well beyond economics; indeed, it could have a major impact, geopolitically, upon Australia's future. What are the stumbling blocks and how will or have they been negotiated? The protesting groups have adopted the stance of suggesting that China's close cultural allies, including Australia, should use their influence ahead of the Beijing games to prompt the Chinese to embark on a phase of social and political reform, particularly in regard to human rights. These campaigns are based upon the premise that the Olympic Games, as global social events conducted under the gaze and scrutiny of the entire international community, are ideal vehicles to promote a specific cause. Host cities and host nations use the games to 'showcase' themselves to the world, with political, economic and cultural outcomes in many ways superseding the sporting goals and legacy of the games. [118] Thus any viable campaigns that can derail the big messages a host nation is promoting are taken seriously. Amnesty International has published its 'Olympic Countdown', which reviews any recent developments with regard to specific human rights issues it has been monitoring, and maintained that China had just a single year to keep the human rights promises it made ahead of the 2008 games. [119] Amnesty International's manifesto, which is embodied in its Olympic Countdown, embraces a wide-ranging agenda including death penalty reforms and changes to detention without trial, particularly in those instances where the upcoming Olympics have been used as a justification on security grounds, and to China's continued strict media controls. However, they do applaud the fact that foreign journalists will have greater freedom to cover news stories up to and during the Olympics. Even so, it has been pointed out that Internet controls have actually increased in some provinces, such as Xiamen in recent years. [120] Amnesty International's manifesto includes a series of recommendations to the Chinese Government and censure of the IOC, which it believes has demonstrated a reluctance to 'take a more proactive stance on human rights issues in the run-up to the Olympics ... [and its lack of action] appears to have weakened as the Olympic Games approach'. [121] In July 2001 Jacques Rogge, the president of the IOC, after Beijing had been declared winner of the bid to host the 2008 Olympics, indicated that the IOC knew there were serious human rights concerns in China, though he felt that, 'it was not up to the IOC to interfere in this issue. But we are taking the bet that seven years from now, we sincerely and dearly hope we will see many changes in China'. [122] The 'bet' does not appear to be safe two months from the opening ceremony, though the Australian government's palpable silence on human rights issues may well indicate, as Charles Woodard, former Australian Ambassador to China, suggests, 'that the Australian government places too much weight on trading relations and economic aspects of Australia's relationship with China and ignores human rights abuses occurring in China ... [and] that Australia had watered down its stand on the protection of human rights in China because of other considerations'. [123]

In July 2007 a group of Australian activists, the Coalition to Investigate the Persecution of Falun Gong [124] in China', which includes the ex-leader of the Australian Democrats, Senator Andrew Bartlett, and other community leaders and rights advocates, called for the cessation of the persecution of the members of the Falun Gong sect. In July 2007, in an article in *The Age*, Senator Bartlett said that people should start talking about such issues ahead of the Beijing games. He also pointed out that 'China's human rights record is appalling and I don't see a lot of evidence that it has improved significantly since the Olympics were awarded'. [125] The call for a boycott of the Beijing games has not gained any real support in parliament, though Australian Green Party leader Senator Bob Brown has called on the government to pressure China about human rights as the Beijing Olympics draw near. Neither the government nor the opposition would or probably could support the boycott as 'the calls could bring negative publicity to the Games and confront the athletes with a moral quandary'. [126] Strange that such fundamental human rights and international relations issues should become a matter for individual athletes to reconcile. However, there is a historical precedent in Australian Olympic history and one that would caution against any attempt to boycott Beijing. In 1980 the Australian government formally supported US President Jimmy Carter's call for an international boycott of the Moscow Olympics in protest against the Soviet Union's invasion of Afghanistan. The government, led by Prime Minister Malcolm Fraser, could not insist on the withdrawal of the Olympic team, and individual athletes and sporting bodies independently decided upon their participation. The reaction of politicians and athletes, irrespective of the moral rights and wrongs of the rationale underpinning the call for a boycott, turned this attempted boycott into a tawdry affair. The government bribed athletes not to attend, individuals withdrew on grounds of stress and little national pride was garnered as the Australian team entered the stadium at the opening ceremony behind the Olympic flag and not the national flag – an action viewed by critics as an ignominious and shameful act. [127] Doug Booth and Colin Tatz decried Australia's semi-participation in the Moscow games, suggesting it gave support to 'an obnoxious regime and system on the verge of disintegration'. [128] Interestingly, 28 years later, and with Australia much more enmeshed with host nation China, there is absolutely no hint of federal government sanction or any mention of direct pressure being brought upon the Chinese government in relation to human rights concerns ahead of the Beijing games.

In 2005 human rights problems in China were viewed by Prime Minister John Howard not as generic concerns but as things that Australians should not become obsessed with, as they are among, as he says, the 'things that make us different'. [129] The Australian Olympic Committee has summarily dismissed any talk of boycotts as far as the national Olympic body is concerned. Dan Silkstone reports that:

> The Australian Olympic Committee secretary-general Craig Phillips said that boycotts were not successful, punished athletes unfairly and could result in subsequent reverse boycotts. 'The Olympics do bring greater scrutiny of the host nation,' he said. 'But it's not a matter for us, it's a matter for governments and other organizations to press if they wish to.' [130]

With so much at stake outside the realm of sport, even Olympic sport, there is little chance of the Australian government exerting any hard-power political energy in an attempt to persuade China to meet some, if any, of the promises it has made to improve human rights as a feature of the lead-up to the Beijing games. In its bid for the 2008 games China asserted it would enhance social conditions, including education, health and human rights; Liu Jinmin, Vice President of the Beijing Olympic Games Bid Committee, supported this in an interview reported in the *People's Daily* in which he reflected that:

> Beijing's bid is the common aspiration of the 1.3 billion Chinese people. To try to help realize their wish means respect to their human rights.

> Everyone has the right to take part in what they are concerned about, which is required by both the Olympic Movement and human rights protection. Now the Chinese have the aspiration to hold the Games in China, this is just their human right.

> We do more than work out a bidding blueprint, but also get down to work. We are taking environment-friendly measures and improving traffic conditions. We have done many things that bring tangible benefits to the broad masses. [131]

These sentiments still underpin the beliefs of the current president of the IOC, Jacques Rogge, who stands firmly behind China's ability to address concerns, such as the imprisonment of journalists and press censorship in China. Rogge stated that 'We [the IOC] believe the Games are going to move ahead the agenda of the social and human rights as far as possible, the Games are going to be a force for good'. [132] He did qualify his statement by further suggesting that the Olympic Games were not a panacea for human rights issues. [133] However, as Bowan stresses, having awarded the 2008 games to Beijing on the understanding that human rights issues will be addressed, the IOC cannot stand by with little more than the 'pretension of statesmanship'; [134] they must make sure that the Chinese will not tarnish the Olympic image, the responsibility for which now lies their hands. [135] How much the IOC can influence the Chinese government on matters that China's global trading partners find difficult to even address, let alone demand, is a matter for conjecture.

On 28 August 2007 the IOC's Coordination Commission for the Beijing Games finished one of its final major reviews of the planning and preparations for the Beijing games when it audited the performance of the Chinese at the 'Good Luck Beijing Sports Events' held in Beijing, the Hong Kong SAR and Qingdao. No hint of concern has been heard from the delegation, and the venues, organization and performance of the officials were given a pass mark by the IOC commission. [136] The poor air condition that caused Jacques Rogge such concern two weeks earlier [137] was not mentioned in the commission's final press report. The games will go on, and the underlying sentiments Rogge evoked in his comments at the Quangzhou meeting with President Jiang Zemin on 11 November 2001 certainly have not changed. He said that the IOC has 'great confidence with your ability to deliver the games' [138] and the reason he gave for the IOC's choice of Beijing, that 'there are a billion three hundred thousand good reasons to do so', [139] could be viewed as representing the IOC's confidence in Beijing and possibly its positioning of China as an emerging superpower.

Australia, as China's major Olympic collaborator and supporter, is equally committed to the Beijing games' smooth passage and, cynical as it may seem, has begun to appreciate China's different form of governance and its perception and treatment of human rights issues. It has, apparently, been recognized that the two countries function under two very different belief systems in regard to individual rights, as Professor Colin Mackerras said: 'China favours the communitarian approach to human rights, emphasizing the history and experience and community welfare of specific peoples, while Australians tend to far more support the individualistic approach, which stresses the universality of individual human rights.' [140] The current Australian government has long adopted a passive human rights dialogue with China, which reflects the countries' growing economic and political ties, [141] and Australia has grown to appreciate that China does not bow to the pressure of the West, particularly in regard to the management of its people.

The overlap of Australia's increasing economic and cultural practices, which is encapsulated in the collaboration in the preparations and forthcoming production of the Beijing games, has allowed both nations, through direct example and osmosis, to review their own governance. The growing public diplomacy both have embraced is most apparent in their Olympic activity. Though the two nations are closely allied in this and the domain of trade, Australia still openly supports human rights reforms and can, because of its closer relationship with China, raise such issues with them in a non-paternalistic or xenophobic manner. This manner of diplomatic interface, which does not judgementally frame China in terms of its governance or which categorizes them as a growing strategic or environmental threat, has the potential to not only enhance the areas in which we agree but also to allow us to be able to discuss and, hopefully in the future, reduce the areas in which we disagree. As Australia and China enthusiastically embrace the 2008 Beijing Olympics, Australia has assumed a major role in helping China achieve its central goal for Beijing 2008, which is to change the perception the rest of the world has of it or, in marketing terms, how 'brand China' is globally perceived. [142] As a marketing tool the Olympic Games are unrivalled in promoting a message or a product, and the Beijing Olympics offer the Chinese an outstanding opportunity to continue their 'charm offensive' [143] with perhaps their most ambitious strategy yet. [144] BOCOG's general goal, to host a 'high level games and high level Olympics', [145] implicitly embraces the notion of creating a new image in its strategic theme of 'New Beijing, Great Olympics' (*xin Beijing, xin Aoyoun*). [146] Australian involvement in the conceptualization, planning, construction, organization and operational aspects is significant and underpins the three concepts that drive the Beijing Olympics: 'the Green Olympics, the High-tech Olympics and the People's Olympics' (*luse Aoyun, keji Aoyun, renwen Auyon*). [147] If China can achieve these aims, even partially, it will go a long way to achieve the national plan of reshaping the nation as a harmonious socialist society, [148] and in doing so further its ambition of establishing China's legitimacy as a global power. If this effort succeeds, Australia will have played an important role in this critical stage of

China's shift to a possibly more harmonized global world; but whether the 'One World, One Dream' [149] will have been attained with China, as J.A. Mangan suggests, having once again re-established itself at the centre of the world, [150] is too speculative a notion to consider; there is a lot of geopolitical tension ahead. [151] However, if the issues emanating from the major stumbling blocks that have surrounded the preparation of the Beijing Olympics can be ameliorated, then Australia's ambivalence may have been worthwhile.

Notes

[1] Fishman, *China, Inc.*
[2] Doug Bandow, 'China Rising: The Next Global Superpower', available online at Antiwar.com, accessed 10 Aug. 2007.
[3] China has increased military expenditure in 2007 by 17.8% to US$44.94 billion: it now matches that of the United Kingdom and France (See Chinese Government, 'China's Defense Budget to Rise 17.8% in 2007', available online at http://www.gov.cn/english/2007-03/04/content_541127.htm, accessed 11 Aug. 2007). For its development of a 'blue water' naval fleet, centred, some say, around newly developed aircraft carriers, see Peter Brookes, 'Pacific Power Play: China's Naval Expansionism', review of reviewed item, The Heritage Foundation, (2007), available online at www.heritage.org/Press/Commentary/ed032007a.cfm, accessed 11 Aug. 2007; and for the continued development of its missile program see, 'US official: Chinese test missile obliterates satellite', available online at http://www.cnn.com/2007/TECH/space/01/18/china.missile/index.html, accessed 14 Aug. 2007.
[4] It has been widely reported that China will soon overtake Germany as the world's third largest economy. See 'China Set to overtake Germany', *China Daily*, available online at http://www.chinadaily.com.cn/china/2007-07/16/content_5435569.htm, accessed 11 Aug. 2007.
[5] See Hunter, 'China: Soft Power and Cultural Influence'; Schmidt, 'China's "Soft Power" Re-Emergence'; Kurlantzick, *Charm Offensive*; Ramo, *The Beijing Consensus*; Joseph S. Nye, 'The Rise of China's Soft Power', *Wall Street Journal Asia*, 29 Dec. 2005; Bates and Yanzhong, 'Sources and Limits of Chinese "Soft Power"'.
[6] See Nye, *Soft Power.*
[7] Ibid., 5–6.
[8] Ibid.
[9] Trudy Rubin, 'China Replacing US in Art of Using "Soft Power"', *Philadelphia Inquirer*, 1 Aug. 2007.
[10] Kurlantzick, *Charm Offensive*, 5.
[11] G. Bates and Yanzhong, 'Sources and Limits of Chinese "Soft Power"', 17.
[12] Bowan, 'The Beijing 2008 Olympic Games', 13–17.
[13] Fan Hong, 'Communist China and the Asian Games', 488.
[14] Xin Xu, 'Modernizing China in the Olympic Spotlight', 93.
[15] Kurlantzick, *Charm Offensive*, 20
[16] Shambaugh, *Power Shift.*
[17] See Terry McCarthy, 'Reef Wars', *Times ASIA*, 8 March 1999..
[18] Sutter, *China's Rise in Asia*, cited in Kurlantzick, *Charm Offensive*, 39.
[19] Rubin, 'China Replacing US'.
[20] Xin Xu, 'Modernizing China in the Olympic Spotlight', 92.
[21] Ibid., 91.
[22] Fan Hong, 'Communist China and the Asian Games', 485.

[23] See ibid., 484–5.

[24] Xin Xu, 'Modernizing China in the Olympic Spotlight', 93.

[25] Guttmann, *The Olympics*, 91–4.

[26] See ibid., 85–163.

[27] Fan Hong, 'Communist China and the Asian Games', 488.

[28] Ibid.

[29] Chinese Olympic Committee, 'China and the Olympic Movement: Olympic Bids' (2004) available online at http://en.olympic.cn/china_oly/olympic_bids/2004-03-27/121850.html, accessed 13 Aug. 2007.

[30] Xin Xu, 'Modernizing China in the Olympic Spotlight', 94–5.

[31] Huntington, *The Clash of Civilizations.*, cited in Xin Xu, 'Modernizing China in the Olympic Spotlight', 95–6.

[32] Cashman, *The Bitter-Sweet Awakening*, 6.

[33] David Uren, 'China Emerges as Our Biggest Trading Partner', *The Australian*, 5 May 2005.

[34] See Fan Hong, 'Communist China and the Asian Games'.

[35] Australia, 'Opportunities and Challenges', Section 16.9, 295.

[36] Ibid.

[37] See Stewart *et al.*, *Australian Sport, passim.*

[38] Australia, 'Opportunities and Challenges', 293.

[39] Kwang-kuo Hwang, 'Face and Favor', cited in Yanjie Bian and Soon Ang Bian, '*Guanxi* Networks and Job Mobility'.

[40] Yanji Bian and Soon Ang Bian, '*Guanxi* Networks and Job Mobility', 984.

[41] Xioa-Ping and Chen, 'On the Intricacies of the Chinese *Quanxi*, 321.

[42] See, Australia, 'Opportunities and Challenges', ch. 13, *passim.*

[43] Ibid., 306.

[44] See Dan Silkstone, 'Activists Propose Olympic Boycott', *The Age*, 12 July 2007.

[45] Amnesty-International, 'The Olympics Countdown – One Year Left to Fulfil Human Rights Promises', Amnesty International on-line Library 2007, available at http://www.amnesty.org/en/library/info/ASA17/024/2007.

[46] See http://www.grouchos.org/, accessed 14 Aug. 2007.

[47] See Brohm, *Sport, a Prison of Measured Time;*. Brohm, 'La Tyrannie Sportive'.

[48] 'Air Quality Could Force Rescheduling of Games Events: Rogge', *The Age*, 10 Aug. 2007.

[49] See Robertson, *Globalization.*

[50] See Gordon, *Australia and the Olympic Games.*

[51] Fan Hong *et al.*, 'Beijing Ambitions', 518.

[52] Cashman, *The Bitter-Sweet Awakening*, 124.

[53] Fan Hong *et al.*, 'Beijing Ambitions', 518.

[54] Howell and Howell, *Aussie Gold*, 301.

[55] Booth and Tatz, *One-Eyed*, 175.

[56] Ferguson, *More Than Sunshine and Vegemite*, 24.

[57] Daly, 'Australian Institute of Sport', 31.

[58] Barns, 'Going for Gold Via the Eastern Bloc'.

[59] Fan Hong *et al.*, 'Beijing Ambitions', 519.

[60] Ibid., 518.

[61] Ibid.

[62] Kurlantzick, *Charm Offensive*, 61.

[63] Ibid., *passim.*

[64] Ibid., 62.

[65] Aoyama, 'Chinese Public Diplomacy'.

[66] 'Wuxing hongqi wo wei ni jiao'ao: relie zhuhe woguo tiyu jianer zai aoyunhui shang qude youyi chengji' [I Am Proud of the Five Starred Red Flag: Congratulations for the Victory of Our National Sports Heroes in Athens'], *Renmin ribao* [People's Daily], 30 Aug. 2004, 1, cited in Fan Hong *et al.*, 'Beijing Ambitions', 518.
[67] Cited in Miller, *From Athens to Athens*, 340.
[68] Fan Hong *et al.*, 'Beijing Ambitions', 520.
[69] Cushman and Wakefield, 'Asia Report', 2.
[70] Dong Jinxia, 'Women, Nationalism and the Beijing Olympics', 537–8 and, Fan Hong *et al.*, 'Beijing Ambitions', *passim*.
[71] Jennings, *The New Lords of the Rings*, 199–213.
[72] Cashman, *The Bitter-Sweet Awakening*, 117–23.
[73] See, Kurlantzick, *Charm Offensive*.
[74] Ibid., 176.
[75] Ibid.
[76] For a review of the extent of diplomatic relations between China and Australia, see, in PRC Embassy, Australia, 'China and Australia'.
[77] Ibid., 6.
[78] PRC Ministry of Foreign Affairs, 'President Jiang Zemin Met with Australia Prime Minister'.
[79] Ibid.
[80] Australia, 'Opportunities and Challenges'.
[81] Ibid., 304–6.
[82] Ibid., 304.
[83] Ibid., 310
[84] Richard Tan, Committee Hansard, 1 Aug. 2005, 35, cited in ibid., 270.
[85] Endeavour Consultancy is the largest Canberra-based political lobbying and public relations consultancy, established in 1998 a product of the merger of a number of prominent Canberra lobbyists. It has very strong links at all levels of Australian government and particularly with the public service in Canberra.
[86] Cashman, *The Bitter-Sweet Awakening*, 119.
[87] 'The Australian Trade Commission (Austrade) is a statutory agency within the portfolio, established by the Australian Trade Commission Act 1985. Austrade's mission is to contribute to community wealth by helping more Australians succeed in export and international business by providing advice, market intelligence and support to Australian companies to reduce the time, cost and risk involved in selecting, entering and developing international markets. In addition Austrade provides advice and guidance on overseas investment and joint venture opportunities. Austrade also administers the scheme that provides financial assistance to eligible businesses through partial reimbursement of the costs of specified export promotion activities. Austrade is represented in around 140 overseas locations in over 60 countries and in Australia. Austrade's domestic network comprises 18 Austrade offices and 54 Tradestart offices including eight Export Hubs': From http://www.austrade.gov.au/About-Austrade1351/default.aspx, accessed 23 Aug. 2007.
[88] Cashman, *The Bitter-Sweet Awakening*, 122.
[89] The following list outlines the major activity of Australian companies and consultants in the Beijing Olympic Games preparations:

- Sydney company PTW Architects designed the $140 million 'watercube' Beijing Olympics National Swimming Centre, with engineering design input from Arup in Sydney. PTW also secured the design of the $600 million Beijing Olympics athletes' village and was appointed by BOCOG to work on the development of Olympics overlay.

- Bligh Voller Nield was hired to master-plan the Olympic green; designed the Beijing Aquatic Park which was subsequently placed in the hands of a local design institute; designed the Beijing International Tennis Centre; designed temporary venues for the archery and hockey; and designed the Shunyi Water Park regatta centre.
- Cox Architects developed the Olympic sailing base in Qingdao. URS designed some related foreshore areas.
- EDAW (Aust) Pty Ltd, working with Bligh Voller Nield, provided landscape design for the Shunyi Water Park as well as its swimming centre work with PTW Architects: Arup (Aust) provided engineering services for projects including a new CCTV Tower at Beijing Airport.
- Bluescope Steel provided steel panels for the Tianjin Olympic Sports Centre that will be used for football qualifying matches.
- Sydney architects Group GSA won the design competition for the Beijing Olympic Shooting Centre, which was subsequently placed in the hands of a local design institute.
- Bowral architects Timothy Court and Company designed the 2008 Olympic Equestrian Centre in Hong Kong. It includes a 20,000-seat competition arena and 250 new air-conditioned stables; construction and management consultants Turner & Townsend Rawlinsons were appointed by the Hong Kong Jockey Club to provide project cost and budgeting advice for the equestrian facility.
- Engineering consulting firm Northcroft Australia provided advice on bid assessments for construction of the Beijing Olympic Stadium and the National Swimming Centre. It also provided financial consultancy to the Beijing Urban Construction Group for the National Indoor Stadium and the Olympic Village projects.
- Two Sydney specialists in transport planning, engineering and consulting, GHD and Parsons Brinckerhoff, provided Olympics-related advice to Beijing agencies. Parsons Brinckerhoff was engaged by BOCOG to undertake pedestrian movements modelling for the Beijing Olympic green and is providing design services for the Wukesong Cultural and Sports Centre.
- Bostik is providing architectural adhesives and sealants for the National Indoor Stadium.
- David Churches of Major Event Planning is advising the Hong Kong Government on planning and coordination matters relating to the equestrian venue.
- Telstra is advising BOCOG on telecommunications strategy.
- Macquarie Bank advised the Beijing State-Owned Asset Management Company on Olympics project finance issues.
- Macquarie Real Estate provided financial services to the Beichen Group for the International Convention Centre which will house the International Broadcast Centre.
- Ogden International, linked with the Telstra Stadium management company, is providing advice to the Beijing National Stadium Company in relation to venue operations planning and management.
- Bob Elphinston was appointed as a sports consultant to BOCOG. He was physical education officer for the Sydney 2000 Olympic Games and secretary-general of the Australian Olympic Committee, and is sports consultant for the International Olympic Committee (IOC) and president of the International Basketball Federation (FIBA).
- George Davey, director general of the NSW Food Authority, was appointed as the lead international expert on the Beijing Olympics Food Safety Advisory Committee, operating under the auspices of the Beijing Municipal Food Authority. The NSW Food Authority is engaging with the Beijing Municipal Food Authority on a range of planning, management and technology matters.
- Australian Nick Morris was appointed adviser to BOCOG for the 2008 Paralympic Games.
- Real Brand and Business secured merchandising assignments with Olympic sponsor VW China, relating to the VW and Audi brands.

- Maxxam International was appointed by BOCOG to manage the planning of the torch relay.
- Great Big Events is working on sports presentation and medal ceremonies.
- Australian David Payne was appointed to plan and manage all official games, BOCOG hospitality and athletes' catering facilities and associated requirements.
- Australian Sandy Hollway was appointed by BOCOG as training adviser with particular reference to BOCOG and volunteers training.
- Australian Richard Palfreyman is advising BOCOG and the Beijing Municipal Government on matters relating to media operations.
- TAFE NSW secured a leadership training contract for the Hong Kong Olympics Equestrian Organizing Committee.
- Sports Technology International (STI) secured work to provide five hockey venues with surfaces and also a venue in Shanghai. Source: www.business.**nsw**.gov.au/industry/sports/nsw_success_beijing2008.htm, accessed 14 Aug. 2007.

[90] David Uren, 'China Emerges as Our Biggest Trade Partner,' *The Australian*, 5 May 2007.
[91] Australian Government, 'Australia-China FTA Negotiations'.
[92] English *et al.*, 'An Australian-China Free Trade Agreement', 2.
[93] Ibid.
[94] Ibid.
[95] Mary-Anne and Ben Cubby Toy, 'Toxic Soup on Games Menu', *Brisbane Times*, 22 May 2007.
[96] See, http://www.abc.net.au/news/stories/2007/08/15/2006272.htm, accessed 24 Aug. 2007.
[97] See Kell, *Good Sports* and Cashman, *The Bitter-Sweet Awakening*.
[98] Australia, 'Opportunities and Challenges', ch. 16, 293–310.
[99] Tkacik, 'A Chinese Military Superpower?', 7.
[100] Ibid.
[101] Paul Keating (in interview), *The 7.30 Report*, ABC Television, 23 Aug. 2007.
[102] Bowan, 'The Beijing 2008 Olympic Games', 1.
[103] Ibid.
[104] Ibid., 3.
[105] Ibid.
[106] See Australia, 'Opportunities and Challenges', ch. 16, 297–8.
[107] Bates and Yanzhong, 'Sources and Limits of Chinese "Soft Power"', 23.
[108] See Australia, 'Opportunities and Challenges', ch. 18 ('Political Links').
[109] Kurlantzick, *Charm Offensive*, 5.
[110] Australia, 'Opportunities and Challenges', section 16.4, 293.
[111] Cook, *Australians Speak 2005*.
[112] Ibid., 7.
[113] Ibid., 13.
[114] Ibid., 21.
[115] See Collective for the Boycott of the Beijing Olympic Games, 'Call for a Boycott of the 2008 Olympic Games in Beijing' (2007), available online at http://www.grouchos.org/070328 pekin.htm, accessed 9 Sept. 2007.
[116] See 'The Race for Tibet', available online at http://www.atc.org.au/index.php?option= com_content&task=blogcategory&id=56&Itemid=113, accessed, 27 Aug. 2007.
[117] See 'Countdown to Olympics Fails to Stop Killing in China', available online at http://www.falunau.org/indexArticle.jsp?itemID=2032, accessed, 27 Aug. 2007.
[118] See Cashman, *The Bitter-Sweet Awakening, passim*.
[119] Amnesty International, 'The Olympics Countdown'.

[120] ESPN, *Olympic Reports*, 14 July 2001)., cited in Bowan, 'The Beijing 2008 Olympic Games', 13.

[121] Ibid., 8.

[122] Ibid., 13.

[123] Charles Woodard cited in Australia, 'Opportunities and Challenges'

[124] This brief description of the sect comes from the Falun Dafa Information Center: 'Falun Gong (also called Falun Dafa) is an ancient form of qigong, the practice of refining the body and mind through special exercises and meditation. Like tai chi, qigong is a vital part of many people's lives in Asia; almost every Chinese park is brimming by the break of dawn with people practicing these arts. Only a few years after its public introduction in 1992, Falun Dafa quickly grew to become the most popular form of qigong ever in Chinese history. The major reason for this is that Falun Dafa distinguishes itself from other qigong practices by emphasizing not only physical cultivation, but also cultivation of one's moral character in daily life according to higher principles taught by Mr Li Hongzhi, Falun Dafa's founder. Falun Dafa's effectiveness in improving health and its profound principles have quickly made the practice immensely popular throughout the entire world. Since being introduced to the general public by Mr Li, Falun Dafa has attracted tens of millions of people in over 60 countries. Most major cities and universities in the United States, Canada, Australia, and Europe have English-speaking Falun Dafa practice groups. The people who practice Falun Dafa come from every imaginable walk of life, as Falun Dafa transcends cultural, social, economic, and national boundaries. The practice has spread largely by word of mouth, as those who learn it usually find the benefits simply too good to keep to themselves.' See http://www.faluninfo.net/, accessed 20 Aug. 2007.

[125] Quoted in Silkstone, 'Activists Propose Olympic Boycott'.

[126] Ibid.

[127] Booth and Tatz, *One-Eyed*, 179.

[128] Ibid., 178–9.

[129] Transcript of the Prime Minister, the Hon. John Howard MP. Address to the Asia Society Lunch (12 Sept. 2005), available at http://www.pm.gov.au/news/speeches/speech1560.html, accessed 18 Aug. 2007.

[130] Silkstone, 'Activists Propose Olympic Boycott'

[131] Liu Jinmin, Vice President of the Beijing Olympic Games Bid Committee, reported in 'Beijing: Olympic Bid Helps Develop Human Rights', *People's Daily Online*, 7 Feb. 2001, Available at http://english.people.com.cn/english/200102/07/eng20010207_61746.html.

[132] Jacques Rogge, 'Hosts Say Beijing Preparations on Track' (2007) available at http://news.ninemsn.com.au/article.aspx?id=94520, accessed 29 Aug. 2007.

[133] Ibid.

[134] Bowan, 'The Beijing 2008 Olympic Games' 15.

[135] Ibid.

[136] IOC, 'Coordination Commission for the Beijing Games' (2007), available at http://www.olympic.org.uk/games/athens2004/home/full_story_uk/asp?id=2300-.

[137] Jacques Rogge, cited in 'Air Quality Could Force Rescheduling of Games Events: Rogge'.

[138] 'Jiang Zemin Meets IOC President', *People's Daily*, 12 Nov. 2001.

[139] Ibid.

[140] Professor Colin Makerras, cited in Australia, 'Opportunities and Challenges', ch. 14, 253.

[141] Ibid.

[142] Berkowitz *et al.*, 'Brand China'.

[143] Kurlantzick, *Charm Offensive*.

[144] Doctoroff, *Billions*, cited in Kurlantzick, *Charm Offensive*.

[145] Official website of the Beijing 2008 Olympic Games, BOCOG, 'Goals and Concepts' (2007) available at http://en.beijing2008.cn/bocog/concepts/, accessed 2 Sept. 2007.
[146] Ibid.
[147] Ibid.
[148] Xin Xu, 'Modernizing China in the Olympic Spotlight', 104.
[149] BOCOG, 'Goals and Concepts'.
[150] Mangan, 'Epilogue: Empire in Denial', 1196.
[151] J.A. Mangan, personal communication, 23 Oct. 2007.

References

Aoyama, Rumi. 'Chinese Public Diplomacy in the Multimedia Age: Public Diplomacy and Civil Diplomacy'. In *Waseda University Collection*. Waseda, Dec. 2004.
Australia, Commonwealth Government of. 'Opportunities and Challenges: Australia's Relationship with China', edited by Senate Foreign Affairs Defence and Trade References Committee. Canberra: The Senate Printing Unit, 2005.
Australian Government, Department of Foreign Affairs and Trade. 'Australia-China FTA Negotiations', 1 Nov. 2007.
Barns, Greg. 'Going for Gold Via the Eastern Bloc'. *On Line Opinion*, 2006, available at http://www.onlineopinion.com.au/view.asp?article=4254.
Bates, G. and Yanzhong Huang. 'Sources and Limits of Chinese "Soft Power"'. *Survival* 48, no. 2, (2006).
Berkowitz, Pere, George Gjermano, Lee Gomez and Gary Schafer. 'Brand China: Using the 2008 Olympic Games to Enhance China's Image'. *Place Branding and Public Diplomacy* 3, no. 2, (2007): 164–78 (15).
Booth, D. and C. Tatz. *One-Eyed: A View of Australian Sport*. St Leonards, NSW: Allen & Unwin, 2000.
Bowan, John. 'The Beijing 2008 Olympic Games: China in the Limelight'. In *Asia Pacific Program*. Sydney: Lowy Institute for International Policy, 2004.
Brohm, Jean Marie. *Sport, a Prison of Measured Time: Essays*. London: Ink Links Ltd., 1978.
———. 2006. 'La Tyrannie Sportive. Théorie Critique D'un Opium Du Peuple'. Groupe Contre l'Horreur Olympique et Sportive, available online at http://www.grouchos.org/tyranniesportive.htm#1, accessed 7 Sept. 2007.
Cashman, Richard. *The Bitter-Sweet Awakening: The Legacy of the Sydney 2000 Olympic Games*. Sydney: Walla Walla Press, in conjunction with the Centre for Olympic Studies, University of Technolgy, Sydney, 2006.
Cook, Ivan. *Australians Speak 2005: Public Opinion and Foreign Policy*. Sydney: Lowy Institute for International Policy, 2005.
Cushman and Wakefield Inc. 'Asia Report: After the Games Are Over: Famine or Feast'. Shanghai 7 Oct. 2007.
Daly, John D. 'Australian Institute of Sport (AIS)'. In *The Oxford Companion to Australian Sport*, edited by W. Vamplew *et al.* Melbourne: Oxford University Press, 1992.
Doctoroff, T. *Billions: Selling to the New Chinese Consumer*. Basingstoke: Palgrave Macmillan, 2005.
Dong Jinxia. 'Women, Nationalism and the Beijing Olympics: Preparing for Glory'. *The International Journal of the History of Sport* 22, no. 4, (2005): 530–44.
English, Tony, Curt Anderssen and Geoff Upton. 'An Australian-China Free Trade Agreement: Managing an Elephant'. Adelaide: Research Paper Series, School of Commerce, Flinders University, 2005.
Fan Hong. 'Communist China and the Asian Games 1951–1990: The Thirty-Nine Year Struggle to Victory'. *Sport in Society* 8, no. 3, (2005): 479–92.

Fan Hong, Ping Wu and Huan Xiong, 'Beijing Ambitions: An Analysis of the Chinese Elite Sports System and its Olympic Strategy for the 2008 Olympic Games'. *The International Journal of the History of Sport* 22, no. 4, (2005).

Ferguson, Jim. *More Than Sunshine and Vegemite: Success the Australian Way.* Sydney: Halstead Press, 2007.

Fishman, Ted C. *China, Inc.: How the Rise of the Next Superpower Challenges America and the World.* New York: Simon & Schuster, 2005.

Gordon, Harry. *Australia and the Olympic Games.* Brisbane: University of Queensland, 1994.

Guttmann, Allen. *The Olympics: A History of the Modern Games.* Urbana, IL and Chicago: University of Illinois Press, 1992.

Howell, Max and Reet Howell. *Aussie Gold: The Story of Australia at the Olympics.* Brisbane: Brooks Waterloo, 1988.

Hunter, Alan. 'China: Soft Power and Cultural Influence'. Coventry University: Centre for Peace and Reconciliation Studies, 2006.

Huntington, S. *The Clash of Civilizations and the Remaking of World Order.* New York: Simon & Schuster, 1996.

Jennings, Andrew. *The New Lords of the Rings: Olympic Corruption and How to Buy Gold Medals.* Sydney: Pocket Books, 1996.

Kell, Peter. *Good Sports: Australian Sport and the Myth of a Fair Go.* Sydney: Pluto Press, 2000.

Kurlantzick, J. *Charm Offensive: How China's Soft Power Is Transforming the World.* Melbourne: Melbourne University Press, 2007.

Kwang-kuo Hwang. 'Face and Favor: The Chinese Power Game'. *American Journal of Sociology* 92 (1987): 944–74.

Mangan, J.A. 'Epilogue: Empire in Denial: An Exceptional Kind of Imperialism'. *The International Journal of the History of Sport* 22, no. 6, (2005): 1194–97.

Miller, David. *From Athens to Athens: The Official History of the Olympic Games and the IOC, 1896–2004.* Edinburgh: Mainstream, 2004.

Nye, Joseph S. *Soft Power: The Means to Success in World Politics.* New York: Public Affairs, 2004.

PRC Embassy, Australia. 'China and Australia: Bilateral Political Relationship in Retrospect', 2003, available at http://au.china-embassy.org/eng/zagx/sbgx/t157240.htm, accessed 19 Aug. 2007.

PRC Ministry of Foreign Affairs. 'President Jiang Zemin Met with Australia Prime Minister', 2001, available at http://au.china-embassy.org/eng/zagx/sbgx/t57240.htm, accessed 9 Nov. 2007.

Ramo, J.C. *The Beijing Consensus.* London: Foreign Policy Centre, 2004.

Robertson, R. *Globalization: Social Theory and Global Culture.* London: Sage, 1992.

Schmidt, J.D. 'China's "Soft Power" Re-Emergence in Southeast Asia'. Paper presented at the international workshop 'China World', Copenhagen 2006.

Shambaugh, David. *Power Shift.* Berkeley, CA: University of California Press, 2005.

Stewart, Bob, Matthew, Nicholson, Aaron Smith and Hans Westerbecek. *Australian Sport: Better by Design: The Evolution of Australian Sport Policy.* London: Routledge, 2004.

Sutter, Robert G. *China's Rise in Asia: Promises and Perils.* Lanham, MD: Rowman and Littlefield, 2005.

Tkacik, John J. 'A Chinese Military Superpower?.' WebMemo, The Heritage Foundation, 8 March 2007, available at http://www.heritage.org/Research/AsiaandthePacific/wm1389.cfm, accessed 24 Aug. 2007.

Xin Xu. 'Modernizing China in the Olympic Spotlight: China's National Identity and the 2008 Beijing Olympiad'. *The Sociology Review* 54, suppl. 2 (2006).

Xioa-Ping and Chao C. Chen Chen. 'On the Intricacies of the Chinese *Quanxi*: A Process Model of *Guanxi* Development'. *Asia Pacific Journal of Management* 21 (2004).

Yanjie Bian and Soon Ang. '*Guanxi* Networks and Job Mobility in China and Singapore'. *Social Forces* 75, no. 3, (1997): 981–1005.

The Dish Might Be Overspiced: Fears, Doubts and Criticisms in French Perceptions of Chinese Olympic and Other Successes

Thierry Terret

Economic experts give the impression that they are only now discovering the fact that China is 'the' new superpower of the twenty-first century. Specialist books and reviews are decoding, by means of statistics and reports, the ingredients of what seems to be an undeniable success. [1] The banking system, domestic market, investment, industrial fabric and, in particular, the conquering of foreign markets are being studied as much for their characteristics as for their effects on what has now become a global market. [2] Nevertheless, faced with this Chinese growth, Europe is torn between three attitudes. The first is to observe the challenge that all this offers to the United States – a political as well as economic struggle being predicted by American commentators, but in which old Europe does not seem to have a decisive role to play. [3] Next, this passive attitude is leaving more and more room for the explicit ambition which consists of modifying this new economic balance by imposing a three-way system implicating Europe, China and the United States. The last posture, which goes far beyond economic considerations, [4] also reveals the fear of seeing a new cultural, political and economic system, backed up by 1.3 billion people, imposing its own values on Western society. Indeed, as far back as 1973, Alain Peyrefitte, French politician and intellectual, announced in a remarkable book (with an alarmist title) *Quand la Chine s'éveillera … le monde tremblera* ('When China awakes, the world will shake') that the Chinese could, once they have reached a sufficiently high level of culture and technology, impose their ideas on the rest of the world. [5] In other words, this growing fear of the 'yellow peril' is a mixture of fear of Communism, fear of the masses and fear of the economy.

Since the ping-pong diplomacy of the early 1970s and the readmission of the People's Republic of China to the IOC in 1979 at a time when the Chinese Government was moving towards economic reform, [6] the sport issue has deeply reflected the ambivalence of these European perceptions. Beijing's bid for the 2008 Olympic Games offered an opportunity to journalists and observers to adopt an attitude that alternated between fascination, criticism and fear. France, the auto-designated birthplace of human rights, is a particularly illustrative example of these ambiguous perceptions. [7]

1. From Economic Success to Olympic Consecration

The 'two-China' question poisoned the country's Olympic affairs for 30 years before a temporary solution was found in 1979 with the IOC's acceptance of the Taipei Chinese Olympic Committee alongside that of the People's Republic of China. [8] The door was thus opened for the Chinese government to instrumentalize sport in order to consolidate its image not only in socialist countries but also in the eyes of the Western world. [9] This movement is an incontestable part of a much larger policy. International relations specialists use this to demonstrate that Beijing's Olympic Games candidatures of 2000 and 2008 are part of a process of political reform begun in 1978 and which, in particular, heralded China's more outward-oriented policy of participating more actively in various political, economic and cultural organizations such as the United Nations, the World Bank and the International Monetary Fund. [10] This policy has continued, leading *Le Monde Economie* to state in May 2007 that 'China's currency reserve war treasury, together with its colossal appetite for energy and raw materials, is forcing the Chinese Empire into playing a more and more important role in regional and international financial institutions'. [11]

Economists consider that China's economic health is due to its enormous domestic market, the extent of its own resources, the reduced cost of labour, its controlled outward-looking policy in terms of foreign capital and its investments in foreign markets. The continual reinforcement of China's presence in Africa and, more recently, South America, by rolling back in Africa's case the historical influence of Europe and in South America's that of the United States, is helping the Chinese economy to become an unavoidable presence. Thus China posted a positive commercial balance of US$150 billion in 2006 – an increase of almost 50 per cent compared to the previous year. [12] Such results are propelling the country towards the summit of the economic hierarchy. China is steadily climbing the ladder, overtaking firstly France and Great Britain, followed by Germany, to finish in fourth place in 2006, then third in 2007 with a net GNP figure in excess of $3,100 billion, according to the global power classification issued by the World Bank.

Since the end of the Cold War and the ensuing break-up of the Soviet Union, China has found itself in a position to defy the United States in terms of its economy. It would certainly be useful to note here that this success is progressively spreading to the sporting economy. Chinese sport brand names such as Li Ning, Peak, Anta and Double Star are transforming the Beijing games into a commercial opportunity to promote Chinese clothes, shoes and other items, well beyond their domestic market possibilities. [13] Moreover, the ambition of becoming a superpower [14] is leading China to extend its efforts beyond the economy, to include other parameters of recognition such as sporting supremacy. Since the 1980s, China has increased its efforts to select and prepare the best athletes, giving rise on the way to a few doping scandals (particularly demonstrated by Chinese female swimmers in 1994 and 1998), and the selection of overly young athletes. [15] There have been successes nevertheless, and Chinese progress in the world of sport is an almost perfect mirror image of the effects of its position on the economic scene. China finished fourth in Atlanta in 1996 with 50 medals, including six gold. It finished third in Sydney in 2000 with 28 gold medals out of a total of 59. The Athens Olympics in 2004 are another example of this increasing power: 32 titles (of which two-thirds were won by women), just behind the United States, who came first with 35 gold medals. The bookmakers cannot see anything else but a Chinese victory in 2008, particularly since the games will take place in the country. [16]

By simultaneously demonstrating both China's will to become part of the great international organizations, as well as its ambitions to increase prestige through medals won by hyper-motivated athletes in a competition taking place on Chinese soil, China's candidature is evidently part of a political strategy aimed at recognition and a symbolic challenge for large and traditionally strong nations such as the United States and Japan. [17] This junction between the world economy and the Olympic Games in a period of apparent commercial outward orientation inspired the French journalist Samuel Pisar, after Beijing's successful bid, to write:

> China has become the theatre of a gigantic reform movement which could, more quickly than we imagine, redefine the world's economic, political and cultural boundaries. By rallying the cause of the World Trade Organization and the games of 2008, she has taken a decisive step towards her opening up to the community of

nations. This process is now accelerating under our very eyes, at the same time as the next Communist Party congress in the world's most populated country is readying itself to appoint a new generation of leaders. [18]

2. Admiring Economic Success: 'Getting a Slice of the Cake'

The West's attitude to China's economic success is anything but fatalist. Rather it is realistic, progressively transforming the condescending, indifferent or sceptical attitudes of the 1970s into a more ambiguous perception in which two strategies are becoming evident. In 1973, economic circles remained oblivious to the warnings contained in Alain Peyrefitte's *When China Awakes*. The sporting world was completely indifferent to the prospects described by a politician for a country which was not even a full member of the IOC. Fifteen years later, the political, economic and sporting situation has totally changed. A symbol as well as the means of her economic success, China's membership of the World Trade Organization (WTO) reflects these difficult debates, begun in the mid-1980s and resulting initially in 2001 in a 900-page document that would soon pave the way for Beijing's membership of the organization. From then onwards, 'An enormous market [is] now open to all the countries of the world'. [19]

Nevertheless, the superficial admiration of observers, economists and political leaders cannot hide the underlying fear and desire: the fear of the effect of Chinese economic ambitions on national economies and the desire to 'get a slice of the cake', the 'cake' being a new market of more than a billion people thought to be – often hastily and no doubt naively – open to Western products and culture. This dual phenomenon manifests itself by occasionally contradictory opinions.

Thus the risk of a flood of Chinese products and equipment into European and American markets, which could potentially destabilize whole sectors of the economy – the sports goods market to give but one example – provoked various containment strategies in order to undercut Chinese ambitions. The best-known example remains the quotas imposed on Chinese textile exports. Their suppression on 1 January 2005 was even announced as a commercial tsunami against which the European Union would be powerless to react. [20] In an alarmist article printed six months later, journalists Serge Marti and Jean-Michel Bezat saw this issue as marking the end of the admirative and understanding attitude that Europeans had thus far shown towards the Chinese:

> China is imposing herself in all sectors and in all markets. … The deluge of textile products, which is threatening to submerge Europe and the United States in the form of low-priced pullovers and trousers from the Chinese Empire, has changed our perception of China, this soon-to-be economic giant, which now frightens as much as it fascinates. 'Sino-mania' suffered a hard blow. [21]

These fears have also led to the use of the WTO's entire legal arsenal. Thus Peter Mandelson, in charge of trade in Brussels and with close links to Tony Blair, submitted a 'strategic report', dated 24 October 2006, in which he stated that 'Europe must conduct a fair but firm trade policy', while threatening to refer Europe and China's difficulties to the WTO. [22] A threat that the United States would not hesitate to emulate the following year by engaging in proceedings against China for having 'flooded the country with subsidized, thus low cost, goods'. [23]

After the stick came the carrot. The Europeans had no intention of letting the Americans be the only ones to profit from the opening up of Chinese markets to foreign investment and the exteriorization of industrial production. [24] The case of France is an exemplary one in this context. After decades of economic near-indifference, and despite constant cultural agreements, it took until 1997 before President Jacques Chirac signed a strategic partnership with China. During his 12 years in office, China was the distant country the most visited by the French president in his role of head of state, with a total of four official visits. As the journalists Rémy Ourdin and Bruno Philip would put it almost ten years later, 'For Mr Chirac, the growing importance of China on the world scene imposes the development of close ties with her, given that France's fundamental interests are at stake'. [25] The comments concerning his third visit to Peking, in October 2004, demonstrate remarkably well the will to shift from the 'good political and cultural relations' of the 1970s and 1980s to a 'trade partnership'. In an article entitled 'Paris is only the eleventh highest commercial partner of Beijing', the conclusion offered by Le Monde's Beijing correspondent is presented in the form of regrets:

> The fact that Jaques Chirac decided that a strong economic flavour would be used for his 1995 visit to China, the third since his becoming president, is not a coincidence. Relations between Paris and Beijing are excellent on a political level, but France's position in Chinese markets is not what it could be. The third European supplier, far behind Germany and Great Britain, France is only in eleventh position worldwide [and] her trade deficit remains heavily detrimental; almost 5 billion euros. [26]

At the same time, the French President called upon French companies to conquer Chinese markets and pleaded for a 'specific Franco-Chinese partnership'. [27] Nevertheless, this positivist policy did not always pay off. In 2005, France was the tenth largest investor in China with $6.8 billion – only 1.2 per cent of total investments in China. France was the third largest recipient of Chinese investment in Europe, and the tenth worldwide. [28]

Even though the sports equipment and clothing markets had already played an active role in the general strategy consisting of conquering the Chinese market since the 1990s, the perspective of the Beijing games gave a solid boost to investment. European and American multinationals such as Nike, Adidas, Reebok and Puma 'are placing themselves in battle order to be sure they profit from product-hungry urban Chinese youth'. [29] Bric Pedroletti also remarks that 'attracted by the perspective of the games, advertisers worldwide, sports clothing producers, sporting events organizers and other sports marketing gurus are converging on China'. [30] For

Mickael Payne, advisor to Bernie Ecclestone, head of Formula One and former marketing director for the International Olympic Committee, 'There has never been so much interest shown in the Olympic Games by business as there is for the Beijing Games'. [31]

French companies tried hard not to be left behind in this market segment, but their efforts came too late and proved too limited. In 2003, the national leader, Décathlon, timidly declared that it 'hoped to profit from China's new-found interest in sport'. [32] Tibor Sillinger, general delegate of the Federation of Nautical Industry in France said in 2005 that 'The Shanghai Nautical Salon has existed for ten years and the whole world has attended ... except the French. We need to act, and quickly!' This led, at long last, to the sending of representatives from 34 leading companies such as Bénétau, Dufour, Fountaine, Pajot, Nautitech, Zodiac, Wichard and others, which represented 80 per cent of turnover for the French nautical industry. [33]

3. The 1989 Turning Point

The conquest of Chinese markets and Western representation in China have not always evolved in an uninterrupted manner since the 1970s. Western opinions of China were, indeed, deeply affected by the dramatic events that took place in Tiananmen Square in 1989. This resulted in numerous and lasting consequences for the Olympics issue. It all started in April 1989 with the death of the ex-general secretary of the Chinese Communist Party, Hu Yaobang. His successor, Deng Xiaoping, decreed a state funeral with the highest honours. Hu Yaobang had been forced to resign in 1987 after having trouble controlling student protests. On 17 and 18 April 1989, students in Beijing demonstrated in order to demand the truth concerning this resignation. [34] The protest gained momentum in the following days in spite of police intervention, and 100,000 people were now in Tiananmen Square, where Hu Yaobang had paradoxically become a symbol of the desire for a more liberal society. [35] On 22 April, the day of the funeral, the challenge to government power reached new heights and gave rise to the first regional riots. [36] Ignoring government banning orders, the largest demonstrations for 40 years increased in number over the following two weeks, and became synonymous with direct criticism of Deng Xiaoping. Despite tentative efforts by the Chinese government to negotiate with the demonstrators, the crisis worsened during the visit of Mikhail Gorbachev to Beijing on 17 May. [37] Martial law was imposed during the night of 19 May, the army was sent into Tiananmen Square and foreign media coverage of events was forbidden. [38]

After five weeks of crisis, Western governments began to react officially and sympathy demonstrations for the Chinese students were held in European capitals. In Paris, correlations between the revolution of 1789 and the events in Beijing exactly two centuries later were beginning to be transformed into slogans, while the Chinese living in Paris, soon to be supported by many sympathizers, paraded symbolically on the Esplanade des Droits de l'Homme. [39]

Meanwhile, in Tiananmen Square, the crowds forced the army to retreat several times, while the government hesitated as to what action to take; but the hardliners finally imposed their will. Between 3 and 4 June the army crushed the rebellion in a bloodbath, instantly provoking a unanimous reaction of horror among all foreign observers and governments. Beijing's relations with Washington and the European Union deteriorated. The numerous death penalties inflicted upon Chinese students in the capital in the days following the revolt finally destroyed the image of the country in the eyes of the West. 'The events unfolding in China at this moment are absolutely vile, and those in power, or rather those who are pretending to be, are governing under the double credo of vengeance and elation' declared Alain Jacob in *Le Monde*. [40]

Criticism was nowhere stronger than in France, where preparations were under way for the bicentenary of the 1789 revolution and the universal declaration of human rights. However, China was spoiling the image and obscuring what should have contributed to repositioning France as the country of human rights. In what was an unhappy coincidence, the festivities planned long beforehand began in Paris less than a week after the Tiananmen massacre, and culminated with the 14 July celebrations. [41] The carefully orchestrated parade organized for the occasion by Jean-Paul Goude, and broadcast to televisions in hundreds of countries, underwent slight programming modifications. At the head of the cortege marched the Chinese students of Paris, pushing their bicycles and ringing their bells as a tribute to the bloody deaths of their compatriots. Three days later, Beijing sent Paris an official protest which denounced what was considered to be inappropriate symbolic interference. [42]

As was illustrated by the BBC correspondent in Beijing at the time, James A.R. Miles, the consequences of the Tiananmen Square drama for national unity and long-held ideas of a certain osmosis between the people and their leaders was enormous, [43] and the effects on the image of China abroad were doubtless even more serious. Since 1989, press freedom and human rights organizations have commemorated, at the beginning of June, the intervention of the Chinese army against the demonstrators in Tiananmen Square. Western public opinion generally adopted an accusatory stance provoking, in the 1990s, anti-Western and even more anti-American attitudes in China. [44]

This chain of events led to a complex and ambiguous situation, causing friction in the West between commercial aspirations and condemnation of the Beijing regime's abuses. Nevertheless, during this sensitive diplomatic period, the predominance of political considerations rapidly led to questions of democracy being put on the back-burner, as was recently demonstrated by Pierre-Etienne Will and Mireille Delmas-Marty, [45] or revealed by Taiwanese concerns that economic realism could result in democracies forgetting the real issues. [46] However, if there is one area where mistrust and criticism have surprisingly persisted, it is sport. The successive candidatures of China for the Olympic Games in 1993 and 2001 were thus clearly impregnated with the ambiguity of political and economic policies after 1989.

4. Beijing's Victory: Ambiguous Perception

The wish to hold the Olympic Games in China goes back to the beginning of the Olympic movement and intensified in 1945 but the civil war, followed by the 'two-China' issue, countered Beijing's ambitions until 1979. The conditions were then right to send a team to the 1984 games, and later to become a candidate in 1993 for the 2000 games, which were awarded to Sydney, with two more votes than Beijing. The candidature presented by China on 13 July 2001 profited from this experience, and China won comfortably with a majority of 56 votes in the second ballot.

Several studies have demonstrated that these candidatures are the logical conclusion to a policy of internal development and the promotion of the nation's image, as well as that of its capital, abroad. [47] Not only that, but the sporting and political victory of 13 July 2001 came at a moment when commercial interests were losing sight of or minimizing the intensity of questions concerning freedom. Strong contradictions remained, however. Grant Jarvie has reduced the debate concerning the perception of Beijing's candidature for the organization of the Olympic Games to two opposing points of view. One was that the games represented a wonderful opportunity of bridging the gap separating China from the rest of the world by modernizing Beijing and responding to the new expectations of young Chinese. The other contended that giving the games to China was in total contradiction with the definition of human rights. This was notably confirmed by the handling of the Tibetan question, the Tiananmen Square massacre and the limits imposed on foreign television stations concerning access to information. [48] These points of view were also well made by the *Le Monde* journalist Francis Deron a few days before the IOC's vote:

> We shall know where we are ... when the IOC takes the decision to attribute or not the 2008 games to China – because that is, after all is said and done, the essential issue. For: Integrating the international community, according to Olympic theorists. Against: The unknown – represented by a regime with confirmed totalitarian tendencies being in charge of one of the most colossal social transformations in history. [49]

Yet, before 13 July, most of the criticism came from organizations involved in human rights and freedom issues, as well as prominent anti-Chinese government dissident groups. In April 2001, for example, a delegation of Tibetans, Uygurs and Chinese democrats, led by Wei Jingsheng, [50] went to Geneva to denounce certain Chinese actions against human rights and to use the opportunity to protest against Beijing's candidature at IOC headquarters. [51] A few months later, on 12 June, the organization Reporters Without Borders launched a campaign against the Chinese candidature, notably by driving around Lausanne, home to IOC headquarters, in three 'sandwich-vans' upon which two of the five Olympic rings had been transformed into handcuffs, alongside the accusing slogan 'Olympic Games in Beijing? China, gold medal in human rights violations'. [52]

Criticisms reached their high point as the decision day, 13 July, approached, and came from ever-more diversified sources. In France, *Le Monde* even picked up on particularly sickening similarities recounted elsewhere concerning the Berlin Olympics of 1936, given to Hitler's Germany in a growing atmosphere of anti-Semitism, and the 2008 games which could be attributed to Beijing in a context of curtailment of human rights. [53] But the intensity of French criticism, which also concerned other issues such as Chinese lobbying of IOC members, may also be explained by the fact that Paris was one of the fiercest candidates opposing Beijing. [54]

For all this, the question of human rights was absent during the debate held on 13 July, unless journalists preferred to remain silent on the matter. [55] Nobody was so naive, however, as to think that the Chinese would not use the Olympic Games to present a new image of themselves.

This was confirmed by the journalist Frédéric Bobin the day after the IOC's decision:

> Some images obliterate others. That is, of course, a power calculation. The wonderful present, that of Beijing celebrating a political regime constantly looking for new sources of legitimacy! You only had to look, on the evening of Friday 13th, at the astonished face of President Jiang Zemin to understand that, for the Communist Party, the happy event was not only a question of the technical organization of sporting events. [56]

5. The Olympic Games as a Pretext for a Critique of Chinese Society

As far as human rights watch groups are concerned, since 2001, the Olympic Games have become a particularly interesting and visible means to question Beijing on its engagement towards the IOC and, more widely, towards the international community. Olympic Watch (Committee for the 2008 Olympic Games in a Free and Democratic Country), [57] the Society for the Defence of Human Rights and other similar organizations multiplied their initiatives by often informing the press and conducting information campaigns on the human rights situation in China and the contradictions with Olympic ideals. [58] Within this context, several contacts were established with IOC members. During the Athens games of 2004, several requests were made and systematically refused – examples include requests for one minute of silence for Tibet during the opening ceremony or to defend the rights of Taiwan. Open letters were often sent between 2003 and 2007 to Jacques Rogge, IOC president, asking him to reconsider the decision to give the games to Beijing. [59] Given the impassive attitude of the IOC, Olympic Watch also sent, in August and December 2006, two detailed letters to national Olympic committees to warn them about 'the ongoing human rights violations in China' and to remind them of their obligations in defending Olympic ideals. Contrasting the Chinese government's record on universally defined human rights standards such as the death penalty, torture, freedom of expression and other issues with the Olympic ideals of 'individual dignity' and 'respect for fundamental universal ethical principles', Olympic Watch called on the national committees to respond to the fact that the International Olympic Committee 'has apparently made little effort to actually hold [the Beijing Organizing Committee] accountable for the context in which the 2008 Olympic Games are to take place'. [60]

In France, where sensitivity to human rights issues increased after 1989, the press expressed radical criticism in a debate that perpetuated the memory of what had happened in Tiananmen Square. However, commentary was less virulent in the right-wing press, close to financial circles, which, like *Le Figaro*, supported industrial and political lobbies wishing to re-establish the country and Europe in the race which, for the moment, was between China and the United States only. In *Le Monde*, on the other hand, admiration for a certain efficiency in preparing the games [61] could not stop the series of critiques centred around five large issues in direct relation with the games, and which offered an unbalanced and Eurocentric image of China: human rights, press freedom, pollution and protection of the environment, Chinese culture and, finally, Chinese foreign policy.

The first critique concerned human rights and recounted in general terms the issues of militant organizations, such as torture and the selling of organs. [62] One element in particular was explicitly linked to the Olympic question – the supposed exploitation of Chinese workers hired by companies that had been accredited for the games. Under the banner 'Play fair 2008', a recriminatory campaign was thus launched by the International Confederation of Free Trade Unions (ICFTU) in 2007 with a report which was amply commented on by *Le Monde*. The paper's Beijing correspondent wrote:

> Underpaid workers, 12-year olds on the production assembly lines, 12-hour working days, seven days a week, in dubious hygienic conditions – the report just published by independent international union associations is damning for several Chinese factories which have been accredited for the Olympic Games, companies which will supply gadgets and various other merchandise during the Beijing games in 2008. [63]

As if these accusations were not enough, *Le Monde* also spread suspicion in articles replete with doubts concerning the future results of Chinese athletes. During a symposium organized in 2005 by the World Anti-Doping Agency, the journalist Stéphane Mandard described an imaginary situation in which Chinese athletes won 50 gold medals in Beijing, including 22 world records, thanks to a generalized programme of genetic doping. [64]

The second main critique concerned press freedom, and most of *Le Monde*'s articles on this subject between 2001 and 2007 linked it to the proximity of the games, and the fear felt by Wen Jiabao's government of seeing possible damage being done to the image of China by uncontrolled reporting. This link was made at all levels, whether it was in a speech by the German Chancellor Angela Merkel, during a visit made by Wen Jiabo to Berlin in 2006, [65] or in an Amnesty International report dated 30 April 2007 which denounced ever-increasing censure of the Chinese press as the games approached, [66] at the exact time that the press itself was trying to use the games to reinforce its independence vis-à-vis the authorities. [67]

The third critique linked the Olympic question to that of environmental protection. Prior to its candidature, Beijing had promised ecologically clean games, using – not without a certain irony – Paris as a reference. [68] Six years later *Le Monde*, in turn, had the occasion to ironize about the results obtained by China by noting that, according to the International Energy Agency, China was becoming the largest producer of greenhouse gases in the world, surpassing the United States. [69] Beijing alone held all the records in this field, notably in terms of the number of harmful particles in suspension and floating around in the air. This led *Le Monde* journalists to doubt the conditions in which athletes would find themselves during the games, despite notable efforts made to reduce these problems, such as applying pollution standards to buses and taxis, reduction of steelworks production levels, artificial rain reduction during the games etc. [70]

A fourth kind of critical commentary aimed, in its own way, to 'civilize the Chinese'. The French press emphasized Chinese government efforts to give the impression of an advanced society, not only from an economic and industrial point of view, but also in terms of the population's behavioural patterns. The implicit comparative model used was that of the West. That campaigns aiming to modify Chinese attitudes in order to make them conform to the expectations of tourists and spectators from all over the world existed was one thing. That they be used in an ethnocentric manner to describe ostensibly uncivilized behaviour in Western eyes was another. In this context, Bruno Philip, *Le Monde*'s Chinese correspondent, was the author of the most hackneyed opinions on Asians in a series of articles entitled 'Beijing is learning good manners' and 'Beijing wants to "civilize" its citizens for the games'. [71] The journalist said, first of all, that 'Face-saving is crucial in Asia, where everyone, they say, spends their time trying to save their own. The Beijing authorities are thus making great efforts to protect their reputation. This means impeccable behaviour towards the crowds of foreigners who will arrive in the capital in 2008 for the XXIXth Olympics.' He continued with a description with suspect overtones: 'The *Beijinren* (habitants of Beijing) have a marked tendency to shove and push openly in order to get onto crowded buses, to insult their adversaries during sporting events and to spit all over the pavement.' Evoking the general thrust of the 'educative' programme launched by one of the people in charge of the communication for the Beijing Olympic Games Organization Committee (BOGOC), the journalist spoke about the anti-spitting campaign; the fact that the 11th of each month had been decreed 'waiting line day' in order that people learn how to queue; the campaign launched to stop people rolling up their T-shirts, thus exposing their bellies, during hot weather; English lessons for Beijing policeman and the 'fragrancing' of taxis. He then concluded that, on most of these issues, 'the battle is far from being won'.

The final critique concerned Chinese foreign policy, the Beijing games having become a means of blackmailing certain media chiefs and political figures in France.

Non-recognition of Taiwan, the Tibetan question, even the events in Darfur in 2006, [72] were all linked to the Beijing games in journalists' debates. The flame's itinerary for example, which was supposed to include Taiwan and Mount Everest, provoked numerous reactions that *Le Monde* was quick to echo. [73] This criticism reached a pitch during the French presidential campaign in April–May 2007. François Bayrou, then in second or third place according to pre-election polls, did not flinch from attacking Khartoum on several occasions [74] for its aid to Arab militias by threatening Beijing with a French boycott of the Olympic Games. The threat was even more implicit between the two rounds of voting, where the two remaining candidates, Nicolas Sarkozy and Segolène Royal, went head-to-head in a televised debate on 2 May 2007. During this oratorical battle, watched by more than 20 million French citizens, the socialist candidate considered that 'pressure must be brought to bear on China, including the threat of a boycott of the games'. This provoked a retort in question form from the future president: 'If you are in favour of a boycott for athletes, why didn't you yourself boycott your visit [to Beijing in January]?' [75]

Conclusion

The differing responses offered by the two candidates for the French presidency in May 2007 sum up perfectly the ambiguity of the French standpoint. On the one hand, against a background of humanitarian issues brought up by the memory of the Tiananmen Square massacre and by the tradition of human rights in France, opinions are deliberately critical of the choice of Beijing for the organization of the games. On the other, market realities – represented by Nicolas Sarkozy [76] – put economic considerations before everything else, perpetuating the double standards of Jacques Chirac in the 1990s. If the truth be told, despite a little Chinese diplomatic reaction, China hardly seems to care about French, or even European, concerns. For one thing, offensive talk is not backed up with action. For another, the ambiguity of the general sentiment towards the Olympic Games, between human rights and economic necessity, has left considerable room for manoeuvre for the Chinese government, for whom the principal challenge concerns firstly, and uppermost, the United States – in financial markets as well as in stadiums. Is it not remarkable, moreover, that Paris's bid for the 2012 Olympic Games provoked a wave of sympathy among the Chinese? To the point where, in June 2005, a study carried out by A.C. Nielsen consultants in 27 countries and with 20,000 internet users, put the Chinese in first place, ahead of the Belgians and the Greeks, in preferring that the IOC gave the next games to France. [77]

Notes

[1] Much literature on this issue has been published in recent years. See, for example, Chee and West, *China: Mythos und Realität*; 'Le devenir financier de la Chine'; Marteau, *Le secteur bancaire et les marchés financiers en Chine*; *La Chine: un colosse financier?*; Howie and Walter, *Privatizing China*; Aglietta and Landry, *La Chine du XXIème siècle*.

[2] Mar and Richter, *China: Enabling a New Era of Changes*; 'Chine: les enjeux de la mondialisation'; Gavalda and Rouvin, *La Chine face à la mondialisation*.

[3] Bernstein and Munro, *The Coming Conflict with China*; Bush and O'Hanlon, *A War Like No Other*; Spitaels, *Chine-USA, la Guerra aura-t-elle lieu?*

[4] J. Ruffier, *Faut-il avoir peur des usines chinoises?*.

[5] Peyrefitte, *Quand la Chine s'éveillera ... Le monde tremblera*. The sentence has been attributed to Napoléon I, who is said to have pronounced it in 1816.

[6] Chinese historians generally agree on the political rupture in 1978, which marked the beginning of a new phase in the socialist construction of the Chinese society. See Xingxing, 'Current Status of PRC Studies'.

[7] I have chosen to analyse the French perception of the increasing economic, political and sporting power of China through the daily newspaper *Le Monde*, which remains the reference in France. Although independent, this newspaper is in fact politically oriented centre-left. It coverts the three national and international dimensions that this text endeavours to link: the Olympic Games, human rights and the economy. For the newspaper's history, see in particular Eveno, *Histoire du journal* Le Monde.

[8] On this issue, see especially Brownell, 'Sport and Politics Don't Mix'.

[9] Fan Hong and Xiong Xiaozheng, 'Communist China: Sport, Politics and Diplomacy'.

[10] Segal, *Openness and Foreign Policy Reform*; Quansheng Zhao, *Interpreting Chinese Foreign Policy*; Chan, *China and International Organizations*; Chan, '"Three Chinas" and International Organizations after 1997'; Necker, *La politique étrangère de la Chine populaire aux Nations Unies*. The Chinese historiography considers the work of Kirby and Dayong (*China's Interaction with the World*) as one of the most significant on this issue. See Dayong and Lan, 'International Historical Studies in PRC during the Post-WWII Period'.

[11] B. Pedroletti, 'La Chine dans le jeu de quilles des agences d'aides multilatérales', *Le Monde Economie*, 22 May 2007.

[12] 'Nouvel excédent commercial record pour la Chine', *Le Monde*, 11 Nov. 2006.

[13] B. Pedroletti, 'Les marques de sport chinoises misent sur les Jeux de Pékin', *Le Monde*, 3 Jan. 2007.

[14] B. Philip, 'La Chine s'imagine en grande puissance', *Le Monde*, 6 Feb. 2007.

[15] On these issues, see Riordan and Dong Jinxia, 'Chinese Women and Sport'; Fan Hong, 'Innoncence Lost'.

[16] See, for instance, 'Chine, encore un effort', *Le Monde*, 31 Aug. 2004; S. Bardon, 'Prêts pour Pékin', *Le Monde*, 29 Aug. 2004; F. Potet and G. van Kote, 'La Chine déjà prête pour ses JO à Pékin', *Le Monde*, 22 Aug. 2004.

[17] Analyses of the political background of the bid of Beijing are developed in Close *et al.*, *The Beijing Olympiad*.

[18] S. Pisar, 'La Chine et le Monde', *Le Monde*, 8 Nov. 2002.

[19] J.C. Buhrer, 'Un immense marché ouvert à tous les pays du monde', *Le Monde*, 19 Sept. 2001.

[20] 'Textile: la fin des quotas ne se traduira pas par un raz-de-marée des importations chinoises', *Le Monde*, 8 June 2007.

[21] S. Marti et J.M. Bezat, 'Le défi chinois – fabriquer et vendre tout et partout', *Le Monde*, 15 June 2005.

[22] P. Ricard, 'L'UE menace de porter ses contentieux commerciaux avec Pékin devant l'OMC', *Le Monde*, 26 Oct. 2006.

[23] 'Les Etats-Unis engagent une procédure contre la Chine devant l'OMC', *Le Monde*, 2 Feb. 2007.

[24] During the 2000s, China produced half of the world's production of cameras, 30% of washing machines and 20% of fridges.

[25] R. Ourdan and B. Philip, 'M. Chirac veut consolider le "partenariat" avec Pékin', *Le Monde*, 26 Oct. 2006.

[26] Bruno Philip, 'Paris n'est que le onzième partenaire commercial de Pékin', *Le Monde*, 10 Oct. 2004.

[27] 'Jacques Chirac appelle les entreprises françaises à conquérir le marché chinois', *Le Monde*, 10 Oct. 2004.

[28] *Le Monde*, 25 Oct. 2006.

[29] L. Girard, 'La Chine devient une nouvelle terre de conquête', *Le Monde*, 16 Aug. 2005.

[30] B. Pedroletti, 'La perspective des Jeux Olympiques stimule le "sport business" en Chine', *Le Monde*, 6 July 2005.

[31] Ibid.

[32] S. Lauer, 'Décathlon espère profiter de l'intérêt naissant de la Chine pour le sport', *Le Monde*, 29 Nov. 2003.

[33] M.B. Baudet, 'A Shanghaï, les Français prospectent un marché naissant', *Le Monde*, 13 Dec. 2005.

[34] F. Deron, 'Chine, Hu Yaobang plus encombrant mort que vivant', *Le Monde*, 18 April 1989; F. Deron, 'Chine des milliers d'étudiants ont manifesté en hommage à Hu Yaobant', *Le Monde*, 19 April 1989.

[35] F. Deron, 'Chine, la poursuite des manifestations étudiantes. Le régime contesté en plein cœur de Pékin', *Le Monde*, 20 April 1989; F. Deron, 'Chine l'hommage des Chinoise à "Hu Yaobang le Démocrate". Les manifestations s'amplifient à Pékin en faveur de la libéralisation', *Le Monde*, 21 April 1989.

[36] F. Deron, 'Les funérailles de Hu Yaobang. L'ampleur des manifestations populaires met en difficulté les dirigeants chinois', *Le Monde*, 23 April 1989; F. Deron, 'Après les manifestations de Pékin, des émeutes ont eu lieu dans deux villes de province', *Le Monde*, 25 April 1989.

[37] F. Deron, 'Chine, des milliers d'étudiants ont manifesté à vélo dans les rues de la capitale', *Le Monde*, 12 May 1989; F. Deron, 'La Chine à l'heure des bouleversements. Une marée humaine a envahi le centre de Pékin', *Le Monde*, 18 May 1989; F. Deron, 'Le chaos est complet à Pékin', *Le Monde*, 19 May 1989.

[38] F. Deron, 'Les rumeurs de la place Tiananmen', *Le Monde*, 21 May 1989.

[39] P. de Beer, 'Les manifestations en Chine, Manifestations de solidarité à Paris et dans le monde "1789–1989, Bastille-Tiananmen"', *Le Monde*, 23 May 1989.

[40] A. Jacob, 'Chine: un peuple humilié', *Le Monde*, 23 June 1989.

[41] Y. Agnès, Ombres et lumières', *Le Monde*, 11 June 1989.

[42] 'Pékin proteste contre la présence d'étudiants chinois dans la parade du 14 juillet', *Le Monde*, 19 July 1989.

[43] Miles, *The Legacy of Tiananmen Square*. See also Lui, 'Looking Back at Tiananmen Square'.

[44] Rawnsley and Rawnsley, *Political Communication in Greater China*.

[45] Will and Delmas-Marty, *La Chine et la Démocratie*.

[46] F. Deron, 'Taïwan, victime de la Realpolitik de l'Occident', *Le Monde*, 29 Jan. 2004.

[47] Brownell, *Training the Body for China*; Riordan and Jones, *Sport and Physical Education in China*; Broudehoux, *The Making and Selling of Post-Mao Beijing*.

[48] Jarvie, *Sport, Culture and Society*, 366. The two arguments are highlighted in the American context in chapter 22 of Kennedy, *China Cross Talk*.

[49] F. Deron, 'Votez Pékin!', *Le Monde*, 13 July 2001.

[50] Wei Jingsheng is an emblematic figure of Chinese contestation.

[51] J.C. Buhrer, 'Dissidents chinois, Ouïgours et Tibétains contre la candidature de Pékin aux JO', *Le Monde*, 17 April 2001.

[52] J.C. Buhrer, 'Reporters sans frontières lance une campagne contre l'attribution des Jeux olympiques à Pékin', *Le Monde*, 19 June 2001.

[53] M. Holzman, 'JO: Pékin2008 après Berlin 1936?', *Le Monde*, 11 July 2001.

[54] See, for instance, the criticisms of S. Cypel (avec F. Bobin, à Pékin), 'Le clientélisme olympique de Pékin', *Le Monde*, 11 July 2001.

[55] F. Potet, 'Lors du grand oral du CIO, personne n'a évoqué les droits de l'homme', *Le Monde*, 15 July 2001.

[56] F. Bobin, 'La communauté internationale offre une nouvelle légitimité au régime', *Le Monde*, 15 July 2001. See also 'Le CIO confère à la Chine le rang de puissance reconnue', *Le Monde*, 15 July 2001.

[57] This non-governmental organization is mainly European-based.

[58] Olympic Watch, 'Human Rights Organizations Unveil "Minimum Standards for Beijing 2008"', 29 Aug. 2004, available online at http://www.olympicwatch.org, accessed 3 Sept. 2007.

[59] Olympic Watch, 'After Turin, Focus on Beijing's Human Rights Record', 28 Feb. 28 2006; 'Chinese Human Rights Activists Write IOC', 19 May 2007, available online at http://www.olympicwatch.org, accessed 3 Sept. 2007.

[60] Olympic Watch, 'Two years until Beijing 2008: IOC fails, activists call on athletes, sponsors to act', 7 Aug. 2006; 'Olympic Watch writes National Olympic Committees', 10 Dec. 2006, available online at http://www.olympicwatch.org, accessed 3 Sept. 2007. The second letter mentions that 300,000 inhabitants of Beijing may have been moved for safety reasons, and as a consequence of the Olympic Games.

[61] For instance in F. Edelmann, 'Le stade, premier exploit des JO', *Le Monde*, 12 Jan. 2006.

[62] For instance, B. Philip, 'Chine: le pouvoir reconnaît l'usage de la torture par la police', *Le Monde*, 22 Nov. 2006; B. Pedroletti, 'Des membres du Fa Lun Gong seraient victimes d'un trafic d'organes en Chine', *Le Monde*, 18 Aug. 2006.

[63] B. Philip, 'Des usines chinoises accusées d'"abus flagrants" avant les JO', *Le Monde*, 15 June 2007. See also: 'Les articles de souvenir des JO de Pékin fabriqués par des enfants', *Le Monde.Fr* avec AFP et Reuters, 11 June 2007, available at http://www.lemonde.fr/, accessed 16 Sept. 2007. This report resulted in an official investigation by the organizing committee of the games.

[64] S. Mandard, 'Demain, des athlètes seront génétiquement modifiés', *Le Monde*, 4 Dec. 2005.

[65] A. Jacob and B. Philip, 'Le régime chinois interpellé en Europe sur la liberté de la presse', *Le Monde*, 16 Sept. 2006.

[66] 'Amnesty dénonce une répression accrue en Chine à l'approche des Jeux Olympiques de 2008', *Le Monde*, 30 April 2007.

[67] B. Pedroletti, 'La presse chinoise entend se servir des JO de Pékin pour marquer des points contre la censure', *Le Monde*, 10 Aug. 2006.

[68] 'JO 2008: Pékin promet un air "aussi pur qu'à Paris"', *Le Monde*, 3 Jan. 2001.

[69] 'La Chine en passé de devenir le premier émetteur de gaz à effet de serre', *Le Monde*, 25 April 2007.

[70] B.P., 'Quelques lueurs dans la fournaise polluée de l'été', *Le Monde*, 17 June 2007.

[71] B. Philip, 'Pékin veut "civiliser" ses citoyens pour les JO', *Le Monde*, 28 March 2007; Bruno Philip, 'Pékin apprend les bonnes manières', *Le Monde*, 17 June 2007.

[72] As a summary of this complex issue: China supported the decision of Sudan not to open a humanitarian channel to Darfur.

[73] 'Le parcours de la flamme olympique en Chine fait débat', *Le Monde*, 25 April 2007.

[74] 'Bayrou réitère sa meance de boycotter les JO de Pékin', *Le Monde*, 3 April 2007.

[75] C. Jakubyszyn, 'Darfour: Mme Royal menace Pékin d'un boycott des JO', *Le Monde*, 4 May 2007.

[76] The French president's links with economic and financial circles are well-known. See, for instance, Noir *et al.*, *Nicolas Sarkozy ou le destin de Brutus*.

[77] 'Une incroyable cote d'amour à Pékin', *Le Monde*, Supplément spécial, 6 July 2005.

References

Aglietta, M. and Y. Landry. *La Chine du XXIème siècle: une nouvelle superpuissance?* Paris: Economica, 2007.

Bernstein, R. and R. Munro. *The Coming Conflict with China.* New York: Alfred A. Knopf, 1997.

Broudehoux, A.M. *The Making and Selling of Post-Mao Beijing.* London and New York: Routledge, 2004.

Brownell, S. *Training the Body for China: Sports in the Moral Order of the People's Republic.* Chicago: Chicago University Press, 1995.

——. 'Sport and Politics Don't Mix. China's Relationship with the IOC during the Cold War', in *East Plays West: Sport and the Cold War,* edited by S. Wagg and D.L. Andrews. London and New York: Routledge, 2006: 253–71.

Bush, R.C. and M.E. O'Hanlon. *A War Like No Other: The Truth About China's Challenge to America.* Chichester: John Wiley & Sons, 2007.

Chan, G. *China and International Organizations. Participation in Non-Governmental Organizations Since 1971.* Oxford: Oxford University Press, 1989.

——. '"Three Chinas" and International Organizations after 1997'. *Journal of Contemporary China* 6, no. 16, (Nov. 1997): 435–589.

Chee, H. and C. West. *China: Mythos und Realität. Die Wahrheit über Geschäfte im Reich der Mitte,* trans. C. and M. Stock. Chichester: John Wiley & Sons, 2006.

'Chine: les enjeux de la mondialisation'. *Le Monde chinois* 9 (Winter 2006–7).

Close, P., D. Askew and Xu Xin. *The Beijing Olympiad. The Political Economy of a Sporting Mega-Event.* London and New York: Routledge, 2007.

Dayong, N. and X. Lan. 'International Historical Studies in PRC during the Post-WWII Period: New Perspectives and Limitation'. In *The Present and Future of Chinese Historiography* (Proceedings of Chinese Academy of Social Sciences/Associations of Chinese Historians Symposium, Beijing, 16 Sept. 2007): 73–85.

Eveno, P. *Histoire du journal Le Monde: 1944–2004.* Paris: Albin Michel, 2004.

Fan Hong. 'Innocence Lost: Child Athletes in China'. *Sport in Society* 7, no. 3, (2004): 338–54.

Fan Hong and Xiong Xiaozheng. 'Communist China: Sport, Politics and Diplomacy'. *The International Journal of the History of Sport* 19, nos. 2–3, (2002): 319–42.

Gavalda, E. and L. Rouvin. *La Chine face à la mondialisation.* Paris: L'Harmattan, 2007.

Howie, F.J.T. and C.E. Walter. *Privatizing China: The Rise and Fall of China's Stock Markets.* Chichester: John Wiley & Sons, 2003.

Jarvie, G. *Sport, Culture and Society.* London & New York: Routledge, 2006.

Kennedy, S., ed. *China Cross Talk. The American Debate Over China Policy since Normalization: A Reader.* Lanham, MD: Rowman & Littlefield, 2003.

Kirby, W.C. and N. Dayong. *China's Interaction with the World: Internationalization, Internalization and Externalization.* Henan: People's Press, 2007.

'Le devenir financier de la Chine'. *Revue d'économie financière* 77 (2005).

Lui, A. 'Looking Back at Tiananmen Square'. *Peace Review* 12, no. 1, (2000): 139–45.

Mar, P.C.M. and F.J. Richter. *China: Enabling a New Era of Changes,* Chichester: John Wiley & Sons, 2003.

Marteau, J.L. *Le secteur bancaire et les marchés financiers en Chine.* Paris: éd. Hermès, 2005.

Miles, J.A.R. *The Legacy of Tiananmen Square: China in Disarray.* Ann Arbor, MI: University of Michigan Press, 1996.

Necker, A.M. *La politique étrangère de la Chine populaire aux Nations Unies depuis 1989.* Paris: L'Harmattan, 2006.

Noir, V., D. Demonpion, S. Faure and A. Glaser. *Nicolas Sarkozy ou le destin de Brutus.* Paris: Denoël, 2005.

Peyrefitte, A. *Quand la Chine s'éveillera ... le monde tremblera.* Paris: Fayard, 1973.

Quansheng Zhao. *Interpreting Chinese Foreign Policy. The Micro-Macro Linkage Approach.* Oxford: Oxford University Press, 1996.

Rawnsley, G.D. and M.Y.T. Rawnsley. *Political Communication in Greater China: The Construction and Reflexion of Identity.* London and New York: Routledge, 2003.

Riordan, J. and Dong Jinxia, 'Chinese Women and Sport: Success, Sexuality and Suspicion'. *China Quaterly* 145 (1996): 130–52.

Riordan, J. and R.E. Jones. *Sport and Physical Education in China.* London: Taylor & Francis, 1999.

Ruffier, J. *Faut-il avoir peur des usines chinoises ? Compétitivité et pérennité de l'atelier du monde.* Paris: L'Harmattan, 2006.

Segal, G. *Openness and Foreign Policy Reform in Communist States.* London and New York: Routledge, 1992.

Spitaels, G. *Chine-USA, la Guerre aura-t-elle lieu?* Bruxelles: Editions Luc-Pire, 2007.

UERASFI (ed.). *La Chine: un colosse financier? Le système financier chinois à l'aube du XXIème siècle.* Paris: Vuibert, 2006.

Will, P.E. and M. Delmas-Marty, *La Chine et la démocratie. L'empire métamorphosé.* Paris: Fayard, 2007.

Zhang Xingxing. 'Current Status of PRC Studies'. In *The Present and Future of Chinese Historiography* (Proceedings of Chinese Academy of Social Sciences/Associations of Chinese Historians Symposium, Beijing, 16 Sept. 2007): 34–9.

Creative Tensions: 'Join in London' Meets 'Dancing Beijing' – The Cultural Power of the Olympics

Vassil Girginov

China can no longer be left to the sinologists. We all need to become China experts now, because China, and especially China's future, matters for all of us. [1]

Introduction

Peter Mandelson's words quoted above were addressed to an audience of business people but they succinctly capture the main challenge that China poses to UK sport.

The gist of this message is simple – we need to understand Chinese culture in order to better define who we are and to meaningfully engage in various enterprises. While the message may be straightforward, achieving it presents an uneasy task for the United Kingdom's sport community.

China's rising prominence in the world has attracted significant attention in domestic political, economic and academic circles. Think tanks as well as various political, economic and academic forums have been studying the impact of China's growing influence on the UK. This is quite extraordinary given that Beijing and London only exchanged ambassadors in 1972 and the first visit of a Chinese head of state to the UK was in 1999. What is more, some 200 years ago Emperor Qianlong turned down King George III's request that Lord Macartney be accepted as Britain's first ambassador to China. In his reply to the King on 3 October 1793, he wrote:

> [T]he Celestial Empire ruling all within the four seas, simply concentrates on carrying out the affairs of Government properly.... We have never valued ingenious articles, nor do we have the slightest need of your country's manufactures. Therefore, O King, as regards your request to send someone to remain at the capital, while it is not in harmony with the regulations of the Celestial Empire, we also feel very much that it is of no advantage to your country. [2]

Things could not be more different at the beginning of the twenty-first century: there are 24 joint agreements, memoranda of understanding and statements between China and Great Britain; 'all-round partnership' has become a buzzword and the two countries have exchanged eight diplomatic missions (five British and three Chinese). The UK is by far the largest European investor in the People's Republic of China (PRC), with 3,013 projects in 2001 worth US$9.62bn and a record high direct export to China reaching £3.3bn in 2006. Similarly, China puts the largest share of its investments in Europe into the British market, doubling them from 27 projects in 2006 to 52 projects in 2007 [3] and has more than 100 companies listed in the UK.

Recently, the China impact has become the focus of a series of Westminster hearings addressing a range of political, economic and cultural issues. In 2006, the Scottish Executive published a 'Scottish Strategy for Stronger Engagement with China', while the Smith Institute (2005) released an influential report entitled *China and Britain: The Potential Impact of China's Development.* [4] Sport has also been an integral part of cultural exchanges between the two countries and in 2005 was given prominence when John Steele, chief executive of UK Sport, accompanied Prime Minister Tony Blair on a sport-themed visit to Beijing.

The fact that China has contributed more to world economic growth since 2001 than the G7 countries put together provokes many commentators to promote the idea of a new Chinese economic imperialism. These claims tend to present economic achievements as floating above and detached from the value systems and cultural milieu within which they occur. [5] Economic success is primarily a moral enterprise. This is also true of success in sport. This is because every interaction that takes place in sport is by people who are making choices based on their values and beliefs. The moral values that underpin their behaviour originate in culture. While the link between economic success and national culture has been well documented, [6] there is a dearth of studies on the relationship between culture and national success and associated sport models. [7]

The aim of this article is to investigate the significance of the 'soft power' exerted by the cultural diplomacy of the 2008 Beijing Olympics on the British model of sport, the organization of the London 2012 games and the provision of sport studies within the higher education sector. In doing so, it responds to a challenge posed in 2005 by J.A. Mangan, who considers the 2008 Beijing Olympic Games 'simply a "down-payment" on a longer term investment' [8] and calls for a better understanding of the Chinese psyche and the significance of the games beyond sport. The investigation is organized into four interrelated parts. The first provides the context of the study by examining the Olympic cultural biographies of Britain and China and their interpretations of Olympic philosophy; the second looks at the impact of the 2008 Beijing Olympic Games on the British model of sport; the third outlines some of the challenges which the 2008 games present to the organizers of the 2012 London Olympics; finally, the implications of Sino-British cultural exchanges on sport studies in the UK are considered.

Olympic Cultural Biographies of Britain and China

To better understand the Olympic cultural biographies of Britain and China, we need initially to examine the nature of the Olympic project as a particular type of ideology. From its very inception in 1894, Olympic ideology was charged with an ambiguity in accommodating its common appeal for bettering the world with a process of recognition of different cultures. Behind the claims of Pierre de Coubertin's Olympism for universalism lies a logic of exclusion which, under various guises, remains largely unchanged today. It can be discovered at three levels – national cultures, class division and gender. [9]

The twenty-first-century Olympic ideology is not substantially different from what it used to be more than 100 years ago and, as John MacAloon rightly points out, 'there has been next to no progress made in the last decade in refining, deparochializing, and re-energizing Olympic ideology itself'. [10] A number of studies provide ample evidence for this claim with regard to the exclusive character of the Olympic programme, [11] women's under-representation in the Olympic movement [12] and the pressure exerted to transform the non-Western Olympic sport of judo along Western competitive lines. [13] Even for de Coubertin himself Greece's membership in the family of civilized West was far from fully established. As he remarked surprisingly after his first visit to Athens, he 'expected to find the Greeks reduced to orientalized Albanians'. [14]

Modern Olympism emerged in an increasingly materialist Western culture and advocated a 'transmission model' of culture that treats audiences as a residual category and places the explanatory responsibility on the International Olympic

Committee (IOC), which is the most important agency destined to spread the tenets of the project. Hence the source of value is not sought in the lived experiences of those engaging in cultural practices promoted by Olympism but is identified in the judgements of the IOC, which is supposedly equipped to judge. This reveals Olympic ideology as a set of ideas pertinent to the social needs of the West that emerged as a specific cultural product at the end of the nineteenth century in Europe. Similar to the Enlightenment, it represents a 'cultivating process' that relates civilization to culture and seeks to promote standardization and universalism with a strategy from above. As Smith notes, 'many of the associations between the culture and historically and socially specific logics of western societies were developed through the oppositions that emerged as result of encounters with other cultures'. He further argues that 'as a result, European societies could understand their conquest of the rest of the world as a cultivating process'. [15] This process is epitomized through the notion of the 'civilized man' who could exercise judgement concerning matters of aesthetics, morality and epistemology. Thus Pierre de Coubertin's Olympic Games have become a manifestation of the 'civilized sport' model towards which all nations should aspire to. It is precisely this implicit suggestion of Olympic ideology to which China has always refused to subscribe.

From a cultural perspective, the development of sport is a cultural and cognitive process. Sport must not only be organized in various forms but also be marked culturally as traditional or modern, professional or amateur. Borrowing from Arjun Appadurai's notion of the social life of things, [16] it is proposed that the differences between social history and cultural biography are in the temporality (short vs. long-term processes), the class identity (Olympic, 'Sport for All') and the social scales of sport (larger and local). For example, the Olympic cultural biography of China tells us much about what it means in society at a particular time, its rituals and symbols, the athletes' and public's perceptions, its role in forming national identity or its use by the state and individuals. At the end of the nineteenth century, the Western notions of physical education and sport did not have linguistic equivalence in China. The Chinese borrowed the Japanese word *taiiku* to construct their term *tiyu* (physical education, physical culture, sport) in order to translate Spencer's concept of physical education. Similarly, Song Ruhai introduced the concept of Olympism to the Chinese with the help of an ingenious transliterative device which renders its essence to 'I can compete! (*Wo neng bi ya*) [17] However, this does not mean that the idea of competition is alien to Chinese culture. On the contrary, Johan Huizinga argues that 'the agonistic principle plays a part in the development of Chinese civilization far more significant even than the *agon* in the Hellenic world'. [18]

It is also important to note that in constructing the cultural biography of traditional Chinese physical activities, such as martial arts, dragon boat races and wrestling, the West classes them not as sports but as religious festivals. Modernization is a buzzword characterizing the current sport policy discourse and practices both in Britain and China. However, the meaning attached to this concept is very different. Whereas in China modernization concerns largely the reconciliation of traditional and contemporary forms of sport through collective solidarity and community spirit, in Britain the same concept implies individualizing and 'responsibilizing'. These interpretations produce two very different policies and experiences in sport. The social history of the Olympics tells us a lot about the key factors shaping its structure, membership and financing over different periods. Susan Brownell discussed the social histories of sport in Britain and China and outlined the role of three key factors – parental attitudes, intellectualism and athleticism – that were at work but in different configurations. Interestingly in both countries citizenship has been constructed through a combination of religion and physical activities (games and martial art), but 'muscular Buddhism' in China preceded the ideology of muscular Christianity by at least 1,200 years. [19] While the social histories of sport in Britain and China are very different, the cultural biographies of both countries have many similarities.

China was a 'late-comer' to the Olympics and first competed at the 1932 Los Angeles games. In contrast, Britain was a founding member and a regular participant. However, China's absence from the games between 1959 and 1979 was in large measure due to the Western-dominated IOC. There were heated debates between the Chinese Olympic Committee (COC) and the IOC president Avery Brundage (USA) leading to China's withdrawal from the Olympic movement. The IOC member He Zhenliang's memoirs reveal previously little known information about the Chinese position at the time. In a letter to Brundage from 19 August 1958, Mr Dong, president of the COC, exposed his ignorance of Chinese history and international declarations about the status of Taiwan, condemned the American plot of creating 'two Chinas' and concluded: 'A man like you, who are staining the Olympic spirit and violating the Olympic Charter, has no qualifications whatsoever to be the IOC president. All who are faithful to the Olympic spirit will surely oppose your shameless acts.' [20]

China's response to Western imperialistic interests in sport during the Cold War period was to withdraw. This time, however, China is using the 2008 games to assert a different interpretation of Olympism. MacAloon, among others, questions the capacity of Olympic ideology to promote cross-cultural learning, wondering whether this is due to hypocrisy or a contradiction in ideology. Indeed, as he observes, 'recognizing that contemporary sport practice itself may become a barrier to cross-cultural learning requires not only the courage to stand up to powerful institutional interests, but first of all a thoughtful questioning of the "common sense" rhetoric that may conceal the contradiction in the first place'. [21]

In China's view the main means of challenging the Western rhetoric is through deploying the 'soft power' of culture. As the Minister of Culture, Sun Jiazheng, puts it, 'Cultural diplomacy, along with political diplomacy and economic diplomacy, are regarded as the three pillars of Chinese diplomacy'. The minister further elaborates that 'culture is soft but powerful … because its essence is like water. It can exert a subtle influence on people. … Under economic globalization, cultural exchange plays an increasingly important role in international relations.' [22]

The above vision of culture underpins the strategy of the Beijing Organizing Committee for the Games of the XXIX Olympiad (BOCOG). BOCOG's general goal is to host high-level Olympic Games with distinguishing features. Those distinguishing features

> refer to Chinese style, cultural splendour, contemporary spirits and mass participation. The Beijing Olympic Games will be a perfect occasion to fully display China's 5,000-year history and its resplendent culture, a grand ceremony that will gather athletes from all over the world and present diverse and brilliant cultures. The Beijing Olympic Games will fully express the common aspiration of the Chinese people to jointly seek peace, development and common progress together with the peoples of the world, and it will highlight the fact that the 1.3 billion Chinese people of 56 ethnic groups, along with 50 million overseas Chinese, are all most enthusiastic participants in the Beijing Olympic Games. [23]

It is worth noting the prominence given to history, tradition and cultural diversity in Chinese official public discourse.

The development of Olympism has been dominated by standardized recipes for fabrication including a charter, rules, protocol and promotional campaigns. Recently, the urge for standardization culminated into two new universal programmes – the Olympic Games Knowledge Transfer (OGKT) and the Olympic Games Image Protection (OGIP). British input in those initiatives has been instrumental. [24] These programmes not only codify various aspects of Olympic knowledge and images into standardized manuals and guiding principles but also formulate and enforce a system of property rights for their use. The Olympic growth expressed in various forms of commodification of Olympic ideology has not been unproblematic. Kopytoff's brilliant treatment of the cultural biographies of things and commodification process helps us to understand this issue: 'The counter drive to this onrush of commoditization is culture. In the sense that commoditization homogenizes value, while the essence of culture is discrimination, excessive commoditization is anti-cultural.' [25]

China has always questioned the Enlightenment mentality of the West rooted in anthropocentrism and scientific rationality and driven by aggressive individualism. Weiming even maintains that 'the enlightenment can hardly provide guidance for human survival, let along human flourishing'. [26] His modern interpretation of Confucianism succinctly captures the essence of China's alternative reading of Olympic ideology with its insistence on universalism and standardization:

> The Confucius way of life embodies self, community, nature and heaven in an ethic of care and responsibility, is the Confucius idea of humanity ... although culture diversity is taken for granted, the Confucian quest for *harmony without uniformity* is predicated on the belief that great unity through education of global citizenship is not only desirable but realizable. [27]

China's vision for the 2008 Beijing games is very different from the two previous Asian hosts of the Olympics: the 1964 Tokyo Games helped Japan regain its place among the world's important nations, while the 1988 Seoul Games were used to encourage Korea's transition from a military dictatorship to a modern democratic nation. This compels us to pay attention to Beijing's proclaimed intent ostensibly to reinterpret the fundamental Olympic principles by challenging the established Western ontology and norms of sport and 'to promote the harmonization of world civilizations'.

The above goal is clearly hinted at in China's President Jiang Zemin's letter to the IOC in 2000 presenting Beijing's bid for the 2008 Olympic Games:

> It will be of extremely great significance to promoting and carrying out the Olympic spirit in China and across the world and to facilitating the cultural exchanges and convergence between East and West if the Games of the XXIX Olympiad are held in China, a rapidly developing country with a long-standing civilization and 22 percent of the world's population. [28]

Thus the three major themes of the Beijing games are 'Green Olympics', 'High-Tech Olympics' and 'Humanistic Olympics'. The concept of 'Humanistic Olympics' is a creative idea seeking to redefine humanism as a core Chinese cultural value. The wider aim of this concept is both to construct a moral order to counterbalance the materialist tendencies in China's rapid march to modernization and to produce an alternative to the excessive commercialization and 'spectacularization' of the games. The main difference between the British and Chinese Olympic cultural biographies would appear to be in the interpretation of Olympic ideology and its claims for universality in particular. Table 1 summarizes some key selective elements of British and Chinese Olympic cultural biographies. If China's involvement in the Olympic movement was in some measure a result of China seeing itself through the eyes of the West, the 2008 Beijing games will challenge the West to abandon the occidental interpretation of Olympism and to embrace the oriental view. This is a cultural challenge.

The 2008 Beijing Olympics and the British Model of Sport

It is beyond the scope of this study to undertake a comprehensive analysis of the impact of the 2008 Beijing games on the British sport model. A similar task requires a complex longitudinal study. Therefore the link is to be sought at ideological and policy levels, as there is sufficient evidence for the ideological direction and main policy priorities of both countries. Three interrelated factors deserve consideration: (1) China's performance as a host country in terms of an effective organization of the games and the success of its sport model; (2) the interplay between global and local which Olympics performances exemplify; and (3) ethics, concerning the commercialization and mediatization of Olympic sport largely driven by the West. These three factors are briefly examined below.

Most commentators rightly see a link between Beijing's readiness to host the Olympics and China's sport model. The latter is analysed in detail by Hong, Wu and Xiong [29] and has been systematically studied by the UK sport authorities. [30] UK

Table 1 Selected key elements of Olympic cultural biographies of Britain and China

Olympic cultural biography	Britain	China
Involvement with modern Olympic movement	English public-school model of sport has significant conceptual/ideological impact on de Coubertin's visions Two IOC founding members plus 3 new appointments in 1897, 1901 and 1906	1894 Coubertin and the Greek prince issue an invitation to Qing Dynasty rulers through the French Embassy in China to send athletes to the first modern Olympiad, to be held in Athens in 1896, but the Qing government didn't reply. 1947 – first IOC member
Participation in the games	Every modern games since 1896	First in 1932 to 1952 and from 1980 to day
Meaning of Olympism	1920 – calls from 45 BOA senior members for complete withdrawal from Olympic movement due to its professionalization 1948 – lack of interest among general public 2008 – general public largely sceptical about the benefits of London 2012 Games	1920 – Olympism first translated as 'I can compete' 1907 – Tianjin YMCA congress sets 3 strategic objectives to: • win an Olympic medal • win a team medal • host an Olympic Games 2008 – all country support for the Beijing games
Construction of Olympic cultural biographies	Through own/occidental sport history publications	Until 1980s mainly through Western accounts
Use of Olympic sport	Nation-building and prestige Promoting own values Instrument of social policy	Nation-building and prestige Promoting own values Instrument of social policy
Goals for Beijing 2008	To be the most successful sporting nation	To be the most successful sporting nation

Sport has developed a good collaborative partnership with the China General Administration of Sport and in April 2007 signed a second memorandum of understanding. This document envisages cooperation and exchanges in the areas of sports science and medicine, talent and coach development and drug-free sport. However, as the impact of the Eastern European model of sport (on which the Chinese is largely modelled) on British gymnastics shows, cooperation entails not only benefits but conflicts as well. [31] In Beijing, British and Chinese badminton players will compete for superiority in a direct clash. The strategic plan of the Badminton Association of England (2005) envisages five gold and ten other medals from seven major international tournaments including the Olympics. [32] To this effect, a top Chinese expert was employed as a national coach. China, however, has no lesser ambitions as currently four Chinese men and women are in the top five in the world.

The second factor concerns the interplay between global and local. Peter Taylor's notion of a three-tier model of the world political system allows us to examine the relationship between British performance at the 2008 Beijing games and sports development nationally. [33] In Taylor's model, the three scales represent a national scale of ideology, a local scale of experience and a global scale of reality. The scale of experience is interpreted as the scale at which people live their daily lives, which encompasses all basic needs and interactions. In contrast, the scale of reality refers to the concrete world economy, the one that 'really matters', which incorporates the other scales. The scale of ideology represents a partial view of the world aiming at channelling public perceptions and support in favour of particular political projects. The interplay between these three scales involves an interpretation of the reality of the world system through nation-centred ideologies, which produce contrasting world-views and political practices. In other words, what separates the day-to-day practices of British athletes (the scale of experience), from the competitive world of the Olympic Games (the scale of reality) is the scale of ideology, that is, the way elite sport is constructed at national level.

British sporting ideology has evolved over the years, but in all its manifestations the international importance of elite sport has always been present. This is evidenced in an influential government policy document, *The Value of Sport* (1999), where the international value of sport is put even before its social, economic and environmental value. More specifically the document promotes the view that 'successful sports people are part of our country's history and folklore. The sense of pride and the positive "boost" that people feel when our teams and individuals achieve international success cannot be quantified but they are real'. [34] It is worth noting that differences in political ideologies in Britain (e.g., the Conservative from the mid-1990s and Labour of the 2000s) never resulted in significant shifts in sport ideology with its dual emphasis on school and elite sport. [35]

The day-to-day practices in which British athletes and officials are engaged, however, are not sustained locally. The British government policy document *A Sporting Future for All* amply illustrates the point: 'The success or failure in achieving milestone targets in performance plans will be an important factor in deciding future levels of funding'. [36] The impact of this policy is real and has been hardly felt at the level of experience. For example, when the British swimming team failed to deliver medals from the 2000 Sydney Games its funding was cut by £1,3000,000. The same occurred to UK Athletics after the 2004 Athens games for 'failing' to deliver its target of five to seven medals by 'only' winning three gold medals. UK Athletics' punishment was double – a reduction in funding of some £1,100,000 for its elite athletes for the period 2005–9 and a further cut by Sport England for 2005–6 developmental programmes – from £2 million to £1.35 million. The key point is that reduced levels of funding impact directly on athletes' and organizations' potential, which reinforces the view that winning international competitions is critical for sustaining sports development locally. A similar conclusion provides justification for even greater government intervention in sport, which undermines the autonomy of the UK voluntary sport sector in general.

The third factor that links the 2008 Beijing Olympics to British sport concerns the ethics of sport. The overriding motive for foreign companies to invest in China's economy, through an association with the Olympic Games, is to gain access to its large domestic market. This is particularly pertinent to the IOC's top sponsors, which include companies such as Coca-Cola and McDonald's. Dickson and Schofield express concern that the increased presence of these two companies in particular on China's market is going to intensify China's already looming health crisis or what they called 'globesity' – spreading the Western epidemic eastwards. [37] Obesity costs the UK economy £2 billion a year. [38] As these authors maintain, 'the argument put forward here is that the 2008 Olympics will assist a number of companies to market to the Chinese population calorie-dense food and beverages as well as devices associated with reduced energy expenditure'. [39] Moreover, each McDonald's restaurant sends 100 tonnes of waste to landfill each year. With its 800-strong China network and plans for opening some 100 new restaurants each year, this Olympic sponsor is set to make a rather dubious contribution to China's development. [40]

The above concerns become an issue for British sport authorities because they have a duty to protect the integrity of sport. What is more, the real negative effects of the global commercial presence in China will become evident in time for the 2012 London Olympics and will inevitably require the London Organising Committee of the Olympic Games (LOCOG) to address them. The next section examines the implications of the 2008 Beijing Olympics on the 2012 London games.

'Join in London' Meets 'Dancing Beijing'

There is little doubt that China will raise the bar for organizing the Olympic Games to a new height. We should also have little doubt that London organizers will be well prepared to meet this challenge. BOCOG and LOCOG have been working closely together and a number of British experts perform key roles within the Beijing games, acquiring valuable knowledge and skills to be applied four years later in London. However, the real test for London 2012 will be on two fronts – (1) to deliver its vision for an inclusive Olympics, thus living up to the image of Beijing's 'People's Games', and (2) to mobilize the country's support.

The 'Dancing Beijing' and 'Join in London' are the official emblems of the 2008 and 2012 Olympic Games. Both emblems represent core cultural values of two civilizations. The 'Dancing Beijing' is a static image, a seal of identity, which epitomizes the Eastern way of thinking and conveys the unique cultural quality, elegance and credibility of Chinese civilization. 'Join in London' is a dynamic image that has been designed to inspire youth and reflects the multicultural nature of British society. It holds a promise to build a legacy from the games by increasing participation in sport and boosting community sport across the country. Join in London's design cost £400,000, and was met with massive public disapproval, triggered early-day motions from MPs, an online petition with 49,000 signatures to force the LOCOG to remove the logo [41] and the hasty withdrawal of a promotional video that caused seizures among epilepsy sufferers. This was a rather disappointing start for a successful Olympic bid centred on the notion of inclusion. In contrast to President Jiang Zemin's message emphasising the harmony of civilizations, in his letter to the IOC ON 11 July 2003, the British Prime Minister Tony Blair projected his government's key aspiration for social inclusion: 'The British Government also wants to use this unique festival of sport as a catalyst to promote sports participation and physical activity in all communities throughout the celebration through the fundamental principles of the Olympic movement of respect, friendship and fair play.' [42] The chairman of LOCOG, Lord (Seb) Coe, echoes this agenda: 'The vision of the London 2012 Olympics is to stage inspirational games that capture the imagination of young people around the world and leave a lasting legacy.' [43] To illustrate this vision the jagged 2012 logo, according to its designers Wolf Ollins, projects ahead into the future: 'The audience you're addressing are kids between the ages of, say, eight and 16, and in a few years' time they're going to be 12 to 20. Those kids look at the web all the time, and what they look at is things that move.' [44]

Delivering social inclusion both as a political and sport-specific project has already proved an insurmountable hurdle. Despite ten years of Labour government, the gap between poor and rich is widening and poverty continues to grow. [45] To expect the 2012 Olympics to redress this situation would be naïve. Rowe, Adams and Beasley's 2004 analysis of sport participation makes this point plain clear:

> [S]ports participation rates in England remained broadly unchanged over the last two decades or so and that sport in England has continued to be characterized by considerable social inequalities. The 1980s and 1990s saw the development of the recreation management profession, an increase in sports development officers, an expansion of local authority leisure departments, a number of national campaigns, a national junior sport development programme, improved support and training for volunteers and a number of coaching initiatives. And still participation rates did not go up or inequalities become narrowed. [46]

The vision of London 2012 sets an admirable goal, but successful Olympic legacies can be achieved by adopting a longitudinal, multi-agency and historic approach to understanding the processes that contribute to their sustainability over time. Sofield and Li's study on *Gokh Chin*, an 800-year-old Chinese festival, vividly illustrates this point. [47] The construction of Olympic legacy is primarily a matter of culture as it concerns organizers' attitudes to time. As the views of Coe and Ollins demonstrate, British culture is forward-looking and tends to view time as racing by (time as sequence). A similar attitude to time is more likely to adopt a short-term orientation and to emphasize quick results. [48] In contrast, Chinese culture is more backward-looking in that it takes account of the past in order to project the future. As a result the Chinese think of time as recurrent and generative (time as synchronization), and they are likely to develop more long-term strategies.

Delivering a lasting legacy may prove even harder in the current policy climate where funding for grassroots sports development opportunities is being clawed back in order to provide further support for the country's elite athletes. LOCOG's vision has been questioned by the chair of Sport England, [49] Derek Mapp, who asks how such significant cuts in funding 'can be squared with the clear commitments the Government has already made about the wider benefits the Games will bring'. [50] To make the point even more explicit, he adds:

> Our commitment for the 2012 [Olympic] Games is unquestioned and we know the Government has had to make tough choices. However, the decision to divert a further £55.9 million of Sport England's share of lottery income between 2009 and 2012 to fund the 2012 Olympic/Paralympic Games is a cut too far and seriously endangers the creation of a sporting legacy from the 2012 Games. [51]

The capacity of LOCOG to mobilize political and social support needed to deliver its visions has been seriously undermined by two key factors: government involvement and public opinion. This is in sharp contrast with China's *jugo tizhi* ('whole-country support for the elite sport system') policy. Jiang Zemin, the general secretary of the China Communist Party, articulates it clearly: 'The success of American sport depends on its economic power; the success of Russian sport depends on its rich resources and experience of training elite athletes; the success of Chinese sport depends on *jugo tizhi*.' [52]

Historically the British government has always been reluctant to come up with support for the Olympics. An excerpt from the 1948 London Olympic Games Report illustrates this point:

> [I]n England we have hitherto been deprived of one form of assistance which is common, I believe, to the rest of the world; for we never have been able to count upon any Financial contribution from the public funds through the channels of Official Administration nor have we been able to avail ourselves of the patronage of the Government in raising money, by any officially supported scheme, for these objects. [53]

The long deliberations of British government before committing to the 2012 Olympic project suggests that some 60 years later little has changed. A recent *Guardian* headline reads: 'Before the end of next January, a foot-dragging government has to decide whether to throw its weight behind London's bid for the Olympic Games of 2012'. [54] Although British Prime Minister Blair's personal lobbying among the IOC members proved instrumental for winning the bid, he left the government to deal with a spiralling cost of the games and a growing public disillusionment. [55]

The Olympic enthusiasm of the British public has been waning. As the latest YouGov survey for the TaxPayers' Alliance shows, 44 per cent of people think the stated £9.35 billion cost would be put to better use in schools and hospitals and only 28 per cent believe that the benefits of the London games will outweigh the financial risks. Interestingly, 38 per cent of the respondents expect that the budget would soar to at least £15 billion. Matthew Elliott, chief executive of the TaxPayers' Alliance, sums the point: 'This is the first concrete evidence that the British public has fallen out of love with the 2012 Olympics.' [56]

The legacy and public support are two important issues for LOCOG also because the IOC will scrutinize the Beijing games to produce the first comprehensive Olympic Games impact study. Previous studies have concentrated on the look of the games and their economic impact and paid only cursorily attention to social legacies. The challenge for London 2012 will be not only to match but to improve on the 2008 Beijing results. Outdoing the *jugo tizhi* policy both at rhetorical and practical level will be extremely hard.

The 2008 Beijing Olympics and Sport Studies in the UK

The link between an Olympic Games and a subject area such as sport studies is multifaceted and difficult to pin down in a neat description. As far as it can be ascertained no similar studies exist. *The Contribution Of The Higher Education Sector To The Sydney 2000 Olympic Games* [57] represents an encouraging first step in analysing the role of the higher and tertiary education in staging the Olympics. A key finding of this report suggests that despite some benefits for the academic community in Australia, the games largely failed on two counts – to produce educational innovations and to bring educationalists together. However, we can begin to understand the relationship between the Olympics and academia by placing it in the wider economic context and by examining the epistemological and ontological challenges that the 2008 Beijing games pose to sport studies in the UK. Higher education (HE) is a lucrative export industry for the UK. In a speech at the Academy of Social Sciences in Beijing, the Chancellor of the Exchequer clearly acknowledged this: 'In just five years the value of British education as an export has almost doubled, from £6.5 billion to £10.3 billion. … Indeed, I believe that if we continue to make the right decisions, by 2020 education exports could contribute over £20 billion a year to the UK economy.' [58] At present there are 330,080 foreign students in Britain, of which some 51,000 are Chinese, accounting for almost one in six overseas students. International students bring in £3.6 billion, of which £2 billion is from fees. The economic impact of higher education institutions in 2003–4 had a total output of just over £45 billion. [59] Education and education-related services are the UK's fastest-growing export earner and have already eclipsed food, tobacco, drink, insurance, ships and aircraft. China's potential to contribute to the UK HE sector is significant, as it aims to have 15 million students in higher education by 2007, which only represents around 15 per cent of the relevant age cohort.

The Beijing Olympics have served as a catalyst for enrolling hundreds of Chinese students on sport- and Olympic-related courses in the UK. The 2012 London Olympics will further stimulate the interest in this subject area. With growth, however, come issues of quality, standards of provision and the need for innovation and creativity. Recently concerns have been raised that economic considerations are taking over the academic integrity of some British HE institutions [60] in their policies towards Chinese students. The UK higher institutions, and the area of sport studies in particular, don't have to lower their admission or assessment criteria to meet revenue targets. Instead, we need to better understand the ontological and epistemological premises on which the study of sport in both countries is based, and how those differences can be creatively used to advance knowledge. This is a cultural challenge.

The 2008 Beijing games will help the realization that the Chinese understanding of physical culture is based on an approach to studying physical education and sport as a complex social, educational and political process. It is deeply rooted in Confucianism with its emphasis on the correct observation of human relationships within a hierarchically-oriented society. [61] Five core Chinese cultural characteristics facilitate this process: emphasis on perception of the concrete; non-development of abstract thought; emphasis on particulars not universals; practicality as central focus; and concern for reconciliation, harmony and balance. [62] The widely held perception within UK academia of Chinese students as mechanical or rote learners is a myth which has been persuasively dispelled by Chan [63] among others. Building on a range of Western and Eastern studies, she demonstrates that learning is a question of style and that far from being mechanical learners Chinese students use sophisticated decomposition and deep-learning strategies. Chinese educational culture requires a substantial period of imitation before creativity can be contemplated. British sport lecturers therefore should not be discouraged when their Chinese students memorize texts. This is the first step in the learning process, which enables them to attach meaning to the material. Delza (1967) captured neatly the essence of Chinese-style learning by noting that in practising the fixed forms of Taichichuan, 'although this composition is not an original for anyone, the participator, in re-enacting the structure, creates it anew, so to speak, and is transformed by it'. [64]

Chinese insistence on harmony, family relationships and self-effacement can be discerned in the above approach to studying physical culture, which is in contrast with Anglo-Saxon personal and private traditions in sport. As the English historian Richard Holt points out:

> The British amateur tradition has worked against the idea of *studying* sport. ... Physical culture as a discipline was marginalized in terms of the wider educational and social development of the nation. The British *played*, the Germans drilled; sport was supposed to be moral and spontaneous. To this day the term 'science' seems to strike the wrong note – although, increasingly, physical educators tend to see sport in such terms. [65]

Interestingly, after the end of the Cold War, which provided impetus to China's openness, the concept of 'physical culture' has been gaining currency in the West. Similarly to the Chinese who introduced new terms to describe Western concepts of sport and physical education, David Kirk documents the reverse process of the disappearance of the term physical culture from the lexicon of the English-speaking world. He proposes the recovery of a notion of physical culture which implies that 'systems of exercise were more than mere movements, but instead were embedded in beliefs, knowledge and broader individual and social practices'. [66] The main advantage of reconstructing this notion through a relational analysis, according to Kirk, lies precisely in its potential to reveal complexity. Furthermore, it would provide a measure of continuity in discussions of the relationships between past and contemporary forms of physical activity. Kirk's argument lends support for the historical and process-oriented approach to a sustainable legacy established earlier.

From an ontological point of view, the appeal of the 2008 Beijing 'Humanistic Olympics' for harmony of civilizations goes well beyond the call for peace and international understanding and has far-reaching implications. At stake is the ultimate source of Olympic wealth, the intellectual property rights. These were formalized by the IOC only in the 1980s to protect its economic interests. The Olympic Games is the most expensive cultural commodity in the world: the cost of the 2008 Beijing broadcasting and sponsorship rights exceeds $3.5 billion. [67] Property rights, writes Weimer, 'are relations among people concerning the use of things', and 'property rights systems, which include the rights themselves and formal and informal institutions that create them, structure economic transactions, including decisions concerning the exchange and accumulation of physical, human and intellectual capital'. [68]

The critical question becomes who really owns the Olympic idea and how should the profits it generates be allocated. The Chinese approach to creativity based upon imitation is at odds with the Western idea of intellectual property rights. For example, Chinese culture does not emphasize attribution of a cited text, as this is usually considered as a route to achieve competency in writing. The new digital age, which is central to the 2012 London Olympics communication and economic strategy, creates a conjuncture where the notion of 'intellectual property' has increasingly been questioned. What is proposed instead is the idea of 'intellectual value'. [69] Esther Dyson suggests that in the new economy of ideas dominated by the Internet, what really matters is not the content (information and images) but the process and the relationship which this content generates through follow-up services and other activities. The gist of this argument is that most information is not unique and that creativity is a mixture of common routines and innovative spurts. As Chris Shei maintains,

> to claim 100 per cent text ownership is to claim 5 per cent ownership of the library, 5 per cent ownership of published books and journals, 5 per cent ownership of daily-read newspapers, 5 per cent ownership of language in other people's brain, and so on. In other word, reuse of text is the norm of human communication. [70]

The study of 2008 Beijing Olympic Games already features prominently in the research plans of a number of British scholars. It is hoped that research will interrogate the issue of exclusivity, offered by the IOC to broadcasters and sponsors and the ownership of Olympic idea.

Join in London' meets 'Dancing Beijing' – the Cultural Power of the Olympics

The 'Dancing Beijing' and 'Join in London' logos symbolize a Western and an Eastern civilization which we distinguish by their attitudes to other people, time, activities and natural environment. In concluding this study, Samuel Hungtington's argument raised in *The Clash of Civilizations* is recalled: 'In the politics of civilizations, the peoples and governments of non-Western civilizations no longer remain the objects of history as targets of Western colonialism but join the West as movers and shapers of history.' [71] For a long time British culture and its sport model have been responsible for promoting a moral and structural order in world sport based on Western values and beliefs. This order is no longer sustainable. MacAloon's 1992 examination of the link between science, Olympism and intercultural relations criticized the positivist claims of Western European science: 'It does not now nor has it ever transcended cultural space and time to the degree it claims. Its ontology, like the essentialist internationalism that follows from it, is only one among many ontologies organizing the experiences of the people of the world today.' [72] The British sport community has to accept this realization if it sincerely subscribes to the lofty Olympic principles. China, too, has to make adjustments. There is no need to insist on the false dichotomy between Western function and Eastern essence as these are mutually constructive and complementary. This entails writing and rewriting the two countries' Olympic cultural biographies as this time they are likely to be constructed from a very different vantage point. To what extent the 2012 London games' cultural biography will be constructed through Asian lenses represents a challenging research and educational issue.

As demonstrated, the 2008 Beijing games are going to exacerbate the trend for further centralization and state intervention in British sport. This will undermine the long-established amateur tradition and autonomy of sport governing bodies. This trend poses also an important ethical challenge for London 2012: can the Olympic Games deliver the purported benefits to everyone and keep developing a highly competitive, commercialized and undemocratic international elite sport system? This question is particularly potent for the LOCOG as it has to reconcile its present-future cultural orientation entailing short-term results (the lifespan of an Olympic organizing committee is eight years) with its long-term visions requiring a sustainable government commitment and public support, both of which are far from certain.

Indeed, there are important lessons to be learned from Beijing 2008 and China in general. There are merits in Chinese learning culture and approach to creativity. Under the slogan 'linking up with the international track', learning from and imitating the West has become an official policy in China since 1987. As Wang [73] elaborates, this is manifested through three interrelated discourses – political, public and academic. The moral of this policy is that the Chinese clearly differentiate between different types of international norms and that they are more open to norms in the economic and technical realms than to those governing political and military matters and social sciences. This is because, as Wang argues, 'most Chinese reformers today seem to believe in learning Western functions while preserving Chinese essence'. [74] This is an example for reconciliation of different values.

Peter Mandelson is right in saying that we all have to become China experts. This holds true for politicians, sport administrators and academics. The remarks of Tessa Jowell, former Secretary of State for Culture, Media and Sport and now Minister for the Olympics, at the NESTA Conference ('Making Innovation Flourish') are a proof that we still have a long way to go. Drawing on Adam Smith's economic teaching of 200 years ago, that trade means wealth, Jowell delivered an enlightening message to her audience:

> My visit to China just a few weeks ago showed me just how much we could benefit from positioning ourselves; not in competition, but in a complementary way with China. That focus on commercialization and *the Chinese education system's historic failure to encourage creativity* means that there is an innovation gap. The potential is there for *our creative industries to add value.* [75]

Similar political messages only hinder our understanding of Chinese culture. Indeed, Chinese education is creative and as values represent differences they cannot simply be added, as Jowell suggests; they can only be reconciled. This entails accepting China's position.

As Robert Kagan writes in 'The Illusion of "Managing" China', 'Yes, the Chinese want the prosperity that comes from integration in the global economy, but might they believe, as the Japanese did a century ago, that the purpose of getting rich is not to join the international system but to change it?' In answering this question he asserts that 'we need to understand that the nature of China's rise will be determined largely by the Chinese and not by us'. [76] Indeed, the wisdom of Lao-tsu, the founder of Taoism, bears forcefully on the 2012 London Olympic Games and British sport: 'The way to control the new is to go along with it and to master it through adaptation.' [77]

Notes

[1] Peter Mandelson, 48 Group Club Icebreaker Lecture, London, 12 Oct. 2004, 1, available on-line at hppt://ec.europa/commission_barroso/mandelson/speeches_articles/sppm002_en.htm, accessed 18 June 2007.

[2] Cited in ibid.

[3] Source: China-British Business Council, 'China's Economy: Key Developments, Trends & Pointers', 10 July 2007, available online at www.cbbc.org/the_review/trade_figures.html, accessed 5 Sept. 2007.

[4] De Burgh, *China and Britain.*

[5] See for example, Chow, *The Chinese Economy*; Lardy, *China in the World Economy.*

[6] For example, see Hampden-Turner and Trompenaars, *The Seven Cultures of Capitalism* and Hampden-Turner and Trompenaars, *Building Cross-cultural Competence.*

[7] One noticeable exception is the PMP and Loughborough University Report *Studies on Education and Sport, Sport and Multiculturalism.*

[8] Mangan, 'Epilogue', 1196.

[9] For an extended discussion on the relationship between Olympic ideology and multi-culturalism see Girginov, 'Does One-world Olympic Ideology Lead to Multiculturalism?'.

[10] MacAloon, 'Sponsorship Policy and Olympic Ideology', 73.

[11] Landry, 'The Olympic Games and Competitive Sport'; Parry, 'Sport, Universals and Multiculturalism'.

[12] Hargreaves, *Sporting Females: Critical Issues*; Henry et al., *Women, Leadership and the Olympic Movement.*

[13] Villamon et al., 'Reflexive Modernisation and the Disembedding of Judo'.

[14] Coubertin, *Un Campagne de 21 ans*, 112–13.

[15] Smith , *Culture*, 6.

[16] Appadurai, *The Social Life of Things.*

[17] Cited in Moris, 'I Can Compete!', 545.

[18] Huizinga, *Homo Ludens*, 55.

[19] Brownwell, 'Sports in Britain and China, 1850–1920'.

[20] Cited in Brownell, 'Globalization is not a Dinner Party', 12–13.

[21] MacAloon, 'Intercultural Education and Olympic Sport', 15.

[22] Cited in Hilton, 'Culture and Cultural Power', 53–4.

[23] Cited in the BOCOG website, http://en.beijing2008.cn/bocog/concepts/index.shtml, accessed 25 Sept. 2007.

[24] London is home to the IOC Olympic Television Archive Bureau and Getty Images, both of which are critical to promoting the 'look of the games' and for standardization of Olympic images.

[25] Kopytoff, 'The Cultural Biography of Things', 73.

[26] Tu Weiming, 'Toward a Dialogical Civilization', 40.

[27] Ibid., 42 (emphasis added).

[28] Cited in Xin Xu, 'Modernizing China in the Olympic Spotlight', 96.

[29] Fan Hong et al.,. 'Beijing Ambitions'.

[30] For example, see Shibly, 'Predicting the Performance of China'.

[31] Girginov and Sandanski, 'From Participants to Competitors'.

[32] Badminton Association of England, *Whole Sport Plan Strategy.*

[33] Taylor's model has been used in the study cited in note 31.

[34] Sport England, *The Value of Sport*, 10–11.

[35] For an extended discussion on this issue see Green 'National Sport Governing Bodies in Sports Development'.

[36] DCMS, *A Sporting Future for All*, 44.

[37] Dickson and Schofield, 'Globalisation and Globesity'.

[38] Vlad, 'Obesity Cost UK Economy £2billion a Year'.

[39] Dickson and Schofield, 'Globalisation and Globesity', 170.

[40] BBC News 24, 19 Sept. 2007, available online at http://news.bbc.co.uk/1/hi/england/south_yorkshire/7002100.stm , accessed 19 Sept. 2007.

[41] The petition is online at http://www.gopetition.co.uk/petitions/change-the-london-2012-logo.html.

[42] British Olympic Association, 'Tony Blair letter to IOC', 11 July 2003, available online at http://www.olympics.org.uk/contentpage.aspx?no=268, accessed 9 Sept. 2007.

[43] Seb Coe, cited at www.london2012.com, accessed 1 Sept, 2007.

[44] Wolf Ollins, quoted in *Metro*, available online at http://www.metro.co.uk/news/article.html?in_article_id=51690&in_page_id=34&expand=true, accessed 1 Sept. 2007.

[45] For an excellent treatment on sport and exclusion see Collins, *Sport and Social Exclusion*.

[46] Rowe *et al.*, 'Driving up Participation in Sport', 12.

[47] Sofield and Fung Li, 'Historical Methodology and Sustainability'.

[48] Hampden-Turner and Trompenaars, *Building Cross-cultural Competence*, and Morden, 'Models of National Cultures'.

[49] Sport England is charged by the government with the responsibility of being the main coordinating agency for delivering the Olympic vision.

[50] Cited in Sport England, Online document (2007), available at www.sportengland.org.uk, accessed 13 Sept. 2007.

[51] Ibid.

[52] Fan Hong *et al.*, 'Beijing Ambitions', 513.

[53] British Olympic Association, *The 1948 London Olympic Games Report*, 388.

[54] *The Guardian*, July 7 2005.

[55] The words of two senior IOC members testify to that: 'This is down to Tony Blair. If he hadn't come here I'd say that six to eight votes would have been lost and London would not be sitting here today (as) winners' (Patrick Hickey, Ireland); and 'You should get down on your hands and knees and thank your prime minister' (Dick Pound, Canada). However, the government was left to deal with the spiralling cost of the games and a growing public disillusionment. (John Goodbody, 'Tony Blair's Sporting Legacy Will Never be Forgotten', *Times* (Lonodn), 9 May 2007, available online at http://www.timesonline.co.uk/tol/sport/london_2012/article 1768660.ece, accessed 13 Sept. 2007.

[56] Daniel Bentley, 'Poll Blasts Olympic Costs', *London 2012 News*, available online at http://www.sportinglife.com/london2012/news/story_get.cgi?STORY_NAME=others/07/09/11/manual_080011.html, accessed 27 Sept. 2007.

[57] Cashman and Toohey, *The Contribution of the Higher Education Sector To The Sydney 2000 Olympic Games*.

[58] UK Treasury Committee, cited in 'Impact of China on the World and UK Economy – Memorandum from Universities UK', available at www.universitiesuk.ac.uk/parliament/showEvidence.asp?id= 26, accessed on 1 Oct. 2007.

[59] Diana Warwick (Universities UK Chief Executive), 'The Economic Impact of Higher Education Institutions', House of Lords debate on the economic impact of higher education institutions, 19 April 2007, available online at http://www.universitiesuk.ac.uk/speeches/show.asp?sp=74, accessed 30 Sept. 2007.

[60] For example, see 'Chinese Students Oust UK Pupils from Top Universities', *Sunday Times*, 13 May 2007.

[61] Oh, 'Understanding Managerial Values and Behaviour among the Gang of Four'.

[62] O. Nakarama, cited in Redding, *The Spirit of Chinese Capitalism*.

[63] Chan, 'The Chinese Learner'.

[64] Cited in Shei, 'Plagiarism, Chinese Learners and Western Convention', 3.

[65] Holt, 'Sport and History', 8.

[66] Kirk, 'Physical Culture, Physical Education and Relational Analysis', 65.

[67] BOCOG 'Strategic Plan', available online at http://en.beijing2008.cn/culture/, accessed 11 Sept. 2007.

[68] Weimer, *The Political Economy of Property Rights*, 1.

[69] Dyson, E., 'Intellectual Value', *Wired* 3 (1995), available online at http://www.wired.com/wired/archive/3.07/dyson.html, accessed 18 Sept. 2007.

[70] Shei, C. 'Plagiarism, Chinese Learners and Western Convention', *Online document* available at http://www.northumbrialearning.co.uk/newsletters/issue1/Chinese%20Learners%20and%20Plagiarism%20-%20Issue%201.pdf, retrieved 20 September 2007.

[71] Huntington, 'The Clash of Civilizations?', 23.

[72] McAloon, 'Sport, Science and Intercultural Relations', 14–15.
[73] Wang, '"Linking up with the International Track": What's in a Slogan?'
[74] Ibid., 22.
[75] Tessa Jowell, speech at NESTA Conference, 'Making Innovation Flourish', 26 Oct. 2006, available online at http://www.culture.gov.uk/what_we_do/Creative_industries/QuickLinks/minister_speeches/?expand=Tessa_Jowell&extra=true, accessed 30 Sept. 2007 (emphasis added).
[76] R. Kagan, 'The Illusion of "Managing" China, *Washington Post*, 15 May 2005, B07.
[77] Fan Hong and Tan Hua, 'Sport in China', 207.

References

Appadurai, Arjun. *The Social Life of Things. Commodities in Cultural Perspective.* Cambridge: Cambridge University Press, 1986.

Badminton Association of England.*Whole Sport Plan Strategy for Badminton in England 2005–2009.* Milton Keynes: BAE, 2005.

British Olympic Association *The 1948 London Olympic Games Report.* London: BOA, 1948.

Brownwell, S. 'Sports in Britain and China, 1850–1920: An Explanatory Overview'. *The International Journal of the History of Sport* 8, no. 2, (1991): 284–90.

——. 'Globalization is not a Dinner Party: He Zhenliang and China's 30-Year Struggle for Recognition by the International Olympic Committee'. Paper presented to Conference on Globalization and Sport in Historical Context, University of California, San Diego, March 2005.

Cashman, R. and K. Toohey. *The Contribution of the Higher Education Sector to the Sydney 2000 Olympic Games.* Sydney: Center for Olympic Studies, University of New South Wales, 2002.

Chan, S. 'The Chinese Learner – A Question of Style'. *Education and Training* 41, no. 6/7, (1999): 294–304.

Chow, G. *The Chinese Economy.* Hackensack, NJ: World Scientific, 1987.

Collins, M. *Sport and Social Exclusion.* London: Routledge, 2003.

Coubertin, Pierre de, *Un Campagne de 21 ans (A campaign of 21 years).* Paris: Libraire de l'Education Physique, 1909)

DCMS, *A Sporting Future for All* (London: DCMS, 2000)

de Burgh, Hugo, ed. *China and Britain: The Potential Impact of China's Development.* London: The Smith Institute, 2005.

Dickson, G. and G. Schofield. 'Globalisation and Globesity: The Impact of the 2008 Beijing Olympics on China'. *International Journal of Sport Management and Marketing* 1, no. 1/2, (2005): 169–79.

Fan Hong, Ping Wu and Huan Xiong. 'Beijing Ambitions: An Analysis of the Chinese Elite Sport System and its Olympic Strategy for the 2008 Olympic Games'. *The International Journal of the History of Sport* 22, no. 4, (2005).

Fan Hong and Tan Hua. 'Sport in China: Conflict between Tradition and Modernity, 1840s to 1930s'. *The International Journal of the History of Sport* 19, no. 2, (2002).

Girginov, V. 'Does One-world Olympic Ideology Lead to Multiculturalism?' *Olympica*, forthcoming.

Girginov, V. and I. Sandanski. 'From Participants to Competitors: The Transformation of British Gymnastics and the Role of the Eastern European Model of Sport'. *The International Journal of the History of Sport* 21, no. 5, (2004): 815–33.

Green, M. 'National Sport Governing Bodies in Sports Development'. In *Management of Sports Development*, edited by V. Girginov. Oxford: Elsevier, 2008.

Hampden-Turner, C. and F. Trompenaars. *The Seven Cultures of Capitalism*. London: Piatkus, 1993.

——. *Building Cross-cultural Competence*. London: Yale University Press, 2000.

Hargreaves, J. *Sporting Females: Critical Issues*. London: Routledge, 1994.

Henry, I., W. Radzi, E. Rich, C. Shelton, E. Theodoraki and A. White. *Women, Leadership and the Olympic Movement*. Loughborough: Institute of Sport and Leisure Policy, Loughborough University and the International Olympic Committee, 2004.

Hilton, I. 'Culture and Cultural Power: Where Goes China and Does it Matter to Us?' In *China and Britain: The Potential Impact of China's Development*, edited by Hugo de Burgh. London: The Smith Institute, 2005.

Holt, R. 'Sport and History: British and European Traditions'. In *Taking Sport Seriously*, edited by L. Allison. Aachen: Meyer and Meyer, 1998.

Huizinga, J. *Homo Ludens: A Study of the Play Element in Culture*. Boston, MA: Beacon Press, 1950.

Huntington, S. 'The Clash of Civilizations?' *Foreign Affairs* 3 (1993).

Kirk, David. 'Physical Culture, Physical Education and Relational Analysis'. *Sport, Education and Society* 4, no. 1, (1999).

Kopytoff, I. 'The Cultural Biography of Things: Commoditization as Process'. In *The Social Life of Things*, edited by A. Appadurai. Cambridge: Cambridge University Press, 1986.

Landry, F. 'The Olympic Games and Competitive Sport as an International System'. In *Proceedings of the International Olympic Academy* 24. Athens: IOA, 1984: 157–67.

Lardy, Nicholas. *China in the World Economy*. Oxford: Blackwell, 1994.

Loughborough University and PMP?? *Studies on Education and Sport, Sport and Multiculturalism (Lot 3) Final Report*. Brussels: European Commission, 2004.

MacAloon, J. 'Intercultural Education and Olympic Sport' (1986 Challenge Address to the Olympic Academy of Canada). Montreal: Olympic Academy of Canada, 1986.

——. 'Sport, Science, And Intercultural Relations: Reflections on Recent Trends in Olympic Scientific Meetings'. *Olympika: The International Journal of Olympic Studies* 1 (1992).

——. 'Sponsorship Policy and Olympic Ideology: Towards a New Discourse. In *Proceedings of the International Olympic Academy* 32. Athens: IOA, 1992.

Mangan, J.A. 'Epilogue: "Empire in Denial": An Exceptional Kind of Imperialism'. *The International Journal of the History of Sport* 22, no. 6, (Nov. 2005).

Morden, T. 'Models of National Cultures: A Management Review'. *Cross Cultural Management* 5, no. 1, (1999): 19–44.

Morris, A. '"I Can Compete!" China in the Olympic Games, 1932 and 1936'. *Journal of Sport History* 26, no. 3, (1999).

Oh, T.K. 'Understanding Managerial Values and Behaviour Among the Gang of Four: South Korea, Taiwan, Singapore and Hong Kong'. *Journal of Management Development* 10, no. 2, (1991): 46–56.

Parry, J. 'Sport, Universals and Multiculturalism'. In *Proceedings of the International Olympic Academy* 40. Athens: IOA, 2000.

Redding, G. *The Spirit of Chinese Capitalism*. New York: Walter de Guyter, 1990.

Rowe, N., R. Adams and N. Beasley. 'Driving Up Participation in Sport: The Social Context, the Trends, the Prospects and the Challenges. Cited in *Driving up Participation: The Challenge for Sport*. London: Sport England, 2004: 12.

Shei, C. 'Plagiarism, Chinese Learners and Western Convention'. Available online at http://www.northumbrialearning.co.uk/newsletters/issue1/Chinese%20Learners%20and%20Plagiarism%20-%20Issue%201.pdf, accessed 20 Sept. 2007.

Shibly, Simon. 'Predicting the Performance of China in Beijing 2008'. Paper presented at European Sport Management Congress, Turin, Sept. 2007.

Smith, M. *Culture: Reinventing the Social Sciences*. Buckingham: Open University Press, 2000.

Sofield, T. and Fung Li. 'Historical Methodology and Sustainability: An 800-year-old Festival from China'. *Journal of Sustainable Tourism* 6, no. 4, (1998): 267–92.

Sport England. *The Value of Sport*. London: Sport England, 1999.

Trompenaars and Hampden-Turner, 2003 ???.

Tu Weiming. 'Toward a Dialogical Civilization: Identity, Difference, Harmony, Part I'.In *The Harmony of Civilizations and Prosperity for All*. Peking: Peking University Press, 2006.

Villamon, M., D. Brown, J. Espartero and C. Gutierrez. 'Reflexive Modernisation and the Disembedding of Judo from 1946 to the 2000 Sydney Olympics'. *International Review for the Sociology of Sport* 39, no. 2, (2004): 139–56.

Vlad, I. 'Obesity Cost UK Economy £2billion a Year'. *British Medical Journal* 6 (Dec. 2003).

Wang, H. '"Linking up with the international track": What's in a Slogan?' *The China Quarterly* 189 (March 2007): 1–23.

Weimer, D., ed. *The Political Economy of Property Rights*. London: Cambridge University Press, 1997.

Xin Xu. 'Modernizing China in the Olympic Spotlight: China's National Identity and the 2008 Beijing Olympiad'. *The Sociological Review* 54, no. 2, (2006).

Preparing to Take Credit for China's Glory: American Perspectives on the Beijing Olympic Games

Mark Dyreson

American observers of sport in the Far East have long seen the outline of a 'new China' in the growing interest of the Chinese in Western, and, in particular, American, athletics. In 1911 an American correspondent writing from Shanghai praised the rapid conversion of China to the gospel of American sport, arguing that basketball, football, baseball, track and field and other games had seized Chinese imaginations. Chinese fans, claimed the American commentator, were as conversant with the stars, statistics, rules and other nuances of sport as any US devotees. In one generation Chinese attitudes had been transformed by athletic exposure, catapulting the nation from feudal tradition to vital modernity at breakneck pace. Sport served as China's new *lingua franca*, binding the vast and disparate nation together through a common devotion to the shared experiences of athletic spectacles. Just like the United States, China seemed to be forging a national identity through sport, the American reporter trumpeted. Indeed, in large part due to the influence of American sport in the region, the 'new China' seemed to be moulding itself into a distinctively American form. Peering into the future, the China expert wondered aloud: 'When will the world's Olympic Games be held in Peking?' [1]

Since 2001, when the International Olympic Committee (IOC) met in Moscow and voted for Beijing over Osaka, Paris, Toronto and Istanbul, the world has known the answer to that question. [2] In the summer of 2008 Beijing will stage the Olympics. If readers did not pay close attention and missed the 1911 publication date of the essay from Shanghai and then skipped over the use of the archaic 'Peking' instead of Beijing, they could easily imagine that the story of the 'new China' invigorated by American sport had been written no later than the 1980s or 1990s, when tales of a Chinese athletic renaissance conjoined to rapid economic, social and political changes in a post-Maoist world filled the popular press and represented important new scholarly insights into the rise of the Pacific Rim in global affairs. [3]

Instead, the early twentieth-century observations of China's conversion to American-style culture through sport were penned by W.W. Lockwood, the general secretary of the powerful Shanghai Young Men's Christian Association (YMCA) for the liberal Protestant weekly *The Independent*. [4] Lockwood credited American athletic missionaries [5] with breathing life into a 'new China'. He rapturously described the creation of national games in China modelled on the 1904 Olympic Games held in St Louis as part of a grand American world's fair. [6] Lockwood argued, offering no evidence beyond mere circumstance, that these new Chinese 'Olympics' were causally linked to the creation of a national legislature for China – a major step forward, in his opinion, in the modernization of the Chinese polity. [7]

Lockwood admitted that the performances turned in by Chinese athletes in these new games would not inspire widespread fear among the Americans or the British. Still, he insisted the 'results were creditable considering the few years the sons of the Middle Kingdom have applied themselves to athletics'. The 'old China', Lockwood asserted, had detested physicality. Labouring under the spell of decadent Confucianism, they 'exalted the mind and despised the body'. The YMCA changed all of that, Lockwood proclaimed, introducing an American-invented 'new gospel of the value of the body and its importance to manhood'. China had been converted, Americanized and modernized. '"When will China be represented in the Olympic Games?" This question is being asked in all seriousness by China's modern literati,' Lockwood revealed. 'Others, looking farther into the future, ask, "When will the world's Olympic Games be held in Peking?"' [8]

Nearly a century later, another American scribe, seeking to comprehend China and knowing that Beijing will hold an Olympic Games in 2008, penned an essay with eerie similarities to Lockwood's 1911 article. S.L. Price, who visited Shanghai, Lockwood's old stomping ground, as well as Beijing and several other locales, sought to unravel the mysteries of the China in a 2007 *Sports Illustrated* tale entitled 'Olympic China'. Like Lockwood 96 years earlier, Price found the 'new China' a land of contrasts, open and closed, rich and poor, traditional and modern, capitalist and communist.

Underneath his musings runs a crucial subtext. Are the Chinese like us? Price constantly wonders. Can China, he muses, become an American-style society? His questions lie just beneath the surface of his quest to make sense out of a China he regards, as do many Americans, as mysterious, exotic, unintelligible – the enigmatic 'Orient' of Western lore and history. [9]

Price discovers in the $400 million 'Bird's Nest', the graceful new stadium transforming Beijing's skyline, a metaphor for how sport is rapidly pushing China from feudal tradition to radical modernism. Rural peasants come from the ancient rice paddies to build the 91,000-seat coliseum and the rest of the edifices and infrastructure on which China plans to spend at least $60 billion. The workers are transformed instantaneously into a proletariat for a market economy expanding at a dizzying pace. Urbanized and modernized, the workers become consumers in China's sprawling capitalist endeavours, buying among other things the accoutrements of contemporary sports, from tickets to athletic spectacles; from Nike shoes to flat-screen televisions on which to watch games. Indeed, Price insightfully notes, Chinese athletes have been rapidly transformed into national commodities – just like American athletes. Price ruminates on whether markets or the police state ultimately control their fates, buying and selling them for different ends. He admits an uncomfortable parallel to the commodified American athletes of big-time intercollegiate and professional sports. [10]

Price differs from Lockwood in some details of the 'new China' produced by modern sport meta-narrative. Where Lockwood credited the Christian zeal of the YMCA, Price identifies the compelling commercial power of the market forces of the Olympic Games as the causal agent. Where Lockwood saw moral transfiguration, Price sees economic transformation. Where Lockwood saw only beneficent progress in the Americanization of China, Price expresses considerable uncertainty concerning the benevolence of the process. Still, both meta-narratives of American-style sport giving birth to a 'new China', though separated by nearly a century, share an important set of common assumptions. The Olympic Games give China a crucial opportunity for shaping its national identity. The Olympic Games will bring China into the international community. The Olympic Games reveal China moving towards a more Western, or more specifically a more American, future. The Olympic Games will render the 'inscrutable Orient' intelligible to the West in general and especially to Americans.

If the Chinese perceive the twenty-first century as the era in which they ascend to world leadership and plan the 2008 games as a stage to herald their coming dominion, as Price and American neo-Orientalists constantly warn, [11] they are following a custom established by the United States in the preceding century. US leaders and the public routinely hailed the twentieth century as the 'American century' and used the Olympic games as stages to demonstrate and signify their status as the globe's leading power. Whether as host nation (1904, 1932, 1960, 1980, 1984, 1996, 2002) or as an athletic powerhouse, the United States endeavours to use the Olympics to project images of strength, virility and superiority to the rest of the world. The US also uses the Olympics to attempt to convert the rest of the world to American lifestyles. [12] In these scripts that Americans concoct about the Olympic Games as showcases for US global superiority, China and other nations played roles as either threatening villains, loyal sidekicks or comic jesters. In the first half of the twentieth century the Chinese generally appeared in American Olympic tales in the latter two roles. After the Communists won the long mid-century civil war and gave birth to the People's Republic of China, mainland China orbited between villain and jester in American interpretations of the Olympics, while the Nationalist republic that fled to Taiwan appeared as the stalwart ally, basking in the sunlight of American favour. [13]

In the process of crafting these Olympic scripts Americans have engaged in a thorough and a paradoxical 'Orientalism'. Orientalism, as the historian Edward Said has explained in detailing how the West made the East the non-modern 'other' in its modern mania for self-definition, has long characterized Western cultural interactions with the non-Western world. [14] The American brands of Orientalism emerged in the long history of US perceptions of China as the exotic and inscrutable 'other'. China becomes, in various versions of this trope, the 'sick man' in contrast to the robust athleticism of the US in so many American imperial visions of China and itself. At the same time, China becomes the 'sleeping giant', an untapped market of athletic talent and sports consumers that threatens to both enrich and overwhelm the benevolent Americans who allegedly bequeathed the gift of modern sport to ancient China. Adding another layer to the paradox, China also becomes in these interpretations the 'new China', beholden to the American gift of modernity that rapidly propels it towards a radical transformation into an American-style society. Americans, as the historian Paul Carter has observed, recognized by the mid-twentieth century that the world was moving towards global interdependency, 'if not a "global village," then perhaps a global shopping mall'. [15] An Americanized China, the US has long hoped, would serve as an 'anchor store' in a US-designed global mall devoted to the culture of consumption. The US has long employed sport to make sure that happens.

Since the revival of the Olympics in 1896 Americans have used the Olympics to tell stories about themselves to themselves, to borrow the brilliant expression the anthropologist Clifford Geertz employed to explain to story of Balinese cockfights. [16] Clearly, American interpretations of the Chinese at the Olympics reveal more about the US than China. Other scholars, most notably Susan Brownell, Fan Hong, Dong Jinxia and Andrew Morris have ably chronicled the stories that the Chinese tell themselves about themselves through Olympic performances. [17] Much less attention has been paid to stories that Americans tell themselves about themselves through interpretations of China at the Olympics. [18] If China, as Dong has argued, is 'preparing for glory' in Beijing in 2008, [19] a long history of American interpretations of China's Olympian history indicate that the US will seek to take credit for that glory.

American conceptions of Chinese sport date to the late nineteenth and early twentieth centuries, a period during which US missionaries, the US military and US merchants travelled to China in large numbers. As early as 1909 American missionary

W.A. Seavy heralded a 'new China' emerging from the diligent athletic efforts of the YMCA. Faced with a 'deep-rooted aversion to physical exercise' from the Chinese, the muscular Christian evangelists had in short order made a multitude of miraculous conversions. Seavy witnessed Chinese students engaged in an American-style track meet, complete with cheerleaders and hoopla. 'On the field before my eyes the thousand-year-old traditions of China were being wiped out,' the missionary marvelled. Seavy admitted that 'it will be many years before China will send competitors to the Olympic Games', but still found the American transformation of Chinese vigour a profound step forward. [20]

Some reports in the American press insisted that Chinese participation in the Olympic Games was not as far in the future as many assumed. Just two years after Seavy's report, a blurb in the liberal Protestant weekly *The Outlook* promoting the upcoming Stockholm Olympics announced that 40 nations would compete, including China. [21] *The Outlook*'s optimism about a Chinese entry in Sweden proved misplaced. While the Chinese did not make an appearance at the 1912 Olympics, they did send a team to the inaugural Far Eastern 'Olympics', as the American press referred to these novel Asian international contests, held in Manila in 1913. YMCA missionaries contrived these games to promote athletic enthusiasm in East Asia, to foster international amity between the region's nations and to sponsor the eventual inclusion of China, Japan and the Philippines in the greater Olympics. Major General Palmer E. Pierce, then the US military commander in China and a former president of the National Collegiate Athletics Association, heralded the Far Eastern 'Olympics' as a major triumph in modernizing China and the rest of Asia. Ultimate credit, *The Outlook* made clear, should go not to the Chinese or Filipino or Japanese athletes who competed or to the officials who organized the teams but to the Americans, especially the YMCA missionaries, who had envisaged the event. [22]

In 1915, Shanghai hosted the second instalment of Far Eastern 'Olympics'. American observers noted the improved performances of Asian athletes at those games, especially the strides made by the Japanese. Cables from Shanghai reported the Asians had approached the times and distances turned in by Westerners at the Stockholm Olympics. Once again, Americans took credit for the Chinese improvement. A column in *Youth's Companion* magazine, commenting on the 'highly successful' Far Eastern games at Shanghai, concluded that 'certainly they showed the surprising influence of the American athletic spirit on the Orient'. [23] Favourably disposed to the 'new China' that seemed to spring from the cinder and turf, James Edward Sullivan, a long-time leader of American Olympic efforts, invited Chinese athletes to come to his special games at San Francisco's Panama-Pacific International Exposition. With the First World War scuttling the 1916 Berlin Olympics, Sullivan predicted that his 1915 spectacle in California would be the decade's greatest sporting event. [24] Full of alleged American spirit they might have been, but Chinese athletes did not venture to San Francisco to compete. [25]

The Great War disrupted international sport in much of the world, although it did not impact the Far Eastern Championship Games – as the Asian regional Olympics were officially dubbed. They continued on a biennial cycle, going to Tokyo in 1917, back to Manila in 1919 and returning to Shanghai in 1921. [26] American spectators touted the events as crucial to China's transformation to modernity. Political correspondent Katherine Mayo asserted that the Far Eastern Olympics were 'of incalculable political and social significance to the whole Orient' – and especially to China. 'Replacing such lone-hand games as jiu-jitsu by games of brotherly teamwork, they tend to replace selfishness by self-sacrifice, to build character, to raise physique, to inspire national loyalty, to implant good fellowship among hostile tribes and peoples' Mayo contended, lauding the Americanizing force of sport. [27] Elwood Brown, the YMCA leader whom Mayo and others credited with creating the Far Eastern Olympics, argued that the long-haired, long-nailed patricians of American caricatures of Confucian tradition were hardly suited to the basketball court, the baseball diamond or the cinder track. In converting China from its long history of body-hatred, Brown insisted that he and his fellow missionaries had remade China. [28]

During the 1920s, with the Great War ended and international sport on the rebound, rumours of China's entry into the regular Olympic Games repeatedly swirled through the United States. The *New York Times* listed China as a 'probable' competitor for the 1920 Antwerp Games. [29] *Life* magazine sarcastically warned the Americans to watch out for the Chinese. 'Any group of athletes who could succeed in inserting more pins into one shirt than the record established by the Chinese team, would have a clear title to the laundry championship', the journal unpleasantly joked. [30]

China did not send a team to Antwerp for shirt-pinning or for any other contest. In 1924 at Paris, however, an American observer counted a two-man Chinese team, allegedly the first Chinese entry in Olympic history. [31] That claim, like the earlier report about a Chinese entry in the 1912 and 1920 Olympics, proved an illusion. China did not send any athletes to Olympics during the 1920s. The Chinese did, however, prepare for future Olympic entries. Under the tutelage of the YMCA, China had formed a national Olympic committee in 1910. The IOC finally recognized the Chinese petition in 1922. That same year the IOC tabbed Wang Zhengting, China's foreign minister and the chief of the Chinese National Amateur Athletic Federation (CNAAF), as the nation's first IOC member. [32]

China joined the Olympic movement as part of a larger effort to take control of its own sports organizations. A growing 'sports war' that highlighted larger east Asian power struggles between China and Japan provided the impetus to 'nationalize' Chinese sport. After Japan trounced a Chinese team lead by an American YMCA official at the fifth Far Eastern Championship Games at Osaka in 1923, China's sports leaders took control of the CNAAF in an effort to make their nation more competitive in its increasingly intense rivalry with the Japanese. When sporting conflict turned into military conflict in 1931 with Japanese incursions into Manchuria, the battles at the Far Eastern Championships became even more intense. When Japan cleverly sought international legitimacy for its Manchurian puppet-state,

Manchukuo, by seeking to have the regime recognized by the IOC and the Far Eastern Athletic Association, China vociferously objected. Japan managed to win the inclusion of Manchukuo after the 1934 Far Eastern Games in Manila. China's promise to bar the Japanese pawn from the next Far Eastern Championships destroyed the two-decades-old, American-created contests. The 1937 invasion of the Chinese mainland would put the final nail in the coffin of the Far Eastern athletic proxy wars. Actual combat replaced sporting conflicts. [33]

In the midst of China's battles with Japan and its efforts to reach the global stage at the Olympics, some Americans grew nervous that the world's most populous nation might launch a challenge to American Olympic hegemony. The most prolific US foreign correspondent in China during the era, Thomas Millard, constructed a brief history of China to showcase how modern sport and modern medicine had radically transformed the ancient culture. [34] 'When the Western nations forced intercourse on China they found the Chinese in the main an undersized, undernourished and rather mild people, averse to violence, shrinking from rough contests', Millard began. Western medical science and sport had transformed the Chinese into healthy, athletic specimens who might soon contend for international prowess. Millard noted that some nations, most especially Great Britain, fretted that their 'improvement' of Chinese physicality might actually threaten the West. He quoted a 'European scientist' who worried that 'we are sowing seeds in China of which we cannot foresee the harvest'. [35]

Millard contended that the British did not allow the Chinese or other colonies in the Empire to partake in British sports – a typical American caricature of the role of sport in British imperialism. [36] The Americans, Millard revealed with a mixture of pride and anxiety, did include the Chinese in American sports. He praised the Far Eastern 'Olympics' and speculated that baseball might become the national pastime of China as it had of Japan. Over British objections, Millard contended, the US had sponsored the 'physical renaissance of the Chinese'. China stood poised, he concluded to play a much larger role in world sport and in world affairs. [37]

Some American experts did not share Millard's view that China was in the midst of a 'physical renaissance' that would make it a world power. American sprinter Charles W. Paddock, generally labelled in the 1920s as the world's fastest human, won the 100-metre gold medal at the 1920 Olympics and the 200-metre silver medal at the 1920 and 1924 Olympics. In 1925 Paddock toured the world with American teammate Loren Murchison, running exhibition races and commenting on national character. Paddock recounted his 'Sprinting Around the World' adventures for the readers of *The Saturday Evening Post* – a magazine with one of the largest circulations in the US market. His essay combined self-improvement tips for youngsters who sought to emulate his athletic prowess with long discourses on how sport revealed national identity. [38]

In China, Paddock discovered a serious lack of competitive spirit. Though American missionary efforts had produced 'splendid specimens of manhood' among the Chinese, Paddock derisively dismissed them as future rivals for the US or the rest of the West. 'Natural athletes, with a large group of clever strategists in some fields of sport, they seem to lack altogether the ability to meet physical contact and to fight back', Paddock maintained, repudiating Chinese physical and political culture in one sweeping characterization. He insisted that the Chinese took nothing seriously enough, 'according to our standards of civilization and of life'. That fault, Paddock asserted, accounted for chaos in the land of the warlords, preventing China from becoming a 'modern' nation. [39]

In China, the republic's leaders took Paddock's critique to heart. Moving cautiously towards the world athletic stage, China sent an observer but no athletes to the 1928 Amsterdam Olympics. [40] The Chinese observer went to Holland at the behest of Chinese officials rather than under the auspices of the YMCA. Shortly thereafter, Wang Zhengting, China's foreign minister and the nation's representative to the IOC, proclaimed that 'If a nation wants to pursue freedom and equality in today's world where the weak serve as meat on which the strong can dine, they first must train strong and fit bodies'. [41] Immediately following Zhengting's proclamation, American newspapers reported that China was spending millions of dollars to build extensive new athletic facilities in order to spur the national development of sport. [42]

In 1932 the Republic of China sent its first team – one sprinter, one coach, and four sports administrators – to the Los Angeles Olympics. The runner's selection underscored the raging sports war between China and Japan. The Japanese had tried to make the Chinese sprinter the star of the team from its Manchurian puppet state, but he refused and joined China's squad. [43] Americans paid little attention to the first Chinese entry in the modern games. That was a curious oversight, since the US by the 1930s was well practised in taking credit for Chinese sporting progress, and the Olympics occurred on American soil. Notices concerning China's debut appeared as an afterthought in newspaper stories on the Los Angeles spectacle. [44]

At the same time, coverage of Japan, China's Asian rival and its enemy in the burgeoning Manchuria crisis, garnered copious space in American periodicals. [45] Certainly the focus on Japan instead of China had much to do with the fact that the Japanese finished a surprising fifth in the overall medal count while the lone Chinese sprinter was eliminated in the early heats. [46] It also underscored the fact that Americans perceived Japan as their real rival along the Pacific Rim. [47] When Chinese participation was mentioned, it was often dismissed as comic sideshow. One story in a small-town Midwestern newspaper pointed out that the nation with the world's largest population could only find one athlete for the Olympic track meet but that little Wyandotte High School in Kansas City, Kansas, sent 70 athletes to the Kansas Relays. [48]

Undiscouraged by American barbs, the Chinese continued their Olympic project. With a first Olympic experience under its belt, the Republic of China prepared to launch a much larger expedition to Berlin in 1936. Building on Western, and particularly American, models, the Chinese set up an Olympic training camp and committed economic resources to the effort. The *New York Times* reported that China had budgeted $160,000 to prepare and send a team of 136 athletes and officials to Germany. [49] The US, by contrast spent $350,000 to send a team of more than 400 to the Berlin games. [50] The per-capita investment projections were remarkably similar.

As in 1932, the US media paid little attention to the 1936 Chinese entry, even though it was considerably larger and joined with the Americans in refusing to offer a *Seig Heil* to Chancellor Adolf Hitler at the opening parade. [51] Though China entered more than 70 athletes in Berlin, the Chinese team was barely mentioned in the American press. [52] In the few notices of Chinese Olympians, strains of 'Orientalism' prevailed. A picture of the Chinese team arriving in Berlin highlighted their exotic costumes. [53] A few references referred to the Chinese squad adding colour to the opening ceremonies or other events. [54] The sparse mentions of Chinese athletes in action concentrated on the amusing tales of incompetence. The American press laughed at the Chinese boxer who 'won' his bout when his British opponent was disqualified for hitting in the clinch at the very moment the English pugilist knocked the Chinese fighter unconscious. The US media also found delight in the Chinese wrestling team that apparently did not understand Occidental notions of time and failed to show up for their bouts. [55] In the post Olympic wrap-up, China also fell under the unflattering gaze of John Kieran, a prominent Olympic journalist for the *New York Times*. Kieran noted that the nation with the world's largest population ranked last in American 'scientific' studies of per-capita Olympic medal production. [56] As in 1932, China failed to win a single medal at the 1936 Olympics, though it entered 79 athletes instead of just one. That failure disappointed Chinese leaders but did not dissuade them from using international sport to promote the Republic of China. [57] After 1936, however, with the Far Eastern 'Olympics' extinguished by the Sino-Japanese conflicts that erupted in 1937 into full-scale war when Japan invaded China, those opportunities quickly dwindled. The Chinese did agitate to deprive Japan of its hosting rights for the 1940 Olympics. At the 1938 IOC meeting in Cairo, C.T. Wang, China's new IOC delegate and the Chinese ambassador to the US, argued that nations at war should be barred from putting on the Olympics. Wang wanted the Tokyo games moved to another location since Japanese troops were waging total war deep inside China. [58] Whether Chinese lobbying had any impact on the decision remains murky, but soon thereafter Japan abandoned its efforts to stage the 1940 games. The outbreak of the Second World War in Europe, a conflict already blazing in East Asia, scuttled plans to relocate those Olympics as well as cancelling the 1944 games. [59]

After the Second World War the 'new China' changed dramatically. Ripped asunder by civil war, two 'new Chinas' quickly emerged for American observers to interpret through Cold War lenses. [60] In 1948 China, then in the midst of a brutal civil war, sent an Olympic delegation of 32 athletes and 20 officials to the London Olympics. The team, sponsored by the Nationalists in the Chinese power-struggle and funded by wealthy Shanghai and Singapore entrepreneurs, was warmly received in Britain but once again failed to win a single medal. Shortly thereafter, the Chinese civil war ended with the triumph of the Communists over the Nationalists. Much of

China's sporting infrastructure, including the national Olympic committee, fled with the defeated to Taiwan. [61]

The civil war schism produced an enduring conflict between the 'two Chinas' that played out in the Olympics and in a host of other international venues. The People's Republic of China (PRC) on the mainland and the Republic of China (ROC) on the island of Taiwan struggled incessantly for sole recognition as the Chinese representative in Olympic and other sporting competitions such as the Asian Games that emerged as the post-war replacement for the old Far Eastern 'Olympics' and the Games of the New Emerging Forces (GANEFO) that sprouted in East Asia in the 1960s in opposition to the colonialism of the 'Occidentalist' Olympics and Asian Games. [62]

In Olympic arenas since 1952 both the PRC and the ROC have spasmodically entered and pulled out of competitions to protest against the presence of the 'other' China. The ROC pulled out of the 1952 Olympics, then sent teams to the 1956, 1960, 1964, 1968 and 1972 games. The ROC boycotted the 1976 Olympics when the IOC required it to compete as Taiwan, joined the US-sponsored boycott of the 1980 Soviet Olympics and then entered every games thereafter. The PRC sent teams to the Olympics in 1952, pulled out in 1956, then withdrew from the IOC and descended into the internal turmoil of the Cultural Revolution. The PRC rejoined the IOC in 1979, sent a team to US for the Lake Placid winter games in 1980 but not to Moscow for the summer spectacle that same year, and then entered every games thereafter. [63]

In these Cold War Games from 1952 to 1988, American interpretations of Chinese Olympic experiences depicted the ROC as the heroic and loyal allies of the United States. [64] C.K. Yang (Yang Changuang), the 'Iron Man of Asia', played the faithful sidekick to his University of California at Los Angeles teammate and US athletic star Rafer Johnson in American tales of the classic 1960 Olympic decathlon battle in which Yang took silver to Johnson's gold. [65] The PRC, even when absent, played the role of villains to Yang and the virtuous ROC athletes. Indeed, they were literally dastardly in one famous case when PRC intelligence agents at the 1964 Tokyo Olympics recruited two traitorous ROC teammates of Yang's to poison the gold-medal favourite and scuttle his bid for an Olympian decathlon victory. [66]

When the PRC inscrutably, from American perspectives, abandoned Olympic opportunities from 1952 to 1980, US observers treated the decision as the anti-modern backwardness typical of the 'Orient'. In American tales from that era, Communism replaced Confucianism as the causal force preventing China from modernizing. When the PRC returned to the Olympic fold, Americans generally portrayed them as exotic enemies who used their police state to enslave children to grim gymnastic or diving factories – a practice for which Americans could depend on parents rather than the state. As China won increasing numbers of medals in odd contests that the US did not particularly care about, Americans pointed to the fact that the PRC fared poorly in what then were considered by the US the 'real' athletic events – particularly track and field, basketball and swimming. Even when the PRC climbed into the upper echelon of the national medal count, placing fourth in 1996 and third in 2000 and 2004, sparking what the Sinologist Susan Brownell labelled as 'an overreaction by the Western media' to the prospect of China knocking the US off the top of the Olympic podium, they generally fared poorly in those sports. [67]

In the 1990s, when the PRC briefly began to threaten US swimming hegemony, a drug scandal destroyed their team's reputation, making it easy to dismiss the Chinese challenge. In fact, American reports on the drug scandal betrayed the continuing 'Orientalism' of US perspectives, as the Chinese doping efforts were depicted as unsophisticated and amateurish compared to the refined and scientific approaches of the Occidental totalitarians, especially the East Germans and the Soviets, or the thoroughly modern sport science programmes of Occidental free societies. [68] Reports that Chinese athletes mixed Western performance-enhancing chemicals with traditional Chinese medicines, including caterpillar fungi and turtle blood spiked with herbs, added extra flavour to the exotic Orientalism of American Olympic tales. [69]

As the Cold War evaporated in the early 1990s, Americans turned their attention from the 'two Chinas' back to the mainland. As Communism collapsed in Europe and demonstrations against the regime grew in China, the US hoped for major changes in the People's Republic. Rapid economic and social changes as China joined the global market gladdened American hearts and convinced many that another 'new China' was about to be born. The squelching of the pro-democracy movement at Tiananmen Square, an event that captured enormous attention in the US, greatly dismayed the American public and policy-makers. China's leadership, Americans believed, had aborted the birth of a truly 'new China'. The Communist state blocked a leap to modernity in a reactionary quest to maintain power, consigning China to archaic decline. [70]

In this climate, China launched a bid to bring the 2000 Olympics to Beijing. Many in the US media and government announced their resolute opposition to a Chinese games. In addition to the older tropes of Chinese Olympians perfected in the first half of the twentieth century, they employed metaphors from collective memories of the 1930s, comparing Beijing's quest to Berlin's production of the 'Nazi Olympics'. [71] These reinterpretations ignored a few historical details that muddied the comparative waters, such as the fact that the IOC had bequeathed the 1936 Olympics to Germany when the liberal Weimar Republic was in power and not Hitler and the National Socialists. In spite of that and other problems in making such comparisons, the opportunity to lump 1990s China with 1930s Germany in order to crush a Beijing Olympics proved too rich to ignore. Opposition to China's bid became a chance to rewrite history, to undo the mistake done in allowing the Nazis to have the Berlin Games. Robert Lipsyte in the *New York Times* argued that 'denying Beijing is in the best interest of humanity, especially if it is clear why that city is forbidden to be the host'. Lipsyte speculated, grandly if unrealistically, that if the US had pursued a similar course in 1936 Nazism might have withered if confronted by American moral condemnation. [72]

This revisionist notion that an American-led global boycott of the 1936 Olympics would have altered the course of world history and checked the advance of the Third Reich and might have even prevented the Second World War ignored serious analysis of the history of the 1930s, overestimated the power of the Olympics in global politics and contained a host of implausible assumptions, but still proved enormously popular in 1990s American culture. A bipartisan coalition devoted to those tenets quickly emerged. Democratic Congressman Tom Lantos of California, representing a district with a significant population of Chinese refugees from the People's Republic, became the spokesperson of the anti-Beijing movement. Lantos accused the Chinese of attempting to bribe the IOC, detailed the regime's human-rights violations, and explicitly linked Beijing's efforts to the 'Nazi Olympics'. Lantos counselled Americans that they stood, as they had in 1936, at a historical crossroads. He warned them not to make the mistake of once again allowing a totalitarian nation to host the Olympics. [73]

Some American observers took a different view. Instead of linking Beijing to Berlin, they insisted that a better analogy was to the 1988 Seoul Olympics. They argued that South Korean games had opened up and liberalized a repressive regime, leading to a more democratic Asian state. Though this comparison also lacked rigorous analysis, it too proved popular. Adherents such as the *Wall Street Journal* speculated that a Chinese Olympics would have a similar impact on the world's most populous nation. [74]

In the 2000 bid contest Sydney triumphed over Beijing, due to strong US and Western opposition as well as to astute Australian 'purchases' of IOC delegates. Undeterred by defeat, China launched a bid for the 2008 Olympics, developing a more sophisticated and lucrative marketing campaign that employed global movie stars Jackie Chan and Gong Li. [75] American opponents, citing China's human rights record, environmental policies and totalitarian government, once again manned the barricades to block a Beijing Olympics. Interestingly, the 2008 Beijing plan won support from some unlikely realms who in the past had not been supporters, including the exiled Tibetan Dalai Lama and IOC member Alex Gilday of Israel, who in an odd attempt at logic noted that Texas had also executed quite a few people without arousing massive opposition to Dallas's plan to bid for an Olympics. [76]

The new Chinese bid once again evoked strong US reactions. The same questions again shaped the discourse on a Beijing games. Would a 'new China' be more likely to emerge if the world withheld the Olympics or if it granted the prize to the Chinese? Was Berlin in 1936 or Seoul in 1988 a better historical frame from which to interpret the potential impact of the Olympics on China? A host of American prognosticators declared that granting the Olympics to China would replicate the mistake made in giving the 1936 Games to the Nazis. A *St Louis Post-Dispatch* column by Bernie Miklasz chastised American corporations that supported the Beijing bid as cut from the same cloth as American firms that collaborated with the Nazis in the 1930s. The prospects of China's 1.26 billion consumers and $1.1 trillion dollar economy attracted Coca-Cola and other US firms like moths to a flame, just as in 1936 when

Coca-Cola and the rest of corporate America coveted the German market. 'Perhaps the next time the totalitarian Chinese government seeks to punish the protesters in Tiananmen Square, the tanks will be outfitted with NASCAR-like sponsorship labels', Miklaz disgustedly concluded. [77]

The *Washington Post* joined the anti-Beijing coalition. 'Some supporters of China argue that the 2008 Olympics might have the same effect in China as the 1988 Olympics did in South Korea, where an opening to the world led to a broader opening to democracy', the powerful organ of opinion in the US national capital admitted. 'But it seems just as plausible that the critics who cite the example of the 1936 Olympics in Berlin will be right – that the games will prove a platform for a dictatorship to strut its regimented athletes and nationalist agenda before the world', the *Post* concluded. [78] *Boston Globe* reporter Jeff Jacoby, incensed that the Chinese planned to use Tiananmen Square to stage the marathon and other events, predicted the Olympics would embolden the Chinese dictators as much as the Berlin games had emboldened Hitler. [79] An editorial in the *Houston Chronicle* declared that Beijing and Berlin were twin mistakes. The Texas newspaper urged Americans to support the strange-bedfellow coalition of Congressional leaders and arch rivals Dick Gephardt (Missouri Democrat) and Tom DeLay (Texas Republican). [80]

California Democrat Tom Lantos engineered another strange political alliance, teaming with erstwhile enemy Senator Jesse Helms of North Carolina to block China's bid. [81] Lantos again led the cheerleading against Beijing by linking it to the spectre of the Nazi Olympics. [82] 'We only need to look back at the 1936 Olympics in Berlin to see how authoritarian governments use the Games to strengthen their hand', Lantos warned. [83] Henry Wu, a leading Chinese dissident, joined the fray: 'As a native Chinese, I would be both pleased and honored to see the Olympic Games held in Beijing, but only when Beijing is the capital of a free and democratic China', Wu proclaimed. 'The world should heed the lessons of the 1936 Berlin Games in Nazi Germany.' [84] The *San Francisco Chronicle*, inhabiting a metropolitan area that was home to the nation's largest Chinese expatriate community, who were mainly staunch opponents of the PRC, as well as to Congressman Lantos, came out against Beijing's bid. China's crackdowns on dissidents and its penchant for executions marked it as clearly unfit to host the Olympics. If China won, the California daily groused, 'we would grit our teeth and give the nod to China, hoping that seven years in the international spotlight would moderate a regime so needful of the world's respect'. [85]

Unlike the 1993 effort to prevent China from garnering the Olympics, the US government did not take a strong stand on the issue. Congressional leaders and the Bush administration effectively sat the controversy out. [86] When Beijing won, the idea that the Olympics would 'moderate' China and put it back on the path to Americanization, a popular historical notion in the US if not in the PRC, garnered as much support as the earlier efforts to prevent a Chinese games. For those who sought to restore the popular belief that had prevailed in the first half of the twentieth century, that sport would produce an American-style 'new China', the correct comparison was to Seoul in 1988 rather than to Berlin in 1936. Adherents of this perspective came from all sectors of the American political spectrum, mirroring the ideological eclecticism seen in the Beijing games as the new Nazi Olympics faction. In the corporatist *Wall Street Journal*, William McGunn noted that for those determined to contrast the 2008 games to the 1936 games, the vote for China at the IOC's Moscow session was 'bitter news'. McGunn, who had been in South Korea in the 1980s, insisted that the Seoul games had forced moderation and Americanization on that repressive regime. 'It is difficult to imagine this happy [South Korean] ending without the Olympics', McGunn asserted. The Olympics could well spark a similar change in China he concluded. [87]

To those floating the notion of a US boycott after Beijing won IOC favour, Zbigniew Brzenzinski, the former national security advisor to the Carter administration and one of the chief architects of the American walk-out from the 1980 Moscow Olympics, offered a history lesson. Moscow in 1980 and Beijing in 2008 were in no way comparable, Brzenzinski proclaimed. Seoul in 1988 offered a much better parallel. 'The Olympics in Beijing may be a triumph for China, but by intensifying the pressures for change the games are quite unlikely to be a triumph for China's waning Communism' he hypothesized. 'In fact, the Games may accelerate its fading.' [88] Henry Kissinger, another foreign-policy heavyweight, concurred with his former rival Brzenzinski. A moderately reformed China would emerge from the Olympic experience, Kissinger predicted. [89]

A few voices questioned the optimism and the logic of the claims that awarding the Olympics to repressive regimes would liberalize and democratize them. 'With that philosophy, the IOC would have voted for Tehran over Los Angeles for 1984 as an enticement to the ayatollah to change' mocked Randy Harvey in the *Los Angeles Times*. [90] Most Americans, however, have prepared to take credit if the Olympics liberalize the PRC. Conversely, if the optimistic predictions do not come to fruition, Americans certainly have no plans to take the blame. The Beijing-as-Berlin rhetoric has moved to the new lunatic fringe of contemporary American politics, a land that Hollywood's 'glitterati' mainly inhabit, as actress Mia Farrow prophesied that director Steven Spielberg would 'go down in history as the Leni Riefenstahl of the Beijing Games' for signing on as the 'artistic advisor' to the Chinese organizing committee. [91] When Spielberg resigned his position with the Chinese in early 2008, Farrow immediately took credit for the victory. [92] In the main the rest of the nation ignored the celebrity spat and welcomed the news that American national pastimes, from Major League Baseball to BMX stunt biking, have garnered toeholds in the 2008 games. [93] The efforts to take credit for China's glory and to Americanize the Middle Kingdom thus take both old and new paths. Such is the power of Occidentalism in framing the rules for modern games.

Notes

[1] Lockwood, 'The Chinese Olympic Games'.
[2] Wushanley, 'Beijing 2008'.

[3] Susan Brownell's masterful *Training the Body for China* represents the best linkage of the 'new China' scholarship to a post-Maoist athletic rebirth. Other works that heralded to Americans the emergence of another 'new China' include Hacker, *The New China*; Rau, *The People of New China*; Spence, *The Search for Modern China*.

[4] Lockwood, 'The Chinese Olympic Games', 180–5.

[5] 'America's athletic missionaries' represents a label given to US Olympians in the early twentieth century and reveals the American belief that they could convert the world to their nation's way of life. Dyreson, *Making the American Team*; Dyreson, '"America's Athletic Missionaries"'.

[6] Dyreson, *Making the American Team*, 73–97; Dyreson, 'The Playing Fields of Progress'.

[7] Lockwood, 'The Chinese Olympic Games'.

[8] Ibid.

[9] Price, 'Olympic China'.

[10] Ibid. Price's discomfort with the commodification of American athletes is shared most acutely by William Rhoden in his critique of race and exploitation in contemporary American sport, *Forty Million Dollar Slaves*.

[11] Terrill, *The New Chinese Empire*; Mitter, *A Bitter Revolution*; Needham, *A Season in Red*; Pomfret, *Chinese Lessons*, Prestowitz, *Three Billion New Capitalists*.

[12] Dyreson, 'Marketing National Identity'; Dyreson, 'Globalizing the Nation-Making Process'; Dyreson, *Making the American Team*.

[13] For an introduction into how the American media wrote these scripts see Dyreson, 'Scripting the American Olympic Story-Telling Formula'.

[14] Said, *Culture and Imperialism*. In applying Said's model to US interpretations of Chinese Olympic history I am following the insightful leads of Susan Brownell in 'Challenged America: China and America'.

[15] Carter, *Revolt Against Destiny*, 233.

[16] Geertz, 'Notes on a Balinese Cockfight'.

[17] Brownell, *Training the Body for China*; Brownell, 'Challenged America: China and America'; Fan Hong, *Sport, Nationalism and Orientalism*; Hong, *Footbinding, Feminism, and Freedom*; Dong Jinxia, 'Women, Nationalism and the Beijing Olympics'; Dong Jinxia, *Women, Sport, and Modern China*; Morris, *Marrow of the Nation*.

[18] An insightful comparative history of Chinese and American interpretations of Olympic meaning can be found in Brownell, 'Challenged America: China and America'.

[19] Dong Jinxia, 'Women, Nationalism and the Beijing Olympics'.

[20] Seavy, 'Public Opinion'.

[21] 'By the Way'.

[22] 'Athletics in the Orient', *New York Times*, 16 Dec. 1912; 'Far Eastern Athletes', *New York Times*, 1 Feb. 1913. For historical analyses of the early Far Eastern Championship Games, as they were officially dubbed, see Fan Hong, 'The Origin of the Asian Games', xiii–xxiv; Morris, *Marrow of the Nation*; Gems, *The Athletic Crusade*.

[23] 'Fact and Comment'.

[24] 'Oriental Athletes Coming', *New York Times*, 30 Aug. 1914.

[25] Todd, *The Story of the Exposition*, 175–85.

[26] Fan Hong, 'The Origin of the Asian Games'.

[27] Mayo, 'Fair Play for the World'.

[28] Brown, 'Teaching the World to Play'.

[29] '30 Nations in Olympics', *New York Times*, 10 July 1920.

[30] 'The New Olympic Games'.

[31] Jessup, 'The Greatest Olympiad'.

[32] Morris, *Marrow of the Nation*, 167–76; Morris, '"I Can Compete!"', 545–8.

[33] Morris, *Marrow of the Nation*, 69–78, 96–8, 161–6; Fan Hong, 'The Origin of the Asian Games'.

[34] Millard wrote more than 20 books on China and East Asian issues, including one of the many tomes on the 'new China': Millard, *The New China*. For an assessment of Millard's enormous influence on American views of China in the first half of the twentieth century, see Hamilton, 'The Missouri News Monopoly and American Altruism in China'.

[35] Thomas F. Millard, 'Physical Change Affecting Chinese', *New York Times*, 6 Sept. 1925.

[36] For trenchant analyses of the complexities of British colonial sport policies see Mangan, *The Games Ethic and Imperialism*; Guttmann, *Games and Empires*.

[37] Millard, 'Physical Change Affecting Chinese'.

[38] Paddock, 'Sprinting Around the World'; Paddock, *The Fastest Human*, 201–16.

[39] Ibid.

[40] Morris, *Marrow of the Nation*, 167–76; Morris, '"I Can Compete!"', 545–8.

[41] As cited in Morris, *Marrow of the Nation*, 167; Morris, '"I Can Compete!"', 545.

[42] 'Nanking Athletic Plant Costing $2,000,000 to House Chinese National Meet in October', *New York Times*, 29 March 1931.

[43] Morris, *Marrow of the Nation*, 167–76; Morris, '"I Can Compete!"', 545–50.

[44] '100 Far East Athletes Arrive', *New York Times*, 7 July 1932; Arthur J. Daley, 'Curtis Will Open Olympics Saturday', *New York Times*, 24 July 1932; Arthur J. Daley, 'New Delegations Bring 300 to Camp', *New York Times*, 26 July 1932. A search covering July and August 1932 on NewspaperArchive.com, a site with more than 2,800 newspapers from across the United States, reveals only a score of stories that mention the Chinese at the Los Angeles games. The stories are wire service reports that merely list China among the participants.

[45] Welky, 'US Journalism and the 1932 Olympics'; Yamamoto, 'Cheers for Japanese Athletes'.

[46] Morris, *Marrow of the Nation*, 167–71; Morris, '"I Can Compete!"', 547–50.

[47] Iriye, *The Globalizing of America*.

[48] 'Over-Size Entry', *Portsmouth* (Ohio) *Times*, 25 May 1936.

[49] 'China to Compete in Olympics', *New York Times*, 14 Oct. 1934.

[50] 'Olympic Fund Problems'; 'Forth To War'.

[51] Morris, *Marrow of the Nation*, 177; Morris, '"I Can Compete!"', 556. The US press did notice that Bulgaria, Iceland and India had joined the US in refusing to dip national flags to Hitler. Reports made no mention of the Chinese refusal to offer the Nazi salute. Alan Gould, 'Hitler Opens Berlin Games; US Stars Get Cool Greeting', *Washington Post*, 2 Aug. 1936.

[52] A search covering July and August 1936 on NewspaperArchive.com found no stories that focussed on the Chinese entry and fewer than ten that even mentioned a Chinese presence.

[53] 'Athletes in Olympic Games', *New York Times*, 2 Aug. 1936.

[54] Arthur J. Daley, 'US Is Favored to Gain Major Honors in Berlin Olympics Opening Saturday', *New York Times*, 26 July 1936; Frederick T. Birchall, '100,000 Hail Hitler; US Athletes Avoid Nazi Salute to Him', *New York Times*, 2 Aug. 1936; Albion Ross, 'Attendance Tops the Million Mark', *New York Times*, 8 Aug. 1936.

[55] 'Wilson, Kara and Scrivani Gain in Boxing, But Rutecki Is Beaten', *New York Times*, 12 Aug. 1936; Frederick T. Birchall, 'Young Olympic Diving Champion Gives Grown-Up Radio Interview', *New York Times*, 13 Aug. 1936.

[56] John Kieran, 'Sports of the Times', *New York Times*, 28 Oct. 1936. Kieran added China to a list created after the 1936 Olympics physiologist Charles Snyder of Johns Hopkins University. Snyder's allegedly scientific studies of the Olympics declared Germany a victor of the US and northern Europeans superior to all other groups. Snyder, an ardent eugenicist and committed scientific racist, wrote elaborately on the subject, but did not even bother to include the Chinese in his studies since they had never medalled in Olympic history. Snyder, 'The Real Winners In The 1936 Olympic Games'; Snyder, 'A Study In The Demographic Distribution of

Cultural Achievement'. For an interpretation of Snyder and this sort of scientific racism see Dyreson, 'American Ideas About Race and Olympic Races'.

[57] Morris, *Marrow of the Nation*, 177–84; Morris, '"I Can Compete!"', 550–61.

[58] 'Nothing in China', 20.

[59] Collins, 'The Missing Olympics'.

[60] For an overview of the Cold War politics of the Olympics see Torres and Dyreson, 'The Cold War Games'.

[61] Morris, *Marrow of the Nation*, 236–7.

[62] Fan Hong, 'Communist China and the Asian Games', 76–7.

[63] Senn, *Power, Politics, and the Olympic Games*, 99–100, 105–17, 164–79; Torres and Dyreson, 'The Cold War Games'.

[64] Slack *et al.*, 'The Road to Modernization'.

[65] See Yang's iconic image on the cover of the *Sport's Illustrated* special 1963 issue on 'Sport in the Orient – World's Best Athlete: C.K. Yang'; also Creamer, 'The Cobra and C.K. Yang'; Maule, 'Yang of China Is World's Best Athlete'. Another interesting interpretation is offered by Rafer Johnson in his autobiography: Johnson, *The Best That I Can Be*.

[66] Morris, *Marrow of the Nation*, 239.

[67] Brownell, 'Challenged America: China and America', 1174.

[68] Amy Shipley, 'On Doping, China Faces a Host of Questions', *Washington Post*, 8 Aug. 2007; Alan Abrahamson, 'Drug Testing Impacts Chinese', *Los Angeles Times*, 7 Sept. 2000; Keith Richburg, 'China Getting Back in the Swim of Things', *Washington Post*, 13 April 1996; Philip Hersh, 'US Wants to Ensure Chinese Come Clean', *Chicago Tribune*, 11 May 1995; Karen Allen, 'US Swimmers Plunge Ahead Without China', *USA Today*, 10 Aug. 1995; John Powers, 'Chin's Medals Seem Tarnished', *Boston Globe*, 12 Sept. 1994; Senn, *Power, Politics, and the Olympic Games*, 265–8.

[69] Duncan Mackay, 'Suspicions Rest on China as Dark New World Looms', *The Guardian*, 24 Oct. 2003; Guterl and Liu, 'A Natural Advantage?'.

[70] Gittings, *The Changing Face of China*; Mitter, *A Bitter Revolution*; Terrill, *China in Our Time*.

[71] In this interpretation I take the trail blazed in sport history by Dan Nathan in *Saying It's So*.

[72] Robert Lipsyte, 'Olympics: Tug of War Emerging Over 2000 Games', *New York Times*, 1 Aug. 1993.

[73] Tom Lantos, 'Scratch Beijing from the Olympics Wish List', *Los Angeles Times*, 20 May 1993.

[74] Luke Cyphers, 'US Activists Try to Put Hurdles in Way of Beijing's Bid to Host 2000', *Wall Street Journal*, 2 April 1993.

[75] Wushanley, 'Beijing 2008'.

[76] Philip Hersh, 'Olympic Gold for Beijing?', *Chicago Tribune*, 12 July 2001.

[77] Bernie Miklasz, 'Corporations Ignore Beijing's Tarnish in the Hunt for Gold', *St Louis Post-Dispatch*, 19 July 2001. For a history of American corporate designs on the Berlin Games see Keys, 'Spreading Peace, Democracy, and Coca Cola'.

[78] 'China and the Olympics', *Washington Post*, 8 July 2001.

[79] Jeff Jacoby, 'Olympics 2008: Say No to Beijing', *Boston Globe*, 7 May 2001.

[80] 'China Unworthy of Being Site for International Games', *Houston Chronicle*, 24 May 2001.

[81] Hersh, 'Olympic Gold for Beijing?'

[82] Tom Lantos, 'IOC Should Reject China for 2008', *New York Times*, 8 July 2001.

[83] Michael Hedges, 'US Unopposed to China's Bid', *Houston Chronicle*, 13 July 2001.

[84] Ibid.

[85] 'China's Execution Frenzy', *San Francisco Chronicle*, 9 July 2001.

[86] Jere Longman, 'Mixed Messages', *New York Times*, 12 July 2001; Hedges, 'US Unopposed to China's Bid'.

[87] William McGunn, 'The Games Could Make China a Better Place', *Wall Street Journal*, 16 July 2001.

[88] Zbigniew Brzenzinski, 'Can Communism Compete With the Olympics?', *New York Times*, 14 July 2001.

[89] Randy Harvey, 'Beijing Win No Moral Victory', *Los Angeles Times*, 14 July 2001.

[90] Ibid.

[91] Danna Harman, 'Activists Press China with "Genocide Olympics" Label', *Christian Science Monitor*, 26 June 2007.

[92] Ronan Farrow and Mia Farrow, 'One Olympic Victory', *Wall Street Journal*, 19 Feb. 2008.

[93] Adam Thompson, 'Beijing Olympics 2008: The People's Republic of Ban Qiu?', *Wall Street Journal*, 17 April 2007; Dan Giesin, 'Next Up for BMX: Some Heavy Medal', *San Franciso Chronicle*, 9 Sept. 2006; Robert Marquand, 'Even Pop Culture Must Get a Stamp of Approval in China', *Christian Science Monitor*, 14 June 2005.

References

Brown, Elwood S. 'Teaching the World to Play'. *The Outlook* 129 (28 December 1921): 689–693.

Brownell, Susan. 'Challenged America: China and America – Women and Sport, Past, Present, and Future'. *International Journal of the History of Sport* 22 (November 2005): 1173–1193.

——. *Training the Body for China: Sports in the Moral Order of the People's Republic*. Chicago: University of Chicago Press, 1995.

'By the Way'. *The Outlook* 99 (2 December 1911): 836.

Carter, Paul A. *Revolt Against Destiny: An Intellectual History of the United States*. New York: Columbia University Press, 1989.

Collins, Sandra. '1940 Tokyo and the Asian Olympics in the Olympic Movement'. *International Journal of the History of Sport* 24 (August 2007): 955–976.

——. 'Special Issue: The Missing Olympics: The 1940 Tokyo Games, Japan, Asia and the Olympic Movement'. *International Journal of the History of Sport* 24 (August 2007): 955–1148.

Cover Illustration, 'Special Issue: Sport in the Orient – World's Best Athlete: C.K. Yang'. *Sports Illustrated*, 23 December 1963.

Creamer, Robert. 'The Cobra and C.K. Yang'. *Sports Illustrated*, 23 December 1963, 66–77.

Dong, Jinxia. 'Women, Nationalism and the Beijing Olympics: Preparing for Glory'. *International Journal of the History of Sport* 22 (July 2005): 530–544.

——. *Women, Sport, and Modern China: Holding Up More than Half the Sky*. London: Frank Cass, 2003.

Dyreson, Mark. '"America's Athletic Missionaries": Political Performance, Olympic Spectacle and the Quest for an American National Culture, 1896–1912'. *Olympika: The International Journal of Olympic Studies* 1 (1992): 70–91.

——. 'American Ideas About Race and Olympic Races from the 1890s to the 1950s: Shattering Myths or Reinforcing Scientific Racism?' *Journal of Sport History* 28 (Summer 2001): 173–215.

——. 'Globalizing the Nation-Making Process: Modern Sport in World History'. *International Journal of the History of Sport* 20 (March 2003): 91–106.

——. *Making the American Team: Sport, Culture and the Olympic Experience*. Urbana: University of Illinois Press, 1998.

——. 'Marketing National Identity: The Olympic Games of 1932 and American Culture'. *Olympika: The International Journal of Olympic Studies* 4 (1995): 23–48.

——. 'The Playing Fields of Progress: American Athletic Nationalism and the St. Louis Olympics of 1904'. *Gateway Heritage* 14 (Fall 1993): 4–23.

——. 'Scripting the American Olympic Story-Telling Formula: The 1924 Paris Olympic Games and the American Media'. *Olympika: The International Journal of Olympic Studies* 5 (1996): 45–80.

——. 'Selling American Civilization: The Olympic Games of 1920 and American Culture'. *Olympika: The International Journal of Olympic Studies* 8 (1999): 1–41.

'Fact and Comment'. *Youth's Companion* 89 (24 June 1915): 332.

'Forth To War'. *Literary Digest* 116 (16 December 1936): 33–35.

Geertz, Clifford. 'Notes on a Balinese Cockfight'. In *The Interpretation of Cultures.* New York: Basic Books, 1983, 413–453.

Gems, Gerald R. *The Athletic Crusade: Sport and American Cultural Imperialism.* Lincoln: University of Nebraska Press, 2006.

Gittings, John. *The Changing Face of China: From Mao to Market.* New York: Oxford University Press, 2005.

Guterl, Fred, and Liu, Melinda. 'A Natural Advantage? Who Needs Drugs?' *Newsweek*, 18 September 2000, 68.

Guttmann, Allen. *Games and Empires: Modern Sports and Cultural Imperialism.* New York, 1994.

Hacker, Jeffrey. *The New China.* New York: Franklin Watts, 1986.

Hamilton, John Maxwell. 'The Missouri News Monopoly and American Altruism in China: Thomas F.F. Millard, J.B. Powell, and Edgar Snow'. *Pacific Historical Review* 55 (February 1986): 27–48.

Hong, Fan, Ping, Wu, and Huan, Xiong. 'Beijing Ambitions: An Analysis of the Chinese Elite Sports System and Its Olympic Strategy for the 2008 Games'. *International Journal of the History of Sport* 22 (July 2005): 510–529.

——. *Footbinding, Feminism, and Freedom: The Liberation of Women's Bodies in Modern China.* London: Frank Cass, 1997.

——, ed. *Sport, Nationalism and Orientalism: The Asian Games.* London: Routledge, 2007.

Iriye, Akira. *The Globalizing of America, 1913–1945*, v. 3 in *The Cambridge History of American Foreign Relations.* Warren I. Cohen ed. New York: Cambridge University Press, 1993.

Jessup, Elon. 'The Greatest Olympiad'. *The Outlook* 137 (August 13, 1924), 571–572.

Johnson, Rafer. *The Best That I Can Be: An Autobiography.* New York: Doubleday, 1998.

Keys, Barbara. 'Spreading Peace, Democracy, and Coca Cola®: Sport and American Cultural Expansion in the 1930s'. *Diplomatic History* 28 (April 2004):165–196.

LaFeber, Walter. *Michael Jordan and the New Global Capitalism.* New York: W.W. Norton, 1999.

Lockwood, W.W. 'The Chinese Olympic Games'. *The Independent* (26 January 1911): 180–185.

Mangan, J.A. *The Games Ethic and Imperialism: Aspects of the Diffusion of an Ideal* (New York: Viking, 1986; and 2nd revised ed., London: Frank Cass, 1998).

Maule, Tex. 'Yang of China Is World's Best Athlete'. *Sports Illustrated* 6 May 1963, 26–27, 66–67.

Mayo, Katherine. 'Fair Play for the World'. *The Outlook* 129 (21 December 1921): 650–653.

Mitter, Rana. *A Bitter Revolution: China's Struggle with the Modern World.* New York: Oxford University Press, 2004.

Millard, Thomas F. *The New China.* New York: Scribner's, 1906.

Morris, Andrew D. '"I Can Compete!" China in the Olympic Games, 1932 and 1936'. *Journal of Sport History* 26 (Fall 1999): 545–566.

——. *Marrow of the Nation: A History of Sport and Physical Culture in Republican China.* Berkeley: University of California Press, 2004.

Nathan, Daniel A. *Saying It's So: A Cultural History of the Black Sox Scandal.* Urbana: University of Illinois Press, 2003.

Needham, Kirsty. *A Season in Red: My Great Leap Forward into China.* Crows Nest, NSW: Allen & Unwin, 2007.

'The New Olympic Games'. *Life* 76 (9 September 1920): 445.

'Nothing in China'. *Time* 28 March 1938, 20.

'Olympic Fund Problems'. *Literary Digest* 28 (18 April 1936): 43–44.

Paddock, Charles W. *The Fastest Human.* New York: Thomas Nelson & Sons.

——. 'Sprinting Around the World'. *The Saturday Evening Post* 198 (December 5, 1925): 27, 62–68.

Pomfret, John. *Chinese Lessons: Five Classmates and the Story of China.* New York: Henry Holt, 2006.

Prestowitz, Clyde V. *The Billion New Capitalists: The Great Shift of Power and Wealth to the East.* New York: Basic Books, 2005.

Price, S.L. 'Olympic China'. *Sports Illustrated*, 13 August 2007, 72–80.

Rau, Margaret. *The People of New China.* New York: J. Messner, 1978.

Rhoden, William. *Forty Million Dollar Slaves: The Rise, Fall, and Redemption of the Black Athlete.* New York: Crown, 2006.

Said, Edward. *Culture and Imperialism.* New York: Alfred A. Knopf, 1993.

Seavy, W.A. 'Public Opinion'. *The Outlook* 91 (13 March 1909): 588–589.

Senn, Alfred Erich. *Power, Politics, and the Olympic Games.* Champaign, Ill.: Human Kinetics, 1999.

Slack, Trevor, Yuan-min, Hsu, Chiung-tzu, Tsai, and Hong, Fan. 'The Road to Modernization: Sport in Taiwan'. *International Journal of the History of Sport.* 19 (July 2002): 343–365.

Spence, Jonathan D. *The Search for Modern China.* New York: W.W. Norton, 1991.

Snyder, Charles D. 'A Study In The Demographic Distribution of Cultural Achievement'. *Scientific Monthly* 46 (March 1938): 261–267.

——. 'The Real Winners In The 1936 Olympic Games'. *Scientific Monthly* 43 (October 1936): 372–374.

Todd, Frank Morton. *The Story of the Exposition: Being the Official History of the International Celebration Held at San Francisco in 1915 to Commemorate the Discovery of the Pacific Ocean and the Construction of the Panama Canal,* V. III. New York: Published for the Panama-Pacific International Exposition Company by G.P. Putnam's Sons, 1921.

Torres, Cesar, and Dyreson, Mark. 'The Cold War Games'. In *Research in the Sociology of Sport: Olympic Journeys*, Volume III, ed. Kevin Young and Kevin Wamsley, pp. 59–82. Amsterdam: Elsevier, 2005.

Terrill, Ross. *China in Our Time: The Epic Saga of the People's Republic from the Communist Victory to Tiananmen Square and Beyond.* New York: Simon & Schuster, 1992.

——. *The New Chinese Empire: And What It Means for the United States.* New York: Basic Books, 2003.

Welky, David. 'U.S. Journalism and the 1932 Olympics'. *Journal of Sport History* 24 (Spring 1997): 24–49.

WuShanley, Ying. 'Beijing 2008'. In *The Historical Dictionary of the Modern Olympic Movement*, rev. 2nd ed. John Findling and Karen Pelle, eds. 263–268. Westport, Conn.: Greenwood Press, 2004.

Yamamoto, Eriko. 'Cheers for Japanese Athletes: The 1932 Los Angeles Olympics and the Japanese American Community'. *Pacific Historical Review* 69 (August 2000): 399–429.

Epilogue: Sideshow Beijing 2008 – An Absence of Euphoria beyond the Southern Clouds

Kevin Caffrey

The Observation

It has been observed elsewhere that the Beijing Olympics is a performance of political spectacle that shows the direction of China's geopolitical intentions. In itself, this example demonstrates key aspects of international political spectacle in general, while also illuminating some of the particular Chinese ways Beijing 2008 is unique. But there is another observation to be made that has much to do with the changing Chinese sociopolitical landscape and its neoliberal dress – one that has to do with the price China is paying for Beijing 2008. As with many things Chinese and market-oriented, there is some haggling over the price – only this *jiangjia* (literally 'talking price') has some further-reaching ramifications than whether one is paying too much for cabbage. The staggering cost of the spectacle Olympics, despite its euphoric support in the urban east, has come to strike some Chinese citizens very differently. In some margins and on the frontiers of the country, the issue of the Beijing

Olympics is remarkably free of this hysteria and unquestioned support. Instead, the games stand as a meaningful sign of something else that is bothering the people – a 'something else' that has more to do with the hard and immediate realities of life than the abstract concerns of international *mianzi* ('face'). In Yunnan, as will be shown, the Olympics are often understood as a sign of misguided priorities on the part of Beijing. Alternately, it is sometimes thought of as a sign of corruption in officialdom – indeed, as an especially high profile example of a systemic problem facing the developing population giant. It is even perhaps occasionally understood by intellectuals as a sign of 'business-as-usual' neoliberal inequalities where those less well-placed in the new market society *are also valued less*. In general, the situation of the Olympics and their hidden costs has come to look like a new neoliberal nation-state version of the tendency to marginalize frontier areas and peoples that characterized the historical mode of Chinese empire. But let us begin with a revelatory incident from the frontier near China's border with Burma.

The newspaper headlines in the Yunnan town of Lijiang on the day China was awarded the Olympic Games for 2008 read *Women Yinle!* ('We won!'). The verb *yin* ('to win') is used to describe the successful competition outcome of contests, games and wars – much as in English. The martial connotation of this usage is clear, and if we needed evidence that China is playing by something like American rules, this would suffice. With the possible exception of British muscular Christian sensibilities, this understanding of *award* as being a kind of *conquest* strikes one as almost exclusively American. Indeed, the 'performed' state of drunken happiness many of the celebrants displayed that night reminded the author of a football game seen in southern California, only without the traffic. After a decade of working in China, the Americanness of the Chinese (and vice versa) never ceases to amaze. In this small tourist centre the author happened to be in that day, this is how the majority of tourists conceptually situated the outcome of the award. They were mostly middle- and upper-class urbanites from eastern cities who were in Yunnan to happily drink, eat and take in some of the famous 'ethnic flavour' of the area; and they had brought their own sentiments with them. What the games would mean for China was a popular topic of discussion that day, with feelings of pride, patriotism and confidence represented there in abundance. For example, a few choruses of some kind of drinking song heard that night included references to *weidade zhongguo* ('Great China') and *bishang meiguo* ('beat the USA'). There was some local appreciation for the event as well, and celebrations were to be heard going on into the evening at local bars and restaurants.

Importantly for our analysis, however, Yunnanese people often reacted differently to this Olympics news and imported eastern sentiment. Aside from embarrassment at their compatriots' aggressively patriotic singing when they saw that the Chinese-speaking American was listening, they expressed hesitation at the euphoria with which the Beijing games were being described. Also voiced in sentimental terms, this reaction was caught somewhere between disgust, studied lack of concern and suspicion. Local people were sometimes visibly sullen about the idea of (yet) another grand symbolic *yundong* ('movement') that had all the earmarks of a political movement and (they suspected) would have little or no positive impact on the relatively (vis-à-vis the eastern coast) underprivileged Yunnanese. '*Yinle? Shei yinle? Ye bushi wo yinde*' ('Won? Who won? It sure wasn't me who won') was the reaction of one local businessman. '*Zheige liwu shi **songde***' ('This present was *gifted*'), he said, invoking the very Chinese recognition that gifts come with various subtle and bitingly meaningful reciprocity costs. Going into some detail, this local restaurant owner suggested that the situation was very much like a Chinese wedding where the newlyweds may get some fine gifts, but in order to live up to their standard the wedding banquet had to be lavish indeed. 'Who is the newlywed here?' he mused, asking in effect who was going to repay this gift of the Olympics awarded to Beijing. Beijing may have received the gift, he noted, but someone other than Beijing was going to have to pay for it in order for the Chinese as a whole to live up to its standard. Furthermore, the extractive relationship the centre has to marginal Chinese areas such as Yunnan implies that the middle and upper classes who occupy the population centres in the east are not going to be the ones picking up the tab.

The picture emerging here is far from the harshness of historic peasant revolts that one thinks of as the traditional activity of peasant dissent, but that past is not entirely unconnected from the present-day social unrest. The kinds of disgruntled sentiments seen in this single Yunnanese situation are consequences of urban/rural socio-economic bifurcation and accompanying corruption, and their incidence has caused current Communist Party unease – both in muted tones of policy concern and exasperated calls for immediate action. Micro-scale local events in which these sentiments can be voiced provide the mystery through which to enquire into the assumed agreement that the grandiose 2008 Olympic Games are necessarily a common bonding ritual of a now internationally great China. The evidence from the Chinese hinterland location of western Yunnan is that not all Chinese are euphoric in acclaim for the Beijing miracle, nor are they chauvinistically enraptured by the possibility of outdoing the Western sporting juggernaut. The hysterical climate of national self-congratulation that had overtaken Beijing after the award is called into question from this unassailably Chinese but marginalized quarter – a segment of the population not at all interested in challenging the greatness of China. Rather, the interest from this vantage is focused on ensuring Chinese greatness well into the future – an inspiration for a future in which all Chinese citizens can participate equally rather than just those chosen few tapped by the magic wand of market reform in the hands of the structurally secure eastern elite. This position is not without its supporters, driven by experience and voiced in muted sentiment.

The fervour of having been awarded the Olympics has subsided somewhat in the eastern population centres as the realities of sacrifice to the Olympian gods of neoliberal development have started to impact the otherwise malleable mass nationalism in the Chinese east. This is perhaps not surprising given the startling material price tag for the 2008 games – currently at $40 billion and rising. [2] What is more surprising than it should perhaps be is that this rising sentiment of questioning the cost-to-benefit ratio of Beijing's pseudo-governmental Olympics *is not new to many*

Chinese. The inland, western and frontier populations have something of an ambivalent tolerance of Beijing's grand gestures when they know from history that *they* will more often than not be the ones who pay for all the hand-waving. This inquiry uses a revelatory event through which we can see Chinese ambivalence that balances the more lauded popular fervour – a precarious poise that rests upon the negotiation of material, regional and social inequalities simmering behind the symbolic Olympics 'banquet'. The divisions are margin-to-centre and underprivileged-to-privileged on social and economic registers, and the image to be brought into focus is that of frontier Yunnanese sentiments regarding central Beijing activities. These sentiments represent a possible response to central authority that is always latent in Chinese mass activity – a latency given shape by a cursory look at historical pattern.

Historical Background: Frontiers and Margins

The present-day argument over priorities involving the 2008 games is in some ways connected back through history to past Chinese forms of confrontation between centralized potency and relative local impotency – and between self-serving bureaucrats and put-upon commoners. It is occasionally said of China that in the past the emperor and his officialdom looked upon the rural population (*laobaixin*) [3] as something like a 'force of nature'. The implication was that the general population, not being developed enough by *wenhua* ('culture' – lit. 'literary transformation') to completely understand the complexities of good governance and public well-being, was instead prone to being too readily influenced towards unpredictable and potentially destabilizing unrest that could interfere with the proper functioning of the empire. However, there was also another concern relating to this notion of the Chinese masses being as unpredictable as the weather. The 'force of nature' trope also involved a sense of 'feedback from heaven' built into prevailing epistemes of governance that lay at the centre of imperial government. The unrest of the *laobaixin*, thought in this way to be as irrational as the weather by a usually patronizing and far removed bureaucracy, was also said to reflect an evaluation by heaven. Governance in the land was continually under review, as it were – something like a mandate of heaven, the maintenance or loss of which was both signalled and exercised by when unrest occurred, its degree and how it was handled. Like dangerous weather, rural unrest was a feared event among officials, and it was to be guarded against both because it was bad for the state and bad for them personally.

More than a few of my Naxi, Yi, Hui and Han friends on the north-west Yunnan frontier who were proud of the work they did under the early Communists (1945–70) cited the change in Beijing's attitude towards the people as the most important foundational shift in political thinking during the revolutionary transformation led by the Communists. This mindset had shifted from looking upon the *laobaixin* as unpredictable and potentially dangerous force of nature to seeing them as that population *on behalf of which* the government serves. The first republic – that of the Nationalist Kuomintang – had tried and failed to really achieve this, but the proud activists of the peoples' movements in the 1950s and 1960s remember Mao's government as having managed it. [4] This seemingly simple shift in the way representatives of state conceptualize the people represented a foundational shift in the Chinese epistemologies of government. This mindset can perhaps be an illuminating indicator for how 'imperial' or 'national' China is at any one time, and the focus on unrest locates our concern.

Turmoil in the *laobaixin* meant turmoil in Beijing's soul – a situation with an interesting and revelatory precedent. The practical mechanics of the earlier episteme of governance are visible in the intriguing example of a soul-stealing rumour in the Qing dynasty. In 1768 a rumour spread in China's south central coastal region (*Jiangnan*) that there were those who were stealing souls. Like many similar places, such rumours and fear of magical attack were not entirely unusual in the Chinese popular imaginary. But this one got out of control, and the unrest it caused attracted the attention of higher officials all the way up to the Qianlong emperor himself. Philip Kuhn's analysis of the rumour, its social and political economic conditions of possibility and the manner in which it was handled (in great detail, all the way up to the very hands-on emperor) show the soul-stealer unrest to have been a multivariate sign with somewhat different meanings assigned by different groups involved. [5] Common people saw the event as a sign of threat to their families (especially their children), while lower level officials correctly judged that it meant their positions – and therefore their livelihoods – were in flux. Higher officials correctly surmised that their positions were under immediate threat from events as difficult to control as the weather, and the imperial court saw the unrest as a threat to social stability that could easily get out of control and threaten its rule if left unaddressed. One can assess the event by concluding that the farther removed from the event, such as those in the imperial court, the more likely that it would be viewed as a product of the stresses of proto-industrial transformation. But this may have been small comfort to the average Jiangnan peasant whose soul was in danger. The unusual quarter from which the unrest began – a rumour based on a popular superstition about how to build a strong bridge – shows something of the range of potential sources for unrest. The rioting, sheer numbers affected, official reaction and violence provide an example of how precarious social stability can be in times of stress caused by socio-economic transformation such as that proto-industrial revolution centred on Jiangnan's then silk industry. But it is what the example suggests about the relationship between governing attitude towards common people and what that attitude demonstrates about how officialdom sees unrest in the populations that is useful here.

Kuhn writes about the political-economic and historical factors that served as conditions of possibility for those events, but more importantly for our point he also discussed the attitudes of the various levels of officialdom towards the rumours, actions and general instability of the events – and in particular who was to blame for them. [6] A few 'ringleaders' were always punished, but for the most part the people involved in the unrest were thought to have been something like gullible innocents moved to disorder by the few 'bad apples'. Substantial blame was *also* placed on officials who, in the rhetoric used by the emperor in his unvarnished blaming of provincial officials, were seen to have failed their primary responsibility of maintaining order and stability. The imperial court tended to conclude – at least rhetorically – that the occurrence of this unrest in their districts was a direct indictment by heaven of their ability to do their jobs, and many officials deemed responsible were ultimately demoted or sacked outright. Though just one example, the soul-stealers event serves to show how officialdom viewed the failure of provincial and local officials to maintain order.

Hevia notes that empires are preoccupied with their centres, whereas nation-states attend largely to their borders. [7] Imperial frontiers are where civilization ends in diminishing degree, while national boundaries are where one is faced with a different type of place, being and essence mathematically demarcated by an abstract line. [8] The nature of the modern Chinese nation state is something of a palimpsest in which can be seen an enduring imperial dynamic between China's centres and its peripheries. For most of its history, China's imperial form relied on prevailing understandings of difference that were organized around degree rather than type – human difference that went hand-in-hand with the geo-cosmological sovereignty understandings of empires being preoccupied with centres rather than borders. This cosmology was ordered around the emperor in concentric rings emanating out from his location, becoming less civilized – which is to say 'less Chinese' – the farther out one got until the people were unrequited and un-Chinese *yi* ('barbarians'). The 'glue' that held this civilizational polity together was a usual mix of political economy and social institution, but the unusual aspect of it all was that society and its efficacy was always voiced, narrated and acted upon as if the real glue was the attraction powers of the civilizing, transformational 'light' (*wenming*) of the Son of Heaven. While it would be wildly incorrect to suggest that the empire had no coercive elements – which the very militaristic polity had in abundance – it was this 'soft' power of attraction that dominated the *discourse* of power. [9] We know that Lattimore maintained, counter to much inherited understanding about Chinese political interaction, that Chinese-non-Chinese relations on the northern and western frontiers were usually expansionist and dominating in practice. [10] But the 'word,' as opposed to the deed, of interaction ritual was couched in the rhetoric of civilizational attractiveness drawing all unto its brightness.

The historical trajectory that puts historical frontiers and marginal populations at the *centre* of nation-state concerns thus takes us up until the present day – a day rife with unrest in these and other areas, due in large part to neoliberal stresses during *gaige kaifang* ('reform and opening'). This neoliberal shift is situated within the processes of transformation from imperial to national forms of state and cannot be taken lightly. The nation-form transformation has reshaped the way discord is spoken about today, though the conditions for potential unrest may in broad strokes be similar. The arrival of the nation-form around the turn of the twentieth century brought with it a move to a new preoccupation with borders and demarcating territory. This new practice was an elemental part of the prevailing new notion of sovereignty as primarily territorial rather than primarily jurisdictional (though both sense were likely always present at all times). Interestingly, this nation-form move was also a move away from the soft power emphasis of imperial notions of civilization (*wenming*) towards the hard power emphasis on controlling territory – which then becomes the most legitimate indicator of sovereignty. Whether or not the practicalities of Chinese international interactions changed significantly from its previous course is unclear, but the way in which international relations – the theory – is now usually conceptualized is in accordance with the realist school that dominates Western interaction rituals. [11]

The 2008 Beijing Games, then, might be seen as an Olympian ritual to that new deity in the pantheon – the nation state. With it is displayed the muscular Christian nationalism with Chinese characteristics that we are seeing in the rhetoric of world harmony through competitive spectacle – a neoliberal dream of sorts that belies a host of contradictions latent in transforming-as-we-speak Chinese society. In a political-economic return of the repressed, the stresses of neoliberal transformation result in disgruntled alienation that can bubble up into unrest that takes many strange and interesting forms. [12] Our inquiry seeks not to highlight today's unrest by focusing on a particular event in some pointed way. Rather, what follows will be a laying out of conditions – both historical and present-day – that illuminate how certain sentiments expressed from China's margins might be a more subtle component of more alarming unrest. Below we will further examine the case of the Yunnanese who are suspicious of the notion of Beijing 2008 as an unmitigated good, an example of exactly this more subtle component that can be thought of as a necessary but not sufficient condition for greater unrest. In order to make sense of this, however, it is useful to understand what 'unrest' can mean in China.

Unrest/Dissent

The manner in which unrest comes to be expressed can also serve as an indicator for the shift from empire to nation state. Historically, unrest was a result of a failure in the balance between extractive/exploitive tax farming by officialdom vs. the benefits of being *Hua* or *Han* (Chinese) subjects. These benefits could be economic, symbolic or political. State protection for businessmen on the rough frontier would have been an economic benefit, with a related symbolic advantage being association with the local Confucian temple society that would assist in efforts to educate one's children in preparation for a profitable official position. An example of a political benefit would have been anything from positive association with a powerful polity capable of exercising substantial violence, to the more straightforward opportunity to hold official position in the Confucian structure of Chinese polity. [13] Whatever the case, these benefits were enjoyed by subjects of the empire who could be more *or less* Chinese by their cosmological position. On the frontiers at least, people also had the option of turning away from China to become something else – Burmese, Thai or Manchu, perhaps. The tie to 'Chineseness' ('Hanness' or 'Huaness') was sociopolitical and ultimately fluid, with the state concerned with gaining subjects (i.e., making *and keeping* them Chinese).

After the nation-form transformation, unrest was still – like its earlier avatar – an issue of resistance to and disgust with unchecked resource extraction and neo-tax farming. However, the nature of the benefits due to them was that of the privileges of Chinese *national citizens*. Again, these benefits could be economic, symbolic or political, but they are enjoyable as obligations due to them by the nation state by the fact that they are all equally Chinese – as defined by nationality policies. According to the powerful new nationality episteme, they cannot, unlike before, become something other than Chinese. 'Chinese' had become an ethnic formulation registering differences of type rather than a sociopolitical category measured in degree. In both cases, too stark an inequality between that which is taken from them and that which they receive in return serves as the condition of possibility that leads to dissent/unrest. As mentioned, a subject of empire might (however improbably) choose not to follow established Chinese ways in the margins and on the frontiers of the empire, electing instead to be something else. This escape does not exist under the nation-form, where Chinese nationality has come to be felt as an essential and unchangeable quality. Recourse for Chinese citizens must necessarily take the form of engagement with the state *as its citizens*, and that engagement tends to be formulated in the discourse of petitioning to ensure that they receive the privileges due them under the responsibilities of the nation state. Historically, the unrest of the *laobaixin* took the form of riots, bandit activity and rebellions. Examples were grain riots and other kinds of protests, the romantically named groups of roving bandits and full-blown rebellions. [14] Today this unrest commonly appears as rioting over exploitation, corruption, arbitrary enforcement of law and mismanagement. [15] Dissent is commonly voiced as the demand that the state live up to its announced responsibilities, which is a sense of entitlement very much in keeping with the nation-form's notion of the tax-paying citizen.

China is not now and has never been the kind of monolithic authoritarian state that most in the West have tended to think it was, despite its strong centralization. Even today with immediate communication technology mediating throughout the chain of control and representation from Beijing all the way down to the village, innumerable levels of savvy official operators and sheer inertia militate against any monolithic operation. Such a large polity has always been faced with sometimes extreme difficulty of negotiation up and down the chain of control leading from the capital to the frontiers, and even the radical efficiencies of the nation-form have not done away with this obstacle. Rather, the shift from empire to nation state has witnessed both a continuation of some forms of obstacle (peasant riots and self-serving officials, for example) and an exchange of certain imperial forms of complication for new national ones (the Internet, for example). In this atmosphere of precarious balance, the great bargain and the inherent destabilizing energies of neoliberal values as they refigure and solidify social cleavages and forms of alienation, the political spectacle of the Olympics all too easily (and perhaps appropriately) gets appropriated by these dissent narratives. In several narratives heard in the quotidian world of Yunnan, Beijing is too preoccupied with the games to pay attention to corruption – a ready explanation for corruption that at the same time justifies more of it if the opportunity to get away with it presents itself. Officials are reported to (corruptly) insist that newly levied (and illegal) taxes on an already heavily taxed peasant base are to pay for the Olympics. Even elements of the Public Security Bureau reported to the author that stricter controls on what foreigners are writing about China have been put into place – a claim that was accompanied by a demand to see field notes. [16] This last appropriation of the Olympics for personal reasons of *mianzi* ('face') – he was training a new officer and wanted to demonstrate how one dealt with resident busy-body Americans – was all the more interesting because it was exactly the opposite of what China had officially promised the International Olympic Committee, which was that strict controls on journalists and foreigners writing about China would be *relaxed*. [17] In each case of appropriation, however, Beijing 2008 becomes a reason for doing something more immediately to hand – corruption, manipulation and saving face respectively. It is these more immediate issues that make up the practices of everyday life, and from the vantage of the margins these interactions and their conditions of possibility are very much centred.

The grand Beijing Olympic Games become in these circumstances a sideshow. They become something of a performance to the world – a Chinese Madison Avenue by other means that asserts that 'we mean what we say about China being great again'. As with the political-economic conditions of possibility that built Madison Avenue, the realities we see hidden in the sentiments of frontier Chinese towards the games point to the cost of this advertisement. The China scholars who have taken up the cause of social justice for the masses have correctly pointed out that the real work of building greatness is less neon and requires more intellectual and economic bravery than China has so far mustered – at least since the 1950s. Real greatness, they maintain, has no place for the massive wealth disparities neoliberal development generates, along with other structures of inequality that lead to the creation of capitalism's second- and third-class citizens.

Sideshow Beijing 2008

In western Yunnan, where the social landscape is that of many different minority peoples whose relationship with the Chinese centre is marginal, the world of Beijing is so far away that an almost relaxed disregard for it is captured in the popular saying: 'The mountains are high and the emperor is far away' (*shan gao huangdi yuan*). The western region of Yunnan is populated by a mix of different Chinese peoples, no less Chinese than those of central and eastern Chinese for the fact that they may not be members of the Han nationality. Indeed, if we are to take the prevailing (relatively) impoverished state they share with *most* rural Chinese and labour migrants everywhere in the country as a sign of unity, they are a lot more 'Chinese' than those well-heeled and well positioned urban elite (mostly Han) in Beijing. Class is key here – in exactly the Marxist sense of those who share the same relationship to the means of production. The concerns of Yunnan are not necessarily the concerns of Beijing. Rather, this relatively poor province is constrained by the need to maintain the natural beauty of the area so as not to upset its dominating tourist industry, weighed against the need to seek other kinds of development that will benefit those without income from tourism. Its relationship to Beijing has historically been tenuous, and more recently akin to benign neglect on the centre's part, with the province left somewhat to its own devices.

The now glaring division is between urban China and rural China – now often narrated as separate places. This unintended malformation of the 'one China, two systems' rhetoric relating to Hong Kong cannot be ignored, and its political-economic realities are driving newly forced governmental attention to the inherent instabilities of the country. The muted tumult of growing protest violence, increasing corruption feeding it and officials' wilfulness about attending to their own priorities rather than those of the people they govern, each manage in their own ways to bring these issues of disparity and division further into view. Recent international image-building attempts by Beijing have been seen to improve China's image in some quarters, but the very public nature of these events also necessitates that they become readily available to the Chinese people, who are then prone to evaluate their claims against their own experience and priorities. The Olympics are a revelatory issue in this regard, and one where a thoughtful attention to the ripples of dissent and difference it is throwing off in the Chinese population can be repaid with an illuminated look into that other China in 2008. This second China, the one where most Chinese live, is one where the grand Olympic Games is but a sideshow.

This decidedly less euphoric view of the games can be seen revealed in the awkward celebration event in Yunnan the day of the announcement that the Olympics had been awarded to Beijing. Given the prevailing attitude in Yunnan about distance from the centre, the location provides a vantage on the Olympics where local concerns and their political-economic conditions of possibility tend to obscure some of the grandiosity of Beijing 2008. The revelatory incident from Lijiang with which we began this study shows sentiments that each direct us towards some of the meaningful reactions marginal and marginalized peoples have about the way they see China being run. Some of these sentiments are positive. Along with the eastern tourists, friends and acquaintances also exhibited a strong degree of pride in being Chinese. This was felt and reported as indirect pride that China has, as a whole, brought itself up into the status as a significant country in the world once again – a sentiment generally voiced simply as that of *jinbu* ('improvement'). This kind of pride was substantially different from the 'We won, we are great, only a great country gets the Olympics!' enthusiasm loudly demonstrated by the relatively wealthy eastern Chinese visiting Yunnan that day – many of whom were from Beijing. Both senses of pride, however, were related to and often indistinguishable from the motivating sentiment of patriotism, a notion translated into Chinese as *aiguo*, or 'love of country'. During the evening festivities that day, the drinking games, the informal feasting and the singing carried the sentiment that China is great – *weidade zhongguo* – long into the night. The logic found therein was simple: China is great because it was awarded the 2008 Olympics, a success that shows international recognition of its greatness. The confidence built into this assessment also often carried the more vocal celebrants well into several long choruses of a song involving the words *women hui bishang Meiguo* ('we will beat the USA'), [18] and the entire atmosphere of the event would be immediately recognizable to anyone who had happened in their youth to attend and understand the spectacle of an American high-school football game.

And yet, as mentioned above, some of the same people who were happily serving these celebrants their food and drink were not particularly in agreement with this reason for celebrating. What they were feeling and thinking about the newly awarded Olympics was occupied with variously intertwined forms of angst at the misguided priorities of their political leaders. One proprietor of a teashop wondered out loud to me about whether it was the appropriate time for China to be so disproportionately concerned with its international image. This, he said, was like a poor farmer taking a loan to buy a Mercedes (*nongming jiaqian mai Benz*); even if the bank will lend you the money (and Chinese banks will almost always lend you the money if you have the right connections) you still do not know how to drive the thing. More reluctantly, it costs a great deal of money and it will not help you or your neighbours grow enough to eat. Hidden here is a fairly sophisticated sense that societies and states develop according to a sequence that should not be too readily tinkered with lest something bad happen. Associated with this, though perhaps his personal understanding, was the idea that development had a certain propriety to it where everyone should benefit before those who had already benefited take the next step up. Wanting everyone to have the chance to be elevated before the wealthy get even wealthier seems to be a sense of justice that is very popular in the lower echelons of Chinese society, where the notion that Beijing is often trying to run before it can really walk due to issues of face is popular. The grandiose spectacle of an Olympics held in eastern China does not, so the sentiment goes, bring basic necessities to those in western China. Access to medical care has actually got worse than it was under the Communists, [19] and the disparities of relative poverty are often more sorely felt than general universal poverty. Indeed, several informants who were themselves low-level officials in the provincial government scoffed at the whole situation, and criticized Beijing for causing its own problems. One of the most substantial social problems in Yunnan, they point out, is the trafficking in high-grade heroin. The government is very noisy about trying to control this problem, but the trade is dominated by poor and underprivileged people who have no access to eastern China's development benefits. If Beijing were really concerned with stopping the heroin problem, they say, then instead of wasting money trying to interdict the drug supply and sale, they would help the province develop so that poor people would not turn to drugs as their own route to development. Rather than do this, Beijing chooses to spend a massive amount of money on the *Beijing aoyun qiye* ('Beijing Olympics industry') –

an industry they know to be predicated on official manipulation and kleptocratic corruption.

Corruption is a theme that runs through most discussion of politics in China, at least that which looks up from the lower levels of society. It is listed as the cause of much misery for the people today, and is nearly always thought of as beyond all hope of improvement. This sentiment was somewhat humorously demonstrated in 1999 when an acquaintance of the author very uncharacteristically said, when talking about the graft element of a local road-building project, that he knew the English word for the way it was being organized. The word had been taught to him by an engineer from Illinois ('the state where Chicago is') while they were working together on a small hydro-electric project in southern Yunnan. Yet at that point he could not quite remember the word – though he promised he would think of it as we went along. For some time after that whenever the issue of corruption came up in conversation, he would mention that he knew the English word, but could never quite remember it. When it was widely known that party officials in an area north of Lijiang were manipulating villagers into moving off certain parcels of land that only they knew were eventually going to be used for road-building, he mentioned that the profit from compensation to villages went to these officials – a *fubai* ('corrupt') situation for which he insisted he had the English term on the tip of his tongue. He could not quite produce the word when news of the massive corruption regarding land speculation over the sites of the Beijing games trickled over national broadcasts. Nor could he quite produce the term from memory when reports passed through family and friends that one of the officials who was in charge of organizing the Olympic Games in Beijing was found to have become so wealthy that he kept a house full of beautiful women for his own personal use in the resort city of Dalian. He almost came up with it once when discussing news of police raids on migrant labourer communities in Beijing suburbs, and he was very animated about almost thinking of it when he heard from a news source that hospitals in Beijing and elsewhere on the east coast were overcharging *laobaixin in advance* for unnecessary tests and procedures. But it was not until one day in late 2001 when the government head of Yunnan and his family were rumoured to have been arrested for graft and corruption that he finally blurted out the word 'boondoggle!' He was ultimately correct about many of the situations to which he applied the term, and it was somehow fitting that of the handful of English words he knew this was the one he was proudest to be able to recite. It was even more fitting that he tended to associate the term with Chicago, Mayor Daley's protestations to the contrary notwithstanding. The author did not have the heart to tell him that it was actually a slang term, and he kept using it.

The real-estate and construction profiteering in Beijing has recently become amplified by the efforts of many to shamelessly get their piece of the action, as the narrow Olympics window of opportunity (both temporally and socially) is fast closing. The increasing obviousness of these attempts cannot be kept out of the news, and the impact this news is having on those in the far reaches of the country – areas already somewhat skeptical about the whole boondoggle aspect of the Olympics industry – draws into sharp focus the fractures in society brought on by economic development with Chinese characteristics. The neoliberal inequalities inherent in the system are becoming more visible in the backstage events of Beijing 2008, and our view from the frontier alerts us to the shape of both this backstage and the inequalities. We in the West tend to argue that society operates on the metaphor of the market – a utility-maximizing system model with its own built-in controls. This is likely an error based on our assuming that our society – which tends to operate this way because it is a product of our long and thorough relationship with individualizing capitalism – should in fact be the order that underpins all societies. Yet whatever the case, the notion of the market as an assumed ideal where market rules should order access to resources seems to lie at the heart of China's neoliberal reforms, even if the government refuses to admit as much. Those who are poorly positioned to take advantage of the growing market forces inescapably serve as its reserve army of labour – flowing towards work and having their relationship with place severed or transformed. Frontier and marginal populations are disproportionately represented in the reserve army of labour. Advantageously positioned citizens who have the means, however, escape the need to serve in the reserve army of labour. Those who manage to thrive are disproportionately urban, middle-class eastern Chinese who can adapt to the 'time-space compression' [20] that leaves the underprivileged worker eternally outside the possibility of upward mobility.

This returns us to the issue of the 'unwanted wedding gift' view of the 2008 games. Something like this notion was on the minds of more than a few people in Lijiang that day, but this local fellow's metaphor of the gifted Olympics seems revelatory. His disgruntledness born of a life spanning several such locally questionable 'movements' – a category in which he included all such things gifted from Beijing whether they were wanted or not – is an ethnographic entry into a picture of centre-periphery relations in China. It should be noted that he was no reactionary limited only to negative assessments of the situation. He explained, for example, that he had originally been opposed to Beijing's intervention into the lumber and wood products industry in Yunnan as well. Yet he later recognized that shutting the industry down and stopping the timber cutting in the region had been a forward-thinking and wise move on Beijing's part for both environmental and economic reasons. Nevertheless, his recognition of Beijing's wisdom did not extend to the issue of the Olympics. Hosting the games, he thought, was a display of sociopolitical greatness acted out by wealthy and powerful states that had elevated their national condition to such a point where the next logical step would be to display itself confidently to the world as a self-sufficient actor by international norms. The US, he noted, was such a place with money and confidence to burn. This rosy picture of American stature he held as a given allowed him to suggest that American strength in games came from inherent American success as a country and a society. Chinese strength at games, however, came from a concerted effort to produce good athletes, and did not emerge naturally from societal excellence. Rather, China was putting the cart before the horse with only a facile strength being displayed towards the world. Emphasis, he maintained, should have been placed on organizing resources towards making Chinese people and their life conditions great rather than making China's images great. No amount of image alone is going to do the job that naturally elevating the Chinese people would do, and in the end the excellence in games that emerged from a truly great society would far outshine the manufactured success of the Chinese Olympic present.

Conclusion

This analysis has tried to offer some marginal insight into the hysterical climate of national self-congratulation that has characterized Chinese and other coverage of the 2008 Olympics. Using a revelatory incident from the far Yunnan frontier where sentiments about the Olympics being awarded to Beijing were witnessed, the mystery of why these sentiments stand in subtle opposition to eastern Chinese euphoria energize our investigation into the conditions of this dissent. The historical background of relations between the Chinese centre and the common people who populate the giant polity has been briefly outlined in order to establish a trajectory of transformation in the way that relationship has manifested itself in the past. A very brief discussion of unrest and dissent then situated the Yunnanese sentiments in changing epistemes of disagreement with Beijing, while bringing into focus the conditions of possibility for the alternative understandings of Beijing 2008 seen to be held by the common people of Yunnan. And the neoliberal conditions of division and opposition that underpin this particular disagreement over the world's grandest games are here shown to be a sideshow to the real work of making a great China – at least from the vantage of distant Yunnan and people distant from the palaces of power in Beijing.

   Without making too much of the etymology, we note that the games' namesake can illuminate something of the situation's sentimental element. Mount Olympus was the abode of the gods to the Greeks, and their concerns were quite apart from those of the people. Indeed, as Zeus's escapades and Hera's vindictiveness demonstrated, when the gods become involved in the affairs of man, it was often a very bad thing. Some of the ordinary peoples in Yunnan Province look upon their own modern Olympus – for a time in 2008 to even be located in Beijing by something like the same name – with a similar mixture of awe at the greatness of status it represents, dread at its costs (both opportunity and in real terms) and hopefulness that its attention to Yunnan would take the form of its just responsibilities to this peripheral place. The alternative is attention that takes a more extractive and demanding form that, formulated as the need for a grand display of greatness, appears nonetheless to be another of the gods' fickle escapades to glorify themselves at the expense of ordinary people.

   In conclusion, Beijing 2008 opened with a Prologue reflecting upon the Beijing Olympics as viewed by Chinese Officialdom as a political spectacular resonant with Chinese geopolitical ambitions for greatness beyond the nation's boundaries and closes with an Epilogue reflecting on the Beijing Olympics as a political sideshow as viewed by those Chinese citizens who would prefer Chinese Officialdom to concentrate on less spectacular ambitions for greatness within the nation's boundaries. Thus the circle is closed.

Notes

[1] The author wishes to acknowledge that the idea and need for an analysis of this kind, however limited, was the outcome of a characteristically fruitful discussion with Prof. James Mangan. Originally begun as an inquiry into what the dissenting opinions obscured behind the admirable rhetoric of global harmony – an imperial-flavoured discourse not entirely unfamiliar to historically minded Britishers and any American currently paying attention – might be, the investigation and its author have no interest in diminishing China's grand achievement (for they are many). Rather, the exercise was designed to illuminate the sentiments behind certain recurrences (too patterned to be random) of a enunciated desire to *bishang* ('outdo' or 'to beat') traditional Olympics powers, and more importantly to understand why those sentiments so expressed were considered misguided or just 'tacky' by a subtle but audible section of the Chinese population. The revelatory examples narrated herein bring these themes and these people into a relief that, as the title says, makes the songs of global harmony spun by official Beijing something of a sideshow to the real issues of bare life in a tumultuous China.

[2] The actual amount, however, seems to be either entirely unknown or something like an embarrassing state secret. The $40 billion price tag is what the media have been using in the final week of this writing.

[3] This is now usually glossed as the 'peasantry', though the strictly class-oriented term is misleading.

[4] It is strange, then, that today we once again see the pendulum of history swinging back to an earlier predisposition towards viewing the population in a more imperial episteme – as a potential threat to governmental stability.

[5] Kuhn, *Soulstealers*.

[6] Ibid.

[7] Hevia, *Cherishing Men From Afar*, quoted in Lipman, *Familiar Strangers*, xxviii.

[8] Winichakul *Siam Mapped*.

[9] Nye's definition of soft power, from his book of the same name, is stated as 'The basic concept of power is the ability to influence others to get them to do what you want. There are three major ways to do that: one is to threaten them with sticks; the second is to pay them with carrots; the third is to attract them or co-opt them, so that they want what you want. If you can get others to be attracted, to want what you want, it costs you much less in carrots and sticks' (Nye and Myers, *Soft Power*, introduction). Interestingly, the implicit return to an attention towards soft power that is reflected in China's new attention to its image through the vehicle of the games appears to be something akin to a return to China's old attention to itself as an 'attracting' centre – only the new civilizing light of the Son of Heaven is the symbolic capital of the Chinese nation state as a market society success. Possibly accompanying the 'reenergizing the old to be new again' dynamic is the resurgence of the tendency to think of marginalized Chinese as akin to dangerous weather – forces of nature that are unpredictable and something best controlled rather then led. If China persists in this predisposition – which at this nation-state point in time constitutes a bad imperial habit – then we might justifiably be concerned that things will get worse before they get better.

[10] Lattimore, *Inner Asian Frontiers of China*.

[11] As an anthropologist, the author suspects that the so-called common international interaction mechanics of the realist school are not so much common to all cultures as they are part of European sensibility projected onto the rest of the world over time along with industrial capitalism; a fact that may explain some of the recent interest in mapping out 'Chinese capitalism' or 'Chinese modernity'.

[12] Among the stranger of these is the event that occurred just as the final galley proof of this article was due. This was a protest involving thousands who had gathered to pressure the government into providing some relief for those who had lost money in an investment scheme involving an aphrodisiac made from ants on the grounds that officials had so publicly honoured the company that it somehow amounted to a guarantee. See Chris Buckley, 'Thousands Protest Over Ant Aphrodisiac Scheme,' Reuters, 21 Nov. 2007, available online at http://uk.reuters.com/article/oddlyEnoughNews/idUKPEK27392320071121, accessed 20 April 2008.

[13] Giersch *Asian Borderlands.*

[14] Perdue, 'Insiders and Outsiders'; Kuhn, *Rebellion and its Enemies in Late Imperial China*; Atwill, *The Chinese Sultanate.*

[15] See, for example: 'China's child fines "spark riot"', BBC News, 21 May 2007, available online at http://news.bbc.co.uk/1/hi/world/asia-pacific/6677273.stm, accessed 20 April 2008; '"Thousands riot" in China protest.' BBC News, 12 March 2007, available online at http://news.bbc.co.uk/1/hi/world/asia-pacific/6441295.stm, accessed 20 April 2008; Benjamin Lim Kang, 'Over 50 policemen injured in rural riot', *The Standard* (Hong Kong), 12 April 2005; Preetan Singhani, 'Increasing Internal Riots in China – the Dragon is Shaking from Inside', *India Daily*, 11 April 2005; 'Labour Rights Group Reports Riot at China Factory Producing Toys for McDonald's', AFX News Limited, 27 July 2006; Edward Cody. 'A Chinese Riot Rooted in Confusion: Lacking a Channel for Grievances, Garment Workers Opt to Strike', *Washington Post* Foreign Service, 18 July 2005, A01. This is just a very brief and random selection, and according to multiple reports, the incidence of unrest in today's China is accelerating. See, for example, Edward Cody. 'China Growing More Wary Amid Rash of Violent Protests', *Washington Post*, 12 Aug. 2005.

[16] This demand was eventually complied with because the author knew the man, knew he could not read English, and refused to allow the notes to be copied.

[17] Of course, very recent reports from Amnesty International suggest that China has not lived up to its agreement to improve its human rights situation. One might conclude from this that the Beijing may also have trouble living up to its agreement on international press freedom as well, but this remains to be seen.

[18] Though it must be said that these kinds of more blatantly competitive voices were always to be found in the larger groups of celebrants, usually fuelled by significant amounts of famous Yunnanese *baijiu*, and usually not when they saw any American-looking people around.

[19] 'Missing the Barefoot Doctors', *The Economist*, 11 Oct. 2007. The reference to 'the Communists' is not a mistake. Many informants have a tongue-in-cheek tendency to refer to the pre-1970 government as 'the Communists' while refusing to speculate about what the form of government has become after that. 'Whatever it is', one informant suggested, 'it doesn't look Communist from where I am standing.'

[20] Harvey, *The Condition of Postmodernity.*

References

Atwill, D. *The Chinese Sultanate: Islam, Ethnicity, and the Panthay Rebellion in Southwest China, 1856–1873.* Stanford, CA: Stanford University Press. 2006.

Giersch, C. *Asian Borderlands: The Transformation of Qing China's Yunnan Frontier.* Cambridge, MA: Harvard University Press, 2006.

Harvey, D. *The Condition of Postmodernity: An Enquiry into the Origins of Cultural Change.* Oxford: Blackwell, 1991.

Hevia, J. *Cherishing Men From Afar: Qing Guest Ritual and the Macartney Embassy of 1793.* Durham, NC: Duke University Press, 1995.

Kuhn, P. *Rebellion and its Enemies in Late Imperial China: Militarization and Social Structure, 1796–1864.* Cambridge, MA: Harvard East Asian Series. 1970.

——. *Soulstealers: The Chinese Sorcery Scare of 1768.* Cambridge, MA: Harvard University Press. 1990.

Lattimore, O. *Inner Asian Frontiers of China.* New York: American Geographical Society, 1940.

Lipman, J. *Familiar Strangers: A History of Muslims in Northwest China.* Seattle, WA: University of Washington Press, 1997.

Nye, J. and J. Myers. *Soft Power: The Means to Success in World Politics.* New York: Carnegie Council, 2004.

Perdue, P. 'Insiders and Outsiders: The Xiangtan Riot of 1819 and Collective Action in Hunan'. *Modern China* 12, no. 2, (1986): 166–201.

Winichakul, T. *Siam Mapped: A History of the Geo-Body of a Nation.* Honolulu, HI: University of Hawaii Press, 1997.

Index

ABC News 93
academia 43, 155–6, 158–9
Academy of Social Sciences 155
accounting 64
accreditation 92, 135
Adams, R. 153
Adidas 130
administration 38–40, 46, 48, 159, 172
advertising 9, 91, 130, 193
aesthetics 146
Afghanistan 102, 115
Africa 21, 60–1, 63–4, 68, 72, 128
age 40, 48–9, 66, 155
The Age 114
Ahmad Al-Fahad Al-Sabah, Sheikh 92
Ai Dongmei 44
aid 21, 101–2
AIDS 63, 65
air quality 104, 110, 116
airports 62
Albanians 145
alienation 2, 22, 77, 96, 107, 191–2
all-round partnerships 144
alliance haze 70
amateurism 156, 158, 175
ambassadors 5, 13, 114, 144, 173
ambiguity 133–4, 137
ambitions 111–13
ambivalence 101–18
Amei 96
America *see* United States
Americanisation 167, 170, 177–8
Americans 4, 17, 29–31, 61, 65
   British perspective 147, 154
   French perspective 127, 129–30, 132
   role 165–78
   Taiwanese perspective 80, 89, 91
   Yunnanese perspective 186, 193, 195, 197
Amnesty International 21, 104, 113–14, 135

Amsterdam Olympics 172
anchor stores 168
Anglo-Americans 62
Anglo-French 12
Anglo-Saxons 156
Anta 128
antecedents 77, 79–81
anthropocentrism 148
anthropology 59, 168
Anti-Secession Law 94
Anti-Semitism 134
Antwerp Olympics 170
Appadurai, A. 146
Arabs 137
archery 44, 90
architecture 4, 13
arms race 70
art 13–14
Art of War 59
artificial rain reduction 136
artistic advisors 178
arts 109
Aryans 58
Asia 21, 29, 35, 50, 62, 68, 70–2, 95, 112, 136
Asia Highway 62, 71
Asian Baseball Championships 91
Asian Championships 36
Asian Games 84–5, 92, 103, 174
Asian Games Organising Committee 85
Asian Winter Games 45–6
Asians 31–2, 43, 69–71, 136, 148, 158, 169–70,
   172, 176
aspirations 29–50
association football *see* football
Athens 145
Athens Olympics 2, 21, 29–30
   Australian perspective 106
   British perspective 151
   French perspective 128, 134

gender relations 36, 38, 45, 47
Taiwanese perspective 90
Athens Paralympics 92
athletes 2–3, 9, 13, 17
  Australia 102, 106, 110, 115
  creative tension 146, 148, 151, 154
  French perspective 128, 135–7
  gender relations 32–4, 36–48
  mixed messages 20–2
  politics 58, 72
  Taiwanese perspective 80, 83–4, 89, 91
  US perspective 166–7, 169–70, 172–3, 175, 177
  Yunnanese perspective 197
Athletes Commission 40
athleticism 147, 166, 168
athletics 32, 48, 151, 165–7, 169, 171–2, 174
Atlanta Olympics 38, 89, 105, 128
attribution 157
Austrade 109
Australia 48, 101–18, 155
Australia China Business Council 109
Australia Tibet Council 113
Australia-China Council 112
Australian Institute of Sport (AIS) 105–6
Australian Olympic Committee 21, 115
Australian Open 40–1
Australian Sports Commission (ASC) 107
Australians 176
Australians Speak 2005 112
automobiles 71

back channel politics 59, 71
badminton 35, 40, 45, 67, 90, 150
Badminton Association of England 150
Balinese 168
Balkash, Lake 12
bandwagons 77, 93, 96
banking 5, 126, 195
barbarians 10–11, 18, 190
Barcelona Olympics 38, 59, 105
Barclay, St J. 80
barefoot doctors 65
Barmé, G. 14
Bartlett, A. 114–15
baseball 81–3, 91–2, 165, 170–1, 178
Baseball Federation of Asia 92
Baseball Tonight 91
basketball 32, 34, 38, 47, 81–2, 87, 91, 165, 170, 174
Bates, G. 112

Bayrou, F. 137
BBC 132
Beasley, N. 153
Beijing 130, 144, 150, 166–7, 186–9, 192–8
Beijing Airport 62
Beijing Asian Games 84
Beijing Olympic Games Bid Committee 116
Beijing Olympics
  Australia 101–18
  creative tension 143–59
  culture 143–59
  France 126–37
  gender relations 29–30
  nationalism 8–24
  politics 1–5, 57–73
  sideshow 185–99
  Taiwan 76–97
  UK 143–59
  US 165–78
Beijing Organising Committee for the Olympic
  Games (BOCOG) 88, 109, 117, 135–6, 147,
  152
Beijing-Lhasa railway 62, 67, 70
Beijinren 136
Beiping 84
Belgians 137
Belgrade 15
Bénétau 131
Berlin 135
Berlin Olympics 32, 49, 134, 169, 172–3, 175–8
Best Ten Athletes of the Year 36
Bezat, J.M. 129
bias 45, 62, 92
Bird's Nest Stadium 4, 21, 167
black people 30
blacklisting 96
blackmail 136
Blair, T. 129, 144, 153–4
BMX stunt biking 178
Bobin, F. 134
bobsleighing 89
Bombardier trains 67
bonuses 40–4, 46
bookmakers 128
boondoggle 196–7
Booth, D. 115
Boston Globe 177
Bowan, J. 111, 116
boxing 173
boycotts 58, 80, 92, 104, 115, 137, 174, 176, 178

branding 4, 112–13, 117, 128
bribes 115, 176
brinkmanship 85
Britain 18, 113, 128, 130, 143–59, 171, 173
British 16–18, 29, 156, 158–9, 166, 173, 186
British Empire 18, 171
broadcasting 157–8, 196
Brohm, J.M. 104
Brown, B. 115
Brown, E. 170
Brownell, S. 60, 147, 168, 175
Brundage, A. 147
brush-fire method 62–3, 66, 68
Brussels 129
Brzenzinski, Z. 178
Buddhism 147
bureaucracy 188
Burma (Myanmar) 62, 70, 72, 186
Burmese 191
burping 18
Busan 92
Bush, G.W. 177

Caffrey, K. 57–73, 185–99
Cai Chenwei 88
Cai Jizhou 91
Cai Yingwen 88
Cairo 173
Calgary Winter Olympics 89
California 169, 176–7, 186
California University 174
Cambridge University 40
Canadians 44, 67
Canberra 111
capital 127
Capital Spiritual Civilization Office 18
capitalism 57, 62, 64, 77, 166–7, 193, 197
Caribbean 93
Carter, J. 115, 178
Carter, P. 168
catharsis 2
celebrities 40, 42, 178
censorship 116
Central Asia 12, 71
Central Committee 30
Central Propaganda Department 30
Central Sports Committee 36
centralisation 39–40, 45–6, 158, 188, 192
Centre on Housing Rights and Evictions 17
centre-periphery links 197

Challenging 2008 Golden Plan 90
Chan, J. 176
Chan, S. 156
chatrooms 21
chauvinism 2, 11, 59, 95, 187
cheating 80
cheerleaders 169
chemical spills 71
Chen Huinuo 21–2
Chen Jing 89
Chen Lu 43
Chen Shixin 90
Chen Shuibian 86, 90, 92, 94–5
Chiang Ching-kuo 83
Chicago 196
Chile 80
China 1–5, 8, 11–13, 16–22
    Australian perspective 101–18
    creative tension 143–59
    French perspective 126–37
    gender relations 29–50
    nationalism 8–24
    politics 1–5, 57–73
    Taiwanese perspective 76–97
    US perspective 165–78
    Yunnanese perspective 185–99
China Basketball Association (CBA) 87
*China and Britain: The Potential Impact of
    China's Development* 144
China Fragile Superpower 3
China General Administration of Sport 150
China Taipei 88
China Taiwan 87
The China Times 83
China-Europe railway 62
China-mania 84
Chinese 1–5, 9, 12–13, 15–17, 19–22, 29–50, 83,
    143–59
Chinese Australians 108
Chinese Century 30, 32, 50
Chinese Football Association 47
Chinese National Amateur Athletic Federation
    (CNAAF) 170
Chinese Nationalist Party (KMT) 79, 84, 88, 96
Chinese Olympic Committee (COC) 9, 79–80,
    82, 89, 103, 107, 147
Chinese Olympic Committee, Peking 82
Chinese Olympic Committee, Taipei 82
Chinese Security Service 3
Chinese Taipei 86–7

Chinese Taipei Baseball Association 83
Chinese Taipei Olympic Committee (CTOC) 82, 86, 88–9, 127
Chirac, J. 130, 137
Christianity 4, 57, 60, 147, 167, 169, 186, 191
Chung Wah Association 109
citizenship 60, 147–8
civil war 32, 78–9, 84, 168, 173–4
civility contests 18
The Clash of Civilizations 158
class 145–6, 186–7, 193, 197
Clausewitz 59
Clinton, B. 18
Closing Ceremonies 103
cloud-seeding 17
club system 39, 41
coaching 9, 32, 34, 38
  gender relations 40, 42–8
  Taiwan 90
  UK 150, 153
  US 172
'Coalition to Investigate the Persecution of Falun Gong in China' 114
Coca-Cola 152, 176–7
Coe, S. 3, 153
Cold War 30, 58, 71, 106, 128, 147, 156, 173–5
Coles, A. 105
Collective for the Boycott of the Beijing Olympic Games 104, 113
colonialism 21, 60, 67, 70–1, 106, 158, 171, 174
Comité Olympique de la République Chinoise 79
commercialism 22, 42, 47–8
  Australia 109, 112
  France 128–30, 133
  Taiwan 82
  UK 149, 152, 158–9
  US 167
commodification 148, 157, 167
Commonwealth 109
communication 94, 104, 136, 157
communism 5, 32, 36–7, 65
  France 127
  Taiwan 78–84, 94
  US 166, 168, 173–5, 178
  Yunnan 188, 195
Communist Party 15–16, 19
  Australia 107
  France 129, 131, 134
  gender relations 30, 32
  Taiwan 78

  UK 154
  Yunnan 187
Communist Strategy 82
communitarianism 104, 117
comparative model 136
compensation 67
competition 146, 151, 158, 170–1, 174, 186, 191
computers 61
Confucianism 10–12, 22, 43, 104, 148, 156, 166, 170, 174, 191
Congress 176–7
conservatism 5
Conservative Party 151
consuls 13, 18
consumerism 62, 77, 167–8
containment policy 71
contextualisation 60
contractors 67
The Contribution of Higher Education to the Sydney Olympics 155
Cook, I. 112
Coordination Commission for the Beijing Games 116
corporations 41–2, 47–8, 109, 176–8
corruption 21, 63–5, 68, 186–7, 192–3, 196
cosmology 190–1
cosmopolitanism 11
costs 185–7, 193
Coubertin, P. de 145–6
creative tension 143–59
credit 62–3
cricket 93, 106
Cricket World Cup 93–4
criticism 126–37
Cuba 83
cultivating process 146
cultural genocide 68
Cultural Revolution 34, 174
culture 9–14, 16, 18, 22–3
  Australia 101–2, 104–6, 108–10, 112–14, 117
  creative tension 144–9, 152–3, 156–9
  France 127, 129–30, 135
  gender relations 31–2, 35, 43, 46, 48
  politics 60, 62, 68
  power 143–59
  Taiwan 93, 95
  US 171–2, 176
  Yunnan 188
currency reserves 127

Daily Telegraph 29
Dalai Lama 68, 96, 176
Daley, R. 196
Dalian 196
Dallas 176
dams 68
'Dancing Beijing' 143, 152–5, 158–9
Darfur 5, 137
Darwinism 13
death penalty 114, 134
decathlon 80, 174
Décathlon 131
decentralisation 39, 41
declamations 1
decomposition 156
deep-learning strategies 156
defections 80
degrees 43, 63, 90
Dehring, Chris 94
DeLay, T. 177
Delmas-Marty, M. 132
Delza, - 156
democracy 60, 62, 89, 91, 102–3, 132, 149, 158, 176–8
Democratic Progressive Party (DPP) 85
Democrats 114, 133, 176–7
demography 105
Deng Xiaoping 78, 81, 131
Deng Yaping 40
Department of State and Regional Development (DSRD) 109
Deron, F. 133
detention without trial 114
developing nations 111
Dickson, G. 152
DiCosmo, N. 12
dictatorships 21, 149, 177
digital technology 157
Ding Maoshi 84
Ding Ning 45
Ding Shanli 82
diplomacy 3, 10–12, 16, 30
  Australia 101–18
  France 127, 132, 137
  politics 61, 68–71
  Taiwan 78, 80–2, 91–3, 96
  UK 144–5, 147
discrimination 58
disqualification 89
dissent 133, 177, 187, 191–4, 198

distraction 110
diversity 41–4, 48, 148
diving 35, 42, 45, 174
domino effect 81
Dong Jinxia 29–50, 59, 66, 147, 168
doping 128, 135, 175
Double Star 128
doubts 126–37
dragon boat races 146
dragons 59, 61, 69, 95
Dufour 131
Dunning, E. 58
Dyreson, M. 165–78
Dyson, E. 157
dysphoria 3

early-day motions 153
East 5, 19, 21–2, 31, 91
  UK perspective 149, 152, 156, 158
  US perspective 165, 169
East Asia 14, 38, 83, 169, 173–4
East Asian Games 92
East Germans 175
East Timor 102
Eastern Bloc 106
Eastern Europe 150
Ecclestone, B. 131
ecology 136
economic growth 4, 14, 22, 45, 62–3, 95, 101–2, 126, 144
economics 1, 4–5, 9–10
  Australia 101–2, 104, 106–7, 109–14, 117
  creative tension 144–5, 147, 151, 155, 157, 159
  France 126–31, 137
  gender relations 30, 37–8, 41–5, 48
  imperialism 144
  mixed messages 16–17, 21, 23
  politics 60, 62–4, 68, 70–1
  Taiwan 81–2, 89, 94
  US 166–7, 172, 175
  Yunnan 187–9, 191–4, 197
Economist 95
economy 40, 45, 127–8, 151–2, 155, 157, 159, 167, 176
education 13–14, 18, 30, 43
  Australia 101–2, 112, 116
  France 136
  gender 43
  politics 63, 65
  Taiwan 87

UK 155–6, 159
  Yunnan 191
educationalists 155
elections 96, 137
Elias, N. 58
elites 2, 11, 13, 21–2, 64
  Australia 105–6
  UK 151, 154, 158
  Yunnan 187, 193
Elliott, M. 155
emancipation 32, 35, 44, 50
emperors 188, 193
empires 190–2
Endeavour Consulting 109
endorsements 42
energy 21, 70
engineering 63, 66–7, 70
England 13, 106, 153–4
English 3, 156, 173
English language 86, 90, 136, 157, 186, 196
English, T. 110
Enlightenment 146, 148
entrance exams 43
entrepreneurs 173
environment 3–4, 9, 21–2, 63
  Australia 107, 113, 116–17
  France 135–6
  politics 71
  UK 151, 158
  US 176
  Yunnan 197
epidemics 63
epilepsy 153
epistemology 146, 155–6, 189
Esplanade des Droits de l'Homme 131
ESPN 91
ethics 104, 135, 148–9, 152, 158
ethnic cleansing 12
ethnicity 78, 86, 89–90, 148, 186, 192
ethnocentrism 21, 136
ethnography 69
euphoria 2, 9, 185–99
Eurocentrism 135
Europe 13, 21, 31, 48, 62
  Australia 113
  France 126–30, 135
  UK 144, 150
  US 173, 175
European Union (EU) 111, 129, 132
Europeans 4, 31, 129–31, 137, 144, 146, 158, 171

evangelists 169
Everest, Mount 67, 137
evictions 21
exclusion 145
exclusivity 158
expatriates 177
exports 129, 144, 155

factories 135
fair play 21, 60, 153
Falun Dafa 113
Falun Gong 114
famine 34
Fan Hong 21, 105–6, 149, 168
fans 9–10, 17, 21, 165
Far East 165, 169
Far Eastern Athletic Association 171
Far Eastern Championship Games 169–71, 173–4
Farrow, M. 178
farting 18
fashion 13, 84
favoured nation status 113
fears 126–37
Fédération Internationale de Football Association
  (FIFA) 80
Federation of Nautical Industry 131
fencing 35, 44, 81
Ferrari 67
field notes 193
Fifth World 80
Le Figaro 135
film stars 42
first nation status 106
First World War 169–70
five zone (*wu fu*) theory 10
Flame Relay 3, 5, 17, 67, 79, 88, 94, 137
flooding 71
folklore 151
football 21, 35, 42, 47–8, 80, 88, 92, 165, 186, 195
footbinding 32, 35
Forbes 500 67
Forbidden City 33
forefathers 84
foreign policy 10, 21, 30, 102, 135–6, 178
Formosa 80
Formula One 131
Fountaine 131
France 126–37
Fraser, M. 115
free trade agreements (FTAs) 110, 113

freedom of expression 134
freedom of press 135
French 104, 137
French Revolution 132
Fu Ying 5
funding 41–2, 47, 58, 109, 151, 154
Fung Li 153

G7 144
Games of the New Emerging Forces (GANEFO) 174
Gaoxiong 92–3
gaze 19, 87, 114
Geertz, C. 168
gender relations 32, 35, 40–1, 44, 48, 50, 58, 145
Geneva 17, 133
geography 1, 50, 105, 113
geopolitics 1–5, 57–60, 68–73
    Australia 102, 107, 110, 112–13, 118
    gender 50
    Yunnan 185, 198
George III, King 144
Gephardt, D. 177
Germans 58, 135, 156
Germany 47, 128, 130, 134, 173, 175, 177
Gilday, A. 176
Girginov, V. 143–59
global warming 71
globalisation 5, 21, 23, 31, 66, 71, 105, 147
globesity 152
GNP 128
Goffman 69
Gong Li 176
'Good Luck Beijing' Sports Event 116
Gorbachev, M. 131
Gothenborg 61
Goude, J.P. 132
governance 63–4, 66, 117, 188–9
graduates 63, 65
grassroots 154
Great Britain *see* Britain
Great Leap Forward 33–4
Great Pumpkin 62
Great Wall 9
Great War *see* First World War
great-power status 9
Greater China Federation 95
Greece 145
Greeks 58, 137, 145, 198
green issues 8

Green Party 115
greenhouse gases 136
Grenadines 93
Gries, P.H. 16
gross domestic product (GDP) 30, 45, 63–4
guanxi 104, 108
Guardian 154
Gujarat 70
Guo Jingjing 42
Gwadar Deep Water Port 70
gymnastics 34–5, 42, 44–5, 48, 150, 174

Hainan 9
Han Chinese 79, 188, 191, 193
Han Dynasty 10–11, 36
handball 44, 47
Hao Longbin 88
hard power 94, 101–2, 112, 115, 191
Hardt, M. 60
Harvey, R. 178
have nots 67
Hawke, B. 111
He Zhenliang 1, 87, 106, 108, 147
health 65, 67, 116, 152
Hebei 34
hegemony 30, 85, 94, 96, 104, 171, 175
Hellenism 146
Helms, J. 177
Helsinki Olympics 37, 79
Hera 198
heritage 106
heroin trafficking 195
Hevia, J. 190
hierarchy 10
higher education (HE) 43, 145, 155–6
highways 62, 71
Himalayas 70
Hirofumi, D. 34
Hiroshima Asian Games 92
historians 156, 168
history 10–15, 21–3, 31
    Australia 105–6, 115, 117
    creative tension 147–8, 151, 153, 157–8
    France 128, 133
    gender relations 38–9, 48–50
    politics 59–60, 66, 69–70
    Taiwan 77–81, 95
    UK 146
    US 171, 175–8
    Yunnan 187–91, 194, 198

Hitler, A. 58, 134, 173, 175, 177
Hobsbawm, E 97
hockey 47
Hohhot 16
Holland 172
Hollway, S. 109
Hollywood 72, 178
Holt, R. 156
Hong Kong 21, 86, 88, 96, 116, 194
Horton, P. 101–18
Howard, J. 108, 110, 115
Hu Jintao 49
Hu Yaobang 131
Huan Xiong 21, 149
Huang Dazhou 86
Huang Debei 76
Huang Zhifang 92
Hui Chinese 188
Huizinga, J. 146
human rights 5, 21, 102, 104, 109–10, 113–17,
    127, 132–5, 137, 176
Human Rights Watch 21
humanism 21, 149, 157
humanitarianism 5, 137
Hunan Provincial Sports Administration 40
Huntingdon, S. 38, 158
hypocrisy 147

identity 3–4, 14, 35–6
    Australia 106
    creative tension 146, 152
    Taiwan 89–94, 96–7
    US 165, 167, 171
ideology 11, 31, 33, 68, 106, 145–9, 151, 178
Illinois 196
imagined communities 90, 97
imitation 156–7
immigration 81
imperialism 3–4, 9–14, 18
    Australia 104
    gender relations 30–1
    mixed messages 21–3
    politics 61, 67, 69
    UK 144, 147
    US 171
    Yunnan 188–92
improvement campaigns 18
inclusion 153
Independent Olympic Participants (IOP) 88
India 21, 62–3, 65, 69–70, 72

Indian Ocean 60
indicators 64, 106, 191
individualism 148, 197
industry 130–1, 135–6, 197
inequality 4, 22, 42–3
    politics 63, 65, 67
    UK 153
    Yunnan 186, 188, 192, 197
infrastructure 49, 62, 64, 71, 94, 107, 167, 174
Inner Mongolia 12, 16
instrumentalisation 73
intellectual property rights 157
intellectualism 147
intelligence 174
International Confederation of Free Trade
    Unions (ICFTU) 135
International Cricket Council 93
International Energy Agency 136
International Monetary Fund 127
International Olympic Committee (IOC)
    Australia 103–4, 106, 109, 114, 116
    Charter 82
    Commission for the Culture of Olympic
    Education 1
    creative tension 145–7, 149, 152–5, 157–8
    France 127, 129, 131, 133–5, 137
    gender 29, 33–4, 37, 40
    politics 58, 65
    protocol 87–8
    role 2, 8, 16–19
    Taiwan 76–7, 79–82, 84–9, 92–3
    top-down structure 85
    US 166, 170–7
    Yunnan 193
International Paralympics Committee (IPC) 92
international relations 69–70, 111, 115, 127, 147,
    191
Internet 2, 5, 21, 114, 137, 157, 192
interpretation 147, 149, 168, 173–5
'Invest in Beijing' campaign 107
investment 5, 21, 31, 38
    Australia 103, 107, 110
    France 126–7, 130
    gender 45
    Taiwan 82, 89, 93–4
    UK 144–5, 152
    US 173
Iran 81, 102
Iraq 102
irredentism 96

Islam 21
Israel 58, 80, 176
Istanbul 166

Jacob, A. 132
Jacoby, J. 177
Japan 1, 21, 29, 31, 35–6
    Australian perspective 103, 113
    French perspective 128
    gender relations 38
    politics 69, 71–2
    Taiwanese perspective 81–3, 92
    UK perspective 148
    US perspective 169–73
Japanese 17, 34, 81, 95, 159, 169–71, 173
Japanese language 146
Japanese Table Tennis Association 102
Jarvie, G. 133
Jiang Enzhu 70
Jiang Xiaoyu 88
Jiang Zemin 108, 116, 134, 149, 153–4
Jiangnan 189
jiu-jitsu 170
jogging 85
Johnson, R. 174
'Join in London' 152–5
Journal of the Beijing University of Physical Education 17
journalists 13, 21, 65, 114, 116, 127–30, 133–7, 173, 193
Jowell, T. 159
judo 35, 45, 90, 145
jugo tizhi 154–5
Junwei Yu 76–97

Kagan, R. 159
Kansas Relays 172
Keating, P. 111
Khartoum 137
Kieran, J. 173
Kirk, D. 156–7
Kissinger, H. 80, 102, 178
kleptocracy 63–5, 196
KMT *see* Chinese Nationalist Party
Kongur Jiubie Shan 34
Kopytoff, I. 148
Koreans 47
Kuhn, P. 189
Kulantzick, J. 106
kung fu 72

Kunlun Mountains 34
Kunming 16
Kuomintang 188
Kurlantzick, J. 21

labour costs 127
Labour Party 151, 153
laissez-faire 11
Lake Placid Winter Olympics 174
land bubbles 63
landfill 152
Lantos, T. 176–7
Lao-tsu 159
Laos 62
Latin America 64
Lattimore, O. 190
Lausanne 82, 133
leadership 2–3, 5, 15, 21–2
    Australia 103, 108, 113–14
    France 129, 132
    politics 59, 64
    Taiwan 78, 84, 91–2, 94–5
    US 167, 172–3, 175, 177
    Yunnan 195
learning styles 156, 158
lecturers 156
Li Denghui 85, 89–90, 92, 95
Li Jieying 37
Li Na 45
Li Ning 128
Li Shen 32
Li Ting 40
Liabnhebao (United Daily) 84
Liang Qichao 9, 13
liberalisation 176, 178
liberals 62, 64, 131, 166, 169, 175
libraries 157
Life 170
lifestyle 168
Lijiang 186, 194, 196–7
Lin Chienyu 90
Lin Hongtan 80
Lin Zhongbin 95
lingua franca 165
Lipsyte, R. 175
literature 13–14
little league baseball (LLB) 81
Liu Jinmin 116
Liu Kai 91
Liu Xiang 36

Liu Xuan 42
Liu Zhihua 64
living standards 38
lobbying 113, 134–5, 154, 173
local-global links 151
Lockwood, W.W. 166–7
logos 153, 158
London 3, 5, 16, 143–59
London Olympic Games Report 154
London Olympics 4, 145, 152–5, 173
London Organising Committee of the Olympic
   Games (LOCOG) 152–5, 158
long-distance running 43
loose-rein policy 11
Los Angeles Olympics 58, 76, 83, 107, 147, 172,
   178
Los Angeles Times 178
lotteries 154
Lovell, J. 2, 8–24
Lowy Institute 112
Lü Xiulian 85
Luo Xuanjuan 47

Ma Family Army 42–3
Ma Qingshan 80
Ma Yanhong 35
Ma Yingjiu 96
MacAloon, J. 58–9, 71, 145, 147, 158
Macao 86, 88, 96
Macartney, 144
McDonald's 152
McGunn, W. 178
machismo 14
Mackerras, C. 117
Madison Avenue 193
magazines 80, 169–71
magic 189
Mainland Affairs Council 88
Mainland Female Football Team 88
Major League Baseball 178
management systems 41, 45–6, 48, 66, 117
Manchu 11–12, 191
Manchukuo 171
Manchuria 170, 172
Mandard, S. 135
Mandarin 86
Mandelson, P. 129, 143, 159
Mangan, J.A. 1–5, 29–50, 76–97, 118, 145
Manila Far Eastern Championship Games 170–1
Manila Games 169

manuals 148
manufacturing 111
Mao Tse Tung *see* Mao Zedong
Mao Zedong 2, 4, 13–14, 19, 33–4, 102–3, 189
Maoism 105, 166
Mapp, D. 154
marathon 44, 177
marginalisation 185–91, 194, 197
market economy 4, 40, 42, 45, 48, 102, 105, 167,
   186–7, 197
marketing 48, 77, 91, 117, 130–1, 152, 176
Marti, S. 129
martial arts 38, 90, 146–7
martial law 84, 89, 131
martialism 2, 186
Marxism 194
mascots 59
materialism 149
Mayo, K. 170
Mbeki, T. 78
medals 2–4, 9, 13, 19–21
   Australia 105–6
   France 128, 133, 135
   gender 29, 34, 36–40, 42–5, 47
   politics 63, 67
   Taiwan 80, 82, 84–5, 90, 92, 95
   UK 150–1
   US 171–4
media 2–3, 5, 17, 19
   Australia 104–5, 110, 114
   France 131, 136
   gender relations 40, 42–3, 46
   mixed messages 21, 23
   politics 65, 67–8, 72
   Taiwan 77, 83, 87–8, 93–4
   US 173, 175
mega-stars 91
Melbourne Olympics 79
memoranda of understanding 107–8, 144, 150
memory 77, 137, 156
merchandise 135
Merkel, A. 135
meteorology 17
middle class 66, 186–7, 197
Middle East 60, 68, 71
Miklasz, B. 176–7
Miles, J.A.R. 132
militarism 190
military 2, 11, 70, 78–9, 94–5, 101–2, 111, 149,
   159, 168–70

Millard, T. 171
minerals 111
Ming Dynasty 60
mining industry 64–6
Minister of Foreign Affairs 84
Minister of Sport 37, 107
minorities 193
missile shields 71
missionaries 166, 168–71
Missouri 177
mixed messages 3, 8–24
models 149–52
modernisation 9, 62, 64, 106, 146, 149, 167, 174
Modi 70
Le Monde 130, 132–7
Le Monde Economie 127
Mongolia 12, 16
Mongols 10–12
Montevideo 82
Montreal Olympics 105
morality 144–6, 149, 156, 158, 167, 175
Morris, A. 168
Moscow 109, 166, 178
Moscow Olympics 58, 115, 174, 178
Motherland Female Football Team 88
mountain climbing 34, 67
multiculturalism 12, 21, 152
multinational corporations 72, 130
Munich Olympics 58
Murchison, L. 171
muscular Buddhism 147
muscular Christianity 57, 60, 147, 169, 186, 191
Muslims 61
Muztag Mountain 34

Nagoya 82
Nanjing 61, 71
NASCAR 177
Nathu La Pass 70
National Amateur Athletic Federation 79
National Chengchi University 89
National Collegiate Athletics Association 169
National Day Rally 94
National Games 33, 38, 45
National Olympic Committees (NOCs) 40, 58, 85, 89, 134–5, 170, 174
National Paralympics Committee 92
National People's Congress 64, 70
National Sports Administration 41
National Sports Commission 43

National Sports Committee 37
National Tennis Association 40
nationalisation 170
nationalism 2–4, 8–24, 30
  Australia 105, 111–12
  gender relations 37, 49–50
  Taiwan 78, 90, 95
  US 177
  Yunnan 187, 189, 191
Nationalists 168, 173, 188
NATO 15
nautical industry 131
Nautitech 131
Naxi Chinese 188
Nazis 58, 175–8
Negri, A. 60
neo-imperialism 67, 104
neo-Orientalism 167
neoliberalism 62, 65–6, 68, 185–7, 190, 192–3, 197–8
NESTA conference 159
'New Beijing, Great Olympics' 117
New China 1, 32–3, 35, 165–9, 173, 175–7
new public diplomacy 106
New South Wales (NSW) 109
new world order 60
New York Times 170, 172–3, 175
New York Yankees 91
New Zealand 113
newspapers 17, 58, 60, 66, 83–4, 157, 172, 177, 186
Nielsen, A.C. 137
Nike 130, 167
Nixon, R.M. 80, 102
no-go policy 84
Nobel Prizes 13
non-governmental organisations (NGOs) 82, 87, 92, 107
norms 159
North Carolina 177
nostalgia 61
Notice on Further Developing Sports and Physical Education 37
Nye, J. 94, 102

obesity 152
obfuscation 110
officials 21, 46, 63–4
  Australia 103
  Taiwan 87, 89, 92

US 172–3
Yunnan 186, 188–93, 195–6, 198–9
Oh, Sadaharu 83
Ohmae, Kenichi 95
Ollins, W. 153
Olympic Council of Asia (OCA) 81, 92
Olympic Countdown 114
Olympic Formula 81–4, 86, 91
Olympic Games Image Protection (OGIP) 148
Olympic Games Impact Studies 155
Olympic Games Knowledge Transfer (OGKT) 148
Olympic Honour-winning Plan 38
Olympic industry 104
Olympic Legacies 5
Olympic Strategy 37, 47
Olympic Watch 134–5
Olympism 145–7, 158
Olympus, Mount 198
'One China' principle 85–6, 96
'One Country, Two Systems' formula 81, 83–4, 194
'One World, One Dream' 8, 19–23, 95, 118
one-child policy 40
ontology 149, 155–6, 158
open-door policy 44
Opening Ceremonies 4, 87, 92, 96, 104, 113–15, 134, 173
opiates 77
Opinions on how to Correctly Use Propaganda Phrases Involving Taiwan 87
Opium Wars 17, 19
organ sales 135
Orientalism 167–8, 173, 175
Orwell, G. 2–3
Osaka 166
Osaka Far Eastern Championship Games 170
'Our Place in the World' 112
Ourdin, R. 130
Outer Mongolia 12
Outline for Conducting Patriotic Education 30
The Outlook 169
overrepresentation 38
overseas students 155
ownership 157–8
Oxford 5

Paddock, C. 171–2
Pajot 131
Pakistan 70

Palestinians 58
Pan Duo 34
Pan-Pacific Volleyball Championship 81
Panama-Pacific International Exposition 169
pandas 59, 69
Papua New Guinea 102
parachute jumping 34
paralympics 92, 154
parasites 64
parents 147, 174
Paris 130–2, 134, 136–7, 166
Paris Olympics 170
Party Congress 49
Patching, J. 105
patriotism 2, 4–5, 9, 14–17
  gender relations 30, 35
  mixed messages 19, 23
  politics 67
  Yunnan 186, 194
patronage 154
Payne, M. 131
Peace Corps 102
peaceful rise theory 19–22
Peak 128
peasants 167, 187, 189, 192–3
Pedroletti, B. 130
Peking *see* Beijing
Peking University 35
Peng Shuai 45–6
Peng Yeren 21–2
pensions 49
People's Daily 2, 15, 17, 19–20, 106, 116
People's Republic of China (PRC) *see* China
Persian Gulf 70
petitions 153, 170
Peyrefitte, A. 127, 129
Philip, B. 130, 136
Philippines 169
Phillips, C. 115
physical culture 156–7, 172
physical education 14, 21, 36–7, 146, 156
Pierce, P, E. 169
Ping Wu 21, 149
ping-pong diplomacy 80, 102–3, 106, 127
Pisar, S. 128
Plan to Win Glory 44–5
'Play Fair 2008' 135
pluralism 46, 50
Politburo 17
political correctness 59

political economy 190
politicians 2, 38, 77, 85, 96, 103–5, 110, 115, 127, 129, 159
   Australia 103–5, 110, 115
   France 127, 129
   Taiwan 96
   UK 159
politics 48–9, 57–73, 95–6
   Australia 101, 104–6, 108, 110–12, 114, 117
   context 29–31
   creative tension 144, 147, 151, 154, 156, 158–9
   France 127–30, 132–5
   sideshow 185
   Taiwan 77–9
   US perspective 166, 170, 172, 176–8
   Yunnan 186, 189–92, 194–6, 198–9
pollution 9, 21, 135–6
population 40, 49, 66, 78, 149, 152, 172–3, 186–8, 190
post-sport jobs 42–3
postcedents 77, 94–6
posters 18
postmodernism 21–2
Potemkin display 18
poverty 21, 63, 65–7, 153, 195
Price, S.L. 166–7
private property 68
prize money 40, 46
pro-independents 85, 96
pro-unionists 85, 94
process orientation 157
professional model 41
profit 41–2, 77, 104, 107, 109–10, 130–1, 157, 191, 196
profiteering 196
proletariat 167
promotion 148
propaganda 30, 58, 60, 78, 83–4, 87, 91, 106
property rights 148, 157
protection rackets 10
Protestants 166, 169
protests 21, 68, 72, 78, 80, 113–14, 131–2, 177, 192, 194
protocol 148
psyche 31
psychology 5, 23, 49, 83, 95
public disquiet 101–18
public opinion 84, 95, 132, 154
public relations (PR) 3, 17, 61, 91
Public Security Bureau 193

publicity 9, 93–4, 115
pugilism 173
Puma 130
punditry 73

Qianlong, Emperor 12, 144, 189
Qing Dynasty 10–12, 36, 78, 189
Qingdao 116
Qiu Zhonghui 34
qualifications 43, 147
Quand la Chine séveillera...le monde tremblera 127, 129
Quangzhou 116
Queensland University 105
queuing 18, 136

race 58
Race for Tibet 113
railways 62, 67–8, 70
rain reduction 136
rationality 148
real estate 67, 196
realpolitik 4, 69, 72
records 32, 34, 36, 135
Reebok 130
referees 21
refugees 176
registration 39, 41
'Relevant Notification of Further Strengthening Sports Exchanges with Taiwan' 91
religious festivals 146
relocation 17
Report on the Improvement of People's Sport and Physical Education 36
Reporters Without Borders 133
repression 3, 21
Republic of China Olympic Committee 79–80
Republic of China (ROC) *see* Taiwan
Republicans 177
research 38, 157
resource diplomacy 61, 70
retirement 47
reunification 82, 84–5, 94, 96
revanchism 2
revisionism 4, 176
rewards 40, 46
rhetoric 3–5, 11, 14–15
   mixed messages 19, 23
   politics 63, 72
   UK 147

US 178
  Yunnan 190, 194
rhythmic gymnastics 44–5
Riefenstahl, L. 178
right wing 135
ritual 57–9, 64, 67, 69, 146, 187, 190–1
Rogge, J. 29, 114, 116, 134
Romania 82
Rome Olympics 80
Rowe, N. 153
rowing 104
Royal, S. 137
rugby 106
Rugby World Cup 77–8
rural areas 49, 63, 66, 167, 187–8, 193–4
Russia 71–2
Russians 154

Said, E. 31, 168
St Kitts and Nevis 93
St Louis Olympics 166
St Louis Post-Dispatch 176
St Vincent 93
salaries 42–4
Samaranch, J.A. 76, 80, 82, 84, 86, 103
San Francisco 169
San Francisco Chronicle 177
Sarkozy, N. 137
SARS 63, 65
The Saturday Evening Post 171
Schofield, G. 152
scholarship 157, 166, 168, 193
science 1, 16–17, 61, 93, 112, 148, 156, 158, 173,
  175
Scottish Executive 144
'Scottish Strategy for Stronger Engagement with
  China' 144
Seattle Mariners 91
Seavy, W.A. 169
Second World War 71, 173, 176
Security Council 72
semiotics 67
Senate 177
Senate Report 104, 108
Seo Cheong-hwa 82
Seoul Asian Games 82
Seoul Olympics 148, 176–8
Shambaugh, D. 15
Shanghai 63–4, 67, 108
  Communiqué 102

Far Eastern Championship Games 170
  Nautical Salon 131
  Qingpu Martial Arts School 90
  US perspective 165–6, 169, 173
Shanxi 64
Shei, C. 157
Shen Jiaming 82
Shenzhen 16
Shirk, S. 3
shooting 34–5, 45, 90
Sichuan 40, 66, 68
'Sick Man of East Asia' 83
silk industry 189
Silk Road 11, 61, 70
Silkstone, D. 115
Sillinger, T. 131
Sina basketball team 87–8
Singapore 17, 113, 173
Sino-centrism 10–12, 21–2
Sino-Japanese War 13
Sino-mania 129
Sinologists 175
Sinophobia 89
skating 43
small-ball diplomacy 103
Smith, A. 57, 159
Smith Institute 144
Smith, M. 146
soccer *see* football
social sciences 66, 159
socialism 18, 117, 127, 137
Society for the Defence of Human Rights 134
sociology 58
Sofield, T. 153
soft power 94, 101–3, 105–8, 111–12, 145, 147,
  190–1
softball 44, 47, 83
soldiers 68
solidarity 147
Song Ruhai 146
soul-stealers 189–90
South Africa 78, 80
South America 61, 64, 68, 128
South East Asia 50, 69, 102
South Korea 82, 92, 149, 176–8
South Korean Basketball Association 82
Southern Weekly 65
Soviet Union 5, 33, 58, 63, 102, 115, 128, 174–5
speed skating 34, 42, 45
Spencer, 146

Spielberg, S. 178
spitting 18, 136
sponsorship 41–2, 47–8, 93, 152, 157–8, 177
Sport England 151, 154
sport studies 155–8
A Sporting Future for All 151
sports colleges 43
Sports Culture Digest 17
Sports Culture Guide 21
sports federations/organisations 33, 37, 81, 170
Sports Illustrated 166
sports science 150
sports studies 145
sportswomen *see* women
sprinting 171–2
SSA 45–6, 48
stadiums 167
standardisation 148
star-status 91
state 1, 3, 9, 14
  gender relations 30, 40, 49
  politics 58–60, 62–4, 69
  Taiwan 79
  US 174
  Yunnan 186, 189–92, 195, 197
State General Administration of Sport 107–8
State Sports Administration 42, 44
State Statistics Bureau 45
State Tennis Management Centre 40–1
Steele, J. 144
steppes 10–12
stereotypes 11
Stockholm Olympics 169
stumbling blocks 113–18
stunt biking 178
Sudan 72, 102
Suisheng Zhao 15
Sullivan, J.E. 169
Summer Palace 13
Sun Jiazheng 147
Sun Jingfan 40
Sun Tiantian 40
Sun Wen 47
Sun Yat-sen 18
Sun Yingjie 43
Sun-Tzu 59
superior sports 45
superpowers 31, 78, 101, 103, 107, 110–12, 116, 126, 128
surveys 89

sustainability 5, 158
Suzhou 87–8
Suzhou (Taiwanese Investors) Sina Lions Club 88
Sweden 61, 169
swimming 45, 47–8, 105, 128, 151, 174–5
Swiss 62, 82
Sydney Olympic Games Organising Committee (SOCOG) 109
Sydney Olympic Park Authority 109
Sydney Olympics 38, 89, 103, 105, 107–9, 128, 133, 151, 176
Sydney-Beijing Olympic Secretariat 109
synchronisation 153

table tennis 34–5, 45, 80, 84, 89–90, 102
taekwondo 45, 89–90
Taichchuan 156
Taipei 85, 88, 91–2
Taipei Chinese Olympic Committee *see* Chinese Taipei Olympic Committee
Taipei College of Physical Education and Sport 90
Taipei Times 90
Taiwan 9, 12, 31, 33
  Australia 101–4, 110
  Compatriots Visas 87
  Expo 93
  French perspective 132, 134, 137
  Olympic Committee 80
  politics 69–71
  reactions 76–97
  Tourism Bureau 91
  UK perspective 147
  US perspective 168, 174
Taiwanese Foundation on International and Cross-Strait Studies 96
Taiwanese Sports Affairs Council (SAC) 86, 90
talent 47–8
Tan, Richard 109
Tang Dynasty 36
Tang Jiuhong 40
Tang Mingxin 88
Taoism 159
Tatz, C. 115
taxation 191–3
taxis 18, 21, 136
TaxPayers' Alliance 154–5
Taylor, P. 151
technocracy 63

technology 1, 11, 61, 70, 93, 127, 159
Tehran 178
telecommunications 107
television 83, 87, 106, 132–3, 137, 167
temporality 146
'Temporary Provisions Effective during the
    Period of Communist Rebellion' 84
Teng Yi 84
tennis 40–1, 45
Tennis Management Centre 40, 45, 47
tensions 143–59
Terret, T. 126–37
terrorism 58
tertiary education 155
Texas 176–7
text ownership 157
textbooks 14
textiles 129
Thailand 62, 191
think tanks 144
Third Reich 176
Third World 102
three-nos policy 81–3
Tiananmen Square 15–16, 76, 84, 102–3, 131–3,
    135, 137, 175, 177
Tianjin 34
tianxia 10
Tibet 5, 12, 67–8, 101–2, 104, 133–4, 137
Tibetans 12, 68, 70, 96, 133, 176
timber 71
Time 80
time scale 31
Times Weekly 29
Tokyo 173
Tokyo Far Eastern Championship Games 170
Tokyo Olympics 80, 148, 174
torch relay *see* Flame Relay
Toronto 166
torture 134–5
totalitarianism 133, 175–7
tourism 21, 66, 93–4, 109, 136, 186, 194
toxic soup 110
toys 110–11
track and field events 165, 174
trade 10, 12–13, 21, 70
    Australia 101–3, 107, 109–10, 112–14, 116–17
    France 129–30
    UK 159
tradition 148, 156, 158, 169–70
traffic 116

translations 86–7, 90
transmission model 145
treasure ships 61
tribute system 10, 13, 16, 61, 69
Tsinhua University 40
Tu Weiming 148
tuberculosis 63
Turnerian ritual 58
turning points 131–2
two-China issue 127, 133, 147

UK Athletics 151
UK Sport 144, 149–50
unemployment 42, 78
unificationists 85
unions 135
United Kingdom (UK) *see* Britain
United Nations (UN) 72, 80–1, 127
United States (US) 4, 9
    Australian perspective 101–3, 107, 111, 113,
        115
    gender relations 29–33, 48
    mixed messages 19, 21
    perspectives 165–78
    politics 58, 60, 62–4, 68–72
    Taiwanese perspective 80–2, 91
    UK perspective 127–8, 130, 135–7, 147
    Yunnan 197
    Yunnan perspective 186, 195
universal declaration of human rights 132
universities 43, 63, 65
upper class 186–7
urbanisation 167
Urumqi 16
USSR *see* Soviet Union
Uygurs 133

The Value of Sport 151
Van de Ven, H. 11
Venezuela 102
Victorians 18
Vietnam 62
volleyball 19, 34, 38, 40, 47–8, 81
Volleyball World Cup 35
voluntary sector 152

Waley-Cohen, J. 11
Wall Street Journal 176, 178
Wang, C.T. 173
Wang Dexian 43–4

Wang Gungwu 12
Wang, H. 158–9
Wang Jianmin 91
Wang Meng 46
Wang Zhengting 170, 172
war 2–3, 10–13, 17, 19, 21, 32, 58–9, 79, 127
Washington 3, 22, 132
Washington Post 177
waste 152
weather modification 17
websites 19, 21, 153
Wei Dynasty 11
Wei Jingsheng 133
weightlifting 35, 42, 45, 81, 90
Weimar Republic 175
Weimer, D. 157
Wen Jiabao 135
West 1–5, 9–14, 18–22
    Australian perspective 102–3, 117
    British perspective 145–9, 156–9
    French perspective 127, 129, 131–2, 136
    gender relations 31–2, 36, 38, 40–1, 45, 47–8
    politics 61–2, 72
    Taiwanese perspective 80–1, 91
    US perspective 165, 167, 171–2, 175–6
    Yunnanese perspective 187, 191, 197
West Germany 82
West Indies 93
Westminster 144
Westphalia 19
white people 30
Wichard 131
Will, P.E. 132
William Jones Basketball Cup 81
Williamsport 81
Wimbledon 41
women 19, 29–50, 72, 88
women-first policy 38
Women's Football Championship 92
Women's Softball World Championship 83
Women's World Soccer Championships 36
Woodard, C. 114
worker exploitation 135
World Anti-Doping Agency 135
World Bank 127–8
World Cup 21, 36, 42, 47, 58, 80
World Games 93
World Gymnastics Championships 35
World Table Tennis Championships 34, 102

World Trade Organisation (WTO) 13, 106–8, 128–30
World University Games 87, 92
wrestling 81, 146, 173
Wu, H. 177
Wu Jingguo 85, 93
Wu Shaozu 37, 107
Wu Shuzhen 92
Wu Xiaoyang 22
Wyandotte High School 172

xenophobia 59, 68, 117
Xi Yao 34
Xia Dynasty 10
Xianfeng, Emperor 13
Xin Xu 103
Xinhua News Agency 65
Xinjiang 34, 102
Xu Lide 92
Xu Shiquan 86
Xu Yixiong 86

Yan Emperor 84
Yan Xiaozhang 83
Yan Zi 40
Yang, C.K. 174
Yang Chuanguang 80
Yang Yang 42
Yangtze 71
Yanzhong Huang 112
Yao Ming 91
Yellow Emperor 84
Yellow Peril 19, 62, 127
Yi Chinese 188
Yomiuri Giants 82
YouGov 154
Young Men's Christian Association (YMCA) 4, 166–7, 169–70, 172
youth 130, 152–3, 171
Youth's Companion 169
Yuan Dynasty 11
Yuan Weiming 37
Yunnan 66–7, 186–7

Zeng Zhilang 87
zero-sum games 63
Zeus 198
Zhang Baifa 85
Zhang Fengxu 93
Zhang Huimin 9

Zhang Tianyi 45
Zhang Zhenwang 91
Zheng Fengrong 32
Zheng He 60–2, 69
Zheng Jie 40
Zhongguo 86–8
Zhonghua 86–8
Zhou Chunlan 42

Zhou Enlai 37, 80, 102
Zhu Muyan 90
Ziamen 114
Zimbabwe 5
Ziyou shibao 96
Zodiac 131
Zunghar Mongols 12